Lecture Notes
in Economics and
Mathematical Systems

Managing Editors: M. Beckmann and W. Krelle

270

Technological Change, Employment and Spatial Dynamics

Proceedings of an International Symposium
on Technological Change and Employment: Urban and
Regional Dimensions
Held at Zandvoort, The Netherlands
April 1–3, 1985

Edited by Peter Nijkamp

Springer-Verlag
Berlin Heidelberg New York Tokyo

331.12
I61
1985

m R

ISBN 3-540-16478-2 Springer-Verlag Berlin Heidelberg New York Tokyo
ISBN 0-387-16478-2 Springer-Verlag New York Heidelberg Berlin Tokyo

Printing and binding: Beltz Offsetdruck, Hemsbach/Bergstr.
2142/3140-543210

PREFACE

In recent years, the scientific interest in the complex relationship between technological change, employment and regional growth has exhibited a fast growth. Despite the upswing in attention for the interactions between the components of this 'triangle', research efforts in this area are still severely hampered by lack of theoretical and empirical insights.

The present volume aims at providing a refreshing look at this triangle against the background of recent discussions on structural economic changes, technological innovations and labour market dynamics. In particular the attention will be directed toward two focal points, viz.:

- the relationship between technological developments and (qualitative and quantitative) shifts in the labour market. In this framework a review of current theoretical and empirical knowledge on labour saving or labour augmenting technologies, on changes in the secondary and tertiary sectors, and on shifts in external and internal labour markets will be given. It goes without saying that in this context also the relationship between innovation and employment policy will be analysed, as well as the spatiotemporal diffusion pattern of (product, process or managerial) innovations.

- the interaction between the urban or regional production environment and technology changes, with a particular emphasis on labour market dynamics. Spatial potentiality factors, bottleneck effects and incubation functions will also be treated in this perspective, while also much attention will be devoted to empirical evidence and policy prospects in this field.

Altogether the present publication serves to make an inventory of the state of the art in the triangle of technological innovation, labour

market effects and spatial dynamics, as well as to provide a construc-
tive strength-weakness analysis of this important field of research.

This book is the outgrowth of an international symposium on 'Technological Change and Employment: Urban and Regional Dimensions', which
was held in Zandvoort (The Netherlands) from April 1-3, 1985. This
volume contains most of the papers presented at this symposium in an
edited and revised form, while also some new papers have been added in
order to make this volume as coherent as possible. The financial support for this meeting, provided by the Netherlands Organisation for
the Advancement of Pure Scientific Research (ZWO) and the Economic and
Social Research Institute (ESI) of the Free University, Amsterdam, is
gratefully acknowledged. My sincere thanks go also to Dianne
Biederberg, who did the editorial work for this volume.

Amsterdam, February 1986   Peter Nijkamp

TABLE OF CONTENTS

THE TRIANGLE OF INDUSTRIAL DYNAMICS, LABOUR MARKETS AND SPATIAL SYSTEMS
Peter Nijkamp

1. INTRODUCTION

In the recent past much attention has been focussed on the role of technological change in developed economies. Witness a great many publications in the field of innovation, long waves and economic dynamics. Especially the present economic stagnation has induced many research efforts among economists in this area. In this context, increasing attention is called for labour market aspects of long term industrial dynamics. Theoretical knowledge however, is scarce in this respect, and empirical evidence does not show unambiguous results. It is, for instance, still an unresolved question whether innovation favours employment in the secondary or tertiary sector or whether it has totally adverse impacts. Consequently, much theoretical and empirical research on labour saving and labour augmenting technology is needed in order to obtain a full understanding of the complex and interwoven relationship between employment and industrial evolution. Such a closer investigation into the socioeconomic mechanism of industrial dynamics and labour market developments requires a careful analysis of labour saving versus labour augmenting technology in each sector, of the impacts of industrial bottlenecks, of the potential offered by research and development, of the effectiveness of (direct and indirect) labour market policies, and of spatiotemporal diffusion of innovation. In this context, it is increasingly questioned whether conventional macro-oriented economic approaches are still satisfactory and whether disaggregate behavioural approaches at the firm level are not able to provide a better analysis framework. A more thorough investigation of technological, entrepreneurial and employment dynamics is no doubt warranted.

It is interesting to observe that much of the discussion on industrial dynamics (including technological change and innovation) is usually related to the Schumpeterian 'long waves' framework (see also Kamien and Schwarz 1982). This is indeed a plausible approach, although it is worth observing that Schumpeter paid particular attention to the industrial market structure forming the context for innovative behaviour (for instance, his view on monopoly power and entrepreneurial size as one of the roots of industrial innovative behaviour). It is also highly interesting to observe that - after a long period of taboo on 'long waves' analyses in the Soviet economic literature - recently a book on these issues was published by a Russian economist (see Yakovetz 1984). Thus the existence of (long term) structural economic changes is increasingly regarded as a major analysis framework for industrial and labour market dynamics.

Another issue which also deserves close attention is the regional-urban dimensions of industrial developments and related labour market developments. The sectoral shifts in industrial growth patterns in many countries appear to be accompanied by drastic shifts in the role of urban agglomerations in a regional-national framework. For instance, one may wonder whether the breeding place nature (the 'seed-bed' function) of large agglomerations favours industrial growth and employment (the 'incubation' hypothesis) or whether congestion in many agglomerations has adverse impacts. In this context, much attention has to be given to urban and industrial life cycle phenomena (especially the relationship between urban development stages and quantitative and qualitative shifts in employment), the employment consequences of spatial competition (for instance, regional and urban 'depression trigger' phenomena), and the impacts of regional or urban bottlenecks and thresholds. More insight into such questions requires a closer analysis of regional-urban dynamics and of the changing role of cities and regions in a spatial system. It is also worth noting however, that new evolving spatial configurations show much variation among different countries, so that both theoretical and empirical research on the conditions of urban and regional systems for industrial innovation and development, and for related urban and regional labour market dynamics is needed.

In the light of the fact that various large metropolises tend to increasingly lose their innovative potential in favour of medium sized cities, it is conceivable that in several countries also an increasing tendency can be observed to analyse more thoroughly the innovation potential of peripheral areas. Therefore, a closer analysis of urban and regional incubation profiles (the set of spatial pros and cons with respect to geographically determined innovation stimuli) is a meaningful tool in order to provide reliable information for <u>urban and regional industrial and R&D policy</u>. In this framework, it is extremely important for an effective implementation of policies to carefully analyse - at a detailed microlevel - the locational requirements of new firms, R&D centres and new public policy agencies in order to be able to prelude future employment effects.

While there is no doubt concerning the relevance of scientific research undertaken in the triangle of industrial dynamics, employment, and urban-regional systems, it has to be admitted at the same time, that our analysis framework for urban-regional systems is not only incomplete and unsatisfactory from an urban and regional economic viewpoint, but it has also failed to provide a solid basis for (urban and regional) economic and industrial policy analysis. Clearly, several recent developments demonstrate the importance of active favourable locational policies with regard to technology and innovation (for instance, the Silicon Valley development, route 128 near Cambridge/Boston, the satellite development of Tokyo, the Science Park concept near Cambridge and Bristol, etc.). But on the other hand, it is too often taken for granted in policy making that large agglomerations have automatically many economies of scale which will favour the urban and regional incubation functions for innovations and hence for a more favourable employment potential. Conflicting issues and views seem to dominate the scientific scene here, among others by lack of operational scientific research concerning the abovementioned triangle. The present volume serves to fill this gap by providing a representative international inventory of the state of the art in this field, from both a theoretical-analytical and an empirical viewpoint. The first chapter of this volume is organised as follows. In Section 2, some general remarks on the relationship technological change-labour market will be made. Then Section 3 will be devoted to a brief review of spatial implications of the abovementioned relationship, while in Section 4, the main structure of the present volume will be outlined.

2.   TECHNOLOGICAL CHANGE AND THE LABOUR MARKET

The relationship between technological change and employment is a complex one, which cannot be adequately analysed at the macro level of conventional economic modelling. Research in this field is therefore increasingly directed towards the meso and micro level of firms,

sectors, or cities or regions. Despite variations in various countries, the global macro picture shows a fairly uniform pattern of employment changes in the past 40 years: a decline of employment in the
agriculture sector, a relative decline (though not necessarily an absolute decline) of employment in the industrial sector and rise in the
service sector(see Rothwell and Zegveld 1979). In various sectors of
the economy, it is worth noting that increasingly a 'jobless growth'
seems to emerge. For the moment, the employment in the service sector
is still growing in number, but it is questionable whether this trend
will continue in the light of recent developments in the field of
automation, informatics, telecommunications and telematics.

Clearly, the impact of technological progress on economic growth and
employment depends inter alia on the nature of innovations (product or
process innovations, capital or labour saving innovations, etc.). An
OECD report on microelectronics, robotics and job states in this context:

> "To see whether a new specific technology, in this case micro-
> electronics, causes unemployment we must really look at some
> counter-factual time path for the economy - that time path that
> would have been followed if the new technology had not been used.
> We can reason that on this counter-factual path productivity
> would have been lower, but by how much we cannot say. The effect
> on employment depends on whether or not the counter-factual path
> output would have been higher or lower. We have thus the compen-
> sation effects detailed elsewhere to consider. We have argued
> that these effects are not necessarily all positive or positive
> at all moments in time or for all circumstances, thus whether
> they mean higher or lower output relative to the counter-factual
> cannot be stated a priori. We have seen that in the past employ-
> ment has increased and new technology has also been introduced"
> (OECD 1982).

A major question in this respect is whether new technological changes
will only have labour saving effects, or whether indirect (compensat-
ing) employment effects may occur as a result of new technologies embodied in new capital goods.

The abovementioned complex questions require an analysis level at the
micro (firm, enterprise, organisation) scale or at the meso (sectoral,
regional or urban) scale. In this framework, the traditional

neoclassical macro-oriented production model is far from satisfactory, as it neglects the heterogeneity of labour, the often 'embodied' nature of technological progress, and the impact of new technologies on market structures. In a study undertaken by Wragg and Robertson (1978) on micro impacts of technological growth, it is concluded that there is no clear direct linkage between technological development (measured by means of productivity rise) and employment, as the price elasticity for the products of the firm concerned is also of decisive importance. Furthermore, the relationship between income elasticities and the sectoral distribution of production growth caused by innovations has to be mentioned here (see van Bochove 1982).

Another problem concerns the diffusion and adoption of technological changes. In a temporal context, this leads to the well known logistic (S-shaped) growth curve, while at the level of firms or regions hierarchical or distance-decay effects may take place. In this context, the direct and indirect employment effects may be traced by analysing a whole technological trajectory through various sectors (for instance, the impacts of microelectronics upon all firms during the entire life time of this innovation.)

Clearly, spatial and labour market dynamics is strongly affected in the behaviour of firms. The firm provides a starting point for an understanding of labour markets in specific regions. Segmentation of labour markets according to occupational skills, and the emergence of internal labour markets and the formation of primary versus secondary submarkets are essential for functional-spatial differences. Thus, regional economic systems are co-determined by the segmented labour demand of firms, while at the same time, their locational profiles (including bottlenecks) are to be taken into account as bottleneck factors.

In conclusion, new technologies require a specific skill of specialised people, so that they exert a severe claim on specific (mainly highly-skilled) segments of the labour market (implying mainly a filtering-up mechanism) thus causing a selective friction in some parts of the labour market. In various countries this has led to the emergence of so-called internal labour markets marked by in-house training and education at the firm level. This situation leads to the seemingly paradoxical situation that scarcity and abundance can simultaneously co-exist in a national labour market, although clearly in certain professional and urban/regional segments large discrepancies between demand and supply may arise. The latter issues orient again our attention toward spatial aspects of the evolution of technology and employment. These aspects will be further taken up in the next section.

3. SPATIAL IMPLICATIONS OF TECHNOLOGICAL CHANGE AND THE LABOUR MARKET

It was already mentioned that the evolution of technology and of employment has an interwoven relationship with spatial dynamics. Cities and regions are affected in different ways by new technologies, depending inter alia on their locational profile, their breeding place potential and their manpower potential. In this framework, Castells (1985) states:

"We are in the middle of a major technological revolution that is transforming our ways of producing, consuming, organising, living and dying. Cities and regions are also changing under the impact of new technologies. To be sure, technology does not develop in a social vacuum, and its effects are necessarily dependent upon a broader framework of economic, cultural and political processes".

In order to fully understand the underlying processes, it would be necessary to make a clear typological distinction between various kinds of new technologies, as specific technologies (e.g. agro-technology, biotechnology, microelectronics, aircraft) require specific locational conditions which cannot be fulfilled by each city or region. Thus technological change leads to a pluriform spatial development.

In addition, it is also necessary to pay explicit attention to spatial demarcations (e.g. spatial scales ranging from counties or provinces to municipalities, size categories of places, spatial dichotomies like urban/rural or centre/periphery, etc.), as it turns out that inferences on spatial (de)concentration of technologies drawn from empirical research are strongly determined by the spatial aggregation level (implying also the risk of ecological fallacy). This implies once more that micro-oriented technology and employment research focussing on the causes, diffusion patterns and effects of technological change is of utmost importance, as it is the firm which is a driving force in

the process of restructuring the (inter)national economy and regional-
urban economy.

As far as the <u>creation</u> of technological change is concerned, it is
interesting to observe the analogies between (inter)national long term
economic waves (or fluctuations) caused by structural changes and
urban and/or regional cycles (see also Nijkamp 1985). In some cases
spatial cycles may be trend following (e.g., in the case of a successful urban or metropolitan incubation policy). One of the most interesting themes in discussions on long term spatial dynamics concerns
the interrelation of long term industrial dynamics and stages of
urbanisation. Apart from difficulties like time-lags and cross-cultur-
al and geographical differences, the question arises which driving
forces are at work that link these two processes and how long term
industrial dynamics is connected with labour markets and regional evolution. A related phenomenon is the evolution of the service sector,
from which many functions are kept in the main central cities despite
the new modern technological opportunities that widen the locational
margin of tolerance (cf. also Brotchie et al. 1985). In this context,
the spatial aspects of an active conditional social overhead policy
(with special emphasis on technological revitalisation) deserve closer
attention, in order to achieve the highest spatial economic efficiency
of the location of new technological activities.

The <u>diffusion</u> of new technologies is - since the path breaking work of
Hägerstrand (1967) - a favourite topic in spatial research. Diffusion
of ideas, products and so forth has both a <u>point</u> and a <u>network</u> aspect.
The point nature concerns the attraction and repulsion forces of places for new ideas or inventions in geographical space. For instance,
information, science and technology centres in certain areas may provide an appropriate seedbed for (the adoption of) new technologies.
The network nature is related to the spatial channels along which new
ideas or inventions move (for instance, a telecommunication infrastructure, new patterns in logistics and telematics, and so forth).
Both the point and the network patterns may have multilevel geographical functions ranging from an international to a local level. This
also closely related to labour mobility where - depending on the degree of skill or specialisation of manpower - a different geographical
orientation of employees can be observed varying from a local labour
market to an (inter)national labour market. Furthermore, such spatial
evolutionary processes are also linked to the industrial organisation
and the pattern of multiplant companies.

Finally, the _effects_ of technological change are multidimensional, as they may range from impacts on market structures to labour market impacts. Clearly here one may again observe specific impacts on certain segments of an urban or regional labour market. The identification and assessment of all such impacts would require the use of the abovementioned technological path analysis implying an analysis of all (direct and indirect) socioeconomic effects of a specific technology (e.g., microprocessors) upon all sectors in all regions of the economy over a number of years. Such a cross-section study might also take into account a broader set of effects like environmental and energy implications.

After this brief and selective 'tour d'horizon' along various issues regarding technological evolution, employment change and spatial dynamics, the question may be raised whether our specific apparatus is appropriate for analysing the complex nature of the abovementioned phenomena. The main aim of this present volume is to provide a compact state of the art review of current developments in this field, both at the general level of theorising and reflection and at the specific level of empirical insights gathered regarding the abovementioned triangular relationship. The structure of the present book will be clarified in the next section.

4.   ORGANISATION OF THE BOOK

This book on the triangular relationship between technology dynamics, employment and spatial evolution is composed of three main parts. The first part (Part A) deals with general, theoretical and methodological reflections on the abovementioned dynamics. Then Part B attempts to bring together some empirical evidence and policy relevant information on the abovementioned interrelation, while finally Part C presents a set of models which aim at replicating - at least in a formal sense - the complex development processes at hand. Each of these parts will now be briefly introduced.

The first contribution to Part A, written by T.R. Lakshmanan and Lata Chatterjee, presents a systems view on technological and spatial development. The main idea of this paper is that the rate and direction of future technical change and adjustment to it in terms of the organisation of urban activities cannot be separated from the broader economic and political setting within which they take place. In particular, the manner in which a system of rewards and penalties operates in order to promote technical change and appropriate adjustments to it will depend to a considerable degree on the nature of public policy. In this regard, the paper provides an interesting survey of the transition from laissez-faire to highly regulative policies after the Second World War. The paper also argues that once again the conditions for public policy appear to be changing. In particular, there appears to emerge a strong need to deregulation in various areas. Moreover, the public sector should change its own technology of decision making.

The next paper, written by <u>Michael Storper</u>, deals with the complex issue of technology, emerging regional growth centres, and spatial production relations. This paper argues that the development of industries occurs under a condition of disequilibrium, marked by differentiated profit rates among firms and sectors. Industries that produce new commodities arise through technological innovation, but innovation and technical choice are not bound by price-competitive conditions in the early phases of an industry's development. These new industries may therefore be able to develop in places with higher factor costs than if strict equilibrium conditions were to prevail. The places where these growing industries locate are developed by the growing industries, because those industries have a factor-attraction power with respect to the rest of the economy: their factor demands are capable of causing regional factor supply curves to move outward. The author then argues that capitalists favour relatively undeveloped regions as sites at which to establish new regional social structures of accumulation: politics, institutions, and patterns of resource mobilisation that would not be possible in well-developed industrial regions. Through this disequilibrium-led process of developing new regions, the extensive margins of the space economy are broadened and the dynamic process of geographical industrialisation unfolds.

It is clear that in addition to the industrial technology also developments in the service sector may play a crucial role in spatial dynamics. In his paper on technological change in the service sector, <u>Peter Townroe</u> states that the spatial implications of invention, innovation and diffusion in the service sector have been relatively neglected in studies of technical change. Against the background of trends in service sector employment in the United Kingdom, this paper points to some of the ambiguities in analysing the impact of technical change in services, before briefly looking to some of the urban and regional consequences of new technology.

Next, John Goddard and Alfred Thwaites present a paper on new technology and regional development policy. These authors demonstrate the existence of important differences in patterns of technological innovation (at least in Great Britain) and indicate that the most important cause of these differences is the unequal spatial distribution of innovative capacity as reflected in the distribution of R&D activity.

Industrial dynamics is clearly reflected in the rapid expansion of the information sector. In this context, John Brotchie discusses the information technology revolution and its impacts including: the shift from materials and energy to knowledge as the major factor of production; a corresponding shift in employment demand to knowledge workers; reduced constraints on location of industries, services, and housing; greater coordination and synchronisation of production leading to concepts of 'just in time' and 'production on demand'; increased demands for information networks and fast and reliable transport systems to facilitate this coordination; greater flexibility of production and diversity of products leading to flexible manufacturing systems; increased home-based employment and leisure activities; increased importance of amenity, transport, and communication in locational choice of households and non-routine activities; increased diversity of locations and facilities for these activities.Some quantitative models to assist in evaluation of this process are proposed, and solution techniques which introduce intelligence and knowledge into the solution process are discussed. These techniques are capable of finding solutions close to the absolute optimum in facility layout and location problems. They are applicable to location and layout of industrial systems, industrial plants and the processes within them, as well as to the coordination and management of these facilities.

The final contribution in Part A is provided by Dirk-Jan Kamann. He starts his paper on industrial organisation, innovation and employment from the viewpoint that the organisation of industrial production is for a certain product (type) a specific chosen combination, organisation and location of capital and labour; capital with certain technology,labour with certain skills required. After a short discussion of this selection process, this chapter deals with three major causes of change of a production organisation: 1) growth of a firm and economic concentration of the market, both resulting in multiplant and multi-product organisations; 2) changing sociocultural values, resulting in both a changing demand for goods, from mass produced to customised small series, and a demand for more autonomy at the shopfloor level; 3) the increased importance of information based activities and the role of telecommunications, resulting in a 'segmented information net-work' theory. All three changes have their own specific effects on the spatial distribution of economic activities, skills and jobs. These effects may range from a product life cycle type of division of labour along Tayloristic lines (with peripheral areas) to more autonomous flexible operating plants (with increased skill levels in 'halfway' or even peripheral areas).

The first chapter of Part B (Actual Trends) is written by Hans-Jürgen Ewers, and provides a variety of empirical facts on the spatial dimen-sions of technological developments and employments. This chapter con-tains essentially three pieces of empirical evidence, which partly seem to contradict each other. On the one hand, spatial analyses of recent employment trends in Western Europe show that there is a strong urban-rural manufacturing shift, which hits in particular the manufac-turing industry of the large industrial cities with respect to both industrial employment and industrial output. At the same time, several studies of employment growth (better: decline) with respect to firm size show that it is mainly the young, independent single plant firm which creates new jobs, and mainly the great multiplant firm which is losing jobs. On the other hand, spatial studies of innovative activi-ties and of the diffusion of new technologies show, that the innova-tion potential as well as the adoption rates for new technologies are generally higher in urban than in rural areas, and that young and small single plant firms are lagging behind in adopting new technolo-gies. The author then tries to indicate how this complies with the popular view which attributes the creation of new working places to innovative activities and which estimates the small, single plant com-pany to be in nearly every respect more innovative than its larger multiplant counterpart.

In addition to the industrial sector also the tertiary sector deserves careful attention. In a chapter on impacts of innovations on service

employment, David Gleave provides various British and American results
from research projects undertaken in this area. First, impacts of the
information technology are discussed, followed by an impact assessment
of office automation on organisational structures and relationships.
Both studies are based on questionnaire surveys and indepth interviews. Gleave's findings reveal quite a variety of employment changes
in various parts of the service sector. The overall effect of technological change on employment seems to be close to a zero sum play.

Next, Frans-Josef Bade analyses the socalled deindustrialisation process and its spatial incidence in the regions of the FRG. Usually, the
increase of services is measured by the growing share of service firms
and public organisations. In this paper, in addition to the traditional sectoral perspective, a functional approach is used which focusses
on the kind of activity working people are engaged in - regardless
which sectors they belong to. At the national level, the functional
perspective shows that the FRG has been much more developing into a
service economy than is usually assumed. While production activities
have been reduced significantly in the past decades, but consumer and
production oriented services have increased, especially in the manufacturing industry. The empirical results indicate that such services
like R&D, strategic planning, marketing or EDP are an essential precondition for the success of firms and their competitiveness. Furthermore, at the regional level, the intensity of production oriented services largely differs with the metropolitan areas as the dominant centres of higher-valued services. Since 1976 the regional disparities
have even increased. Thus, in 1983 the FRG is characterised by a
strong functional division of labour between its regions. While the
agglomeration cores are more specialised on production oriented services, especially those of higher hierarchical as well as educational
level, their rings and the areas outside the large agglomerations are
more confined to production activities and less-valued services. However, the strong specialisation of metropolitan areas on production
services is not due to an especially strong increase of services -
actually, in peripheral areas production oriented services had the
highest growth rates. Instead, the primary reason was the sharp decrease of production activities in the metropolitan areas, whilst outside the agglomeration cores the production decline was rather small.

The next paper, written by Jan-Willem Gunning, Els Hoogteijling and
Peter Nijkamp is also devoted to the regional employment dimensions of

technological change. After a brief review of the literature on the interactions between technological innovations, employment and their spatial dimensions, results are presented from a large scale postal survey in The Netherlands. These data reveal large differences between sectors and between locations in innovation activities; they indicate that firms outside the older urban areas are growing faster and that they innovate more, and that at the level of firms, there is no significant relation between innovation and employment growth.

An analogous study to the previous one is next presented by Maria Giaoutzi for the Greek situation. She pays attention to the difficulty in tracing the direct effects of technological change on employment patterns (e.g. due to lack of insight in factors which are internal or external to the environment of the firm). The paper tries to identify and assess the order of magnitude of the abovementioned complex relationship in the light of a specific regional case study in Northern Greece. On the basis of questionnaires and interviews an attempt is made to find more precise empirical evidence. The results conform to a large extent to the spatial bias of the product life cycle theory. The results of the technology impact assessment show positive results for employment in most cases, especially for product innovations while negative results appear to take place for some specific sectors in the periphery of the study area at hand.

Next, a set of three specific Dutch case studies is presented. Jan Lambooy and Chris van der Vegt present a study on unemployment and manpower policy in Dutch cities. Their paper deals with the tension in labour market policies, related to the shortage of jobs and the official intentions to help the unemployed. In particular, the effectiveness of instruments in Rotterdam for the year 1979 is investigated. The paper shows that the training programmes were not well-suited for the completely unskilled, especially the migrant workers. Most of the workers who were selected hardly improved their positions on the labour market. The paper concludes that a more successful manpower policy in the private sector may need a temporary subsidy system to get some work experience.

Then, Ad Hendriks presents a brief discussion of results and frictions emerging from local initiatives vis-a-vis central government actions. Local initiatives refer to all activities, projects, schemes, institutions and organisations, initiated on the regional or local level for the purpose of stimulating employment and activity in the area. The Netherlands shows a great variety of such local initiatives. Particularly the number of business centres is growing fast. Despite the advantages of business centres for starting firms, the Dutch government is now confronted with the dilemma of the protection of the interests of already existing firms versus the encouragement of new starting enterprises. This dilemma has caused various tensions between central and local government agencies.

Finally, Huub Bouman and Bram Verhoef present results of a Dutch case study on the spatial employment effects of the high-tech industry. Despite a certain pluriformity in spatial employment patterns, some main lines could be identified. The high-tech appears to be oriented either toward the central urbanised Randstad of The Netherlands or toward a limited set of nodal places at accessible points in the national network. Peripheral location of high-tech activities appears to be clearly an exception. In addition, the authors observe that large high-tech firms are increasingly facing a shortage of highly skilled personnel in regional labour markets, which stimulates the emergence of internal labour markets.

The final part of the book (Part C) is devoted to modelling efforts in the abovementioned triangle. The first contribution in this framework is provided by Richard Day and Kenneth Hanson. Their contribution offers a general framework for analysing adaptive economising, technological change and the demand for labour in disequilibrium. An adaptive economising framework is proposed for analysing labour market aspects of long term industrial development using a dynamic, disaggregate economic model based upon principles of bounded rationality and markets in disequilibrium. The approach is applied to a firm's investment-production planning problem to illustrate how labour demand is related to capital investment and technological change.

The next paper in Part C is written by Dimitrios Dendrinos. This chapter gives a set of reflections on advanced modelling efforts for the analysis of dynamic spatial systems. This paper addresses a basic issue in the spatial allocation of capital and labour. Specifically, spatial shifts in capital and labour quantities demanded and supplied are viewed as the result of responses to appropriate spatial productivity differentials. A major incongruity is observed which has significant implications upon the dynamic stability in spatial labour and

capital mobility. The paper identifies this incongruity and then outlines its key qualitative features. It is shown that events containing
cycles, continuous disequilibrium, possibly chaotic behaviour (i.e.,
turbulence), etc. may result under fluctuations involving the spatially distributed production technologies.

Next, in the chapter written by Günter Haag a dynamic theory for residential and labour mobility is presented. In a stochastic framework,
the decisions of individuals to change their residence or workplace
are modelled by introducing the concept of utilities in a non-equili-
brium system. Using regression analysis the parameters of the model
can be estimated. Commuting costs appear explicitly in the model, thus
introducing a relationship among housing, workplaces and transport.
The stationary solution can be seen as a logit model. The analytical
and numerical tractability of the model enables the user to test the
implications of political decisions.

The relationship between spatial evolution, spatial mobility, employment and technology is explicitly taken into account in the paper by
Peter Nijkamp and Jacques Poot. The authors start from a general spatial interaction framework and include successively dynamic push-pull
effects, migration and labour market impacts, and technological developments. The final model appears to be a more general type of the
well-known May model from population dynamics, which is able to generate a wide variety of stable and unstable spatial equilibrium trajectories.

This paper is followed by a related paper on technological change,
spatial development and employment written by Jan Rouwendal. In this
paper particular attention is given to spatiotemporal dynamics of a
two-region system marked by an endogenous development of technological
change. The related competitive pattern of two regions which is especially determined by the diffusion pattern of new technologies is described in this paper by means of an optimal control model.

In a subsequent paper, Roberto Camagni discusses the issue of innovation and urban life cycles with particular emphasis on production,
location and income distribution aspects. The paper builds on the
well-known urban life-cycle model, mainly with reference to the relationships between the entire metropolitan area and the external environment (or 'countryside'). Many elements are tackled which are

insufficiently explained by the traditional model, viz. the driving force of the entire process; the frequence, length and lags which may be theoretically expected; and the relationships, or 'contradictions' which link the metropolis and the countryside. The main conclusion of the paper is twofold. Firstly, the characteristics of the urban life-cycle are mainly tied to the long waves of basic innovations and national economic development, as the Northern Italian experience seems to confirm. Secondly, an analysis based on 'physical' variables (like population or employment) is not sufficient to deeply understand the nature of the city-countryside relationship, which encompass also domination and power elements; these aspects may be captured through a terms-of-trade and income distribution analysis.

The next model in this context is presented by Börje Johansson and Charlie Karlsson. This paper presents results from a study of labour force competence in regions and the introduction of technological in-novations and new technical equipment into such regions. The empirical results provided here are taken from a pilot part of the study, with a focus on the application of information technology in the machinery equipment industry. One important objective of the study is to assess a set of hypotheses about the dynamics of regional specialisation, product cycle development and technical change in individual estab-lishments. The competence profile of the staff in each production unit, and the spatial and network properties of each unit are related to its introduction and use of information technology equipment in office automation, production process control and product development. The empirical results confirm that competence, education and knowledge intensity are important development characteristics of the individual establishment.

Finally, Ewald Brunner and Uwe Schubert present an interesting growth model that aims at incorporating empirical data for Austrian regions. The authors develop a dynamic multiregional model for incorporating capital mobility, labour demand and R&D investment. Special attention is given to a specification of R&D activities on a regional scale that is consistent with investment and labour demand. In this context, an optimal control model is developed. They also try to estimate empiri-cal regional investment and labour demand functions for Austria.

The volume is concluded with a retrospective view written by Manfred Fischer and Peter Nijkamp on technological change and regional

economic dynamics, followed by the formulation of a set of research
perspectives on the triangular relationship of technology, employment
and growth. Altogether, this volume aims at presenting in a systematic
and coherent way, a series of relevant issues on technological change,
employment and spatial dynamics, which range from general and policy
reflections to empirical evidence and dynamic modelling.

REFERENCES

Bochove, C.A. van, Income Elasticities and Sectoral Distribution of
   Productivity Growth Caused by Innovations, Discussion Paper
   8201/G, Institute for Economic Research, Erasmus University,
   1982.

Brotchie, J., Newton, P., Hall, P. and Nijkamp, P. (eds), The Future
   of Urban Form, Croom Helm, London, 1985.

Castells, M. (ed), High Technology, Space and Society, Sage Publ.,
   Beverly Hills, 1985.

Hägerstrand, T., Innovation Diffusion as a Spatial Process, University
   of Chicago Press, Chicago, 1967.

Kamien, M.I. and Schwartz, N.L., Market Structure and Innovation,
   Cambridge University Press, Cambridge, 1982.

Nijkamp, P., 'Metropolitan dynamics: the survival of the fittest',
   Revue d'Economie Régionale et Urbaine, 1985 (forthcoming).

OECD, Micro-electronics, Robotics and Jobs, ICCP series, no. 7, Paris,
   1982.

Rothwell, R. and Zegveld, W., Technical Change and Employment, Frances
   Pinter, London, 1979.

Wragg, R. and Robertson, T., Post-war Trends in Employment, Productivity, Output, Labour Costs and Prices by Industry, Research Paper
   No. 3, Department of Employment, London, 1978.

Yakovetz, Y.V., Patterns of Scientific and Technical Progress and
   their Planned Use, Ekonomika, Moscow, 1984.

PART A: GENERAL REFLECTIONS

TECHNICAL CHANGE, EMPLOYMENT
AND METROPOLITAN ADJUSTMENT
T.R. Lakshmanan and Lata Chatterjee

1.   INTRODUCTION [1]

A remarkable restructuring of metropolitan space is underway in the
industrialised countries. After two decades of rapid overall growth
and peripheral expansion, the metropolitan areas are undergoing a
transformation usually described as the onset of maturity. The characteristics of maturity include reversal of spatial concentration of
economic activities in metropolitan areas, with stagnation or decline
in metropolitan population growth. The geographical restructuring of
population and economic activity reflected deepseated changes in the
broader socioeconomic context.

The metropolis largely represents an adjustment to and a facet of the
industrial economy of the last century. The emergence of the factory
system with its associated scale and external economies, in the context of the dominant technology of the age, led to spatial concentration of activities. In the last half century, a variety of technological and institutional developments, e.g. the internal combustion engine, electronics and information technology has greatly weakened the
hold of metropolitan areas on economic activities. In Section 2 these
adjustments are briefly highlighted. Future metropolitan outcomes are
likely to reflect the interplay of a variety of technological, economic and social developments and adjustments to them on the part of
households, firms and institutions. Such adjustments will also be powerfully influenced by the forms and types of public intervention.

Section 3 outlines two complementary interpretations of the processes
of long term change in industrialised societies. First, the long wave
theiry envisages periodic 50-60 year waves of development fuelled by
technical change. A second interpretation emphasises continuing structural evolution in the service sector. The joint effects of innovations in science, technology and institutions, in the context of the
emerging information technology are anticipated to have   major

consequences for new products, new forms of organisation of production, service delivery and the household economy.

Such major changes are potentially two facetted; on the one hand they increase the capacity for making adjustments and on the other a resistance to change is brought about by damage, dislocations and obsolescence visited on certain activities, groups and areas. This dialectic between pressures for and the rigidities to structural adaptation is explored in Section 4. First, we present two historical examples of major adjustments: the first transition to an industrial economy and the transition thereafter to a predominantly service economy. The objective here is to focus attention on the mutually supporting complex of social, institutional, cultural and spatial innovations that accompany successful technical change. Second, we review current knowledge on the sources of rigidities to structural change in order to identify the implications for an appropriate role for the public sector to smooth the adjustments. Third, we offer some speculations on the likely effect of these processes of technical change and adjustment on employment in metropolitan areas.

We turn in Section 5 to the role of the public sector in facilitating these adjustments. Since the areas and forms of public intervention vary with the conditions and requirements of the times, our interpretation helps us identify some likely 'postures' and positive adjustment policies that would reduce costs of adjustment.

In this paper, we have adopted the ambitious and high risk strategy of ranging over broad areas of technical change, socioeconomic adjustments and the role of the public sector. In doing so, some readers may find us guilty of some gross simplifications. In the usual choice in such occasions between being precisely wrong or vaguely right our preferences are clear.

2.   EMPLOYMENT IMPLICATIONS OF METROPOLITAN MATURITY

Metropolitan areas in industrialised countries have been experiencing a decentralisation trend in recent decades (Leven 1978, Van den Berg et al. 1980). This decentralisation is stimulated by internal and external factors: aging physical plant has caused goods production and service activity to avoid the high costs of public services and of congestion through the outward movement of economic activities. A variety of technological and institutional developments in production and consumption systems has provided further external stimuli. The combined effects of industrialised stagnation in traditional manufacturing industries and the high congestion costs associated with metropolitan areas has caused spatial shifts in the location of employment from metropolitan areas.

In the US there is evidence of population and employment deconcentration since the 1970s. Social security data document the decline in net migration rates to large metropolitan areas - a loss of 20 per thousand in 1970-75 can be contrasted to the gain of 13.5% per thousand in 1967-70 (EEC 1983). While in the US manufacturing employment in the 1972-79 period increased by 12.7%, in metropolitan New York, Philadelphia and Pittsburg negative growth rates of -15.6%, -5.0% and -3.4% were recorded for the same period. European data confirm similar tendencies. While net employment loss in Great Britain, between 1966-72 amounted to 16%, the metropolitan areas of Greater London, Liverpool, Manchester and Birmingham accounted for 85% of all losses (Massey and Meegan 1980). In Frankfurt and Hamburg in Germany employment declined by -6.1% and -4.6% in 1970-78. Similar patterns exist in Amsterdam and Rotterdam.

This loss partly results from the general decline in the share of the manufacturing sector in the total economy and partly from the greater decline of traditional manufacturing within the manufacturing sector. In all OECD countries employment has adjusted, after differential time lags, to the lower growth rate of industrial activity. Industrial employment was stagnating and even declining in Belgium, The Netherlands, Germany and the UK between 1974-1979 when the average rate of contraction of employment in these countries approached or exceeded 2% per year (OECD 1982).

However, not all metropolitan areas show a loss of manufacturing employment. In Boston, Houston and Atlanta manufacturing employment grew by 14.1%, 51.0% and 24.5% respectively in the last decade. This growth resulted from employment created by new technology and new products and not from a spatial shift of traditional manufacturing employment to these metropoli from other metropolitan areas. This growth in manufacturing employment is associated with new product development in four manufacturing subsectors - consumer electronics, electronic capital goods (e.g., communication equipment, integrated circuits), medical technology (including biotechnology) and military equipment. Product innovation, as a source of new demand, increases employment commensurate with the size of the market and labour intensity in the production process. Since the productivity growth in some of these subsectors have been passed on to the purchasers through lower prices, the size of the market has been rapidly increasing. For example, in the US, 410,500 jobs were created in the computer and telecommunications manufacturing subsectors in 7 years and in France 210,000 jobs were added in the microprocessor industry by 1977 (OECD 1980). This can be contrasted to the accelerating negative trends in traditional manufactures. For example, in the EEC as a whole, the average decline in textiles, leather products, clothing, paper and plastics accelerated from -.4% per year between 1960-70, to -1.1% between 1970-73, to -2.4% between 1973-77.

Some of the downward adjustments in employment in the latter subsectors were designed to raise labour productivity, through process innovation and to maintain the competitive strength of the concerned traditional manufacturing subsectors. New process technology results in redundancies in these sectors. This type of technical change has caused a distortion in employment structures and adversely affected the metropoli that have a concentration of traditional manufacturing employment.

In summary, changes in the performance of the industrialised economies in the last decade flow from structural changes (in which technical change is crucial). The prospects for future growth and welfare in the industrialised world will depend on the nature of adjustments these societies will make to structural changes in the coming decades. Such a perspective puts a premium on a greater understanding than we have now, of the nature of the structural changes in progress and the various adjustments that may be made - for such adjustments may well shape the future international economic system and the metropolitanscape in advanced economies.

3.   COMPETING INTERPRETATIONS OF THE PROCESS OF STRUCTURAL ADJUSTMENT

Two formulations of the processes of long term and progressive change
are briefly reviewed. First, the long wave theory and implications of
that theory for influencing adjustment processes. The second is a
structural formulation for long term employment growth and the identification of necessary adjustment processes.

3.1 The Long Wave Theory

A useful way to view the long wave theory is to accept Van der Zwan's
(1979) notion of periodic major crises of adjustment, varying in their
severity and timing between countries, followed by periods of expansion and prosperity that are far more severe than the usual downturns
and upturns of business cycles. Kondratiev (1925) while analysing long
term indicators, first discovered several long waves of 50 to 60 years
duration in the world economy. He noted the importance of inventions
in initiating the major waves of economic expansion.

Schumpeter (1939) attributed a central role to technical change in
long wave formation. He claimed that behind each Kondratiev cycle lay
a set of major technical innovations, brought in the market by the
ability of innovative entrepreneurs and the following 'swarm' of imi-
tators who generated new investment and created boom economic conditions. The competitive processes set in motion by these swarming imi-
tative entrepreneurs would erode the profit margins (a la Marx) in
that sector. However, before a low level equilibrium trap could be
reached, the destabilising effect of a new wave of innovations would
start the process again. Schumpeter stressed the role of steam power
in the first Kondratiev cycle (1818-42), railroads in the second
(1843-97) and electrical power and automobile in the third
(1898-1949). A neo Schumpeterian would interpret the boom in the quarter century following 1948 as resulting from several technologies -
electronics, synthetic materials, drugs, oil and petrochemicals and
consumer durables.

Thus, in the Schumpeterian framework, the causation runs from science
via technology to the economy. The cumulative exploitation of these
scientific and technological ideas is called the 'natural trajectory'
(Freeman 1982). Different industries have different capacities to exploit these natural trajectories (Nelson and Winter 1975). In the
Schumpeterian framework, it is disequilibrium and dynamic competition
among entrepreneurs engaging in industrial innovation that provide the
basis of economic development. The focus is on the supply side with

autonomous investments. Mensch (1979), also emphasising the supply side, noted the importance of basic inventions in providing the basis of new industries. Mensch's data reveal that innovation peaks precede the bottoms of Kondratiev cycles by two decades and the beginning of a new boom is embedded in a previous downswing.

A second school of long wave theorists emphasise the _demand_ side factors. Schmookler (1966) points out that after the major innovation is made, the role of the set of demand led secondary inventions and innovations may be crucial for several decades. The System Dynamic Group of MIT analyses the role of demand for physical capital in the formation of long waves (Rothwell and Zegveld 1982, Nijkamp 1982).

From the standpoint of large scale economic shifts, it is not the date of a particular basic technical innovation that is important, rather it is a constellation of favourable circumstances - key technical inventions, the availability of large volumes of capital, the presence of entrepreneurs and a number of supporting managerial and institutional innovations. The importance of the managerial and institutional innovations (elaborated in the next section) can be illustrated by the steam engine, the adoption of which required an accompanying reorganisation of the production system.

To understand the role of technical change in the downswing side, one must examine the nature rather than the rate of technical change in existing industries, patterns of investment and demand growth. Utterback and Abernathy (1978) have suggested that the nature of innovations change over the duration of a growth cycle. As new industry grows many new products are created that initially open up new markets and expand business. The product innovation phase is this 'expansionary' mode. As the product demand increases, investments are made in physical capital and for augmenting production efficiency. With decline in demand a number of cost reducing process innovations appear and the industry enters a 'rationalisation' mode. With maturity, modest prospects for demand growth discourage capacity enlarging investment and employment declines. Many 'smoke track' industries (steel, petrochemicals, etc.) in the OECD countries are in this advanced phase.

Since this interpretation of sectoral restructuring fits empirical evidence, the source of new expansion in the next decade or two will lie in the development of new markets in the developing world or the generation of new industries based on technologies currently in their infant or early stages of the development cycle. Potential examples of the latter are the biotechnologies, technologies related to energy and new resource frontiers such as the ocean floor. These technologies could provide fresh investment opportunities, stimulate entrepreneurial activity and power the world economy into the next Kondratiev upswing (Rothwell and Zegveld 1982).

The introduction of technologies such as microelectronics may be critical. New microelectronic control and steering devices provide flexibility and promote automation in small and medium sized production units thereby increasing productivity. Microelectronics will not only affect employment in its production sector but also increase the potential for decentralised production and administration in sectors using the product (Friedrichs and Acheff 1982). Since administration, planning, steering of production and production can all have different locations, there are considerable spatial implications for future metropolitan areas.

3.2 Structural Model of Development

The structural model of long term progressive change advanced by Fisher (1935) and Clark (1940) popularised the tripartite concept of economic structure (in terms of primary, secondary and tertiary sectors) and introduced the idea of structural change involving switching of resources from lower to higher productivity sector. The structural change that accompanies growth proceeds in stages: initially industry and services both increase as agriculture declines; in later stages agriculture reaches a minimum level, industry stabilises and services continue to expand. US was the first 'service economy' - a transition from an industrial to a service economy in the 20th century deemed by Fuchs (1968) as a revolution comparable in importance to the industrial revolution in England in the 18th century.

The reasons for the contemporary growth of the service sector in the Fisher-Clark model are:

-   Engel's law - Increasing incomes in the context of the high income elasticity of services lead to greater demand for services,

- Increasing division of labour in the production processes and the growth in producer services that are used as intermediate inputs to production, and

- The lower productivity of the service sector, which with the growth of the economy shifts relatively more of the employment to the service sector.

While the service sector as a whole has been growing, different sub-sectors evidence different rates of growth. Following some of the functional notions of Browning and Singlemann (1978), and Gershuny and Miles (1983) we can recognise four service subsectors: distributive services (e.g., transport, communications, retail and wholesale), intermediate producer services (e.g., professional and technical services), final marketed services and final (largely) nonmarketed services (e.g., welfare, education, health, etc.). Of these, distributive services appear to be a stationary or slightly declining proportion of total employment, reflecting the differential growth rates of component categories. On the other hand, intermediate services for other primary, manufacturing or service sectors are growing reflecting their contribution to productivity growth in these sectors. The long term trends for the two types of final services do not appear to be encouraging.

A major reason for this differential performance is the effect of relative prices of many services (Table 1). In every country, the relative price of services is higher than that of all private consumption. In the UK, for instance, between 1954 and 1974, the price of services rose 1.72 times as fast as that of durables (Gershuny 1978, p. 79). The rise of the relative price of services over time leads to a decline of service consumption.

Table 1
Rates of Increase of Consumer Prices 1977-78

Country	Total Private Consumption	Services	Country	Total Private Consumption	Services
Germany	2.6	3.8	France	9.3	10.6
Italy	12.6	13.0	Netherlands	4.3	8.3
Belgium	4.5	8.4	Luxemburg	3.1	5.0
UK(1970-73)	7.8	10.4			
Denmark	10.0	11.1			

Source: Gershuny and Miles (1983)

While these price trends put pressure on the growth of marketed final services, one part of the service sector is unaffected by them i.e., the producer services subsector. This is a dynamic sector, the demand for it is directly related to the increasing division of labour and the consequent rise in productivity in the manufacturing sector. Branches of the service sector such as banking and financial services that have grown rapidly in the last two decades show considerable pro- ductivity growth. However, in the largely nonmarketed services sub- sector (e.g., education, welfare, health, etc.), that has also been growing rapidly in the last two decades, there is both high labour-in- tensity and wage pressures for parity with workers in other sectors. As a consequence, there has been a major wage cost inflationary pres- sure leading in turn to pleas for the control of the scale of public expenditures. Such pressures are exemplified by the California Propo- sition 13 and Massachusetts 2 1/2, both of which put a cap on state expenditures. Thus the long term vitality of the service sector de- pends on the ability to reduce costs in the final services subsectors. There is already some evidence of this ability to cut costs through innovative ways of provision of some marketed final services.

Innovation appears to have taken place primarily in the organisation of the final market function (Gershuny and Miles 1983). For example, the market purchase of laundry services has been replaced often by household production whose inputs are capital (washing machines), in- formal labour inputs from household members and enlarged housing space. Thus, the rising price of personal services has led to the de- velopment of new consumer products (e.g., automatic machinery) that can be used with household labour in a 'self service' mode. These modes of social innovation in the delivery of personal services can be greatly augmented by the current set of emergent technologies - com- puters, communications information storage and retrieval.

In summary, the preceding discussion of alternative interpretations of the processes of long term change in the more affluent societies argues that the emerging world economy will likely reflect:

-   the cumulative effects of a cluster of technologies - some emerg-
    ing, others on the horizon - or

- the continuing structural evolution of the dominant service sector.

Indeed one may argue that these two formulations are not competitive but complementary explanations of the shape of things to come, since innovations in science, physical technology, organisation and institutional development all interact in production and service delivery and thus determine the nature of the future world economy. Such a future will in all likelihood include the following characteristics: a plethora of new products; far ranging modifications brought about by the microelectronic information revolution in the organisation of production and services; small and medium sized production units increasing their potential for flexibility, control automation and outreach to markets; the greater spatial separation between various functions in the workplaces - administration planning, steering of production, production, and delivery of goods and services; the increasing restructuring of the service sector by bringing segments of economic activity into the 'informal economy' or the household; the consequent household allocation of time and the organisation of the household economy, etc.

It is important to note that there is no single predetermined world economy awaiting us in the future, but rather a multiplicity of alternatives. The impending changes in science and technology are so diverse and the emerging shifts in attitudes driven by newer values and demographic evolution so uncertain, that it will be foolhardy to assert the primacy of one alternative. Which combination is chosen depends to a considerable degree on which adjustment process becomes dominant, on the nature of collective choices made, and on the type of institutional mechanisms used at various levels to express and effect such choices. We now turn to an exploration of such potential processes of adjustment to technological change and their implications for the metropolitanscape.

4. ADJUSTMENTS TO CHANGE AND URBAN EVOLUTION

Steeply rising costs per unit of a major factor of production under conditions of growing demand lead often to technological change, or the availability of superior techniques provides incentives for technical change (Landes 1969). Whatever the origin, once underway, the pace to technological change is never smooth, since it activates both pressures to adjust societal structures and the resistance to structural adaptation. Technical change calls for fundamental modifications since it involves the replacement of existing methods of production, service delivery and management causing considerable damage to vested interest with accompanying human dislocations. Rigidities to adaptations originate from the accumulation of institutions, rules and procedures (instituted at an earlier period for legitimate social objectives) but in the context of new technical change become sources of ineffectiveness (OECD 1982). Thus major changes are potentially two facetted; disruptive tendencies and human dislocations build up resistance to adaptation while creative elements increase the capacity for making adjustments.

Insights into potential processes of adjustment to the future can be gained by an increased understanding of the dialectic between pressures and rigidities for structural adaptation to technical change. First, we present two examples of broad adjustments that have been made in the past to major changes. The first pertains to the transition from a largely agricultural economy to a large scale goods fabrication economy and the second refers to the transition from the predominantly goods producing to a predominantly service economy. The purpose of this bird's eye view of social, institutional, cultural, familial and geographical factors that accompany successful technical change - indicating as well the resulting (legacy of the) role of the state in facilitating such adjustments.

Second, we highlight available knowledge on the sources of rigidities to structural change so as to set the stage for a discussion of implications for the role of the public sector and the type of appropriate dynamic analyses of metropolitan change.

4.1 Major Adjustments: Two Historical Examples

In the latter part of the 18th century, British agriculture was exposed to the shock of cheap foreign competition (in a manner similar to that being faced by contemporary North Atlantic industrial production), which began to capture a growing share of the potential domestic and international market. Accompanied by technological innovations that permitted improved labour productivity, the demand for farm labour began to decline. Industry and transport (once the latter was mechanised by the introduction of the steam engine) offered enormous

increases in productivity, that were far superior to those available
to British agriculture. The result of all of this was a redistribution
of manpower and capital resources from the rural to the urban sector
and the relative decline of agriculture - the so called first industrial revolution[2].

This massive economic and spatial restructuring became possible by a
complex series of supporting technological, social, institutional,
cultural innovations. The use of machinery and exploitation of new
sources of energy led to a radical transformation of the methods of
production and structure of industry that entailed the move from the
home or workshop to the factory. The technological and economic change
in turn touched off a social revolution, that was relatively slow at
first but cumulatively large, and that had both creative and destruc-
tive elements. These changes disorganised, dissolved and even demol-
ished older social structures. The class society with its horizontal
divisions and alliances permanently succeeded the 18th century society
with its vertical links of dependence and patronage (Briggs 1979,
Crouzet 1980). These changes led to a redistribution of population
both occupationally and geographically to new production centres resulting in rapid urbanisation. The process of rapid urbanisation to
Britain was anarchic and haphazard. New productive capital appeared
but there was no anticipation of the need for corresponding residential capital or social overhead investment. As a consequence, there
were problems that caught contemporaries unawares and overwhelmed them
in the field of housing, health, education, law and order (Briggs
1979).

The dynamic adjustments that were made to technical change in that era
extended beyond those producing an improvement in physical capital.
Equally important factors are (Hartwell 1971):

- structural and sectoral change (from agriculture, to industry and
  services)

- organisational change that occurred in all sectors resulting from
  better management, and

- investments in human capital (in the form of better nutrition,
  education, health, etc.) that made labour more productive.

To an important degree, the above three changes reflect the increasing role of the service sector (that has been growing in the UK and the US from the beginning of their industrialisations). The development of services played a key role in the first industrial revolution in three ways. These services provided:

-   <u>Social overhead</u> capital which facilitated industrialisation (e.g., transport, communications, public administration, medicine, law and engineering profession)

-   <u>Intermediate services</u> which were necessitated by the increasing divisions of labour in production (e.g., banking, insurance, other financial services, real estate development retail and wholesale trade, etc.)

-   <u>Cultural facilities</u> whose demand derived from increasing wealth (e.g., sports, entertainment, literature, journalism, and music, etc.).

The key factor in the structural adjustment was the increasing production of services especially in industrial production and of transport which enormously increased the market for products. The increase in service productivity came from a combination of better personnel (given the increased human capital investments and greater specialisation of skills). Some historians of the industrial revolution suggest that in the UK and USA the productivity in services was probably higher and was growing faster than in manufacturing till the latter part of the 19th century (see Table 2). Only in the 20th century the growth of productivity in services in the advanced economies began to slow down and to rise more slowly than in manufacturing. There is some recent evidence, however, that suggest that productivity, while lower in the service sector than in manufacturing has experienced a recent acceleration (Levinson and Wheeler 1981).[3]

Table 2

Productivity Rise in Various Sectors

Year	Agriculture % of National Employment	Output	Manufacturing % of National Employment	Output	Services % of National Employment	Output
1750	45	45	30	25	25	30
1850	20	20	40	35	40	45

Source: Hartwell (1971)

This rationalisation of some segments of the service sector, through the reduction of labour costs, is our second example of dynamic adjustment. This adjustment has arrived in the form of technical and organisational means of service provision as households. There is an increasing industrialisation of the service sector. The cost reducing intensification, familiar economies of scale and the displacement of an important part of the service production outside the formal economy into the household. Manufactured consumer products (autos, gasoline, TV sets, washing machines) are combined with intermediate service (e.g., repair services, TV programmes), physical infrastructure (e.g., roads, broadcast networks, power transmission,) and unpaid 'informal' labour (household labour) to produce personal services (e.g., transportation and entertainment) (Gershuny and Miles 1983). Such service innovations, developed and diffused through the OECD countries in last three decades, have contributed to the continued growth of the personal final services sector.

It is being suggested that this dual economy comprising of a formal, highly efficient, and internationally competitive sector for the production of goods and an informal, labour intensive, lower wage sector which produces final services traded on a small scale, or not at all, may be a harbinger of things to come (Gershuny and Miles 1983). The possibilities of extending this model to a wide variety of final non-marketed services - entertainment, information, education and medical - look promising when viewed against recent developments in telecommunications, computing, information storage and retrieval technologies. A variety of innovative services can be provided comprising of:

-   new manufactured products in electronics, heavy electrical equipment and communications

-   a variety of intermediate services (computer programmes, entertainment, educational, health care, software, equipment maintenance), and

-   new telecommunications infrastructure linking production sites to service delivery centres, households and community centres.

The application of such innovations in fields such as community or home based long term elderly care will involve major reorientations of the modes of provision of these services.

4.2 Rigidities in Structural Adaptation

Several recent analyses of the future prospects for growth and change
in the industrialised world have drawn attention to:

a)   classes of problems that increase the rigidities in adaptation to
     change, and

b)   trouble spots in existing institutions that reduce capacity for
     adaptation to change (this section draws heavily on OECD 1981).

Four problem areas that augment rigidities appear to be:

-   Demographic evolution
    Aging of the population leads to decreased occupational and geo-
    graphic mobility, increased dependency ratios, needs for costly
    services and attitudes less congential to structural adaptation.
-   Labour markets
    The recent increase in 'structural' types of unemployment derives
    from (besides the absolute growth of the labour force) some long
    term trends such as:
    (i)   the mismatch between the pattern of job supply (increase of
          low wage, flexitime or part time jobs) and the attitudes of
          skills of job seekers (better educated, seeking occupational
          mobility, etc.), and
    (ii) the creation of rigidities by government policies, while
          varying from country to country in the OECD, in the areas of
          social protection and labour costs. Rigidities have in-
          creased overall costs, reduced the supply of jobs and sad-
          dled certain categories of persons with the burden of unem-
          ployment.[4]

-   Patterns of state intervention
    Rigidities are introduced into industrial societies by certain
    forms of state intervention. Adjustments may be necessary in or-
    der to accommodate the changing environment described above. The
    three relevant aspects of state intervention pertain to:

    (i)   many regulatory policies (necessitated by social concerns
          resulting from market failure) have become rigid. It is
          preferable to have policies that modify individual behaviour

       while maintaining decentralisation of the decision process. This will permit continuous and flexible adjustment hence the current demand for deregulation in many areas,

(ii) public expenditure patterns: while the overall growth in the level of public expenditures is being resisted, potentially major conflicts are also rising in the allocation of expenditures among different categories (e.g., defense, welfare , debt servicing, infrastructure, etc.) and between different social and economic groups.

- International trade
  Increasing competition among developed countries, and between them and some rapidly industrialising developing countries, is strengthening moves to neo protectionism in the form of import restraints, and regulation of the international market for certain industries. Such efforts at neo protectionism hamper structural adjustment in the more industrialised countries and the burden of adjustment is transferred to other countries.

While the above four problem areas pose increasing challenges to structural adaptation, the capacity to adjust in our institutional makeup shows also some 'trouble spots'. Examples are provided by:

- Social oligopolisation
  As Mancur Olson (1952) has pointed out, the organisation of various interest groups (e.g., doctors, farmers, businessmen, labour, etc.) in pluralistic democratic societies pushing for their rigidities in international cooperation, inflation control, and deregulation.

- The faltering performance of the market and the welfare state - the two major institutions for the distribution of goods and services. A major current issue is to use both these institutions in a manner that gets the best out of each, improve their functioning and possibly fashion an associative non market, non government sector for delivery of certain classes of services.

- The problem of political institutions

The key issues here are inefficiencies, 'overgrowth' of many government agencies, and the conflicts resulting from demands for
decentralisation and participation.

These characteristics vary from country to country. Further, the
labour markets in Japan and the US appear to be more adaptable than in
many European countries.

4.3 Implications for Urban Development

We present here some highly speculative observations on the impacts of
this broad range of anticipated changes, and their pressures for
structural adaptation noted above, on urban activities and their organisation in space.[5]

While the impacts of such broad changes may be comprehensive (in the
sense of rapid changes affecting large parts of the population), the
consequences on large organisations and social systems (e.g., urban
form, the household economy), may be selective. Different decision
units evidence varying speeds of response. Productive capital, sensitive to changing environment for opportunities, may response in a
short period. Human capital takes a longer response time. Housing capital turns over more slowly and infrastructure capital even more slowly. The speed of evolution of different forms of capital and activities in urban areas will very much depend upon the role of the public
sector.

It may be useful to distinguish between the various urban impacts from
two perspectives. The first type pertains to the impacts on activities
that are urban in location and the second relates to impacts of national economic activities that can be in either urban or rural space
(Lakshmanan and Chatterjee 1977).

The essentially urban activities relate to three elements of the urban
physical environment; shelter for residential and production activities; transport and communication facilities to link up production
sites and residences and a variety of facilities for the provision of
public (or semipublic) services. Corresponding to these elements of
the urban built environment is a complementary management or control
system comprising of skilled individuals, organisations and institutions, that provides the knowledge and control base. Our discussion in

Section 2 of the demographic transition, industrial and residential evolution underway suggests increased spatial choice in the location of all facilities in the urban built environment. The emerging information driven changes in transportation, communication, production and service delivery is likely to lead to further enrichment of choice, e.g., demand activated personalised transport, demand activated production, decentralised activities in the service sector, etc. As the traditional constraints of space and time are progressively loosened by improved decentralised services (e.g., electronic cottage, video conferencing) there may be alterations of a timing of activities. Thus, a combination of structural trends - changes in the organisation of production and service delivery, organisation of the world economy, life styles and human skill evolution, etc. - provide strong forces working towards dispersed urban patterns. As a consequence, the recent trend for highly differentiated, geographically dispersed structure of centres and subcentres is likely to be accentuated.

However, there are also forces at work that promote regional concentration of economic activities: e.g., the need for face to face contact in rapidly evolving (high information oriented) activities; the secular trend towards higher energy costs; the 'pull' of existing public investments; the attraction of the centres of new technology development; the pull of recent gentrification in central parts of the cities.

What is the likely outcome of the interplay of these opposing tendencies? One hint can be gained from the inertia of the existing built environment and the organisational forces guiding it which are likely to dampen any radical spatial change. Consequently, one can speculate that the emerging spatial pattern will be a diversified but integrated pattern of centres and subcentres with complex linkages among them. Perhaps a more reliable approach is to examine the adjustments that the anticipated changes call for from various national activities (whether in urban or rural location), for such adjustments collectively define the future urban form.

A central feature of the anticipated structural changes is the dynamic disequilibrating processes at work. Two outcomes ensue. On the one hand, pressure for increased mobility of factors of production to reflect the changing economic environment build up. Demand for capital and labour in new sectors and regions arises and for new skills and

new materials emerges. While there are clear benefits to the economy
from increasing factor mobility, machinery, plants and labour in some
industries, some locations undergo devalorisation. Residential capital
owned by labour in sectors and locations suffering decline are particularly vulnerable to this devalorisation. Consequently, serious costs
are imposed on specific segments of the community. It results in organised pressure against shifting of capital from regions with declining prospects.

Thus, the dialectic between the pressures for and resistance to increased factor mobility determines the pattern of economic adjustments
in terms of the speed of growth and new activities, the ordered decline of weaker sectors, and the changing fortunes of residential capital in negatively impacted locations. It is on the outcome of this
conflict that the future geography of economic activities will depend.
In such an outcome, the role of the public sector in facilitating an
equitable and efficient solution is clearly crucial. It is to a clari-
fication of the role of the public sector we turn to next.

5.   CONCLUDING COMMENTS: IMPLICATIONS FOR URBAN POLICY

A major argument running through this paper is that the rate and direction of future technical change and adjustments to it in terms of
the organisation and location of urban activities cannot be separated
from the broader economic and political setting within which they take
place. For example, the cost and feasibility of technical changes in
energy extraction, in communications infrastructure, and in materials
usage will be significantly affected by the environmental, occupational safety and social legislation in effect; the potential ability to
provide the broad enrichment of choice for producers, and consumers in
the emerging information rich era, will depend upon the institutional
and organisational responses. The pace and direction of technical and
organisational innovations will be powerfully influenced by the system
of incentives in place. The manner in which such a system of rewards
and penalties operates to promote technical and change and metropolitan adjustments to it will depend, to a considerable degree, on the
nature and forms of public sector intervention.

Various scholars have referred to the important role of the public
sector in major transformations (Polyani 1957, de Brunhoff 1978). The

areas and forms of public intervention have varied, however, with the conditions and requirements of the period. The public sector played a crucial role in the pursuit of commercial capitalism through its 'economic policy' of mercantilist regulations affecting markets. In early industrialisation, the public sector encouraged the laissez-faire system and facilitated the mobilisation of capital. As the factory system developed, the economies of scale and external economies led to the concentration of capital and economic activities in space with a broad range of labour dislocations and environmental externalities. The burden of adjustment fell on certain groups and regions, depending on their factor endowments. There was, on the part of the state, no anticipation of the adjustments that households of the labour force had to make to these wrenching changes. As the breakage and wastage multiplied and social costs mounted, the public sector assumed an ameliorative role guided by notions of antimonopoly, social justice and welfare. A variety of legislations pertaining to labour organisation, minimum wage, welfare payments, safety and environmental quality and investments in public infrastructure was instituted.

The conditions and requirements for public policy are changing again. Features of the emerging socioeconomic context are smaller, 'footloose' high technology units with a bimodal skill distribution (increasing demand for highly skilled and low skilled labour but limited demand for middle skill groups) and with big appetite for vesture capital; a robust 'informal sector' in a variety of service activities with flexible time schedules; considerable changes in the organisation of the household economy; an overall demand for greater mobility of capital and labour and for adaptive reuse of existing built environment. The pressure to retain social protection conflicts against the pressure for deregulations for encouraging dynamism and innovative capacity.

What do these changes imply for the public sector? On the one hand, the public sector is likely to promote efficient adjustments to change through encouraging factor mobility, appropriate institutional innovations and a greater articulation of the local, national and international aspect of policy in what has become a global economy. On the other hand, given the social consciousness of the significant costs of past dislocations, future public intervention can ill afford to be ex post and ameliorative; it needs to be <u>anticipatory</u> and 'developmental'. The likely costs of adjustments on the part of small producers

and households should be anticipated and provided for in order to facilitate factor mobility. This will mean reduction of the costs of
adjustment and hastening of the adjustment process through institutional innovations that consider both elements of the adjustment process through institutional innovations that consider both elements of
the disequilibriating forces. For example, capital mobility can be
aided through measure for risk spreading. The demand for venture capital can be met by risk reduction through insurance and tax writeoffs.
Indeed in this area, practice has outpaced analytical research. Many
states such as Massachusetts, Connecticut and New Jersey, (which have
made positive adjustments, have fostered the provisions of venture
capital long before the flowering of analytically focussed research in
the area (Bearse and Konopco 1979).

In the area of human capital, the demand for technical education in
the provision of frequent upgrading through continuing education process, is needed. For metropolitan areas adaptive reuse of components
of the urban built environment should be facilitated. Such reuse is
exemplified by a conversion of piano factories and textile mills to
residence and workplaces in Massachusetts, actively promoted by various public sector incentives. Such adjustments to new production and
consumption systems will minimise devalorisation of existing capital
or inequitable transfers between groups. More challenging would be the
imaginative reuse of residential capital stock left behind in regions
devalorised by declining primary activities, e.g., mining. With the
high income elasticity for leisure and recreation in the national and
global economy, such areas can be converted to other uses.

To smooth the operation of the 'dual economies' developing in some
segments of final marketed and non marketed service sectors and to
promote institutional competition among private and public service
providers, a number of social experimentation efforts in institutional
innovations will be required. Such experiments (e.g., the housing supply experiment, income maintenance experiment, in the US) help identify efficient innovations in the delivery of final market and non market services.

Discussions on forms of likely future public intervention has a twofold relevance to students of metropolitan dynamics. First, future
outcomes in the course of metropolitan evolution have heavily influenced such public interventions. Second, because of their far reaching

effects, specific forms of intervention will undergo ex ante assessment of their consequences on desired social objectives. Consequently,
many of the policies considered can be components of metropolitan modelling and analytics. Since policy issues in metropolitan contexts
tend to be complex, ill-structured and amorphous our analytical agenda
needs to be modified in favour of interactive decision modelling that
will capture the complex forces of disequilibria embedded in fostering
positive adjustment to metropolitan decline.

NOTES

(1) Earlier version of this paper was presented at the IIASA Workshop
in Rotterdam in June 1984 and at the Universities of Wales and
Sheffield in winter 1985. The authors are very grateful to many
individuals for their comments - particularly Chang-i Hua, Ake
Andersson, Michael Batty, Philip Cook, Patrick O'Farrell and Ian
Masser.

(2) This transfer did not necessarily initially involve a reduction
in absolute terms of output, manpower and capital engaged in agriculture.

(3) Between 1870-1950 the ratio of rates of change of output/worker
in service and manufacturing sector was 1/3. In the 1950-76 period, the same ratio has climbed to 1/2 (Levinson and Wheeler
1981).

(4) Certain forms of social protection are considerably increasing
the marginal cost of labour while reducing labour mobility and
incentive to work. However, other rigidities are closely connected with social justice. A choice may be necessary between the
immediate benefits of redistribution and indirect consequences,
even in terms of social justice, of economic inefficiency (OECD
1981, p. 170).

(5) Noteworthy explorations of effects of the emerging information
driven changes in the workplace on future urban forms appears in
Simon (1980), Brotchie et al. (1985) and Beaumont and Keys
(1982).

REFERENCES

Bearse, P.J. and Kopka, 'A comparative analysis of state progress to promote new technology based enterprise', The New England Journal of Business and Economics, 1979, Vol. 5, No. 2, pp. 49-74.

Beaumont, J.R. and Keys, P.L., Future Cities: Spatial Analysis of Energy Issues, John Wiley, New York, 1982.

Briggs, A., The Age of Improvement 1783-1867, Longman, London, Chapters 1 and 10, 1979.

Brotchie, J., Newton, P., Hall, P. and Nijkamp, P. (eds), The Future of Urban Form, Croom Helm, London, 1985.

Brotchie, J.D., Dickey, J.W. and Sharpe, R., 'TOPAZ - general planning technique and its applications at the regional urban and facility planning levels', Lecture Notes in Economics and Mathematical Systems, 180, Springer-Verlag, Berlin, 1980.

Browning, H.C. and Singlemann, J., 'The transformation of the US labor force: The interaction of industry and occupation', Politics and Society, 8, (7-4), 1978, pp. 481-509.

Channon, D.F., The Service Industries, MacmMillan Publ. Co., London, 1978.

Clark, C., The Conditions of Economic Progress, MacMillan, London, 1940.

Cross, N., Elliott, D. and Roy, R., Man-made Futures: Readings in Society, Technology and Design, Hutchinson and Co., London, 1974.

De Brunhoff, S., The State, Capital and Economic Policy, Pluto Press, London, 1978.

Fisher, A.G.B., 'Economic implications of material progress', International Labor Review, 1935.

Flinn, M.W., The Origins of the Industrial Revolution, Longman, London, 1966.

Freeman, C., The Economics of Industrial Innovation, Frances Pinter, London, 1982.

Friedrichs, G. and Acheff, A. (eds), Microelectronics and Society: A Report to the Club of Rome, Pergamon Press, London, 1982.

Fuchs, V.R., The Service Economy, National Bureau of Economic Research, New York, 1968.

Gershuny, J., After Industrial Society, MacMillan, London, 1978.

Gershuny, J.I. and Miles, I.D., The New Service Economy, Frances Pinter, London, 1983.

Hartwell, R.M., The Causes of the Industrial Revolution in England, Methuen, London, 1967.

Hartwell, R.M., The Industrial Revolution and Economic Growth, Methuen, London, 1971.

Klein, B.H., Dynamic Economics, Harvard University Press, Cambridge, MA, 1977.

Kondratiev, N.D., 'The long waves in economic life', Review of Economic Statistics, Vol. 1, November 1935, pp. 105-115.

Lakshmanan, T.R. and Chatterjee, L., 'Urbanization and environmental quality', Association of American Geographers, Resource Paper 77-1, Washington DC, 1977.

Landes, D., 'The old bank and the new: the financial revolution of the 19th century', in: Crouzet, F., Chaloner, W.H. and Stern, W.H. - (eds), Essays in European Economic History 1789-1914, Longman, London, 1969, pp. 112-127.

Leven, C.L. (ed), The Mature Metropolis, D.C. Heath Co., Lexington, MA, 1978, pp. 3-20.

Levinson, I. and Wheeler, J.W. (eds), Western Economies in Transition, Hudson Institute Studies, Westview Press, Boulder, Colorado, 1981.

Massey, D. and Meegan, R., 'Industrial restructuring versus the city', Urban Studies, Vol. 5, No. 3, 1978, pp. 273-288.

Nelson, R.R. and Winter, S.S., 'In search of useful theory of innovation', Research Policy, Vol. 6, 1977, pp. 36-76.

Nelson, R.R. and Winter, S.G., An Evolutionary Theory of Economic Change, Harvard University Press, Cambridge, MA, 1983.

Nijkamp, P., 'Long waves or catastrophes in regional development', Socioeconomic Planning Sciences, Vol. 16, No. 6, 1982, pp. 261-271.

OECD, A Medium Term Strategy for Employment and Manpower Policies, Paris, 1978.

OECD, Interfutures, Paris, 1978.

Olson, M., The Rise and Decline of Nations, Yale University Press, New Haven, CT, 1982.

Perliff, H.S., 'The central city in postindustrial age', in: Leven, C.L., D.C. Heath Co., Lexington, MA, 1978, pp. 109-129.

Rothwell, R. and Zegveld, W., Innovation and the Small and Medium Firm, Frances Pinter, London, 1981.

Simon, J., 'The consequences of computers for centralisation and decentralisation', in: Dertonzous, M.A. and Moses, J. (eds), The Computer Age, The MIT Press, Cambridge, MA, 1980.

Schaffer, B. and Lamb, G., Can Equity be Organized? Gower, London, 1981.

Schmookler, J., Innovations and Economic Growth, Harvard University Press, Cambridge, MA, 1981.

Schumpeter, J.A., Business Cycles, McGraw Hill, New York, 1939.

Thompson, W., A Preface to Urban Economics, The Johns Hopkins University Press, Baltimore, MD, 1965.

Utterback, J.M. and Abernathy, W.J., 'Patterns of industrial innovation', Technology Review 80, June-July 1978.

Van der Berg, R.D., Klaassen, L.H., Rossi, H. and Vijverberg, C., Urban Europe, Vol. 1, A Study of Growth and Decline, Pergamon, Oxford, 1980.

Van der Zwan, A., On the assessment of Kondratiev cycle and related issues, Center for Research in Business Economics, Rotterdam, mimeo, 1979.

Wigan, M.R. and Morris, J.M.M., 'The transport implications of activity and time budget constraints', Transport Research 15A, 1, 1980, pp. 56-66.

Wilson, A.G., Urban and Regional Models in Geography and Planning, John Wiley Publications, London, 1974.

TECHNOLOGY AND NEW REGIONAL GROWTH COMPLEXES:
THE ECONOMICS OF DISCONTINUOUS SPATIAL DEVELOPMENT*
Michael Storper

1.   INTRODUCTION: DYNAMICS OF THE SPACE ECONOMY

This paper outlines an economic logic for explaining the rise of new
regional growth complexes, or regions where industries associated with
major new product groups undergo their first major phase of growth. In
it, both demand for and supply of spatial factors of production are
seen as endogenous outcomes of the process of competition and technical change under the condition of perpetual economic disequilibrium.
As a result of the development of these complexes, the margins of industrial space economies as a whole are pushed outward. This process
of 'extensification' is a critical phase in the long run dynamics of
spatial production relations. The logic of these dynamics is thus a
key element in the future development of an historically tractable
theory of spatial political economy. This paper assembles a series of
specific concepts with respect to technology, production prices, and
spatial behaviour into a coherent view of new growth centres. It bor-
rows openly from a variety of literatures on these subjects; it is us
synthetic rather than specialised. The purpose of the synthesis is to
construct a solid interpretation of reality, rather than to construct
an aesthetically perfect theoretical edifice. Nonetheless, virtually
all of the constituent concepts in the hypothesis proposed here are
available in mathematical form in the referenced literature.

1.1 New Industry Growth Complexes: Geographical Industrialisation

We can illustrate the dynamic process of spatial development, or what
I prefer to label 'geographical industrialisation', by telling a highly stylised, but still realistic story about the location of an industry associated with a major new group of products.

The story begins with the invention of some major new type of commodity use-value, i.e., a fundamentally new way of meeting a social need.

This can take the form of directly designing the new final output good, or it can begin with the invention of some major new form of motive power or conceptual advance applicable across a broad range of technologies. The former case is exemplified by automobiles, computers, airplanes, the latter by semiconductors, the steam engine and the guided missile. Either of these types of inventions tends ultimately to encourage whole industries or industry groups to grow up to produce them: the former because the form of the final output is radically different from the way that social need was previously met; the latter because new social division of labour, in the form of new branches of production is called into being. Both are opposed to a class of inventions we can loosely call products of 'Learning by Doing'; these become integrated into and ultimately subservient to, existing branches of industry organised for production of already defined output groups (cf. Rosenberg 1982).[1]

In the initial stage of the industry's development, a wide variety of prototypes may come into existence as the result of 'backyard' inventions. Typically, a range of ideas for product or process development is tested out - as in the case of experimentation with internal combustion engines and electric motors for automobiles, and more recently with the many early configurations of personal computers. Alternatively, industrial R & D laboratories may competitively develop a variety of competing conceptions simultaneously, each hoping to take the market. But the diffusion of the product is limited to a few specialised producers and (in the case of consumer goods) a few (usually wealthy) eccentric consumers.

We are more interested in the second major stage of the industry's development where a few major lines of approach to the configuration of the final output, and a basic format for organising production come to dominate the industry's output. The form of the commodity is now somewhat technically reliable and no longer a novelty, but it continues to undergo rapid changes in configuration and, as the market grows in extent, an industrial production process begins to take shape.

In this stage, the locational 'decisions' made by various producing agents in the industry - people who have important roles in the invention/innovation process and its transformation into routinised manufacturing - establish centres of growth for the industry, and these centres of concentration of headquarters, product development and manufacturing (especially of components, as opposed to final output assembly) often become centres for the 'mature' industry over the long run. This stage already brings a significant change in the spatial configuration of production for the new commodity, for the widely-scattered inventors are either eliminated from competition or they begin to migrate to the emerging growth centre to gain access to information and the business networks that are beginning to be established. A process of spatial concentration begins.

Where are these centres? They tend not to be in the largest centres of a nation's urban hierarchy. Nor are they typically actually in the already well developed parts of secondary urban-industrial regions in the urban system. Perhaps the best way to describe their locations is to say that they are often near secondary urban-industrial regions, but not in them; they are in the 'hinterlands' of those regions. Occasionally, they are located in urban regions which are even farther down the national urban hierarchy, the 'third tier' of regions, some of which will rise to the second tier by virtue of the growth of their major industry complex. Both automobiles in Detroit and agricultural implements in Chicago and its environs originally grew in third-tier metropolitan regions and were part of the process that brought them up the hierarchy. Aerospace (in Long Beach and the South Bay area, near Los Angeles), electronics (Santa Clara Valley near San Francisco and Route 128 near Boston), electrical machinery (hinterlands of New York City) all developed near, but not in, major urban regions.

All became the centres of major new regional growth processes, as the industries themselves developed through market widening and standardisation of production. As Scott (1982, 1983, 1985c) demonstrates, these industries set into motion a process of creation of factor supplies - including labour, developed land, infrastructure, and ancillary industrial and non industrial services. Put into neoclassical terminology, the industry causes regional factor 'supply curves' to move outward in response to the demand of the industry.

There are really two, often conflated. meanings of diffusion in geographical literature. On the one hand, we speak of the spatial diffusion of product innovations from some 'point' of origin or some moment in time. On the other hand, there is the related but not identical question of the diffusion of an industry from a point of origin. The story thus far suggests that something is missing in the conventional

diffusionist notion that new industries 'incubate' in well developed
areas and move outward from them. It appears instead that they locate
in not so developed areas and it is in these growth centres that they
subsequently mature and _from_ which they then may eventually decentralise.[2]

Let me advance a _qualitative_ conjecture about the spatial behaviour of
major new industries: new industries seem to 'leapfrog' in space, to
establish new growth centres somewhat discontinuous with highly industrialised regions. This conjecture is not amenable to precise quanti-
fication: the position of these growth centres with respect to a national urban hierarchy depends on the overall shape of that hierarchy,
and so it is impossible to capture this _quality_ of new growth centres
with any set of propositions concerning their empirically invariant
characteristics.

Here it is appropriate to ask why industries jump through space away
from well developed areas. This behaviour must be accounted for in two
ways. First, the logic of the processes by which industries are _en-_
abled to jump through space must be established. This logic is distinctly non neoclassical, based on disequilibrium economic dynamics.
Second, the concrete motivations for this behaviour must be understood. This rich palette of reasons for why actual industries seek out
these new locations can, as I shall argue, be conceptualised only via
attention to the broad social dynamics of regional political economies
in the form of regional social structures of accumulation.

Thus, the story of extensification raises the questions to which the
remainder of this paper is devoted:

1.   What is the economic-technological logic by which we can explain
     how a new industry is _enabled_ to leapfrog is space? Why, in a
     competitive economy, is the industry not constrained from this
     behaviour? (Sections 2 and 3).

2.   Given the possibility of leapfrogging, what are the positive mo-
     tivations that capitalists may have for doing so? (section 4).

2.   INNOVATION AND LOCATION AS FORMS OF DISEQUILIBRIUM GROWTH

In virtually any mode of economic thinking, the capability to locate could be defined as the ability to satisfy a given set of factor demands, or to match factor demands with factor supplies at a particular location such that at least average rates of return on capital invested are reaped: elsewhere we call this the 'rule of profits' in industry location (Walker and Storper 1981). Instead of rejecting the traditional microeconomic categories of supply and demand, they may be resituated at the centre of an enquiry into the dynamics of locational capabilities. Factors, in this usage, denotes all the relationships required for production at a particular location (including markets). An hypothesis concerning dynamics must ask how demands for and supplies of locationally-important factors of production change historically. What regulates the changes in these demands from production and supplies in the locational surface, and how do the two interact? In seeking the answers to these complex questions, we seek to account for spatial economic dynamics, or geographical industrialisation, rather than spatial allocation which is the concern of conventional industrial location.

To explain the locational behaviour described above, we must engage debates in economics, specifically those concerned with production technique and factor demands and location theory, specifically those concerned with the relationships of location to production prices and profit levels.

There are four elements in this hypothesis which we outline here to give a sense of the progression of the broad logic of the argument to be advanced. First, technologies represent particular 'paths taken' because they are developed under conditions of disequilibrium. To theorise these paths, we must have a much richer notion of competition under capitalism than is provided in neoclassical economics (Sections 2.1.1 - 2.1.3). Second, the data that describe particular industries - prices of production, profitability, factor demands and inputs, and market structure - are the outcomes of the specific paths taken in development of the industry's technology, in the light of intersectoral resource flows. Unlike in equilibrium models or structural-functional Marxist approaches, however, these flows do not determine sectoral development (Section 2.2). Third, just as an industry is a specifically-constructed assemblage of resources, so is its spatial growth complex: a congeries of regional factor supplies and prices thereof which attach to the propulsive industry. This, as we shall see, enables us to explain how it is that industries are enabled to create new growth complexes (Section 3). Fourth, we can speculate on the positive motivations capitalists have for locating new industries in new places; these reasons go beyond the strictly economistic (Section 4).

2.1.1 The 'Choice of Technique' Revisited: Scale and Inflexible Outcomes

Most industrial production is amenable to <u>increasing returns to scale</u>. This obvious and simple fact is, if taken seriously, incompatible with equilibrium analysis and demands an entirely different theoretical apparatus for understanding economic dynamics. In any rigorous formulation of neoclassical theory, homogeneous and linear production functions are axiomatic to perfect competition and profit maximisation. And we should remind ourselves of Marshall's attempt through the notion of external economies and the use of partial equilibrium analysis, to accommodate both increasing and decreasing returns to scale within the same model, which was rendered stillborn by Sraffa's famous 1926 article on the Laws of Returns.

The most common definition of increasing returns is that they describe a condition where input costs per unit output decline with increases in the volume of output. This can still have several meanings, however. On the one hand, it can mean that there are <u>indivisibilities</u> in a production technology. In this case, physical integration of manufacturing operations enables costs per unit of output to decrease. Increasing returns from these indivisible technologies become inoperative above certain levels of production, and therefore efficient production could be possible as a particular multiple of indivisible technology. If individual choices of technique were constrained by neoclassical outcomes (which they are not, as we shall see), then even with this type of increasing return, the efficiency frontier of the economy could be a 'jagged surface' while remaining convex (neoclassical) in the large.

Although these kinds of scale economies are important, they do not exhaust the possibilities. Not all causes of increasing returns can be attributed to indivisibility of one kind or another and there is no reason to suppose that economies of scale become inoperative above certain levels of production. This is because, in capitalist economies, there is a steady and stepwise improvement in knowledge gained from experience - the dynamic economies of scale - which have nothing to do with indivisibilities (Kaldor 1972). These increasing returns cannot be isolated as multiples of discrete units of technology or activity; they are 'in the air'. The vast majority of the manufacturing economy is organised around these dynamic returns to scale.

In this more general and enriched definition of returns to scale, the necessity that the outcomes of technological choices be efficient, as in the case of the indivisibility definition of returns to scale, is shattered. In other words, the law of diminishing returns upon which neoclassical economics is premised, makes a <u>fundamentally</u> unrealistic assumption about technology (not merely a convenient simplification of empirical reality).

Even in the rather restricted case of 'technical choice' from a set of known blueprints (and thus not even counting the more complex issue of technological innovation, to which we return shortly), we can see that increasing returns to scale introduce disequilibrium outcomes. To illustrate this I will, quite straightforwardly, reiterate the analysis advanced by Arthur (1983).

Usually there are several ways to carry out any given economic purpose. We can call these ways 'technologies' and we are interested, for the moment, in technologies that can potentially fulfil the same purposes, i.e., that compete for shares of a 'market' of potential adopters. Technologies may exist as pure method or pure information, or they may already be incorporated in physical plant or machinery; or they may be marketed as products. We are considering here the case where two or more superior technologies (products or processes) are competing with <u>each other</u> to replace an outmoded technology (thus, <u>not</u> the standard diffusion case where a new and superior technology competes with an old and inferior one). For example, in the 1890s, the steam engine, the electric motor, and the gasoline engine competed as power sources for the new automobile. In the 1800s and on into this century, spinning mules competed with ring frames in cotton manufacturing. And recently, different configurations of personal computers and videocassette recorders have competed with each other.

A given technology combines a certain vector of economic inputs or factors for a given amount of desired 'output', so that monetary returns in use or payoff to adaptation to a particular agent are simply

the value of the output less factor cost over an appropriate time horizon.[3] A technology that is not adopted due to standard or convention, as in the case of the typewriter keyboard, tends to be fluid.
Rosenberg (1982) calls this fluidity 'Learning by Using'. But for the
purposes of this example, we will abstract from learning by using to
the pure increasing returns case, where returns rise simply with the
numbers who have chosen a technology.[4]

In the standard (neoclassical) textbook case of technical choice, all
the technologies competing for adoption show diminishing returns, and
market sharing is the result. As demand increases, adoption follows a
composite supply curve obtained from the lateral addition of the separate returns curves for each technology. The outcome is completely
predictable - we can determine in advance the market shares after n
choices in this situation - and it is easy to show that the configuration which emerges is efficient. The outcome is also flexible: adjustment of either returns curve can always shift the composite supply
curve and hence market shares.

Where objects with increasing returns compete, the market outcome is
usually indeterminate. With increasing returns present, non convexi-
ties appear in the supply curve, and multiple equilibria are called
into being. Information on preferences, endowments and transformation
possibilities enables us to locate these long run equilibria hypothet-
ically in the form of comparative statistics, but this is insufficient
to tell us which one will actually capture the market. Thus,

> 'From many initial positions of interest, the system - like a
> pencil perfectly balanced on its point - is equally 'attracted'
> by several 'equilibrium' outcomes. We cannot say which way it
> will fall; hence, we cannot predict uniquely which path it will
> follow. Thus, we cannot pursue conventional analysis.' (Arthur
> 1983:7)

Arthur illustrates this point with the example of an island where cars
are introduced, all at more or less the same time. Drivers are free to
choose between the right and left hand sides of the road and have no
inbuilt bias towards either. Each side possesses increasing returns;
as a higher proportion of drivers chooses one side, the very real returns to choosing that side rapidly rise. Casual thought tells us that
we would observe a good deal of randomness to the proportions initially driving on each side, but that if one side by chance got sufficiently ahead, other drivers would 'fall in' on this side, so that

eventually all cars would drive on the same side of the road. Of course the side that 'wins' - that comes to dominate the market - cannot be deduced in advance. The outcome is indeterminate.

Notice four aspects of the outcomes themselves worth investigation. First, in contrast to the usual diminishing returns situation, the outcome need possess <u>no efficiency</u> properties - the side that 'takes the market' need not, from any long run collective viewpoint, be the better of the two. Second, driving is now locked in to the chosen side. The outcome is <u>structurally rigid</u>, in that marginal inducements to individual drivers to change sides would likely prove ineffective and policy would have to find other means. Third, even though we know drivers' preferences and possibilities, ex ante the outcome would be <u>unpredictable</u>. 'Small events' <u>outside</u> the model - perhaps some drivers' reactions, perhaps a dog running onto the road, perhaps the timing or positioning of certain traffic lights - may be crucial in deciding the outcome. And, fourth, ex post, exact causality is hard to assign - it would certainly be a mistake to ascribe it to the 'innate superiority' of the outcome.

Mathematically this means that where the market share of each technology follows a stochastic process - a random walk - and the menu of technologies shows standard diminishing returns, or even constant returns, this random walk has reflecting barriers. The aggregate outcome then may logically be efficient, flexible, predictable and ergodic. But, if technologies show increasing returns, the same random walk has absorbing barriers. In this latter case which, as we have noted, typifies the modern industrial economy, the resulting dynamics have the four principal features we have already suggested: 1) a non ergodic property where small events at the outset are not averaged out and forgotten, but may decide the path of market shares; 2) a potential inefficiency of aggregate outcome even where individual choices are perfectly rational; 3) a potential inflexibility or outcome in that ultimate market shares cannot always be influenced by standard policy measures once they have gone beyond a certain point; and 4) a non predictability, in that knowledge of supply and demand functions does not suffice to predict the path of market shares.

Our tendency when observing economic history is to look for reasons why technologies that ultimately came to predominate are superior, and for the means by which this innate superiority came to be translated into adoption.

> 'But this form of reasoning is only logically valid (not to mention historically valid, another question entirely) only for technologies with constant diminishing returns. Where technologies exist potentially in ever more efficient variants, superiority itself becomes a function of adoption or use. In the neoclassical case of diminishing or constant returns - ergodicity - history is reduced to the status of mere carriers, the deliverer of the inevitable'. (Arthur 1983:25)

In the realistic case, microevents are magnified by positive feedback; _their_ cumulation decides the outcomes and _forms_ the causality. Circumstances become cemented into the technological structure of the economy, and history in a sense becomes destiny.

2.1.2 The Development of Technologies: Search and Adoption in Disequilibrium

It is obviously impossible to attempt any complete and generalised theory of technological innovation here. Instead, I will confine my comments to a few points on the historical 'direction' of technical change.

What happens when capitalists face unstable market conditions - price changes, demand instability, etc. - or, if they sense the possibility of major breakthroughs that would enable them to earn superprofits.[5] Following Nelson and Winter (1982), it would seem that these capitalists engage in search for new technologies. The _search_ for new technologies, i.e., behaviour that would lead to the creation of new product or process options (among which we described the process of choice in the previous section of this paper), has some of the same characteristics of the _choice_ of technique. First, inasmuch as search involves the acquisition or production of information, it is intrinsically _irreversible_. The irreversibility is rooted in the familiar economic fact that the costs of retention and use of a given item of information are typically much lower than the costs of initial acquisition or production. The second fundamental characteristic that distinguishes search is _uncertainty_. The scene surveyed by a decision maker inside the firm may well include identifiable 'alternatives' that could be explored, but these are only dimly perceived and it may not be at all clear which will turn out to be best. The process of exploring perceived alternatives, or simple accidents, may bring to light other alternatives not even contemplated in the original assessments. This is in contrast to the neoclassical model in which equilibrium is reached by choosing from a sharply defined set of alternatives (blueprints from a pseudo-production function).[6] Moreover, the outcomes of uncertainty may be _perverse_:

> 'A metal fabricating firm confronts a sudden rise in the price of its raw materials. It makes routine adjustments to this change by, say, making greater use of odd shaped pieces of material that were formerly treated as scrap. After this adjustment, a severe profit pinch remains, and triggers a search for ways to deal with this situation - a search that would not have been undertaken had the price increase and cost crisis not occurred. The result of the quest is the discovery that new types of _labour_ saving machinery, adaptable to the firm's problems, have become available. The firm buys such machinery and eases its profit problem - but the new machinery is less tolerant of odd shaped pieces of material than were the workers who previously performed the relevant operations. As a result, the raw material intensity of the output _increases_. Search triggered by the price rise has contributed a perverse component to the total response of the firm'. (Nelson and Winter 1982:174)

This is an essential correlate to the uncertainty of search processes.

Finally, search is distinguished by what we may call its _contingent_ character. Real search processes take place in specific historical contexts, and their outcomes clearly depend in part on what those contexts contain in the way of problem solutions that are to be 'found'. What there is to be found consists in large part of the fruits, byproducts and residues of information producing activities elsewhere in the society. The flow of general social history thus impinges directly on the firm through its search activities. These three aspects of search are historical processes, not repetitive, and not readily separable from other processes of historical change. They require that we distinguish routine behaviour within organisations from search, which is strategic, non routine behaviour.

It is unlikely, but still possible, that the aggregate outcome of innovations (across sectors, in a whole economy) could be perverse with respect to factor supplies and relative prices in the aggregate, over the medium run (cf. David 1975). But even when the overall direction of change in factor use is consistent with the direction of changes in aggregate supplies and relative prices, the latter cannot be taken as causes. Indeed, the overall development of prices and quantities of factors in the economy is the consequence of the search and choice dynamics we have described here, and not the other way around. To this issue we now turn briefly.

2.1.3   Expanded Reproduction and Factor Creation

Most economic thinking - including that of all branches of spatial studies - has been almost completely dominated by attention to the allocative functions of markets to the exclusion of their creative functions - 'as instruments for transmitting impulses to economic change' (Kaldor 1972:1240). But a world with the kinds of technological processes we have described above requires an enriched conception of competition, most similar to that advanced by Marx, but shared by all the classical political economists (Kaldor 1982, Robinson 1956, Young 1928).

There are two aspects of resource creation that deserve emphasis in the context of the current discussion. First, when every change in the use of resources - every reorganisation of productive activities - creates the opportunity for a further change which would not have otherwise existed, the notion of an 'optimum' allocation of resources is meaningless and contradictory. This is because, with increasing returns and expanded reproduction, each particular resource can make as great or greater a contribution to output in its actual case as in any alternative use. The 'pattern of use of resources at any one time is no more than a link in the chain of an unending sequence and the very distinction, vital to equilibrium economics, between resource creation and resource allocation, loses its validity' (Kaldor 1972:1245). In other words, the very act of bringing into existence new means of production will, under many circumstances, lead to the 'creation' of new factor supplies, as part of the expanded reproduction of the economy. In growth phases of the economic cycle, when expanded reproduction of capital is occurring, the problem of the economy is not the allocation of scarce resources, but quite the opposite: there tends to be an 'overaccumulation' of capital. Capitalist economies, rather than tending toward states of rest, seem to exist under conditions of dynamic growth and decline, and growth phases are extraordinarily capable of creating all kinds of new factor supplies[7]

Second, the precise content and direction of resource creation and flows of resources under conditions of expanded reproduction cannot be

determined via the analytics of optima or by Marxist functionalism[8]
Reorganisation of production under conditions of increasing returns
means the transfer of some factors to new roles where their contributions to output will be greater than before. The aggregates of supply,
demand and relative prices in the economy depend on the precise ways
that capitalists find to produce commodities, and how they put them
into action. Neither the possibility set for expanded reproduction of
capital, nor the precise choices that will be made from that set, can
be predicted.

2.2 Profits, Prices and Markets: The 'Pull' of Resources to Growing and Innovating Sectors

In the dynamic economy we are portraying here, it is not only the dynamics of the development of technology and aggregate resource flows
that differ from orthodox views. Tied to them is a host of short term
processes of economic behaviour. These processes are: the relationship
of production prices to market prices; the resulting patterns of profitability; the endogeneity of market structures; and the creation of
particular factor supplies. With alternative views of these processes,
we will be prepared to offer an hypothesis in the next section about
the location of innovating industry groups, and the subsequent geographical industrialisation process.

First, we must reject the neoclassical price theory in favour of classical views of price setting. What Smith calls 'natural prices' and
Marx terms 'prices of production', are independent from short run demand and supply. The centre of gravity of prices, in this thinking, is
determined by wages and profits, identified backwards through the entire input chain for a final output. All commodity inputs are eventually decomposed into wages and profits.[9] Long run relative prices
of production are the sum of vertically integrated wages and profits
which are the relative values of direct and indirect labour requirements.[10] In the long run, these change when the social and technical
conditions of the reproduction of a commodity change, and when there
are changes in the weights of different techniques in the overall composition of economic output among industries. The development of these
techniques is subject to the same inflexibility, unpredictability and
contingency pointed out earlier.

Marx refers to a <u>regulation</u> of market prices by the centre of gravity, rather than price <u>determination</u>. Market prices are not equilibrium prices (Semmler 1984). Actual prices are equal top natural prices, labour values or prices of production only by accident and as a result, the profit rates of industries and firms are never equal to the social average. Even though much is made of Marx's dictum that competition tends to equalise profit rates between industries and firms, it is less often recognised that his notion of competition implies that the forces of innovation are constantly defeating the equalisation tendency before it is realised, and as a result, competition produced deviations from the centre of gravity and the normal profit rate as well as tendencies towards them.

It is not difficult to see why. Market prices are subject to the constellation of supply and demand, speculation, restrictions on the mobility of capital and so on, which force market prices to fluctuate around the centre of gravity. In the world of real space and time, there are neither infinite elasticities nor perfect inelasticities of supply and demand. There are only real supplies of commodities (and futures) based on production capacity, and real demands of concrete consumers. Short run supply inelasticities are endemic because capital is not putty, i.e., it is not perfectly mobile. And, as we have noted, the long term result of short run changes to capital stock is inflexible, unpredictable and contingent because technological change is typically involved (cf. Clark and Gertler 1984). Thus, not only is there not perfect mobility of capital in the short run (the assumption made by neoclassical models), but the short run events that occur as a result of the 'opening' created by inelasticities have important impacts on the ultimate outcome. In reality, therefore, competition is as much a force for differentiation of production conditions as it is for their equalisation.

Accordingly, there are profitability differences between firms and industries caused by the deviations of market prices - which reflect sectoral averages - and production prices - which reflect firm or industry specific conditions of production. Firms with better than average techniques capture surplus profits (which are quasi-rents on capital analogous to land rent, but applied here to manufacturing). Also, because the potential for internal scale economies differs between firms of different sizes, there may be production cost and profit rate differentials between big and small firms.[11]

The incidence of surplus profits is most relevant to the case of new regional growth complexes. For industries with increasing volume of output, an opportunity for producers to reap a greater per unit differential between production prices and market prices than the economy wide average presents itself, and the whole sector enjoys superprofits (cf. Markusen 1985). As Schumpeter puts it:

> '...for a considerable time during which the new article is vigorously gaining ground, its price as well as its quantity may be very little sensitive to cyclical fluctuations. Demand may go on shifting upward through several depressions of the Kitchin, possibly even of the Juglar, and there may be no reason for the innovating firms to change their prices...' (Schumpeter 1939:541).

How is it possible that these new products can attract buyers at inflated prices? Especially in high income economies, there are resources available to find new occupations. If incomes are not too unequally distributed, there are usually also incentives even for those with moderate incomes to be interested in consuming technological innovations, in the early stages when prices are very high, and in the later stages there are opportunities for creation of mass markets. This is very different from the neoclassical view in which there are only rational substitutions among fully allocated household incomes.

A further source of profit differentiation arises with respect to individual firms. Since adding capacity often entails changing to a more efficient technique (either through search or due to Learning by Using), the process of 'normal' competition holds out the promise not merely of normal profits, but of superprofits (cf. Schumpeter 1939, Nelson and Winter 1982:201-202, Markusen 1985, Mandel 1978).[12] Note that this differs completely from the neoclassical view in which vintage capital models are reconciled with equilibrium, and with Marxist equilibrium models, where technologies with indivisibilities create below-normal transitional profit rates (cf. Okishio 1961, Roemer 1980). In the disequilibrium view advanced here, the prospect of superprofits is a major motivation to innovation search behaviour: transition opportunities again have long term impacts.[13]

The question arises of how long it takes for industry profit rates above or below the average to develop 'normal' rates of profit. The classical answer is that the time required to adjust supply to demand, market prices to prices of production, and profit rates to the social average, depends on the concrete conditions of production and circulation of a commodity; the time to build up new capacity in industries where the profit rate is above average and to withdraw money capital from fields of employment with low profit rates - that is, the turnover time of capital - is different in each industry and from production technique to production technique. No general theory about adjustment time (i.e., aggregating capital) to equalise profit rates is possible.

Growing industries and innovating firms may be said to enjoy - temporarily - a kind of factor-attraction power with respect to the rest of the economy. Moreover, as Schumpeter points out, along with the innovating entrepreneur (who is the main protagonist of economic development), we find the banker, the architect of the exchange economy, who creates and puts at the disposal of the entrepreneur new purchasing power. The entrepreneur uses this buying power to extract a certain amount of factors from the circular flow, that is, from previous uses.[14] When these are combined using technologies with increasing returns, the extraction of resources becomes creation of new factor supplies.

Most important for our purposes, the precise composition of factors demanded by the industry and extracted from the rest of the economy, is not determined in advance, but it is inflexible and non ergodic once a path is taken. There are two principal reasons for this. First, as we have noted, successful innovation does not require the reduction of use of any particular factor, and outcomes are unpredictable and often perverse with respect to relative factor prices, Second, in the context of innovations, market structure evolves endogenously. Given the capital stocks and techniques of the firms in a particular period, the output for that period is determined. The demand curve then determines market price (within limits, of course) and productivity levels (given input prices) determine production costs. For each firm the ratio of price to unit production cost - the 'price-cost ratio' - is determined. It can be assumed that a firm's desire to expand or contract is governed by its price-cost ratio and its prevailing market share, within constraints set by the ability to finance investment. For firms of a given size, the greater the ratio of price to production cost, the greater the desired proportional expansion. And the greater the price-cost ratio, the greater the firm's retained earnings and the greater its ability to persuade the capital market to provide finance (Nelson and Winter 1982:283)[15] The consequence is that

'it makes better sense to see firms as having 'quantity' policies
rather than as having 'price policies'. Quantity policies are
made operative through the firm's investment decisions. Firms
with large market shares recognise that their expansion can spoil
their own market. The large a firm's current market share, the
greater must be the price-cost ratio needed to induce a given
desired proportional expansion. ...(A) spectrum of possible patterns of investment behaviour may be represented.' (Nelson and
Winter 1982:283)

How may we conclude this discussion? We can sat that, <u>as sectors generate their innovations and market structures, so it can be said that
they generate their own input histories</u>.[16]

3. <u>NEW REGIONAL GROWTH COMPLEXES: PRODUCED INDUSTRIES/PRODUCED
    SPACES</u>

We are now prepared to present the core of our hypothesis with respect
to the development of new regional growth complexes: <u>in the early
stages of growth of a new industry group, the combination of superprofits, imperfect competition due to capital mobility barriers, and
relatively price inelastic demand for the commodity output, make it
possible for the industry to develop successfully whatever region the
industry's innovators happen to settle on</u>. If a firm or industry is
making superprofits, it may have the tactical flexibility to undertake
radically new spatial strategies which are not limited by strict price
competition. The issue of cost minimising location for the initial
growth complex may be, for the most part, simply <u>ignored</u> by the innovators in the industry, as their attention is devoted to other matters. Because of this, there may be invasions of new territories which
are much more dramatic than we might expect from the logic of equilibrium prices. In contrast to the images of highly constrained spatial
behaviour which are implies in equilibrium models (see Section 2
above), the metaphor of spatial 'leapfrogging' seems more appropriate.

The distribution of regional factor supplies is not independent of the
distribution of industry. In the light of the enabling factors described above, we have established logically that the location and
condition of many factor supplies can be altered by the action of capitalists in growing industries Regional development thus becomes a
self fulfilling prophecy for the areas that have these industries: they
can create the conditions for location where they did not before
exist, in the same way that technological change creates resources in

the aggregate. Over the long run, the concrete factor supplies in a region are the historical residue of the concrete factor demands of its industries. The region is a congeries of resources demanded by the industries central to its economy; this demand process is causally 'prior' to demand-supply interactions. Thus, to say that regional factor supplies reflect the demands of regional industries is not merely a commonsense observation of superficial reality, but a theoretical claim that regional development is 'demand based' (demand for factors of production, not consumer demand). Regional economies have the theoretical status of produced historical facts, just as are industry technologies; they are not outcomes that 'had to be', or that followed a structurally predictable line of development.

This hypothesis about the sources of regional development, however, does not rule out a role for regional factor market growth and adjustment processes, to which so much of regional economics has been addressed. I cannot do this enormous subject justice here, but a few comments on the implications of the framework I have elaborated may be useful.

In the orthodox neoclassical approach, regional factor markets tend towards equilibrium, such that the price of a factor in a given region would reflect its marginal rates of substitution with respect to other factors along a given production function of the regional industry, and that this would cumulate to the same result vis a vis total regional factor productivity.[17] In the logic advanced here, industry factor demands are inflexible ex post. Under this circumstance, the demand for and supply of a factor in a given region could be said to be in a sort of 'equilibrium' when regional factor supplies are priced so that the industry or firm in question receives the average rate of profit; that is, the firm's or industry's production prices in the region are identical to the sectoral averages, and the industry or firm thus receives exactly normal profits. But there is nothing in the developmental logic we have advanced that guarantees this; indeed, it would be an extraordinary coincidence since it would require either that the firm employ precisely the average technology and that factor prices be at precisely the average of factor prices used by all firms in the sector, or that factor prices somehow manage to set themselves so as to compensate precisely for different mixes of factor demands among firms - ex post fixed factor demands - in effect creating an ex post 'substitution'. All this seems patently ridiculous.

Under these circumstances, factor markets at the regional level must be seen as outcomes of factor demand dynamics in which supply adjustments play a distinctly secondary role. The chain of events on the demand side, which we have described above, is likely to have powerful long run impacts on the region, and not to be important merely due to a lag in the adjustment of factor supply markets or sectoral production capacity to demand.

3.1 Regional Returns to Scale in the Context of Industry Returns

The importance of regional returns to scale has been acknowledged in the spatial development literature since Myrdal's pioneering observations of the 1950s, and recently some of it has begun to be formalised in more sophisticated ways (cf. Swales 1983). Concurrently, numerous attempts have been made, within the neoclassical regional literature, to view spatial concentration as a consequence of the increases in aggregate regional factor productivity which are supposedly attendant upon these regional Verdoorn effects. In this way, various kinds of optima for city sizes have been worked out, and spatial concentration and urbanisation have been viewed as merely one more example of efficient patterns of resource allocation.

More recently, Scott (1984, 1985c), building on the work of Coase (1937), has begun to show that regional scale economies can be best understood as a consequence of industrial organisation. The specific sectoral structure of transactions between production units rooted in the technical organisation of production and labour processes, generates the demand for - indeed, the necessity of - agglomeration. Growing industries tend to be vertically disintegrated and spatially agglomerated, forming the regional growth complexes we are considering here.

In the light of the logic adumbrated in this paper, and combined with Scott's observations about the relationship between production organisation and agglomeration, it can be seen that the neoclassical interpretation of Verdoorn effects is questionable. There are two sources of Verdoorn effects at issue here: those which apply to the development of the industry as a whole, through the technological search and choice dynamics we have described, and those that are realised through spatial clustering. The former make it possible for the industry - when it is growing rapidly and successful firms are reaping

superprofits - to exercise a certain factor attraction power which is
not limited by neoclassical perfect competition. This disequilibrium
condition, as we have noted, makes it possible for the industry to attract factors to its regional growth complex. The latter type of scale
economy, which is specifically the consequence of the vertically disintegrated structure of production and its dense network of transactions, certainly has the effect of reducing production costs and raising factor productivity, but there is no reason to ascribe to its primacy in explaining regional concentration. It is, indeed, a consequence of, and strictly dependent on, the technical structure of the
production process in the industry.

These regional scale economies may partially offset the possibility
that regional factor supplies are not cost minimising at these stages
of growth, but there is no reason to expect them necessarily to do so.
The regional factor costs that the industry faces are combined results
of several different forces: technological development and the production prices they make possible are primary because they determine
the industry's ability to pay for factors. These determinants are then
secondarily modified by market price competition as it unfolds at different stages of the industry's development, and by the external economies or diseconomies affecting those prices at any particular stage.
Given the nature of technological development and choice, and the
theory of prices outlined previously, adjustments of effects on factor
prices and production prices cannot be presumed to bring the production cost structure of the sector into equilibrium.

The same logic applies to the sequence of events leading up to spatial
decentralisation, consisting of vertical integration, mechanisation,
and the breakup of the regional production complex (Scott 1983).[18]
What were formerly external economies are now internalised. Does this
not imply that industries respond and adapt, technologically and locationally to specifically regional factor supply dynamics? Yes, in that
regional factor price movements may trigger the search for innovations
may eventually result in decentralisation: typically, this happens in
industries where overall growth in output has declined to the point
where market prices are sensitive to business cycles and competition
generally. But, as with all such searches, the precise outcomes are

unpredictable, inflexible, contingent and non ergodic. The production cost structures that emerge do not have to be equilibria, but will be the factual outcomes of interactions between the locational possibilities created by the physical organisation of production processes and their possibilities for creating different forms of linkage systems, and the spatial patterns of factor costs, exploited by capitalists under conditions of competition. Marginal analysis is not likely to be helpful in understanding these technology bound possibilities for concentration and deconcentration.

4. THE ROLE OF SOCIAL PRACTICE: WHY DO CAPITALISTS PRODUCE NEW REGIONS?

To claim that 'small events' are important to the configurations that product and processes ultimately take, and thus to the concrete factor demands of growing industries and to the character of the region in which they locate and grow up, is to claim that human agency, in firms, industries and factor markets is critical to economic history. A full understanding of a concrete phenomenon such as regionalisation can never be had in ignorance of the specificity and complexity of this human agency.

The logical opening we have created for human agency permits us to ask the question: 'why, if there is structural 'room' for agency, do capitalist agents actually develop their industries in new regions?' What are the positive motivations for these locational patterns that are only enabled by the disequilibrium dynamics we have described thus far?

A growing literature on innovation and regionalism suggests that entrepreneurial capitalists perceive important social and institutional rigidities in well developed regions and seek to avoid them (Scott 1985a & b, Hall and Markusen 1985). These include conditions that might be identified in conventional regional science models, such as regional 'factor oligopsony' due to the dominance of developed regional economies by industries with well entrenched advantages: another of the inflexibilities and irreversibilities we have identified (Chinitz 1960). It may also be that an existing, well established entrepreneurial class is a barrier to the establishment of a new group of entrepreneurs associated with new product groups: existing social networks monopolise the attention of creative individuals, funding sources and the local state (Markusen 1985). The social structures of well developed economies may also appear to new entrepreneurs as barriers: labour unions, for example, typically seem to generate at least some spatial pattern bargaining in new industries; they often have important effects on the general climate of class relations in a region even where they take no formal action to organise new industries (Storper 1982). Entrepreneurs may, therefore, unconsciously or consciously, gravitate towards regions where the slate is relatively clean, in which they can situate themselves at the centre of a growing economy and community, and reap all the tangible and intangible benefits thereof. They may also be able thereby to participate in the formation of the social, institutional, legal and political traditions of the area with which they must coexist as long as they are in the region.

I propose that these new growth centres represent distinctive new <u>social structures of accumulation</u>. Above and beyond enabling factors described above - rooted in the structure of production and competition - the region is the essential milieu in which the social, political and institutional resources can be marshalled so as to provide an environment tailored to the growth and development of these industries.

The growing industry's opportunity to be situated at the centre of its 'own' growing region, however, varies greatly from nation to nation; there are different conventions with respect to spatial economic mobility in different political economies. From a casual look at the historical geography of the USA and Western Europe, it appears that in the USA higher levels of individual mobility over longer distances have been the rule for some time than in Europe, and that new industries have had much more freedom to create new metropolitan areas around their agglomerations. In Western Europe, by contrast, new industries have tended to create specialised industrial districts within developed regions (since most regions are developed), or to build an extension onto an existing agglomeration. Still the rise of the spatially separated growth complex for growing industries is evident across Western Europe today. Thus, the precise spatial scales and concrete forms of the search for a clean slate differ, but the basic motivation seems widespread.

We can also now introduce some caution into our claim that new or growing industries have factor attraction power and thus relative 'freedom' to locate. In real space and time, resources cannot be immediately drawn anywhere, regardless of an industry's ability to pay for them. This is especially true with respect to highly skilled R & D or engineering production labour who, regardless of wage incentives, cannot be induced to migrate anywhere. Thus, new regional growth complexes seem to be something of a 'knife edge' phenomenon: often they are near well developed metropolitan regions, or they follow an initial phase of extensive development that paves the way for private investment (as in the case of military spending in the Southern tier of the United States). Tellingly, the Dutch call these areas of their country the 'halfway zone'. The former case suggests Route 128 near Boston, the Santa Clara Valley near San Francisco, the Haute Provence in France, or Prato in Italy (cf. Saxenian 1984). The latter especially suggests Dallas-Fort Worth. Some regions exhibit both characteristics: Orange County and San Diego in Southern California, for example, were initially developed by the military, but Orange County also had early spinoffs from Los Angeles (Scott 1985b). The role of government generally, combined with the proximity to but separation from a major metropolitan area is evident in Tsukuba, Japan.

These new social-spatial forms are thus the result of the enabling dynamics of technology and economic growth identified in the first few sections of this paper, but they cannot be understood fully even with disequilibrium analytics. Disequilibrium conceptions of the economy open up more questions than they answer, and that is how it should be with historically sensitive modes of analysis. These social dynamics must then be given attention in their own right, as legitimate objects of theoretical human geography.

5.   CONCLUSIONS

Factor demand and factor supply in the production of space must be treated as internal components of one dynamic, disequilibrium-led historical process. Factor demand is not determined by adaptations to factor supplies because the overall development of the forces of production continually alter the basis of the space economy, regardless of the initial distribution of factor supplies. Industrial development - guided by the heterogeneity of capital goods, the perversity of

factor demands and the social struggle over wages and profits - involves changes in the absolute availability and relative importance of
factor demand and supply relationships that specify individual location decisions. This means not only a different landscape to describe,
but a new logic of industry location in the course of economic development. There is a strong degree of irreversibility in adjustments,
and previous economic and locational configurations are irrevocably
lost.

In addition to pointing out this historical dimension to the development of spatial production relation I have attempted in this paper to
make some suggestions about the theoretical tools we need to explain
such changes. In particular, I have endorsed a notion of economic
'structure' which is at once more cognisant of the supra-individual
nature of economic forces and yet provides a greater role for human
agency in the construction of concrete economic outcomes, than approaches that take as their point of departure either market processes
or macroeconomic structural aggregates (cf. Giddens 1984). In so doing, I have suggested that the nature of innovations and the changes
associated with them are likely to be much less predictable and much
more dramatic than we are led to believe in most conventional approaches.

ACKNOWLEDGEMENT

*   I wish to thank Meric Gertler, Andrew Sayer and Manuel Castells
     for comments on a prior version of this paper. All errors remain
     my responsibility.

NOTES

(1) Since the precise way an industry is categorised is a matter of
     both the way the industry develops and the way we choose to label
     the industry's output (e.g. the steam engine industry in the lo-
     comotive sector; but actually steam engines are produced in sepa-
     rate factories which may service many different final output sec-
     tors, some unrelated to rail transportation), we cannot provide
     any unambiguous definition of a use-value around which a 'sepa-
     rate' industry grows, on the basis of industrial statistics
     alone. The definition of what a separate branch of production is,

in meaningful theoretical terms, must be made via historical analysis.

(2) For the time being, the reader will have to accept this historical interpretation, as it is not possible to present detailed argumentation on this issue. A literature on the subject is just beginning to appear (cf. Hall and Markusen, eds, 1985). My purpose here is to present this view as part of a stylised but, I believe, essentially accurate story, and then to set forth the theoretical logic that might account for it. Thus, this paper is an hypothesis about both history and theory.

(3) Arthur 1983:5: 'In general it need not be the case that the number of technologies competing for a given purpose is few. If we consider the arrangement of the 40 or so keys on a typewriter as a technology, then in principle 40-factorial or 1048 possible keyboards compete with the standard QWERTY keyboard'.

(4) Not all technologies enjoy increasing returns with adoption. The very popularity of a factor-intensive technology may bid its inputs up in price so that diminishing returns are created upon adoption. Hydroelectric power, for example, or water resource yield, became costlier as suitable dam sites became scarcer and hydrodynamically less efficient (cf. Storper and Walker 1984).

(5) See Section 2.2 for a discussion of superprofits and differential profit rates and pricing practices generally.

(6) Nelson and Winter (1982:201) emphasis added: 'The problems with rectifying the production function as remote input combinations are not satisfactorily resolved by grafting onto the theory a neoclassical model of induced innovation. The graft assumes that 'inventing' or 'doing R & D' is an activity whose outcome can be predicted in advance in final detail. In effect, there is no difference in the amended theory between moving along the production function by increasing one kind of capital (plant and equipment) through physical investment, and 'pushing outward' the production function by increasing another form of capital (knowledge?) through investing in R & D. Both kind of investments are explained by the same behavioural model. <u>The distinction between innovation and routine operation is totally repressed</u>.

(7) Of course, there is no assurance that expanded reproduction will occur: one of the strongest parts of Marx's analysis of capitalism is his identification of the structural contradictions of the capitalist macroeconomic system: labour is both producer of surplus value and consumer of commodities, resulting in contradictory impacts on the real wage; and producers compete with each other, not only generating creative impulses towards greater efficiency, but also generating overcapacity; the combination of these two produces periodic realisation crises that are built into the system, and that interrupt expanded reproduction.

As we have noted, the tendency in much Marxist literature is to emphasise these interruptions, and the Marxist regional literature has followed suit by stressing the cutbacks and rationalisations of productive capital, or its selective 'devalorisation'. In these cases of cutbacks, one could indeed say that the principal business of the economy is to allocate resources away from sectors with profit rates below the social average and towards sectors with profit rates above it.

(8) As, for example, the tendency of many Marxists to assume that there is a direct link between the definitional opposition of interests between capital and labour, and the precise content of technological innovations. This would result in there always being a labour saving bias to innovation. But is completely ignores the complexities of sectors and resembles a neoclassical induced innovation model.

(9) If we assume normal profits and normal or natural wage rates, and neglect rent, then according to Pasinetti (1973), we may write the natural prices or centres of gravity as vertically integrated wages and profits:

$$p = wl + pA + rpA$$
$$p(I-A) = wl + rpA$$
$$p = wlQ' + rpaQ'$$
$$-1$$

where $Q' = (I-A)$ is the Leontief inverse which, multiplied by wl, gives us the vertically integrated wages and multiplied by rpA, gives us vertically integrated profits. I is the identity matrix,

A is the flow matrix (we are ignoring stocks in this case), p the price vector, ro the uniform profit rate, w the uniform wage rate, and 1 the vector of direct labour requirements per unit of output. Price is p(i) = w'(i) + II'(i)where w'(i) and II'(i) are the vertically integrated wages and profits (Semmler 1984 and Shaikh 1980).

(10) That is, following note 9, relative prices are:

$$\underline{p(i)} = \underline{w'(i)} + \underline{II'(i)}$$
$$p(j) = w'(j) + II'(j)$$

(11) These differentials have nothing to do with barriers to entry, as manifested in markup pricing behaviour (Semmler 1984).

(12) On the other end of the spectrum, sectoral decline occurs because, in the real world, there is no such thing as perfectly elastic demand. The notion of infinite elasticity is a fiction produced by taking a real world point of demand and joining it to the vertical (price) axis in the economist's diagram. It is only due to the false assumption of infinite demand line that neoclassical theory can conclude that the supply curve and the demand curve always intersect: but this is an extreme, and therefore, unrealistic, case (Arndt 1984:115). Markets are always subject to saturation, irrespective of price. Finite demand, when combined with capital stock inelasticities, suggests that overcapacity is to be expected under conditions of competition. Capacity cannot be adjusted downward instantaneously. In this case, the market price drops but production prices do not, and the firms with the oldest and least efficient capacity are those whose profit rates decline the most.

This process cannot be derived exclusively from theory, since much will depend on the temporal intersection of demand and firm specific investments in new capacity; if new, highly efficient capacity has been brought into operation just prior to a major overcapacity period in the industry as a whole, the more efficient form may suffer the most because of the burden of higher capital costs (assuming, again, that real relative prices for capital goods or interest rates have risen).

(13) As noted, this also includes Learning by Using, or 'routine' behaviour. Gertler (1984) points out Pasinetti's dictum that what
the neoclassical economist might call substitution of capital for
labour is actually technical progress. The further outcomes of
such 'substitution', however, need not follow neoclassical lines.

(14) Of course, banks have their biases and do make mistakes. And, the
process works the opposite way when profitability or expectations
thereof decline. In this case, firms with positive profits may
find themselves starved of investment capital, so that instead of
having a chance to reinvest, their decline becomes a selffulfill-
ing prophecy (cf. Bluestone and Harrison 1982 for description of
cases). The allocation of social labour is affected by competition for capital, and meeting at least the social average rate of
profit is what matters, not profitability per se.

(15) R & D expenditures, like production costs, reduce the funds
available for investment in production capacity.

(16) Note that we have not ruled out the possibility that innovations
will take the form of reducing inputs of relatively expensive
factors of production; and, there are probably aggregate factor
supply and price trends that tend to direct thinking about technological innovation (or, search, as we have called it) in certain directions.

(17) It is obvious that this logic ignores trade, but it can easily be
extended to the pure Ricardian case of the two-industry model.

(18) Ellinger (1977) attempts to distinguish the behaviour of innovating firms from competitive firms. In initial stages, he shows
that firms are 'indecisive' with respect to location, meaning
that there are no decisive constraints on where they may locate.
In this stage, they are also 'adoptive', meaning that they are
innovators, and innovations are not geared to the supplies and
costs in the spatial surface. Later on, as innovation and market
growth slow, firms become locationally 'decisive', meaning that
they experience serious cost minimisation constraints on locational choices; and they are technologically 'adaptive', indicating that they are gearing their techniques to minimisation of

certain factor costs. He provides some sketchy evidence to support these claims.

REFERENCES

Arndt, H., Economic Theory vs. Economic Reality, Ann Arbor, Michigan State Univerity Press, MI, 1984.

Athur, W.B., 'On competing technologies and historical small events: the dynamics of choice under increasing returns', Stanford University, Stanford , CA, 1983, unpublished paper.

Chinitz, B., 'Contrasts in agglomeration: New York and Pittsburgh', American Economic Review, Papers and Proceedings, 1960, pp. 279-289.

Clark, G. and Gertler, M., 'Adjustment model of regional production, Environment and Planning A, 17, 2, 1984, pp. 231-252.

David, P., Technical Choice, Innovation and Economic Growth, Cambridge University Press, New York, 1975.

Ellinger, R., 'Industrial location behavior and spatial evolution', Journal of Industrial Economics XXV, 1977, pp. 295-312.

Gertler, M., 'Regional capital theory', Progress in Human Geography 8, 1, 1984, pp. 50-81.

Giddens, A., The Constitution of Society, University of California Press, Berkeley, CA, 1984.

Hall, P. and Markusen, A. (eds), Silicon Landscapes, George Unwin and Allen, Boston and London, 1985.

Kaldor, N., 'The irrelevance of equilibrium economics', The Economic Journal, 812, 1972, pp. 1237-1255.

Mandel E., Late Capitalism, Verso, London, 1978.

Markusen, A.R., Profit Cycles, Oligopoly and Regional Development, MIT Press, Cambridge, MA, 1985, forthcoming.

Nelson, R.R. and Winter, S.G., An Evolutionary Theory of Economic Change, Harvard/Belknap, Cambridge, MA, 1982.

Okishio, N., 'Technical change and the rate of profit', Kobe University Economic Review 7, 1961, pp. 85-99.

Robinson, J., The Accumulation of Capital, Macmillan, London, 1956.

Roemer, J., 'A general equilibrium approach to Marxian economics', Econometrica 48, 2, 1980, pp. 505-530.

Rosenberg, N., 'Economic development and the transfer of technology: some historical perspectives', Technology and Culture, October 1970, pp. 550-575.

Rosenberg, N., Inside the Black Box: Technology and Economics, Cambridge University Press, New York, 1982.

Saxenian, A., 'The urban contradictions of Silicon Valley', in: Sawers, L. and Tabbs, W. (eds), Sunbelt-Frostbelt, Oxford University Press, New York, 1984.

Schumpeter, J., The Theory of Economic Development, Harvard University Press, Cambridge, MA, 1934.

Scott, A.J., 'Production system dynamics and metropolitan development', Annals, Association of American Geographers 72, 2, 1982, pp. 185-200.

Scott, A.J., 'Industrial organization and logic of intrametropolitan location I: theoretical considerations', Economic Geography 59, 1983, pp. 233-250.

Scott, A.J., 'The growth and development of the Orange County industrial complex I: theoretical considerations', UCLA Department of Geography, Los Angeles, 1985a, manuscript.

Scott, A.J., 'The growth and development of the Orange County industrial complex II: empirical evidence', UCLA Department of Geography, 1985b, manuscript.

Scott, A.J., 'Location processes, urbanization and territorial development: an exploratory essay', Environment and Planning A, 17, 4, 1985c, pp. 479-503.

Semmler, W., Competition, Monopoly and Differential Profit Rates, Columbia University Press, New York, 1984.

Shaikh, A., 'Neo Ricardian economics: a wealth of algebra, a poverty of theory', Review of Radical Political Economics 4, 1980.

Storper, M., 'Technology, the labour process and the social geography of industrial labor', University of California, Department of Geography, Berkeley, 1982, unpublished PhD dissertation.

Storper, M. and Walker, R., The Price of Water: Surplus and Subsidy in the California State Water Project, Institute of Governmental Studies monograph series, Berkeley, 1984.

Swales, J.K., 'A Kaldorian model of cumulative causation: regional growth with induced technical change', in: Gillespie, A., (ed), Technological Change and Regional Development, Pion, London, 1983, pp. 68-88.

Walker, R. and Storper, M., 'Capital and industrial location', Progress in Human Geography 5, 4, 1981, pp. 473-509.

Young, A., 'Increasing returns and economic progress', Economic Journal, December 1928, pp. 527-542.

TECHNOLOGICAL CHANGE IN THE SERVICE SECTOR:
URBAN AND REGIONAL IMPLICATIONS
Peter M. Townroe

1.   INTRODUCTION

Governments throughout Western Europe now look to the service sectors
of their economies to provide the jobs that will reduce the high levels of registered unemployment of the mid eighties. It is recognised
that a strong resurgence of job availability in the manufacturing sectors of these economies, even with sharp increases in output is extremely unlikely. At the same time, many governments are seeking to
hold back employment in the public sector in state industries and in
local and central government services. Private sector service employment seems to offer the only route to a fully utilised labour force.

The economic recession of the early eighties has made governments,
commentators and academic researchers alike in these same Western European nations very aware that technical change does not stop when
output is static or falling. The pressures on industry to innovate, to
cut costs, to introduce new processes are, if anything, stronger at
such times. Expensive labour overheads in particular have to be closely scrutinised. Labour productivity therefore rises sharply, especially as each economy starts to come out of recession. The unemployment
figures do not fall as soon as or as quickly as anticipated.

Attention paid to the links between technical change and employment
has been closely centred on manufacturing; and to a lesser degree on
agriculture and mining, on the utilities, and on construction. The
services sectors are rarely drawn into the same discussion. Service
industry examples are not quoted. And the only real concern with job
loss in the service sectors has arisen from a realisation of the potential for fundamental change in data intensive industries, change
coming from widespread cheap electronic recording and processing power.

Urban and regional analysts, within and without government, have en-
thusiastically monitored the changing locations of manufacturing activity, noting the relevance of changing factor prices, of government
policies, and of developing technologies. The same enthusiasm is not
to be found in the study of the service sectors of most economies.
'Offices' have become a subspecialism, but at times with little regard
for linkages to non office service activities. This relative neglect
of locational parameters and spatial change in the service sectors
(especially the non basic activities) extends to a relative absence of
research into the processes of technical change within services, as
well as the impact of this change on employment, and the resultant
spatial outcomes. And it has to be remembered that technical change in
the service sectors stretches much wider than the introduction of
electronic data processing machinery.

This paper seeks to identify some of the reasons for this neglect of
technical change in services by considering some of the difficult conceptual and empirical problems in pursuing studies in this area. This
is done against the background of trends in the United Kingdom. But
these are used for illustration and scene setting, no more. Some possible implications for both the processes of regional growth and the
pattern of urban areas then follow.

First, however, some definitions and distinctions. Service sector activities are conventionally presented as those activities in an economy other than agricultureand fishing, mining, manufactures and construction. Utilities and transport services hold an ambiguous transitional position, the latter being more commonly included with other
services than the former. Note that it is possible to argue that retailing and wholesaling activities are not services, in the sense that
they are parts of the production chain of goods, contributing added
value to the final price. They are thus different in kind to (say)
entertainment or health care or insurance services, all of which are
very involved in the transmission of information. It is important also
to distinguish between final demands being made by households and by
levels of government in collective or public goods. Also many services
(e.g. insurance, hotels) obviously serve both final and intermediate
demands simultaneously. And many intermediate services are clearly
undertaken within manufacturing, construction or utility organisations, the relevant output and employment being categorised within
those sectors. The distinction between public services and private

services provision is also important, although difficult to sustain at a conceptual margin when selected services are offered to businesses or to households for sale by government or by public sector agencies.

2.   TRENDS IN SERVICE SECTOR EMPLOYMENT IN THE UNITED KINGDOM

It is a popular conception that as an economy grows and incomes rise, differential productivity trends, changing patterns of consumption and new directions in international trade, will all contribute to a relative fall in employment in agriculture and mining and then in manufacturing, while sustaining a relative rise in the significance of both service sector output and service sector employment. This picture is not inaccurate, but it is incomplete (see also the contribution by D. Gleave in the present volume).

The growth in employment in the service sector has three primary sources: the growth in aggregate expenditure, a shift in the demand for services relative to goods within that aggregate, and the trends in levels of labour productivity within the sector. Many if not most services have a higher degree of income elasticity at the level of household than the majority of goods (Marquand 1979). Within the overall service portfolio of any government, there will also typically be services, such as education and health, for which the income elasticity is high; even though the demand is revealed imperfectly through non price allocation systems. Therefore, as national per capita income rises, so will the demand for services rather than goods.

Labour productivity rises more slowly in most service sectors than elsewhere in an economy. In a slow growing economy in output terms, but one that is still subject to technical change in all sectors (such as the United Kingdom in the past decade), this productivity differential will accentuate the switch in the balance between service sector employment and employment elsewhere. The speed of the change is dependent not only on the relative rates of productivity increase but also on the rates of investment in each sector and the degree to which productivity advance is embodied in the capital (i.e., the incremental capital output ratios, sector by sector). In a fast growing economy the switch will be slower, labour demand in the manufacturing sector in particular being held up by higher aggregate expenditures on goods, unless productivity change and/or investment simultaneously accelerates there. The contrast in relative sectoral labour demands between a fast growing and a slow growing economy fades, of course, when there is a large pool of unemployed labour available for each and every sector.

A secular change in demand, independent of income and of relative productivity changes, may also encourage a switch in expenditures towards service sector outputs over time. This change could come about from a shift in the age distribution of the population (more elderly and retired), high levels of market penetration with household consumer durables, a taste change (that is not associated with rising income), or the development of services which substitute for goods (yoga classes for alcohol and tobacco). There are obvious employment implications here, but at some distance from technological advance.

In the United Kingdom employment in both public and private service activities has increased fairly steadily over the past decade or so. The figures in Table 1 reflect the twin pressures of a long run secular trend and a dramatic recent decline in employment in the manufacturing sector in Great Britain, raising unemployment over the period from just over half a million to of the order to four million (including the unregistered). The tertiary sector in Great Britain employed approximately 27 per cent of the occupied population in 1841, 33 per cent by 1881, 36 per cent by 1911, 49 per cent by 1931 (with the effect then of depression in manufacturing), 46 per cent in 1951 and 61 per cent in 1981. These figures compare with 1970 or 1971 figures of 61 per cent for Canada, 62 per cent for the United States, 48 per cent for France, 42 per cent for West Germany and 38 per cent for Italy. Table 1 shows the especially strong recent employment growth in Hotels and Catering, Banking, Insurance and Finance, Education and Health Care, and in the category 'Other Services' (a mixture of personal and business services).

Against many expectations and in spite of employment growth, expenditure on services by consumers has retained an almost constant share of total consumer spending. As Gudgin (1983) points out, the proportion of consumer demand for services in the overall demand for services has fallen, as the share of services in current government spending has increased (more than offsetting the other component, a falling share of services in imports). In real terms, with a relative price of services to goods rising over the period, the share of services in consumption has fallen: thus indicating how, in the United Kingdom, a positive income elasticity of demand (on average) for services has been countered by a negative price elasticity of demand (Gershuny and Miles 1983).

Table 1

Employees in Employment by Industry, Great Britain 1971-84

('000s, June each year)

Sic	Industry 1980	1971	Change 1971-84		
			360	No.	%
01-03	Agriculture, etc	421	360	-61	-14.5
11-14	Coal, oil and gas	400	286	-114	-28.5
15-17	Utilities	388	330	-58	-14.9
2-4	Manufacturing	7,910	5,443	-2467	-31.2
50	Construction	1,167	973	-194	-16.6
6-9	Services	11,361	13,381	+2020	+17.8
61-63	of which				
67	Wholesale Distribution	964	1,164	+200	+20.7
64/65	Retail Distribution	1951	2,115	+164	+8.4
66	Hotels and Catering	691	1,006	+315	+45.6
71-77	Transport	1,092	866	-226	-20.7
79	Post and Telecom	435	418	-17	-3.9
81-85	Banking,Finance,Insurance	1,318	1,889	+571	+43.3
91-92	Public Administration	1,733	1,823	+90	+5.2
93	Education	1,260	1,463	+203	+16.1
95	Health Care	939	1,301	+362	+38.6
94,96-98	Other Services	979	1,342	+363	+37.1
	All Industries and Services	21,648	20,771	-877	-4.1

 These figures exclude government employees in building, education and health, and in H.M. forces.

Source: Employment Gazette, 93(4), 1985, Historical Supplement, No. 1, Table 1.2.

Within the service industries in the United Kingdom some of the fastest growth rates in output and employment have been concentrated within producer services: banking, insurance, finance, advertising, research and development, etc. Gudgin's (1983) calculations suggest that these intermediate demand services account for over half of all service sector output, if wholesaling and retailing are included as intermediate services. The fall back in the manufacturing sector in Britain over the past ten years has reduced this demand somewhat;

relative to consumer final demand for services which has been held up by the tax reduction benefits of North Sea oil. If employment is assumed to be proportional to output, it is possible to use the national input-output table to estimate the dependence of different service industries on different sources of intermediate and final demand. Table 2 is derived from Robertson, Briggs and Goodhart (1982). This shows how in 1973 almost two million service jobs were tied to non service industry.

Table 2

Sources of Demand for Service Employment, United Kingdom 1972

(in thousands)

| | Geared to level of nonservice activity | Geared to level of service activity | Final demand | | |
			Consumers	Govern-ment	Invest-ment	Export
Transport & Commun-ication	344	357	276	36	59	356
Distribu-tive Trades	501	43	1867	56	35	180
Miscellaneous Services	963	355	1427	495	226	433
Total Private Services	1808	755	3570	587	320	969

Source: Derived from Robertson, Briggs Goodhart (1982), Gudgin (1983).

The regional distribution of service activity in the United Kingdom is uneven. In 1976, the percentages of employees in employment, counting part time women at half a full time employee, in the service sector as previously defined ranged from 65 per cent in the South East region down to 43 per cent in the North West and West Midlands regions. Differences clearly exist due to the different structures of the regional economies. The great significance of employment changes in these economies over just the past seven years is highlighted in Table 3, comparing index numbers of change in the service sector with change in the manufacturing sector, with 1980 taken as 100.

The figures in Table 3 ignore the self employed, both with and without employees. This group has become increasingly important in the British labour force, up from 1.7 million in 1965 to 2.5 million in 1984. The proportions are particularly high in retail distribution (60 per cent in 1984), in hotels and catering (73 per cent), education (61 per cent), and in health care (47 per cent).

Table 3

Employees in Employment by Region, Great Britain, 1977-1984

(June each year, 1980 = 100)

Region	Manufacturing[(i)]		Services[(ii)]		All Industry	
	1977	1984	1977	1984	1977	1984
South East	103.3	86.0	94.8	101.0	96.9	96.3
East Anglia	103.4	90.9	93.7	106.3	101.5	103.0
South West	103.4	85.5	95.5	102.8	97.7	96.7
West Midlands	109.1	77.3	94.6	98.2	102.0	88.0
East Midlands	103.9	84.2	94.9	100.5	99.1	92.2
Yorkshire and Humberside	109.8	77.7	96.3	99.0	101.5	89.7
North West	110.7	76.2	96.5	100.0	101.6	90.3
North	113.6	75.9	98.5	96.7	104.6	96.6
Wales	109.4	74.6	95.5	101.3	100.6	90.9
Scotland	111.4	78.4	95.6	101.6	100.1	93.3
Great Britain	107.3	80.9	95.4	100.6	99.4	93.0

(i) SIC 1980, 2-4

(ii) SIC 1980, 6-9

Source: Employment Gazette, 93(4), 1985, Historical Supplement, No. 1, Table 1.5.

3.   TECHNICAL CHANGE IN THE SERVICE SECTOR

The processes of invention and innovation in society introduce new developments to companies and to public sector institutions in the service sectors, as in the other sectors of the economy. These developments occur both in the product that is sold and in the process of production (although this distinction is not always as clear cut as in technical change in the production of goods). New technology in the service sectors may be embodied within the capital equipment used, or it may improve the use of existing or replicated capital. Normally this technology will be labour saving, but it is often capital saving as well; and it may occasionally be capital saving but labour generating, involving the substitution of labour for capital. Note that the measurement of these biases is difficult in those public sector services which are not priced, necessitating the use of proxy output measures (often being the expenditure on inputs).

Arguably, the response of labour demand to technical change and to associated price changes is faster in private sector services than elsewhere in the economy. Typically employment units are not large, stock building is not an output option for the employer, unionisation is weaker, labour hoarding is likely to be less, and there are frequently opportunities for tapping into and out of the widening market of part time employment. It is easy to think of exceptions, but in general, the labour market in the private service sector is more demand responsive than other sectors.

The labour market impact of technical changes in the service sector depends principally upon the gain achieved in labour productivity in the relevant subsector. The trend rate of growth of labour productivity in the service sector in the UK over twenty five years or so has been of the order of 1.8 per cent per annum, for example. That labour saving impact may be seen initially within a given expenditure level on the service concerned. However, a price reduction brought about by a process innovation may well increase the expenditure in real terms, thereby possibly more than countering the labour saving impact and generating a net increase in jobs. The labour saving impact of microwave ovens in lower priced restaurants and bars may well be an example, where the ability to produce cheaper meals of a given quality has led to price reductions and to gains in consumer appeal. (In the UK, 'eating out' has been the fastest growing component of consumer expenditure over the past given years.) An expenditure gain in one area will be a loss elsewhere; and it is possible that this link will be identifiable between sectors where a service (e.g. rental and hire) substitutes for the purchase of goods (e.g., in garden tools, or cars, or office computers), in so far as the utilisation of the goods purchased by the rental company is higher than in the ownership of individual user companies or households.

Overall, the macroeconomic labour demand effect of a given technical change will depend upon the degree to which an indirect demand arising from that change counters the direct impact (being normally labour saving). Three interrelated effects are at work here: a technological multiplier, especially into the capital goods sector; an income effect, both by level and by distribution to the labour factor; and a price effect, influencing demand. All three elements are subject to leakage in an open economy and are contained by market inflexibilities. All three elements link also to the diffusion sequence of the technical change, across service organisations and to their customers, and hence over space.

The major determinants of the diffusion of an advance in production technology of a service lie in five directions. The first, much stressed by industrial economists concerned with the process change in manufacturing, rests in the market structure of the industrial sector concerned: the number and size distribution of competitors, the strength and nature of competition, the pressure on profits and the gains from growth. This is a 'Structure-Conduct-Performance' view of diffusion.

A second influence arises from the degree of factor substitutability in the production process. Diffusion is faster if this is high, if capital is replaced (or is written off) relatively rapidly, or if the capital is flexible in use (e.g., a shop), and if production is growing so that net investment is high (e.g., fast food outlets). High profitability and a low initial investment accelerate the process; as may degrees of local (i.e., spatial) monopoly.

A third determinant which has been important in manufacturing, and which has had increasing importance in the service sector in the United Kingdom, comes from direct investment by multinational companies. These (normally large) companies bring new technologies with them, they are often large investors in research and development, and the strength of their competitive presence pushes domestic companies to respond. This has been seen for example in fast food, in corporate banking, and in the hotel industry in the United Kingdom.

The fourth determinant is research and development. R & D is rarely a separate budget item or an organisational subheading for service sector companies. Much of the relevant R & D comes from equipment

suppliers. But frequently the service users work closely with the suppliers in improving designs and lowering costs. And they also invest
resources in R & D in 'soft' process and product development: in improving resource utilisation and in designing new service products.
New insurance policies, new forms of company loans, new theatrical
entertainments, new facilities for sports spectators, new 'theme' restaurants, would all be examples. Market research plays a large role in
these developments, often leading to large investments in the skilled
manpower required for the design stage (e.g., in developing a new sur-
gical technique in a hospital, or a new degree programme in a university).

The fifth determinant of both the speed and the direction of diffusion
of technical changes in the service sector comes closer to the central
concern of this paper. The spatial distribution of demand has long
been recognised for its role in the diffusion of new processes in manufacturing and associated new products. Similar considerations influence diffusion in the service sector and provide the theme for the
next section.

4.   THE SPATIAL FACTOR IN TECHNICAL CHANGE IN THE SERVICE SECTOR

The standard urban and regional economics view sees invention and innovation concentrated at the apex of both the regional and urban hierarchies of a nation. Diffusion is then down and out. The regional hierarchy is conventionally specified in terms of per capita income levels, as a direct proxy here for investment and a youthful but growing
capital stock, but as an indirect proxy for both an information rich
environment which generates new ideas and an entrepreneurial environment which seeks resulting commercial opportunities. The largest city
can be similarly defined, adding in an explicit urban scale effect,
reflecting contact intensity and available information exchange. At
the top end of both hierarchies (one apex being normally geographically located within the other), competitive forces may be stronger than
lower down. And access to relevant information sources (libraries,
government departments and research agencies, universities, trade literature, consultants, etc.) is better.

Ideas and applications are therefore seen as being thrown out of the
centre, then to diffuse or to 'trickle down' the hierarchies of both

regions and cities. The imagery is familiar from writings on growth poles in particular but is found also in literature on rank size distribution and urban development strategies. Thompson (1968) for example, linked diffusion in manufacturing to the idea of a product and process life cycle. Diffusion down the hierarchy is associated with 'maturity', with routinisation of production technique, with a slow down in the rate of growth of the product market, with declining skill requirements: a 'filter down'.

How does this hierarchical view of the spatial sequence of technical change hold up for the service sector? Are process and product changes in this sector sufficiently different for another view to prevail? Relevant empirical evidence is all but non existent. And many would not subscribe to this perspective for the manufacturing sector in a fully industrialised economy, with developed communications and media networks and innovation dominated by very large multiproduct and multiplant companies. However,a number of general conclusions may be drawn, focussing on private sector services and ignoring public sector services.

Corporate organisations in private sector services broadly falls into two categories: owner entrepreneurs with normally one geographical base and outlet (from corner shops, to the single architect or lawyer, to the restaurant owner), and larger companies with national chains of outlets (from retail chains, to public houses, hotels, cinemas, retail banks, etc.). The geographical path of diffusion of a technical change is likely to be rather different in the two categories.

A service oriented company with a multiregional or nationwide distribution of outlets will normally have a head office in one of the largest cities in the nation. Although inventions may come in from the branch units of the organisation, to complement innovations pressed upon it by equipment suppliers, it seems safe to assume that most relevant inventions and innovations developed within the company start from the head office. The criteria for the geographical priority of diffusion over time through the network of branch outlets of these innovations are then unclear. It could be outlets where investment or refurbishment is taking place anyway, it could be those outlets run by flexibly minded branch managers, it could be outlets in areas recognised as accepting change and responding well to innovation. In many cases, selection of initial branches must be experimental. Evidence on this is nonexistent; and a priori reasoning does not suggest any clear spatial hypotheses.

Large companies in the service sector (as indeed companies in the other sectors of the economy) employ large numbers of semiskilled and skilled clerical employees. Indeed in some service sectors (insurance, finance) the clerical fraction is the core of the production process. There has been much speculation as to whether developments in electronic information processing technology will result in large scale productivity gains in these clerical areas, leading to a much reduced demand for these categories of labour. Hard evidence is unclear, amid much strong assertion.

In the United Kingdom the Sleigh Report (1979) for the Department of Employment for example, did not foresee a significant employment impact in aggregate, but did foresee a restricting of clerical tasks and a consequent development of new services made commercially viable by the new technology. This report suggested that the theoretical productivity gains were in fact unlikely to be fully realised because of 'behavioural problems' in the introduction and use of the new systems. Braun and Senker (1982) in a report for the Manpower Services Commission point out that over four million employees in the United Kingdom, or nearly twenty per cent of the labour force, are employed in office functions, over 800,000 being classified into manufacturing. They find no strong evidence on the employment impact of micro electronic equipment, but suggest that in many service sectors there will be a swing in the balance of employees away from clerical tasks towards selling. Evans (1979), reviewing experience across Western Europe, also sees a structural impact of data processing equipment, noting the general slow down in growth in employment in banking and insurance in the 1970s compared with the 1960s. In none of these reviews is a strong spatial effect acknowledged.

It is interesting also to note the comments of the Sleigh Report (1979) on the impact of new electronic systems in large retailing organisations. The impact has come in improved stock control, more precise ordering and so a reduction in out-of-stock items, faster and more accurate checkout with more information provided to the customer, a better basis for the analysis of changing demand patterns, and reduced shrinkage due to pilfering. A reduction in clerical staff of the order of 15 per cent is suggested. More centralised warehousing and distribution systems have obvious spatial implications.

Owner entrepreneur single outlet businesses in the service sector will be more constrained by their location, in both knowing about relevant advances in technology and than in having a sufficient incentive to adopt the innovation. For these businesses, local spatial competition will be a significant factor, as well as local information networks in their areas of expertise. Innovations are more likely to be adopted when the owner entrepreneur is sure of his or her market, and when he or she can look to the success of others elsewhere. This suggests initial diffusion through higher income suburbs and outer metropolitan area towns; with certain innovations being initially tested on the very high income residents of the core city, supported by a relevant tourist demand. Innovations are unlikely to commence in rural or small town areas, unless these areas are fast growing in population terms and investment is taking place. An investor in a new outlet of a standard service is perhaps more likely to evaluate the latest innovations in both process and product, than an investor who is upgrading an existing facility, or an owner who is operating profitably and who sees no need to invest.

We know from studies into the choice of technology by companies in the manufacturing sector (Stoneman 1983) that differences in factor prices have relatively little influence on alternatives chosen. We cannot therefore expect the lower costs of labour for service enterprises in small towns and rural areas to lead to different patterns of choice in innovation. Of greater importance, where choices in the factor mix exist (alongside choices in the product specification and quality), will be considerations such as the minimum efficient scale of production, the skill requirements of the process chosen, training requirements where relevant, the search costs in studying alternatives, and the competitive strategy of the business. Much has to depend on the forecast of the market, and hence on the profit. And for small businesses at the end of the day, much depends upon the personal utility function of the owner.

One further aspect of technical change in the service sector which may have a geographical dimension is the influence of technology on births and deaths of businesses and on the planning of branch plant networks. Many final demand service businesses are established in areas where population and/or incomes are growing. Local market opportunities emerge. Innovation may allow further segmentation of a local demand (specialty restaurants, new forms of 'alternative' health care, consultants of all kinds, individual or group entertainers, repair services, travel companies, legal specialists, training establishments, etc). This applies both to 'births' and to new branch outlets. This pattern may in part be countered in non growth areas in a general recession by attempts by those made unemployed to establish themselves in a service business. These market entrants may need a process or product innovation to break into the sales of established concerns.

Intermediate demand service businesses are frequently established by employees from large companies who see a market opening, often in providing a service back to their previous employer. This fragmentation process will tend therefore to be most prevalent around the headquarters and principal plants of large concerns. The key to a service sector birth in this way is usually specialist knowledge, the main requirement being one of 'appropriability' or the ability of an originator of an idea to obtain for themselves the market value of the idea. This spinout process will be countered of course by a reverse pressure on large companies to internalise services previously purchased in an internal market than substituting for an external market. Key considerations here are the transaction costs of operating the external market, together with the security and predictability of supply from an internal source. Again, it is difficult to see a significant spatial dimension.

5.   CONCLUSIONS

Unlike other sectors of the economy, the key determinants of new urban and regional patterns in service sector activities, both in the public sector and in the private sector, will be dominated by the growth of local demand, both from households and from industry and commerce. Employment in these activities will depend upon the path of productivity growth, and the expansion of demand from higher incomes and in response to developments in the products. It is clear that present rapid developments in information processing technologies can be expected to have an impact on numbers in clerical occupations, and a significant impact on the nature of occupations based upon the provision of specialist information (lawyers, consultants, doctors, financial analysts, travel advisers, teachers, etc.). What is not so clear is the extent to which, in a time of recession, jobs in service trades expand in response to lower wages or to higher output (via lower prices), without a counter pressure of technological advance. It is also not clear whether the rise in self employment in service industries can be seen as in part a result of technical change, or whether it is in fact due to other social and economic forces.

It may well be that technical change in the service sector will have more influence over the next fifty years on urban form within cities than on the overall urban and regional hierarchy. Such speculations however, stretch beyond the compass of this paper.

REFERENCES

Braun, E. and Senker, P., New Technology and Employment, Manpower Ser-
     vices Commission, London, 1982.

Evans, J., The Impact of Microelectronics on Employment in Western
     Europe in the 1980s, European Trade Union Institute, Brussels,
     1979.

Gershuny, J. and Miles, P., The New Service Economy, Francis Pinder,
     London, 1983.

Gudgin, G., 'Job generation in the service sector': Position Paper for
     the Industry and Employment Committee of the Social Science Re-
     search Council, Temple Avenue, 1983 (mimeo).

Marquand, J., The Role of the Tertiary Sector in Regional Policy,
     Centre for Environmental Studies, London, 1979.

Robertson, J.A.S., Briggs, J.M. and Goodhart, A., Structure and Em-
     ployment Prospects of the Service Industries, Department of Em-
     ployment Research Paper, No. 30, HMSO, London, 1982.

Sleigh, J., Boatwright, B., Irwin, P. and Stanyon, R., The Manpower
     Implications of Micro Electronic Technology, HMSO, London, 1979.

Stoneman, P., The Economic Analysis of Technological Change, Oxford
     University Press, Oxford, 1983.

Thompson, W.R., 'Internal and external factors in the development of
     urban economies', in: Perloff, H.S. and Wingo, L. (eds), Issues
     in Urban Economics, Johns Hopkins Press, Baltimore, 1968,
     pp. 43-62.

NEW TECHNOLOGY AND REGIONAL DEVELOPMENT POLICY

John B. Goddard and Alfred T. Thwaites

1. INTRODUCTION

Widening regional disparities have been one of the key characteristics
of the current long recession,. The lagging peripheral regions whose
economies have been based on sectors developed in the 19th Century
(e.g. coal, steel, textiles, heavy engineering) have been joined by
other more prosperous and central regions specialising in the industries of the early 20th Century (e.g. motor vehicles, other consumer
durables, chemicals), as these sectors have begun to suffer the consequences of deindustrialisation and job loss. Much of this job loss in
both types of regions has occurred in large corporations who have been
eliminating excess capacity and/or switching investment overseas.
Regional disparities have been exacerbated because at the same time a
limited number of areas have experienced some growth in output and
employment due to the rise of new technology based industries and services, many associated with the emergence of microelectronics technology, with much of this growth taking place in new and small businesses
or within the limited number of multinational enterprises operating in
this field.

As these tendencies have emerged the instruments that policy makers
have traditionally used to tackle the problems of regional industrial
decline have become less and less effective. General capital subsidies
to attract new and potentially mobile investment in large firms to
greenfield sites in lagging regions have no longer produced the desired jobs as the long established relationship between new investment, output and employment growth has broken down in most sectors. In
these circumstances policy makers have turned to the promotion of new
and small high technology firms and the attraction of high technology
investment as a new means of promoting regional development. Recommendations are being made for areas to develop science parks, provide
advanced telecommunication services, to provide venture capital and
other services for small high technology firms, to support local

research into new products and processes and to stimulate the diffusion of new technology amongst firms in particular areas. The assumptions which underlie these policies is that what is happening due to the operation of market forces in the growth areas can be reproduced through public intervention in the crisis regions.

As is so often the case such policy initiatives have run ahead of the research and critical debate which should underpin them. The objective of this paper therefore is to review the evidence both theoretical and empirical which would suggest that the introduction of new technology has a potential to create self sustaining regional growth in presently lagging regions and to indicate why governments, both national and local, should intervene to facilitate the realisation of this potential.

2.   THEORETICAL CONSIDERATIONS

The debate about long waves, particularly the recent work of Freeman, and his coworkers at the Science Policy Research Unit, University of Sussex, provides a useful starting point for the discussion (Freeman, Clark and Soete 1982).

Freeman is optimistic about the potential contribution of technological change to stimulating an upswing in economic activity. He derives his inspiration from the work of Schumpeter who, writing in and about the depressed 1930s, drew attention to the need to look at economic change in a long run historical perspective. Such an approach highlights the role of new opportunities for investment, profits, growth and employment arising from new technologies. However, the whole process implies considerable economic and social disequilibrium. Radical innovations are likely to occur only in a few enterprises and to be concentrated in a limited number of branches of the economy; these innovations may subsequently diffuse into a wide range of other industries and give rise to technological revolutions when this diffusion process transforms the interindustry input/output matrix through creating totally new branches and destroying others. The role of information technology as a product, process and managerial innovation in a wide range of sectors, including its potentiality to create totally new services, suggests that it alone amongst contemporary innovations has the capacity to bring about such a revolutionary transformation.

The way in which technological revolutions induce instability in the interindustry input/output matrix suggests that while additional economic activity may be created in the economy as a whole some enterprises in some regions may lose out at the expense of other enterprises in other regions through a failure to raise productivity by process innovation or by the introduction of new and improved products. Nevertheless it is extremely difficult to specify the time scale over which such process might operate. It is therefore more useful to concentrate on those aspects of Freeman's argument which concern the mismatch between technological and institutional capacity.

A key feature of Freeman's analysis is the emphasis it gives to the interaction between the technological, economic and institutional systems in bringing about revolutionary transformations. He argues that in the downswing a mismatch develops between the emerging technological capacity and what is actually realisable given existing institutional and market conditions. In the case of information technology, "fundamental changes in the education and training system, in industrial relations, in managerial and corporate structures, managerial styles, capital markets and financial systems, the pattern of public, private and hybrid investments and the legal and political framework are all required to ensure the widespread diffusion of the new technology". Also, investments in the infrastructure of information technology, especially telecommunications, is a fundamental condition for its widespread adoption.

From a regional perspective it seems reasonable to postulate that many of these 'mismatches' have a very clear geographical manifestation. Labour skills are far from mobile and are by and large developed in local labour markets, and are very much influenced by the legacy of previous rounds of industrial investment. Areas where skills developed based around heavy engineering may be unable to make the transition to electro-mechanical technologies but will need a heavy investment in training to embrace those parts of pure electronics where the emphasis is upon mental rather than physical skills. Moreover, the training capacity in local institutes of higher education is likely to reflect the needs of earlier periods and take a long time to adjust. In terms of management information, the enterprises' scanning of its business environment will be strongly conditioned by existing personal contact networks which are likely, for simple time and geographic considerations, to have a strong local orientation. Information reaching enterprises in areas dominated by outmoded technologies consequently may not embrace the latest technological knowledge. Lastly, in the context of the information technology revolution, a lack of demand for telecommunication services arising from a failure to use the ability of this technology to provide access to an international store of technological knowledge may lead to an under investment in the infrastructure that is likely to be a necessary condition for the next upswing.

The Schumpeterian perspective suggests that the real economic benefits of a new technology arise with its widespread diffusion to all sectors and by implication all regions of the economy. In the early stages of technological revolution the benefits are likely to be limited both in terms of enterprises and regions. Large gaps are likely to appear between best practice capital productivity and that prevailing elsewhere in the economy; the work of Soete and Dosi on the UK would appear to confirm that this is the present situation (Soete and Dosi 1983). "The radical nature of the new technology - its widespread cross industry application, the lack of reliable, easily accessible information on profitability within the specific user's environment" (OECD 1985) act as a powerful disincentive to investment. It goes without saying that this investment is usually embodied in new products and processes installed into particular workplaces (factories, shops and offices) which are located in specific geographical environments. It also follows that policies designed to ensure the necessary information about new technology tailored to the needs of individual users must be available throughout the national territory; such policies are as fundamental in national economic development as they are in local terms.

However, the capacity to respond to the information about new technology is likely to vary dramatically from area to area and innovation policies need to be tailored accordingly. A number of highly interrelated factors are likely to determine the adoption potential of areas. These include: city size, relative location, industrial occupational structure, previous history of growth and decline and the size of ownership of enterprises in the area.

a)   City Size: Large cities have both strengths and weaknesses in terms of their potential contribution to structural adjustment. Such cities usually contain a wide range of major institutions - headquarters of manufacturing and service companies, financial houses, government departments and universities. Capital cities are unitary states

and provincial capitals of federal countries are usually well endowed
with a wide range of such institutions. Set against this strength is
the very excess of possibly worthwhile combinations of actors who
could bring about change: in such a rich environment significant innovations may not emerge or have the impact that they deserve. But not
all cities are so richly endowed. Many cities which grew to
pre-eminence in the early 20th Century have a population size in the
national settlement hierarchy which their current functional status
would not seem to justify. Many cities have lost the functions that
they once possessed as the control of local enterprises has passed to
other companies with headquarters in other regions.

b)   Relative Location: Small cities can be compensated for their lack
of higher order functions by the close proximity to major centres of
population. Such cities have access to all the advantages of the large
metropolis without directly bearing the cost in terms of congestion,
pollution, high land prices, etc. Even if the decline of the local
industrial base occurs a city which is embedded in a prosperous region
will have greater opportunities to adapt than a similar sized city in
a region of general decline. Finally, and notwithstanding advances in
telecommunications, peripheral locations within a national territory
would still appear to be a major problem for urban economic development.

c)   Industrial and Occupational Structure: The structural changes
that have been influencing advanced economies have clearly had a differential effect on cities. Those cities based around the Industries
of 19th Century - steel, coal, ship building and textiles have experienced a long history of decline. They have been joined more recently
by those cities which experienced a boom in the mid 20th Century based
on the expansion of sectors like chemicals, motor vehicles and consumer durables. On the other hand, cities which have remained as service
centres and have not experienced large scale industrialisation have
proved to be attractive environments for the entrepreneurs leading the
information technology revolution.

Notwithstanding the seeming importance of industrial structure many
studies suggest that it is a factor of declining significance in accounting for the growth or decline of cities. Far more important is
the occupational structure. The cities that have prospered are those
with a strong representation of professional and white-collar

occupations - the information processing and exchange functions in organisations such as research and development, marketing, accounting and a wide range of other services.

d)   History of Growth and Decline: Cities that have experienced a long and gradual history of decline may find it difficult to reverse this trend because of institutional rigidities. Initiatives to tackle the problem are frequently layered one on top of the other and there is little scope for a comprehensive approach to urban regeneration. Representatives of the declining sector of the economy dominate the key institutions (local government, Chambers of Commerce, Trade Unions, etc.). However, in situations where decline is recent and per- haps on the surface catastrophic the opportunities for radical and far reaching attempts at restructuring may be greater.

e)   Size and Ownership Structure of Enterprises: The size and owner- ship structure of enterprises would appear to underpin many of the possibilities for adoption. The most severe problems exist in those cities which are dominated by large branch establishments of enter- prises with their headquarters in other cities or countries. The scope for action in such situations is severely restrained: local managers owe no particular allegiance to the city and may only be in post for a few years. They have no autonomy to purchase goods and services from local businesses. Their factories support a limited range of manageri- al functions and depend on research and development carried out in other areas for the renewal and improvement of products. In such envi- ronments financial institutions are likely to be poorly developed since little capital will be raised locally; few professional and business services will be required. Potential entrepreneurs are likely to have little direct contact with the full range of managerial deci- sion making processes. At their other extreme there will be urban areas where a small business tradition has survived along with the supporting institutions; here rates of new firm formation are likely to be high with new founders having close contact with the day-to-day realities of business management. In such situations the capacity to adapt to changing conditions through innovation and retraining is con- siderable.

Little systematic research is available on which to substantiate the preceding discussions of what Lambooy has called the 'regional ecolo- gy' of technological change (Lambooy 1984). In the following section

of the paper we review our evidence on regional variations in the incidence of products and process innovations and the importance of one
factor, research and development capacity, in accounting for these
variations. However, many other considerations are important in accounting for regional variations in innovativeness and these must be
the subject of further research before fully fledged policy initiatives can be pursued. The evidence we present moves through the innovation spectrum from significant to incremental product innovations
and finally to process innovations.

3.   REGIONAL VARIATIONS IN RATES OF INNOVATION IN THE UK

Researchers at the Science Policy Research Unit (SPRU), University of
Sussex, have recently updated and extended to 1980 an earlier databank
of significant innovations introduced into Britain in the post war
period (Townsend et al. 1981). The data covers nearly 2,300 innovations occurring in over thirty sectors of manufacturing industry defined at the level of Minimum List Heading (HMSO 1968). While not exhaustive these sectors represent a broad spectrum of British industry
and cover a significant proportion of UK manufacturing output and employment. Table 1 illustrates the regional trends in innovation between 1945 and 1980. It shows that the South-East exhibits a share of
significant innovations well above its share of manufacturing employment and more narrowly of manufacturing establishments. In contrast
the Development Areas have a decreasing share of significant innovations and by the last period, this is considerably below what might be
expected on their basis of employment and number of establishments.

The Sussex study also reveals that the area to benefit most from the
transfer of substantial foreign technology into Britain is the
South-East which received approximately 217 innovations by this means
(Table 2). On the other hand the Development Areas have also benefit-
ted from this, largely it would seem at the expense of the non assisted areas outside the South East. This perhaps reflects the high levels
of foreign inward investment to the Development Areas which makes possible technology transfer within corporations. It also suggests that
foreign owned firms do not see any difficulties in transferring and
successfully operating new technologies in the Development Areas
(Haug, Hood and Young 1983).

TABLE 1

Trends in shares of substantial innovations by area

Years	South East	Non Assisted outside the South East	Intermediate Areas	Development Area
1945 - 59	36.7	27.5	19.1	17.5
1960 - 59	31.2	28.4	24.8	14.8
1970 - 80	34.0 (33.1)	24.9 (26.0)	30.3 (28.5)	10.6 (11.9)
Total 1945 - 80	33.7	27.0	25.5	13.7
N =	770	616	583	313
% of manuf. employees*	24.9	30.6	24.6	19.9
% of establishments*	31.0	29.6	23.4	15.9

Source: * PA 1002 Townsend et al. 1981
Figures in brackets denote standardisation of sectors to produce
comparable statistics with earlier time periods.

TABLE 2

% of innovations of foreign origin by receiving area

South East		Non Assisted		Intermediate Area		Development Area		Great Britain	
Foreign	Total	Foreign	Total	Foreign	Total	Foreign	Total	Foreign	Total
42.9	33.7	16.2	27.9	23.9	25.5	16.6	13.7	100	100
							N =	504	2282

Source: Townsend et al. 1981, Table 8.4, p. 83

While substantial innovations are perhaps of enormous value to innovating firms and industries have far reaching effects upon other industries and consumers, less significant and incremental changes can
be very important to the future of individual enterprises and establishments within enterprises. Such changes can lead to product differentiation and the maintenance or enhancement of market shares. It is
therefore not only the major technological changes which are important
to the continued advance of industry in an area but also crucial updating and differentiation of locally produced goods. In the following
paragraphs we provide evidence of regional variations in product

innovations (defined as products 'new' to the establishment over the period 1973-1977) in Great Britain.

The data were obtained from interview and postal surveys of 60 per cent of the establishments in three generally innovative industries well represented in all regions of the country - Metal Work Machine Tools, Scientific and Industrial Instruments, and Radio and Electronic Components (The Innovation Survey).

TABLE 3

Establishment location by status : incidence of product innovation
(% of establishments innovating)

Area	Single Plant Innovation	Group Plant Innovation	Total Innovation
	%	%	%
South East	85	91	88
Non Assisted Outside the S.E.	74	88	82
Intermediate	76	87	82
Development Area	55	87	73
Great Britain	78	89	84

Source: Innovation Survey

Table 3 shows that the South East Region recorded the highest incidence of product innovation while those establishments located in the Development Areas were on average less innovative than their national counterparts. Within these areas the least innovative set of establishments were operating from within the Northern Region and the most innovative plants were operating in the circle of small commuter towns surrounding but not in London. Further analysis indicates that the spatial variations in product innovation are small within that set of establishments which form part of a larger group whereas the most noticeable difference is between performances in the independent single plant sector or enterprise 'indigenous' to specific areas. On this evidence the Development Areas appear therefore to suffer from a local enterprise problem, rather than from the effects of external control.

Although the presence of innovation is important to local economic advance, where the development of these innovations occur may be a

better indicator of longer term potential within a community. Hence,
'in-house' product development may more accurately reflect the innovative and resource base of industrial establishments than the mere introduction of new or improved products. The survey reveals that 83 per
cent of establishments claiming a product innovation also claimed that
the major development work had been performed on site with the remaining respondents (109 cases) obtaining their products from 'elsewhere'.
This latter group may be termed 'dependent' establishments.

The 'dependent' establishments consisted of the 10 per cent of single
plant enterprises and 22 per cent of group establishments that obtained their product innovations from some source external to the
plant. Establishments located in Development Areas and in particular
the North were more inclined to 'import' new products than were establishments located elsewhere (Table 4). While the 'dependence' of independent enterprises upon external sources for innovation proved higher
in Development Areas than elsewhere an even more marked difference was
observed for group establishments in different locations. One-third of
Development Area group plants import technology compared with less
than one-fifth of similar plants located in the South East with the
majority of these sources lying in the same corporation.

TABLE 4

% of establishment with external sources of product
innovation by region

Total G.B. %	South East %	Non Assisted %	Intermediate %	Development %
17	13	17	15	33

Source: Innovation survey

Of the plants claiming an externally developed innovation nearly 50
per cent come from abroad in particular from the USA; the South East
is the greatest beneficiary from this inflow of new products from the
US. Within Britain 60 per cent of external sources noted were in the
South East and only 8 per cent in the Development Areas. In addition
of 30 products developed in the South East and transferred to another
location for production 57 per cent were transferred to other South
East manufacturing plants and only 18 per cent to Development Area
locations: within the UK there is therefore very little interregional
transfer of technology.

The preceding analysis has suggested that in quantitative terms the
South East has some advantage in the development and manufacture of
new products; it is also the chief beneficiary from the transfer of
new products into Britain from abroad. Further examination reveals
that these advantages are enhanced when the quality of innovations are
considered. To achieve this evaluation each innovation mentioned by
respondents in the survey was categorised with the help of industrial
experts as to whether it was 'high', 'medium' or 'low' technology.
Table 5 describes the distribution of locally developed product innovations within independent enterprises according to the technological
classification. The table clearly suggests that few enterprises indigenous to the Development Areas develop their own high technology products; when innovation does occur it is more likely to be low technology.

TABLE 5

Independent enterprise by on-site development of
technology and location

AREA		HIGH	MEDIUM	LOW	TOTAL
South East	Number	35	35	46	116
	%	30	30	40	
Non-Assisted	Number	3	16	20	39
	%	8	41	51	
Intermediate	Number	5	13	14	32
	%	15	41	44	
Development	Number	1	4	11	16
	%		25	69	

Source: Innovation Survey

Firms may be made competitive by the introduction of new manufacturing
processes which reduce the costs and/or improve the quality of existing products. These processes are usually embodied in new machinery of
various types, machinery which itself may be the result of product
innovations on the part of their manufacturers. The adopter usually
purchases the new machinery 'off the shelf' from a sales representative of a supplier and only limited research capacity may be needed in
order to incorporate the technology into the customer's own production.

A further perspective on the spatial aspects of technological change in Britain can therefore be obtained by identifying selected products and examining the pattern of takeup amongst potential adopters. Table 6 reveals the extent of regional variations in the adoption of give advanced process innovations in 1234 establishments in nine metal-working industries (The Diffusion Survey). The techniques are computerised numerical control of metal cutting, removing and joinery machinery, microprocessors for the control of manufacturing processes, such as assembly, monitoring and inspection and the use of computers for the coordination of production and design. By way of comparison with the earlier studies the incorporation of microprocessors into products as a product innovation is also included.

TABLE 6

Adoption of new technology by assisted area status

	Percentage of respondents in each area having adopted				
	CNC	Computers in Commercial Use	Computers in Manufacturing and Design	Micro-processors in Manufacturing Processes	Micro-processors in Products
Development Areas	21.3	60.9	28.2	10.1	13.9
Intermediate Areas	25.4	70.3	31.1	12.6	20.2
Non-Assisted Areas	27.0	64.5	29.8	11.6	22.4
South East	24.5	62.6	22.8	11.4	22.7
Great Britain	24.8	64.3	28.3	11.3	20.1
Spatial variation coefficient*	22.9	14.6	29.3	22.1	43.8

*Calculated as: $\left(\dfrac{\text{maximum \% } - \text{minimum \%}}{\text{mean \%}} \right)$ 100

Source: Diffusion Survey

It will be apparent from the table that the regional variations in rates of process innovation are far less significant than those re-corded for project innovation either in the studies reported previous-ly or when the adoption of, say CNC, is compared with the incorpora-tion of microprocessors into products in this survey. Moreover, exam-ining the cumulative proportion of adopters over time suggests that for certain techniques like CNC the Developments Areas led the South East in 1978 in the proportion of firms that adopted the techniques, a finding probably reflecting the influence of regional capital subsidies in bringing forward the purchase of new equipment.

4.   THE INFLUENCE OF RESEARCH AND DEVELOPMENT

While there are many factors at work we would suggest that regional various in the commitment to R&D is one of the most important explanations of the low rate of product innovation recorded by industry in the Development Areas. Employment of R&D workers demonstrates a commitment to technological advance and clearly increases the chance of success in product innovation. It is therefore not surprising that the Innovation Survey revealed a very strong link between on-site R&D and product innovation; indeed 89 per cent of the establishments recording a product innovation had some R&D effort in the establishment in question. Plants with no R&D on site were a far less innovative group.

Further examination reveals that establishments and in particular small independent enterprises located in Development Areas are less likely to carry out R&D activities on-site as compared with similar enterprises located elsewhere and particularly in the South East of England. Again it is the independent enterprises indigenous to Development Areas which do not appear to pursue technological advance so rigorously or systematically as their southern counterparts. But even within establishment that are part of a large group there appears to be greater commitment to R&D in the South East: 50 per cent of such plants in the North employed less than five R&D workers compared with 23 per cent in the North West and 18 per cent in the South East. The regional variations in the mean size of R&D employment per establishment indicated in Table 7 suggest important implications for the aggregate level of technological expertise present in the economies of more or less prosperous areas.

A manufacturing establishment can supplement, or to some degree substitute for, its own research effort by using sources of technical information from outside the plant. The dynamic establishment will be expected to exploit these possibilities for technological advance. Innovation Survey results suggest a clear difference between manufacturing establishments which are part of a larger group of those which are the sole location location of the company in the extent to which external technical contacts take place. As a whole single site companies record a lower level of external contact; however, the one-third of establishments which were part of a group recording 'other locations within the group' as their principal source of external technical information. This intra group transfer of technical information was of particular importance to manufacturing plants located in the Development Areas. In fact, contacts external to the enterprise as a whole were much less likely in group establishments in Development Areas than in regions like the South East. This may be because of the lack of capability to absorb external information on the part of Development Area plants (i.e. a lack of R&D capability on site) and/or a scarcity of suitable information sources locally.

TABLE 7

Characteristics of R&D by employment establishment location

Region	Number	Mean	Median	Maximum
North	40	9.7	4	60
North West	51	14.9	4	120
South East	55	21.2	5	300
Total	146			

Source: Innovation Survey (interviews)

In terms of location, the South East region is the primary source of external technical information. In general, plants in Development Areas mentioned relatively few local useful technical contacts. They appear to prefer or are forced to use technical sources at a greater distance than are firms located elsewhere. Although, in general, independent enterprises with one manufacturing site are more locally oriented as regards technical information than are plants which are part of a larger group, this relationship does not hold in the Development Areas, again reflecting the possibly limited supply of suitable technical advice.

5. URBAN AND REGIONAL CONTRAST

The urban/rural shift in manufacturing production in Britain has been the subject of much debate (e.g. Fothergill and Gudgin 1983) and for certain industries such as pharmaceuticals there is evidence of a non urban preference on the part of R&D functions (Howells 1983). In addition detached research laboratories in the public sector, although being concentrated in the South East of England, are in the main located in smaller towns and rural areas (Buswell and Lewis 1970). But what of the on-site R&D capacity which the surveys reported in this paper suggest are a major determinant of product innovation? Does the incidence of such facilities vary between urban and rural areas and are such variations greater than those between the North and the South of the country?

Table 8 attempts to answer this question with respect to the 1893 establishments responding to both the Innovation and Diffusion Surveys. Establishments have been assigned to functional regions and the regions specified according to size (conurbations, cities, towns, rural areas), functional status (dominant, sub-dominant and freestanding), economic structure (manufacturing, commercial, services) and regional location (North, South), (Coombes et al. 1982). The table reveals that the proportion of establishments with on-site R&D ranges from 88 per cent in cities subordinate to Greater London to 48 per cent in rural areas in the North. In the case of the conurbations there is clear evidence of lower level R&D activities in the metropolitan centres as compared with surrounding towns and cities, but with the proportion of establishments with on-site R&D being significantly lower in the Northern conurbations and their surroundings towns than is the case of constituent components of the London Metropolitan Region. While there are no real differences in the case of freestanding cities, the North/South contrast between freestanding towns of all types is quite significant. For example only 54 per cent of the establishments in towns classified as manufacturing in the North have on-site R&D compared with 82 per cent of establishments in similar towns in the South. The contrast between rural areas in the North and South is equally marked. So as far as R&D effort is concerned, the preference for smaller towns is only a phenomenon in the London Metropolitan Region and in the regions based on the provincial conurbations; elsewhere R&D is more significant in metropolitan centres whilst in the case of smaller towns of similar type there are distinct North/South contrasts. Indeed, the overall picture is one where these North/South differences would appear to be more significant than those between cities of different size.

106

TABLE 8

On-site R&D facilities and urban status
(% of establishment in each type of area with on-site R&D)

	%	No.
London		
Dominant Metropolitan Centres	78	205
Sub-Dominant Cities	88	67
Sub-Dominant Towns	83	132
Outer Conurbations		
Dominant Metropolitan Centres	58	223
Sub-Dominant Cities	68	145
Sub-Dominant Towns	69	72
Other Metropolitan Centres		
Dominant Metropolitan Centres	76	97
Sub-Dominant Towns	68	76
Freestanding Cities		
South	76	196
North	75	85
Manufacturing Towns		
South	82	61
North	54	70
Service Towns		
South	78	100
North	69	28
Commercial Towns		
South	81	76
North	69	75
Rural Areas		
South	76	50
North	48	44

Source: Innovation and Diffusion Surveys

6. TECHNOLOGICAL CHANGE AND EMPLOYMENT

What do our findings so far imply for jobs in different regions? We would anticipate that a failure to introduce new products within the peripheral regions of Britain will indirectly result in a loss of markets and jobs. At the same time the introduction of new manufacturing processes would directly result in labour displacement. Our Diffusion Survey lends support to this suggestion with, for example, over 90 per cent of the establishments introducing CNC recording a decrease in average job time, a third a decline in setting up time of machines and further third a reduction in inspection time.

In order to provide some indication of the employment changes associated with the introduction of new and improved products the respondents to the Innovation Survey were asked to estimate the number of jobs created or lost as a direct result of the changes in the year following the innovation. These estimates are compared with Table 9 for single and multisite firms in the North and South East regions. The table reveals that the North gains fewer jobs from product innovation but loses more jobs through process innovation than is the case in the South East, with the most significant losses accruing in multi-firms in the North.

TABLE 9

The mean employment effect of product and process innovation
in the first year by region and plant organisational status

	PRODUCT INNOVATION		PROCESS INNOVATION	
	North	South East	North	South East
Single	+ 0.25	+ 1.25	− 0.50	+ 0.20
Multi-	+ 6.00	+ 7.45	− 6.53	− 0.92
Total	+ 4.30	+ 4.92	− 3.81	− 0.49

Source: Innovation Survey Interviews (N = 123)

The overall regional effects of these changes can be estimated by grossing up the sample to give an indication of the possible job gains and losses in the three sectors covered by the survey. Table 9 suggests that when account is taken of the different sizes of the three sectors in the two regions, the North has gained relatively fewer jobs from product innovation than the South East, but lost more jobs through process innovation. Combining the two effects gives a marginal increase of employment in one year of 0.2 per cent of total employment in these industries. On the other hand the South East gains 3600 jobs or 3.1 per cent of total employment. However, these changes need to be seen in the context of the actual trends in employment in the three sectors in the two regions. Table 10 shows that in the three years after the survey the North experienced an actual annual rate of employment loss of 5.2 per cent compared with a 3.4 per cent loss in the South East. These losses may be attributed to a wide range of factors;

however, we may speculate that had firms in the South East also failed
to innovate to the same degree as those in the North, then the former
region may have experienced an equivalent rate of job loss.

TABLE 10

Estimated total annual regional impact of
product and process innovation

	NORTH	SOUTH EAST
Total employment change (annual average 1978-81) %	– 700 (-5.2%)	– 4,000 (-3.4 %)
Product innovation %	+ 160 (+1.1%)	+ 3,900 (+3.3 %)
Process innovation %	– 130 (-0.9%)	– 290 (-0.25%)
Total innovation effect %	+ 24 (+0.2%)	+ 3,600 (+3.1 %)

Source: Innovation Survey and Department of Employment

7. CONCLUSION: PROBLEMS AND OPPORTUNITIES

The analysis that has been presented in the body of this paper has
indicated important differences in patterns of technological innovation in Britain. The single most important cause of these differences
would appear to be regional variations in an innovative capacity as
reflected in the distribution of R&D activity; the peripheral regions
are generally dependent on the core area for sources of technological
knowledge and do not seem to provide a supporting environment for innovation especially amongst the smaller and medium-sized enterprises
which form the focal point of many contemporary regional industrial
development initiatives.

In these circumstances the question arises as to whether public policy
can enhance the technological capacity of lagging regions resulting in
increased local employment opportunities. On the basis of case studies
of firms in central Scotland, South Wales and Berkshire (West of London), Sayer and Morgan question whether it is realistic to expect

"that the success of Berkshire can be produced in other regions on a major scale... ...simultaneously". They suggest the success of this area is the product of the location preferences of entrepreneurs which has built up "a critical mass of high skilled personnel for which there is an international shortage...access to good communication, especially Heathrow...a core of government research establishments, a rural working environment capable of sustaining elite lifestyles and a marked absence of trade union traditions...what distinguishes the area from central Scotland or South Wales is its elite occupational struc- ture and intense decision making network of activities which have the potential for spawning (and sustaining) new firm formation to an ex- tent not readily apparent elsewhere" (Sayer and Morgan 1985).

To set against this rather negative view it is apparent that the ad- vantages of the South East have been produced not only by the private sector but also by the uncoordinated actions of the state - for exam- ple, as regards the location of research facilities, the award of de- fence contracts, the modernisation of communications and strict plan- ning controls which have preserved the quality of the residential en- vironment. Lagging regions may take comfort in the hope that a better managed state in which regional concerns are high on the agenda might also be encouraged by the fact that Berkshire has emerged from a rela- tively backward agricultural region in less than twenty years, achiev- ing its success in part from the migration of a highly mobile elite. Finally, Morgan Sayer's analysis confirms the importance to a success- ful region of social networks in developing the technological capacity of an area and it may be possible for public sector 'animateurs' to build such networks in certain lagging regions. We will therefore wind up this paper by suggesting how an initiative to promote new informa- tion technology in a region might be pursued. Clearly to be successful such a regional strategy would need to fit into a national strategy but for the sake of brevity we concentrate on the regional level.

A regional information technology strategy would need to be overseen by a powerful body containing representatives of all potentially in- terested parties (e.g. the PTT, Industry and Commerce, Trade Unions and Educationalists). A well formulated strategy is needed to monitor developments, bid for resources, encourage and coordinate policy ini- tiatives. The following activities are indicative of the tasks in- volved:

1) Keep abreast of infrastructure investments and new developments in technology and services. Lobby for investment and innovative projects (such as fibre optic experiments and Cable TV networks), so helping to ensure the area is well served and develops expertise in information technology (e.g. interactive cable services).

2) Support the marketing of telecommunications services: publicity and awareness exercises, demonstration projects and resource centres.

3) Lobby for tariff reductions to facilitate access to core regions.

4) Coordinate and give greater publicity to existing initiatives, such as technology transfer; seek out and support new initiatives and projects, such as regional databases on goods and services, tourist facilities and export opportunities. Bid for new projects and 'top-up' resources to support innovation, in addition to those provided through National or European policies which are not regionally differentiated.

5) Set up centres/agencies able to provide, at an accessible 'shop-front' location, a wide range of assistance on the adoption of information technology. This could include access to technical databases, access to facsimile, telex, etc. on a bureau basis also offering use and 'hands on' experience of automated office systems, microcomputers, etc. Such an activity would need field-worker staff, especially to deal with technology transfer activities within manufacturing industry.

6) Demonstrations of telecommunications networking and the inclusion of its potential within promotional efforts to encourage inward investment. It is necessary to show enterprises the capabilities of telecommunications as an aid to branch managements and as a way of facilitating decentralisation of some functions.

7) So far as information technology production is concerned, there is a need to identify specialisms which build on the industrial production strengths of the area and focus efforts on establishing these via indigenous development and inward investment. However, as far a possible, competitive bidding for inward investment should be avoided.

8)   Coordinate information on current and future skill requirements;
       support/lobby for training and retraining programmes.

Obviously, not all these proposals will be relevant to each region,
and some regions may have specific needs which might be unsuitable for
inclusion within an information technology strategy. However, it is
worth noting that one of the strengths of an information technology
strategy is that the technology is of such general applicability, and
has such widespread impact, that it can draw in a multiplicity of
issues and concerns, cutting across boundaries of conventional policy
areas.

The role of the provincial cities in carrying out these strategies in
the less favoured and peripheral regions in undoubtedly crucial. They
are the focal points of their regions, best able to take a leading
role in the diffusion of technological awareness and change. Above
all, they have the institutional infrastructure capable of supporting
policies to stimulate information technology. Although these institutional resources have often become depleted - notably through the erosion of financial and business services - the provincial cities of
Europe generally have higher education institutions, chambers of commerce, regional headquarters of the telecommunications services, local
government and branches of central government. Many have regional development and promotion organisations as well. To successfully implement an IT strategy, these institutions would have to work together
and support each other.

These cities have some particular characteristics especially relevant
to information technology. Certainly their educational institutions
have much to offer information technology producers and users such as
qualified manpower, training and R&D support. In many cases there remains considerable scope for greater involvement of these institutions
in their local economies. The cities can offer environments conducive
to the relocation of clerical work which has become more mobile with
the spread of distance-independent data transmission services. Provincial cities have often plentiful supplies of clerical workers low-cost
accommodation and other services. The cities are very much more likely
to be 'cabled' than small towns (let alone rural areas) and hence may
have the opportunity of participating in the provision of Value Added
Network Services, including city-wide information and interactive services between enterprises.

In a variety of situations the provincial cities would have to play a
key role in establishing, leading and implementing the kind of strategy outlined above. They must show, by example, what information technology can offer and so set in motion a process of diffusion into
their surrounding regions. The cities must service the activities of
their hinterlands - such as agriculture or tourism - acting as brokers
between hinterlands and markets elsewhere. In some ways new information technology may weaken the position of the cities, as hardware
production technology favours greenfield locations and 'remote working' strengthens the attraction of locations outside the city. This
makes it all the more imperative that strategies must be regional and
the mutual dependence of city and region recognised.

Information technology is not a universal panacea for all the problems
of lagging regions or old industrial areas. But is can offer them some
new opportunities - in contrast to the apparently unavoidable and negative impacts on existing employment levels. A coherently structured
strategy, sensitive to a region's specific needs, administered within
the region, - and draw heavily on the resources of the provincial cities - could enable depressed regions to maximise the potential benefits of this new technology. The socalled 'information technology revolution' requires a positive response; it cannot be ignored.

ACKNOWLEDGEMENTS

This chapter draws heavily on research undertaken in the Centre for
Urban and Regional Development Studies, University of Newcastle Upon
Tyne, over the period 1978-1984. Neil Alderman, Tony Edwards, David
Gibbs, Andrew Gillespie, Peter Nash, Ray Oakey and Fred Robinson all
made significant contributions to the research. Support was provided
by the Economic and Social Research Council, the Department of Trade
and Industry, the Department of the Environment and the European Commission. All responsibility for the text rests with the authors.

REFERENCES

Alderman, N., Goddard, J.B. and Thwaites, A.R., Regional and Urban
    Perspectives on Industrial Innovation: Applications of Logit and
    Cluster Analysis to Survey Analysis, Discussion Paper No. 42,
    Centre for Urban and Regional Development Studies, Newcastle Upon
    Tyne, 1983.

Buswell, R.J. and Lewis, E.W., 'The geographical distribution of industrial research and development in the UK', Regional Studies, 4, 1970, pp. 297-306.

Coombes, M.G., Dixon, J.S., Goddard, J.B., Openshaw, S. and Taylor, P.J., 'Functional regions to population census of Great Britain', in Herbert, D.T. and Johnson, R.J. (eds), Geography and the Urban Environment, 5, Progress in Research Applications, Wiley, London, 1982, pp. 63-112.

Fothergill, S. and Gudgin, G., Unequal Growth: Urban and Regional Change in the UK, Heinemann, London, 1982.

Freeman, C., 'Keynes or Kondratiev? How can we get back to full employment', in Marstrand, P. (ed), New Technology and the Future of Work and Skills, Frances Pinter, London, 1984.

Goddard, J.B., Gillespie, A.E., Robinson, J.F.F. and Thwaites, A.T., 'New information technology and urban and regional development', in Oakey, R. and Thwaites, A.T. (eds), Technological Change and Regional Development, Frances Pinter, London, 1985.

Goddard, J.B. and Thwaites, A.T., Technological Change and the Inner City, Working Paper no. 4, The Inner City Context, Economics of Social Research Council, London, 1980.

Haug, P., Hood, M. and Young, S., 'R&D intensity in the affiliates of US-owned manufacturing in Scotland', Regional Studies 17, 1983, pp. 383-392.

Howells, J.R.L., 'The location of R&D: some observations and evidence from Britain', Regional Studies, 18, 1984, pp. 13-30.

Keeble, P.E., 'The industrial decline, regional policy and the urban/rural shift in the UK', Environment and Planning A, 12, 1980, pp. 945-962.

Lambooy, J.G., 'The regional economy of technological change', in Lambooy, J.G. (ed), New Spatial Dynamics and Economic Crisis, Finn Publishers, Helsinki, 1984.

Mensch, G., Stalemate in Technology, New York, 1979.

Rees, J., Briggs, R. and Oakey, R.P., 'The adoption of new technology in the American machinery industry', Regional Studies, 18, 1984, pp. 439-504.

Sayer, A. and Morgan, K., 'The electronics industry and regional development in Britain', in Amin, A. and Goddard, J.B. (eds), Technological Change, Industrial Restructuring and Regional Development, Allen and Unwin, London, 1985.

Schumpeter, J.A., Business Cycles, McGraw Hill, New York, 1939.

Schmookler, J.A., Invention and Economic Growth, MIT Press, Cambridge, 1966.

Townsend, J.F., Henwood, F., Thomas, G.S., Pavitt, K.L. and Wyatt, S.M., Science and Technology Indicators for the UK: Innovations in Britain since 1935, Report prepared for SERC/SSRC Joint Committee, University of Sussex, 1982.

Mensch, G., Stalemate in Technology, New York, 1979.

Rees, J., Briggs, R. and Oakey, R.P., 'The adoption of new technology in the American machinery industry', Regional Studies, 18, 1984, pp. 439-504.

Sayer, A. and Morgan, K., 'The electronics industry and regional development in Britain', in Amin, A. and Goddard, J.B. (eds), Technological Change, Industrial Restructuring and Regional Development, Allen and Unwin, London, 1985.

Schumpeter, J.A., Business Cycles, McGraw Hill, New York, 1939.

Schmookler, J.A., Invention and Economic Growth, MIT Press, Cambridge, 1966.

Townsend, J.F., Henwood, F., Thomas, G.S., Pavitt, K.L. and Wyatt, S.M., Science and Technology Indicators for the UK: Innovations in Britain since 1935, Report prepared for SERC/SSRC Joint Committee, University of Sussex, 1982.

INDUSTRIAL INTERDEPENDENCE VIA INFORMATION TECHNOLOGY
AND TRANSPORT INTERACTION - EMPLOYMENT IMPACTS
John F. Brotchie

1.   INTRODUCTION

The information technology revolution is beginning to affect our patterns of living and working at least as profoundly as did the industrial revolution, only more rapidly. The industrial revolution extended human muscle; the information technology revolution is extending
the human mind and nervous system and will do so at almost all levels of
human endeavour: from manufacturing industry through service industries, to the new information knowledge industries which it is facilitating, and onto the home and leisure activities (Brotchie et al.
1985).

The obvious employment trends of this revolution are a decrease in
employment in the manufacturing sector and an increase in the tertiary-
quaternary sectors. However, the trends occurring at a less aggregated
level are far more complex.

The reduction in employment in manufacturing does not necessarily represent a reduction in goods produced. In fact the process of innovation (including information technology) is increasing the range (diversity), number and quality of goods produced and the labour productivity involved in producing them. It is producing counter currents
such as the conversion of previous services (home help, laundry, food
preparation, information, entertainment, education) into new manufactured goods (home appliances, processed foods, telecommunications systems and terminals, TV, video, personal computers). It represents an
increasing use of knowledge as a resource - in the R & D, design, production control, and management phases and a reduction of materials and
energy (including labour energy) as resources in the production phase.

It is also changing the distribution systems for these goods during
and after processing. Telecommunications and fast and reliable

transport are allowing better synchronisation of intermediate and final production, distribution and marketing, reducing the need for storage facilities and inventories at various stages in this total process - the concept of 'just in time'. The continuation of low inflation and high interest rates increases the need for this inventory control. The net result is greater use of knowledge as a resource, reduced use of materials, energy, and labour (per unit of production and in many cases overall) and greater interdependence between industries, and between production, distribution, and marketing.

In the service-information sectors similar changes are occurring. Electronic networks and processing facilities are increasing productivity (the electronic office, electronic funds transfer, etc.) and increasing interdependence between complementary service functions and between such functions in different geographic areas. This is providing the scale economies for increasing specialisation and the mechanisms for increasing interaction and interdependence between these specialist services. In this way information technology is allowing new types of service to be introduced. The net result is again increasing use of knowledge as a resource, reduced use of (materials, energy and) labour (per unit of production in some cases overall), and increasing interdependence between services and between regions and increasing range, diversity, and number of these services.

High technology industries also fit into the trends above. Hence, increasing use of knowledge and decreasing use of materials, energy, and labour per unit of production are occurring.

Technological change is also producing relative changes between firms - with those adopting an innovation early tending to grow while those delaying change tending to decline.

Routine production in each case is seeking locations of low factor costs (Malecki 1985). However, these factors are changing with increasing technology change. Materials, energy, and labour energy continue to decline as resource factors in production. There is also an increasing effort to reduce transport, storage, and inventory costs as indicated above. Transport costs are reduced if production components are located closer to each other and to markets, and if high quality transport networks including fast rail are developed. Knowledge and to a lesser extent capital tend to increase in importance as factors of production. Proximity to markets is another factor - offset, however, by a trend to centralise (and automate) production in some cases. Hence availability of knowledge workers and the costs of capital (interest rates) will tend to increase in importance as location factors. Thus routine production is tending to be increasingly knowledge and capital intensive and to increasingly seek locations where costs of capital and of transport are low.

Knowledge workers favour areas of high amenity and high access to knowledge centres, communications, and transport. Hence, these areas tend to be favoured for non routine, R & D type industries.

Associated trends include increasing productivity and increasing capacity to carry out many activities from the home - the home work station, the home entertainment centre, teleshopping, home appliances, etc. Consequences include increasing flexibility and informality of employment, and increased sharing of employment tasks - along with increasing flexibility of household arrangements and of work-leisure patterns.

Increasing interdependence between industries also means increasing interaction including telecommunications and (express) freight and passenger transport flows. Increasing emphasis on knowledge will also be reflected in increasing demands for education. Increasing productivity and hence increasing leisure will also mean increasing demands for leisure oriented activities and associated services. Increasing female participation in these activities will also mean increasing needs for home services (Jones 1982).

Thus, the overall trends are towards increasing emphasis on knowledge and to some extent capital as resources, increasing interdependence between industries and between regions, increasing production of goods and services, but automation of the more routine of these. Locationally, routine production will seek areas of low factor costs with capital and knowledge increasing as factors, and political, economic, and social stability increasing in importance. Amenity, communication, and transport are also increasing in importance, particularly for non routine, knowledge intensive industries. Increasing complexity is a factor common to all these changes. Further employment implications of these changes are explored.

2.   EMPLOYMENT EFFECTS

Information technology facilitates its own cost reduction and diffusion. It provides a change in order, or many orders, in the rate and
cost of processing information. A change of even one order in other
systems (e.g. in the case of travel speed from walking to motor car
travel) has brought with it qualitative changes (e.g. suburbanisation
and lifestyle changes). A change of several orders in the speed and
cost effectiveness of information processing can be expected to have
even more profound effects. These effects are already occurring over a
wide range of human activities and at various levels as indicated
above.

The shift in resource needs from materials and energy (including
labour energy) to information and knowledge parallels a move up in
the hierarchy of human needs from physical through the social to the
psychological (esteem, self-realisation, Maslow 1970). It also parallels the change in employment structure. Automation in routine industries is resulting in deskilling and job loss. Factor costs are similarly changing. Information technology and knowledge are displacing
blue collar labour, so that the advantage of low labour costs is diminishing as a factor of production and of its location. Costs of capital (interest) reduce in stable political/economic environments (e.g.
in developed countries). These changes may be expected to reverse the
trend for manufacturing and services to move 'offshore'. It could also
mean reduced industrial growth and employment in the developing world.
Non routine industries such as R & D are increasing in importance and
are increasingly knowledge based. Their locations are increasingly
dependent on availability of knowledge workers, and access to knowledge centres, and to transport and communication nodes (Malecki 1985).
These too are largely in the developed regions of the world.

Information technology is increasing productivity as a consequence of
increasing processing speed. In the secondary sector this means more
goods are produced, and a greater diversity of goods, with less labour.
In the tertiary sector it appears to mean more services (quantity,
diversity) from a still growing service - knowledge workforce. This
growth is not uniform, however, and routine white collar tasks are
also being automated while new services creating employment are being
introduced (Malecki 1985). The dynamics of these changes appears to be
such that new services and jobs are being created in the service

sector more rapidly that the process of job loss through automation is destroying other service jobs.

The further counter trend of substitution of manufactured goods for services previously noted means that both the range and quantity of goods is increasing while the number of people producing them is decreasing.

The employment shift to the service sector is into two main groups: high skills - high technology - R & D (the quaternary sector) i.e., knowledge based services; and low skills - services including home services, (the quinary sector), i.e., personal services, crafts, health, food, leisure, security, gardening, house cleaning, etc., resulting in increasing home based employment - high technology, and low technology (Batty 1985).

Productivity increases are also resulting in higher incomes and living standards for those employed, and increased leisure from reduced working hours introduced to better distribute this employment.

Formality of employment is also reducing - with flexitime, parttime work, job sharing and contract work replacing the previous rigid working arrangements. Automation is also resulting in space savings: where production can occur continuously, and productivity per unit of plant is thereby increased, less space is required, and production can (in some cases) be centralised in a single plant. The aggregated pattern of locations of these plants, however, is generally dispersed. On the other hand, increasing home based activities are requiring more space needs per capita in the home - but the overall effect on house size is offset by reducing household size. The drawing of more activities into the home also provides more time for other activities outside the home.

There is increasingly less distinction between manufacturing and service employment. Systems lore says 'take care of the information and the materials take care of themselves'. Hence, with automation, both manufacturing and service employment is increasingly concerned with processing information - or imparting knowledge to the system - and the basic tools for doing this, the keyboard and VDU, are the same for each sector. In fact the new jobs created in manufacturing industry are service (information/knowledge) jobs.

Locational constraints are reduced with information/communication technology. Time constraints are similarly reduced. Hence a greater diversity of locations for living and working are feasible along with a greater diversity of timing of these activities. The increasing coordination and interdependence between activities, however, represents a further counter trend.

Global telecommunication networks are increasing the spatial scale of markets, and of firms competing in these markets, leading also to the global village or the virtual city (Pressman 1985). At the same time, the microprocessor is allowing increasing diversity of goods and services and lifestyles, resulting in increasing capacity for difference between communities and increasing importance of local issues, local government, and local community developments for common interest groups - including the aged.

Reducing formality of work and leisure (and education) is increasingly tending to blur the differences between them. A longer period of education, initial and continuing, to develop and maintain the knowledge skills required will reduce unemployment directly (Stonier 1979) and indirectly through better matching of these skills and tasks.

The decreasing distinction between male and female employment roles and increasing female participation adds to the workforce supply, but also to demand in creating the need for more home services, fast foods and labour saving appliances. The trend towards deinstitutionalisation of health and other care further adds to the need for home services.

The most important of all shifts in the long term, however, is really just beginning. It is the introduction of intelligence and knowledge (artificial intelligence) into information technology and its utilisation at all levels of industry to provide new and qualitatively better products, goods and services and competitive advantage for them in the market place. This phase of the information technology revolution (currently being pursued by the Japanese in their fifth generation computer project, with responses from other parts of the developed world) can be expected to be the most important and most influential of all in the longer term (Fiegenbaum and McCorduck 1983).

Some spatial implications of these changes are now considered, first conceptually and then mathematically. An early application of a knowledge based technique is also introduced for solution of industrial employment and location-allocation problems.

3. INDUSTRIAL IMPACT - REGIONAL LEVEL MODEL

As noted earlier, information technology facilitates teleshopping for the ordering and purchase of goods and services. It also allows telecommunication for coordination of the various parts of the production and distribution systems for those goods and services and diversity of goods and services produced. Through this coordination, inventories of raw materials and partly processed and finished goods may be reduced along with storage facilities and the costs of each. This results in the concepts of inventory management and control, (processing and shipment of materials) 'just in time', 'production on demand', and flexible manufacturing systems (FMS).

Consequences include a tendency to centralisation of production (but not its location), reducing need for storage warehouse facilities and inventories, and increasing importance of information data networks and of fast and reliable freight transport systems. Increasing capacity to cater for changing demands, needs, and technological impacts and increasing interdependence between industry segments are further consequences.

Some of these changes are indicated on the technology - spatial impact diagram previously introduced (Brotchie 1984) in which dispersal of activities is plotted against dispersal of interactions between them (Figure 1). The triangle ABC represents the feasible space for industrial location and interaction at the metropolitan or regional level assuming an evenly distributed market and/or workforce. Industrial location ranges from centralised at the point B to dispersed at the line AC. Interactions range from 1 to 1 at A, and 1 to many at B, to many to many at C. Interaction distances also increase with movement up the vertical axis. The points A to C represent different ages of technology. Point A represents preindustrial activity, cottage industry, low technology, land, material, and manual resources based activities, crafts, independence, informality and diversity. Point B represent industrial technology, energy based activities, mass production, dependence, formality, and uniformity. Point C represents post industrial activity, the electronic cottage, and global village, virtual

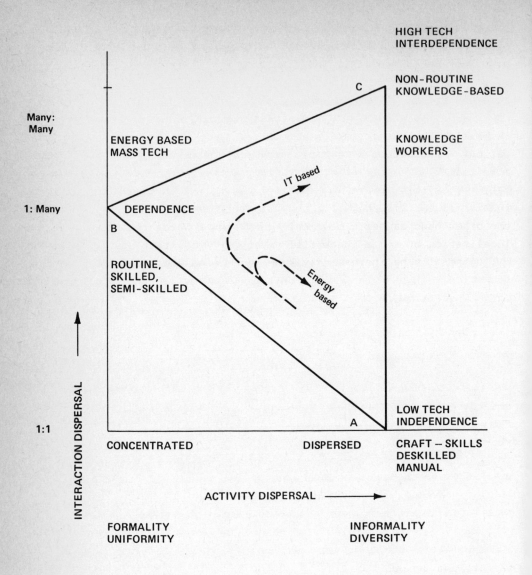

Figure 1   Technology triangle ABC, showing:

    A   low technology - land, material craft based; independent

    B   mass technology - energy based, dependent

    C   high technology - knowledge based, interdependent.

city, information knowledge based processes, information technology, increasing specialisation, small businesses, interdependencies, and a move back to informality, and diversity.

Movement trends within the space are indicated, for both information based high technology and energy based medium to low technology activities. Increased informatics - information processors and telecommunications - facilitate a movement upwards towards the point C. Faster, more reliable, and cheaper passenger and freight transport further facilitates this upward movement increasing the spatial dimensions of industrial systems. Higher transport energy costs for heavy goods on the other hand causes a movement downwards towards the point A and a localisation of these industrial systems. The larger spatial systems will generally be increasingly knowledge based and offer employment to knowledge workers. The smaller spatial systems will tend to employ a large proportion of less skilled workers.

4.   EFFICIENCY VS. ROBUSTNESS - SYSTEM LEVEL MODEL

The knowledge based systems above are complex systems and increasingly interdependent. The trends towards automation, production on demand, FMS, and 'just in time' are based on the premises of increasing reliability of automation of production, and of efficiency resulting from reductions in labour, space needs, inventories, storage and transport costs. Thus efficiency is realised at the expense of robustness.

An increasingly changing environment, labour disruptions, and technical imperfections. however, mean that some robustness in the system is required to cover breakdowns and disruptions and changing production factors and demands.

The relationship between effectiveness, efficiency, robustness and diversity of a complex system was derived (Brotchie et al. 1979) as

$$U = R + S/\lambda \qquad (1)$$

in which U is a measure of the total utility or effectiveness of the system: R is a measure of the total efficiency or resource cost; S is entropy or dispersal of the system and is defined as the log of the number of alternative paths through the production/information process

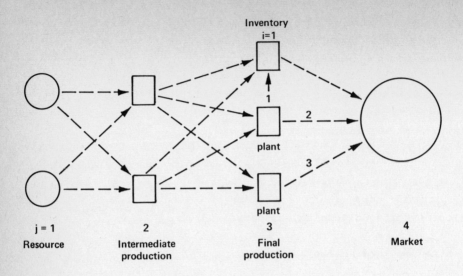

Figure 2 Production system showing resources, intermediate and final
production marketing, and flows of materials between them.
Alternative options (locations/capacities/electronic circui-
tries) are shown.

or of viable arrangements of system components; and $1/\lambda$ is a measure of diversity of component reliability (on the supply side or of diversity of products and services offered from a demand viewpoint); and S/λ is a measure of robustness of the system on the supply side. (It is a premium for diversity/range of choice of goods and services offered on the demand side).

The efficient system has minimal inventories, minimum reserve capacity of production units, uniformity, and concentration and satisfies the criteria of 'just in time' and 'production of demand'. The robust system has inventory reserves, reserve plant units, reserve electronic/information circuits, diversity, dispersal (Figure 2).

For strongly interacting systems without diversity, $1/\lambda$ is zero and total utility is given by the quadratic model

$$U = R = \Sigma\, b_{ijm}\, x_{ijm} + \Sigma\, b_{ijklmn}\, x_{ijm}\, x_{kln} \qquad (2)$$

in which b_{ijm} is the utility of (establishing and) operating a production unit of activity i in location j at time m, x_{ijm} is the portion of production allocated in this way, and b_{ijklmn} is the benefit of interactions between a unit of activity i in site j at time m and a unit of k in l at time n.

Thus b_{ijklmn} includes (transport costs and) inventory and storage costs when time m of (final) production of a good lags that n of its previous (intermediate) stage in the process.

The required solution for the set x_{ijm} is that which maximises U in equation 2 subject to the constraint that all goods i are produced, i.e.,

$$\underset{im}{\Sigma}\, x_{ijm} = 1 \qquad \text{all i,} \qquad (3)$$

and no plant j capacity is exceeded, i.e.,

$$\underset{j}{\Sigma}\, x_{ijm} \leq 1 \qquad \text{all j, m} \qquad (4)$$

Equations 2, 3 and 4 represent a quadratic assignment problem (Koopmans and Beckmann 1957) but in which non integer values of x_{ijm} are acceptable (Brotchie 1969).

Where there is diversity and uncertainty, the term S/λ (equation 1) is also included to provide the necessary robustness required, in which S/λ may be approximated by

$$S/\lambda = \sum_{ijm} x_{ijm}(1-x_{ijm})/\lambda \quad (0 \le x_{ijm} \le 1) \tag{5}$$

Where there is no diversity (full reliability), the optimal solution for maximum utility U requires no reserve capacity and no inventory stocks or storage facilities, i.e., the system is so organised and synchronised that total resource costs of establishment, operation, and transport are minimised, and inventory, storage and reserve plant units are not required, i.e., the concepts of 'just in time' and 'production on demand' apply.

Where there is some uncertainty or variability in the system, the optimal tradeoff between efficiency and robustness is given by equation 1.

On the demand side, some degree of diversity is also desirable to meet the diversity of human preference, and S/λ in equation 1, represents the additional utility to the community that results. Information technology allows this diversity of demand to be met by flexibility of manufacturing systems while still maintaining efficiency on the supply side. This diversity of goods and services and efficiency of their supply is in fact one of the features of the information revolution. In the Annex an 'intelligent' solution technique for the abovementioned specific quadratic assignment problem will be proposed.

5. CONCLUSION

Another major revolution or cycle in the process of innovation, technological development and structural change is upon us. It is providing new patterns of working and living and is penetrating industrial activities faster than its predecessors. Its early impacts are already being felt but as the innovation phase is itself still at an early stage, its major impacts have yet to be felt. These major impacts will come from the introduction of knowledge and intelligence into information technology and their intrusion into virtually all aspects of human endeavour.

Consequences include the shift from materials and energy to knowledge as the major factor of production: a corresponding shift in employment demand to knowledge workers; reduced formality of employment; reduced distinction between male and female employment roles, between manufacturing and service tasks, and between work, education, and leisure activities; reduced constraints on location of industries, services and houses; a reversal of the trend to offshore production (except for reasons of pollution or third world equity and stability); greater coordination and synchronisation of components of the industrial production process leading towards the concepts of 'just in time' and 'production on demand'; increased demands for information networks and fast and reliable transport systems to facilitate this coordination; greater flexibility of production and diversity of products leading to FMS, and adaptability to changing needs and material supplies; increased home based employment and leisure activities; increased importance of amenity, transport, and communication in locational choice of households and non routine activities; increased deinstitutionalisation of health and other community care activities; increased female participation; increased demand for home services and other service activities both high tech and low tech; increased employment opportunities in the knowledge based high tech service areas and in the low tech home based and home services areas, food preparation and service, health care and leisure activities. increased diversity of locations and facilities for these activities; increased needs for education and educators; increased polarisation between knowledge workers and others; increased income differentials (unless redistribution policies are introduced; and increased rates of change and increased opportunities for quantitative and qualitative research of the processes involved in this change.

These trends are demonstrated quantitatively and qualitatively by the models introduced herein.

ANNEX

AN 'INTELLIGENCE' SOLUTION TECHNIQUE

A feature of the quadratic assignment problem is that the function U in equation 2 is non convex so that a number of local optima can exist in the feasible (constraint) space. The robustness term S/λ , however, is convex. This suggests a device for solution of the non convex problem. Hence, if the parameter $1/\lambda$ were treated as an arbitrary constant and a sufficiently large value chosen, the function U could be made convex.

The matrix of coefficients of quadratic terms is positive definite and hence U is convex when $1/\lambda$ is sufficiently large. An iterative procedure for solution of equations 1-5 with stepwise decreasing values of $1/\lambda$ allows the overall optimum for a given real value of $1/\lambda$ including $1/\lambda = 0$ to be approached. In this way the arbitrary robustness term acts as a bridge between local optima allowing the feasible space to be traversed even though the real utility U may initially reduce in the process, i.e., there may be valleys in the real utility surface U between the local optima which may be bridged by the arbitrary robustness term S/λ. In an (initially) robust solution all x_{ijm} are finite. In a (finally) efficient solution zero one solutions emerge.

In design terms, this is equivalent to starting from a general solution in which all options are finite, and systematically eliminating options until a reduced and optimal set specialised to the particular problem is obtained. Utility maximisation is also a basis for human decision making in design. Thus some degree of 'smartness' or 'intelligence' beyond the simple 'hill climbing' techniques of mathematical programming may be introduced into the problem - based on knowledge of the mathematical properties of the system and/or of the process of design.

The technique above is mathematically related to the Metropolis (Metropolis et al. 1953) technique of simulated annealing in which minimisation of energy is the objective instead of maximisation of utility. It is also mathematically analogous to the heuristic technique of Burchard and Bonnigen (1983).

In fact these two solutions are the most effective and efficient so far reported (Burkard and Rendl 1984, Sharpe and Markjso 1985) for quadratic assignment; and both are theoretically underpinned by the robustness theory outlined herein.

This general ability to introduce knowledge and intelligence into computer software will represent the next and most important phase of development of information technology and will be utilised increasingly in all phases and sectors of industrial development to improve production quality and cost effectiveness and to provide comparative advantage in the market place. This increasing emphasis on knowledge and decreasing emphasis on manual processing are features of the post industrial society.

REFERENCES

Batty, M., 'Industrial features: UK', in: Brotchie, J.F., Newton, P.W., Hall, P. and Nijkamp, P. (eds), The Future of Urban Form - the Impact of New Technology, Croom Helm, London 1985, pp. 41-53.

Brotchie, J.F., 'A general planning model', Management Science 16(3), 1969, pp. 265-266.

Brotchie, J.F., Lesse, P.F. and Roy, J.R., 'Entropy, utility and planning models, Sistemi Urbani 3, 1979, pp. 33-53.

Brotchie, J.F., Newton, P.W., Hall, P. and Nijkamp, P. (eds), The Future of Urban Form - the Impact of New Technology, Croom Helm, London, 1985.

Brotchie, J.F., 'Technological change and urban form', Environment and Planning A, 16, 1984, pp. 583-596.

Burkard, R.E. and Bonnigar, T., 'A heuristic for quadratic Boolean programs with applications to quadratic assignment problems', European Journal of Operational Research 13, 1983, pp. 374-386.

Burkard, R.E. and Rendl, F., 'A thermodynamically motivated simulation procedure for combinatorial optimization problems', European Journal of Operations Research 17, 1984, pp. 169-174.

Fiegenbaum, E.A. and McCorduck, P., The Fifth Generation, Michael Joseph, London, 1983.

Jones, B., Sleepers, Wake! Technology and the Future of Work, Oxford University Press, Melbourne, 1982, 295 pp.

Koopmans, T.C. and Beckmann, M., 'Assignment problems and the location of economic activities', Econometrica 25, 1957, pp. 53-76.

Malecki, E., 'North America', in: Brotchie, J.F., Newton, P.W., Hall, P. and Nijkamp, P. (eds), The Future of Urban Form - the Impact of New Technology, Croom Helm, London, 1985, pp. 31-38.

Maslow, A.H., Motivation and Personality, Harper and Row, London, 1970.

Metropolis, N., Rosenbluth, A.W., Rosenbluth, M.N., Teller, A.H. and Teller, E., 'Equation of state calculations by fast computing machines', Journal of Chemical Physics 21, 1953, pp. 1087-1092.

Pressman, N., 'Forces for spatial change', in: Brotchie, J.F., Newton, P.W., Hall, P. and Nijkamp, P. (eds), The Future of Urban

Form - the Impact of New Technology, Croom Helm, London, 1985, pp. 349-361.

Sharpe, R. and Marksjo, B.M., 'Facility layout optimization using Metropolis', Environment and Planning B, 1985, in press.

Stonier, T., 'The Third Industrial Revolution: microprocessors and robots', paper prepared for The International Metal Workers Federation Central Committee Meeting, Vienna, 19 October 1979.

INDUSTRIAL ORGANISATION, INNOVATION AND EMPLOYMENT
Dirk-Jan F. Kamann

1.   INTRODUCTION

This chapter deals with the effect of changes in the industrial organisation on the spatial distribution of labour in conjunction with innovations: the distribution of levels of skills, job opportunities and the quality of work.

The organisation of industrial production is defined as a selected specific combination, organisation and location of capital and labour in order to create a certain product/market combination. We will therefore first discuss some features of this selection process, whereafter three causes for changing organisational structures will be discussed: 1) growth of a firm and concentration of a market, especially the multiplant firm; 2) changing cultural values resulting in changing demand for goods and work situations; 3) the increased importance of information (based) activities and the role of telecommunications and other 'network' linkages, resulting in a 'segmented (information) network' theory. For all three causes, spatial effects will be given.

2.   DETERMINANTS OF INDUSTRIAL ORGANISATION

2.1   Introduction

In order to get a better insight into the process that shapes an industrial organisation, Figure 1 gives a simplified model of factors playing a role in it.

In Figure 1, we see that 'managers' - with a certain 'style' of operating (Johnson and Scholes 1984) decide on certain (new) products (Inglehart 1977) and production processes, given their product/market

combination, their competitive position and the expected development
of the market(s) (Porter 1980). Here questions are raised such as: who
is a market leader and what is he doing? (Knickerbocker 1973); is
there a strong 'demand pull'? (Schmookler 1966); in which stage of the
product life cycle are the products? (de Jong 1981); or - in a wider
scope taking the behaviour of all firms into account - what is the
firm's position in a 'long wave'? (Freeman 1983, Nijkamp 1982)?

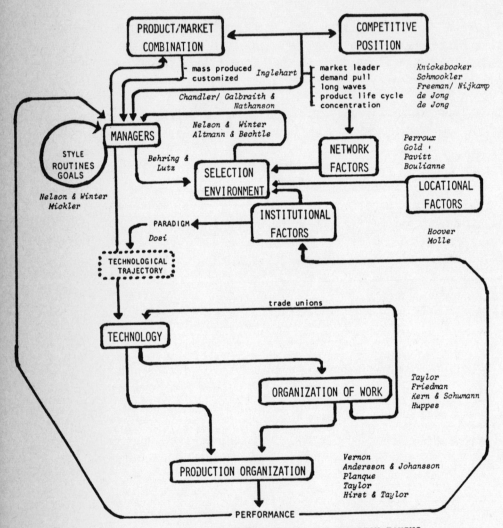

FIGURE 1: DIAGRAM SHOWING VARIOUS FACTORS IN DECISION TAKING

These factors are major causes of a search process for production innovation or process innovation by the manager(s). usually characterised by 'routines' of past experience (Nelson and Winter

1977). New ideas, put forward by suppliers, buyers and (other) interfirms relations - the 'network' - may further direct the choice, as is the case with institutional factors like government regulations, trade unions and so on. Together with location(al) factors, important in the final decision as to where to produce what (Hoover 1971), they are the 'external factors' or 'selection environment' (Altmann and Bechtle 1971, Nelson and Winter 1977). Given a number of technologies to choose from ranked according to a certain 'trajectory' (Dosi 1982, 1983), a new product strategy will be followed, resulting in a specific technology and a specific organisation of work(ers), with certain lines of authority and competence: both intraplant and interplant/intraorganisation, both horizontal and vertical.

This result, a specific combination, organisation and location of capital and labour will be named hereafter as the specific production organisation of a firm.

Finally, the 'performance' of a firm, measured in profits, gives an indication of the successfulness of the managers' attempts to implement the planned product/market strategy. Good performance will satisfy financing agencies (banks, shareholders) and will give more freedom to act. Poor performance will increase outside pressure to improve, 'rationalise' or restructure the firm.

From the many factors mentioned above, we will select some clusters of factors for further discussion. Especially the dynamic aspects of these will be considered: changing markets, shifts in demand, new technologies, network relations and institutional forces, requiring organisational adjustments or restructuring.

The response of the organisation to these 'stimuli' depends, however, on the operating style of the individual organisations and their managers.

2.2 Operating Style and Inertia

Comparable firms in similar situations show different reactions to certain innovative stimuli or, in a wider context, to signals from their product/market 'gatekeepers'. This has first of all to do with the specific management style of a firm or organisation. Is it a 'defender organisation', used to specialise instead of diversify? Is there a innovative policy ('analyser organisation')? Is there an active search for new possibilities - 'niches' - a high rate of diversification and a high propensity to take risks ('prospector organisations') (Johnson and Scholes 1984)?

Another reason for different behaviour in similar situations is that managers and organisations show certain repetitive patterns in their search processes and their problem solving behaviour, based on past experience. 'Organisational memory, representing the present capabilities of a firm'. 'Therefore, firms are usually better equipped to do more of the same than to change their policies on one of their characteristics' (Hagedoorn 1984). These 'routines' (Nelson and Winter 1977) cause certain inertia in the firm's behaviour: the more experience a firm has, the larger the inertia, the less likely it will break with the established problem solving approach and patterns of response to innovative stimuli. Young firms with less or even no experience are supposed to have a small inertia, enabling them to operate in a flexible manner, which is something of importance to survive in new, buoyant markets. The inertia factor could - besides, for instance, financial and risk isolating factors - be one important argument why new initiatives where new markets, products and innovations play a role, are separated from the 'old' organisation into new firms. Drawing on the useful experience - marketing/distribution, finance - of the parent company, the new firm is not loaded with the slowing down inertia of its parent when developing new products or markets. It explains at the same time why large transnational companies often 'sit back and wait' in a new product/market till a small company has shown that a certain product is viable, whereafter a takeover secures the knowhow - built up 'routines' for that product/market - for the transnational.

As we will see later on, a changing demand, leading to more flexibility in a desired output, is a reason for trying to reduce the inertia of an organisation, by reducing the size of organisations, the length of information flows and decision procedures, and giving production units more autonomy.

The loss of 'positive' memory by cutting out decision layers, seems to be compensated by gaining more flexibility.

A third point of importance when studying responses to outside 'stimuli', especially innovation(s), is that managers will evaluate innovations in the light of certain 'goals'. Apart from the usual goals such as profit seeking, continuity, market share and so on, one 'goal' is to <u>control</u> the company they are running (Mickler 1976). Process innovations with a deskilling effect would suit this 'goal', since they would make the production process less dependent on the 'will' and 'skill' of workers. Likewise, the effect of a split up into smaller (production) units is that workers are easier to control and motivate. Since we saw above that more autonomy for production units leads to more flexibility, better market performance and hence higher returns on capital, the apparent paradox of 'more autonomy' and 'control over the organisation' is solved by a careful selection of workers, on the job training, special rewards and fringe benefits for workers in key positions. These measures, to ensure the workers' loyalty is termed 'autonomy regulation' (Christis 1980) or 'responsive autonomy' (Friedman 1977).

The paradox of 'control' and 'profitability', the tradeoff between both management goals, means that sometimes production and organisational solutions are selected that might be less profitably - suboptimal - but which do satisfy the 'need' to control or avoid the perceived risk of giving away decision power.

3.   <u>ORGANISATION DYNAMICS</u>

3.1   <u>Introduction</u>

The abovementioned 'intrafirm' features play an important role in explaining different reactions of firms to outside stimuli like new markets, products, technologies or competitors. These differences in the ability to make full use of certain opportunities result in a dynamic process in which some firms grow, take over other firms, start new initiatives and expand, while others, although being 'winners' in the past, become 'losers' and decline, and are being taken over or closed.

Three aspects, reflected in the structural change of the organisation are 1) growth, 2) economic concentration, and 3) changes in technology, demand or institutional-cultural parameters: the environment.

3.2   <u>Growth and Concentration</u>

A significant growth of a firm causes it to follow the usual evolutional path along 'functional' to 'divisional' and 'matrix' organisation (Chandler 1973, Galbraith and Nathanson 1978). Because of its size, a multiplant transnational organisation becomes feasible with the inherent advantages of 'internal scale economies'. Here, the external economies, important locational factor for industrial plants, have been replaced by internal economies of scale: internal flows and networks of information, internal financial resources, internal labour pools and internal research departments have replaced external sources to a certain extent.

Another important aspect of organisation dynamics is economic concentration. While the geographical term 'concentration' relates to clustering of activities in a certain (urban) centre, the economic connotation of the term relates to the number of independent firms, operating on a certain market, and their market share. The more mergers and takeovers occur, the less independent firms operate on that market, the more 'concentrated' the market.

Here we touch on network theories, describing linkages between firms. These linkages relate to the exchange of goods and services, but in this case also to decision lines, property lines and economic dominance. According to Perroux (1955), firms operate on a specific 'plane' in space. In the network on a 'plane', firms meet competitors having the same activities, buyers of what the firm produces, suppliers of the required input, substitutes of the produced products, and potential newcomers (Porter 1980). Firms may dominate or control a certain 'plane' in a structural manner - for instance, a trading bank - while exercising influence on another 'plane' in the economic space. While one particular company may be market leader in one product of its product mix, another company may be market leader with one of the other products of this product mix. Concentration of a market means then increased dominance over a large or significant part of 'economic space'. It could mean at the same time, that one company has to operate in various networks on planes which have nothing to do with each other. Although satisfying 'megamania', it has organisational and managerial complications (cf. ITT).

The way an industrial organisation adapts to the increased size of the corporation depends - as we saw in Figure 1 - apart from a given 'operating style', on the nature and strength of external factors such as nature of demand, technical possibilities, institutional forces and sociocultural values, 'the selection environment', and so on.

One type of adaptation was very common during the sixties and seventies when more and more companies were split up in 'Head Office activities' (strategic planning, control, finance, marketing), 'Research and Development' and 'Production Plants'. Because of the internal economies of scale, production plants were not always required in urban areas with their external effects, but could be located in rural areas, or Less Developed Countries. Companies did not mind having long routes of supply (Malecki 1980) or being a long distance from their markets, all together resulting in marginal local linkages (McDermott 1979, Kamann 1978). Here, the size of the product did of course play a role: it is easier to ship thousands of chips or watches in a container than larger TV sets, trucks or locomotives.

This phenomenon of geographic separation of organisational functions was characterised as the spatial variant of the product life cycle theory (Vernon 1966).

3.2.1   The Product Life Cycle Theory: Pros and Cons

The product life cycle theory assumes that - along the path of introduction of a product and successive growth, maturity, saturation and decline of the output - production becomes more routinised and standardised. Here, a process of maximal deskilling of each task takes place. In this view, new technologies are selected to serve this purpose. While the required level of skills in the R & D stage is high, the required level of skills in the final standardised production stage(s) is low, with the pilot plant production in between.

A second assumption then states that highly skilled, specialised workers are concentrated in metropolitan areas - in core areas - while (cheap) low skilled labour is available in rural - peripheral - areas or Less Developed Countries, where land prices are also low. The latter locational advantage is important since standardised production plants usually need large sites. Because of this distribution of skills (and land prices), highly skilled work is usually located in metropolitan areas and low skilled work in rural areas. Deskilling of a part of the production process implies then dispersal; an organisational structure along strict 'tayloristic' lines: separation of planning from production.

Andersson and Johannsson (1984) improved the explanatory value of the product life cycle theory by assuming different elasticities to distance of activities with various levels of knowledge. In ranking levels of knowledge, they found at the lowest level pure information (or 'data'), the most elementary form of knowledge. Information can be aggregated or disaggregated, without loss in value. The next - higher - level is knowledge, described as 'ordered information'. 'As a parable, one can see information as variables, while knowledge is a set of equations containing these variables' (p. 35). The third level is 'competence'. This type of knowledge is embedded in patterns of social interaction, in instruments and in other social and physical entities. We can subdivide 'competence' into a) instrument oriented competence, b) sector specific competence, and c) region specific competence.

The highest knowledge level is 'creativity': the ability to order and regroup information in an original manner. It is the combination of all three lower levels of knowledge.

According to Andersson and Johannsson, the 'dispersing' effect of telecommunication is smaller for higher levels of knowledge than for lower levels. 'The social dimensions of knowledge and competence communication seems to be extremely strong, and gives a very large relative efficiency of face to face communications' (p. 36). This statement is in lin with results of other Swedish researchers (see e.g., Erlandsson 1979). Especially those activities dealing with transport and handling of 'information' (data) will be hit by a geographic decentralisation or dispersal.

Table 1 summarises the spatial effects of the various stages.

TABLE 1

THE PRODUCT LIFE CYCLE: Spatial Aspects of the Various Stages

STAGE	SUB-STAGE	RESULT	LOCATION	SKILL LEVEL	URBAN/ RURAL	MARKET
RESEARCH AND DEVELOPMENT	- fundamental research - applied research - development prototype	discovery invention prototype	university company lab. company lab.	high	large urban area's	– – test
PILOT PRODUCTION	- development and testing production process - small scale test production	production process product	'near' HQ and R&D lab			introduction
STANDARDIZED PRODUCTION	- automated, standardized mass production	homogeneous products	'detached' production plants	low	periferal rural area's	growth maturity saturation

3.2.2   Regional Effects on Employment

Rural - peripheral - areas have a chance of being industrialised by means of production plants of large multiplant companies. This means jobs for lower or unskilled workers in the plant, jobs during the con- struction stage and some jobs for cleaning and transport (Kamann 1978). The income multiplier is supposed to be low, because of the lack of high income workers in the factory. Further, the degree of linkage with local suppliers and buyers varies with the degree of de- pendence on the rest of the corporation (internal linkages), but is often low. Negative employment effects on local low wage traditional firms are not impossible.

Industrialisation through production plants does not stop the brain and capital drain from peripheral areas to the central areas, as de- scribed in the cumulative theory (Myrdal 1957, Holland 1976). It leads to a cumulative inability to generate new innovations and jobs (Pfaff and Hurler 1983, Stöhr 1982).

3.2.3   Some Critical Notes on the Product Life Cycle Theory

1.   The product life cycle is geared towards large, multiplant corpo- rations - particularly their foreign branches. Because of their size, their scale economies enable them to establish long dis- tance linkages, taking advantage of the lower factor prices - labour and land - in peripheral regions. When production plants are established abroad, tax advantages and internal accounting practices may further increase the advantage. It should be noted that domestic operating, small and medium sized firms operate differently. Decentralisation of parts of the firm, other than replacing in-house production by buying from a specialised sup- plier, is less likely to occur. For 'new' firms, the 'filtering down' variant applies (Thompson 1968). Firms are 'born' in large urban areas, where they have a high propensity to invent and in- novate and therefore show a higher growth rate, which is typical of a new market. The more a product reaches 'maturity' and   the more it gets into a replacement market, the less - outside - knowledge is required and the more the high wage level and land rents of the innovation areas are felt as burdensome. The firm will filter down to the smaller, less industrial sophisticated areas.

Although empirical research supports this theory (e.g., Ciciotti (1984), we could make a distinction between 'new' activities (like computer programming services) and activities that exist a long time, but continue to introduce new products (like micro electronics). While for both types of activities an orientation towards core areas is found, the latter seems better spread over the various regions (Molle and Vianen 1985). For completely new activities we can say that by the time lower hierarchical cities become an interesting market, local firms or branch offices will be founded (diffusion along hierarchical lines). The problem remains how to explain the behaviour of the small firm that has several products in several stages of the life cycle. The product cycle theory is unsatisfactory here as it 'jumps' from a small one product firm to a large multiproduct, multiplant multinational. Another problem is that 'within rich countries the places of origin of new industries and the sites they choose to undergo their first major stage of growth tend not to be the cities at the top of the urban hierarchy' (Storper 1985, p. 28). The theory is not able to explain these new growth complexes.

2. Although highly educated workers may show a slight preference for urban areas, a lot of empirical research finds no actual differences in urban/rural division, or sometimes even an opposite situation (Gudgin and Fothergill 1984). Furthermore, many large urban areas contain large reservoirs of low skilled workers, and many empty industrial estates. Here, economic cycles or long cycles seem to determine exogenously the 'push' or 'pull' factors of urban areas.

3. Regional differences in wages are an important location factor in the American literature, and likewise the urban/rural differences. For other countries, with central wage agreements like The Netherlands, these differences are, seen against all other location factors, very small or almost insignificant. The presence of labour in these countries, given a low mobility rate, is often a more important location factor than wage differences.

4. Products have changed from mass production to small series. Reason for this change in the nature of demand - sometimes characterised as a shift from a sellers' market to a buyers' market - is a 'deeper rooted' change, embodied in changing cultural

values. It resulted in an increase of 'customised' or small series of products. Tailormade, and yet to be produced on a large
scale, it led to an increase in CNC, CAD/CAM and other types of
flexible programmable discrete manufacturing.

Its consequence was that for an increasing number of products,
the product life cycle did not reach the 'Taiwan' stage. Production takes place 'near' a firm's head office and laboratory where
low(er) skilled workers are also available (see ad 2.). Here,
production 'lines' or 'streets', highly automated, with computerised manufacturing and logistics are established. Toffler's
(1980) computerised 'knitting machine', in 1980 for many still
science fiction, has become reality in many production plants.
This would mean that 'only' products that are still mass produced, are suitable for long distance dispersal; peripheral areas or LDCs. It means at the same time that the peripheral
areas of developed nations should not embark on industrialisation
through mass production plants, since those have only a limited
lifetime. The more advanced CAD/CAM (etc.) using plants, requiring higher skilled workers, seem a better alternative, although,
according to cumulative causation theory, still not ideal.

5. The product life cycle theory is mainly an industry oriented theory. Given that in many countries industry is a decreasing factor in employment, more emphasis should be placed on other sectors, like service sectors, information, government subsidised
and 'fourth' sector activities.

6. The theory follows 'Tayloristic' principles: the division of
planning and production, with highly 'centralised' decision making. Another type of distribution of authority is, however, also
possible; 'Profit Centra', 'Business Units', 'independent daugh-
ters' are examples of this decentralised authority, more according to the 'Human Relations' School. According to Andriessen
(1985), multinationals show a process of reorganisation where
competence to decide on matters like production, marketing and
sales is decentralised, while, at the same time, decisions on
investments, finance, and 'tax management' are centralised. Intermediate layers of decision are eliminated. Whether a sector is
concentrated and an organisation centralised, is of importance
for the geographical distribution of jobs and skills. Taylor and

Hirst (1984) show for the concentration of Australian banking, that it coincided with job losses because of the closing down of branch offices. Further, they found increased centralisation, which 'altered the structure of employment in banks effectively reducing the skill levels required at the branches while central-ising information flows and decision making' (p. 1073). Economic concentration - takeovers, mergers - leads in this way to in-creased centralisation of decision authority, and therefore to geographical concentration of decision taking functions and ac-tivities.

However, as mentioned earlier, alternative decision structures are also possible. Alexander (1983) gives an example of two firms, that, facing the same innovation (CNC), choose for differ-ent organisational structures. While one firm opts for a 'Tay-loristic' approach, the other chooses for a solution with more autonomy and less Taylorism. Given the different nature of the two countries where these firms were located - the USA and Norway - this could be an indication that the sociocultural perception of the desirable working situation is of importance when choosing a certain type of organisational structure. It shows that given a certain choice of innovation, there is a certain band width or room to manoeuvre to choose different organisational structures. It also shows that 'Tayloristic' product cycle behaviour is not the exclusive option.

4. CHANGING ENVIRONMENT: VALUES AND TECHNOLOGIES

Following Ingleharts 'Silent Revolution', the OECD (1979) found a shift from 'materialistic' values towards 'post materialistic values' in the OECD countries: 'an increasing concern for individual self ex-pression', leading to 'workers' demands for reorganisation of the as-sembly line into smaller, more autonomous groups in which each member has a voice in how the job is to be done'.

This 'workstructuring' - or 'job design' - is done by various means like 'job rotation', where one worker is working with various differ-ent machines, 'job enrichment' (Herzberg 1959), where a worker not only has to operate a machine, but also has to maintain and/or program it, or job 'enlargement' increasing 'cycle time'.

The desire for a different type of working situation and the slowness - the inertia - of firms to convert their organisation into the desired type, has contributed to a sharp increase in activities in the 'informal sector'. Gershuny's (1983) definition of 'social innovation' - the shift from purchasing readymade services (theatre, trains, butler, cleaning lady) to consumer capital goods (TV, car, dishwasher, washing machine and Hoover) to produce 'do-it-yourself' services in the informal sphere - adds an extra increase to these informal activities.

The desire for an 'individualistic' orientation of the working situation is culturally determined, and therefore differences occur between the industrialised countries. Japan, with its 'military' industrial system (Kamata 1984), has a different cultural tradition, a fertile medium for the organisation structure that goes with mass production, but less suitable for an industrial organisation based on autonomy and decentralised decision taking. Huppes (1984) states, that Western Europe has a comparative advantage here, and should see this advantage. Or, as Zwart (1985) writes: 'The (US and Japanese systems) will be probably ineffective in our part of the world with its deeply rooted desire for a culture of the 'human standard'.

Besides the working situation aspect of the 'post materialistic' individualistic trend, we find this attitude also reflected in the demand for goods. A change from uniform, identical mass produced products to pluriformity in products. The 'customised' car is one example, the special series of chips for specific purposes is another. Computer Aided Manufacturing, whether or not linked to Computer Aided Design, a Computerised Numeric Control or any other 'flexible' production process enable the producer to meet the different tastes of the customer. At the same time, these processes make it possible to abandon the strict 'Tayloristic' division of work into small, accurately described precise tasks. As a matter of fact, this 'Tayloristic' system proves to be too rigid, and although it enables 'management' to control the production process in details, the required flexibility to meet the new type of demand can only be obtained by leaving the path of Taylorism and introducing more autonomy and decision competence to the workfloor. Huppes labels this return of more autonomy and increase of pluriformity in products with a return to a more 'craftsman' type of industrial production (Huppes 1984).

Table 2 gives some of the features of this new type of industrial production.

TABLE 2

CRAFTSMANSHIP AND INDUSTRIAL PRODUCTION, CHARACTERISED BY
INPUT, ORGANISATION AND OUTPUT

	CRAFTMANSHIP	INDUSTRIAL
INPUT	*LABOUR*	
	- skilled	- simple
	- independent	- dependent
	- creative	- routinized
	CAPITAL	
	- tools; grouped around workers, extension of the worker	- machines; workers grouped around them, as extensions.
ORGANIZATION	- little or no division of work	- division of work (horizontal differentiation)
	- little or no differen- tiation, managing - executing	- formally divided managing - executing tasks
	- small scale	- large scale
OUTPUT	- similar kind of products; 'tailor-made', customized for specific client	- identical mass produced products for anonymous market(s)

Source: Huppes (1984, p.26).

5. SEGMENTED INFORMATION NETWORKS

4.1 Introduction

More and more economic activities are based on 'the part of the economy that produces, processes and distributes information goods and services' (Porat 1977): the information sector. A sector with the largest share of employment in the US since the fifties (Porat 1977) and for the OECD countries since the seventies (OECD 1981).

While this information sector is supposed to consist of public administration, science, banking, insurance, other financial services, trade and industrial services, many information based activities such as decision making, negotiating, advertising, sales, industrial intelligence, research and design (Kowalski 1982) are to be found in any sector of the economy. It would be useful, therefore, to divide 'information' and 'information based activities' into a number of subsets, each with their own field of interest, type of information and

kind of 'actors'. For instance, Leonard-Barton (1984) divides activities in <u>managerial activities</u>, such as finance, marketing, personnel
and <u>technical activities</u> which are product or process development oriented. Each subset has its own network of participants, its own (inner) circle. Other examples of subsets or 'segments' of information
networks are the internal information networks of large multinational
corporations, or the segment of scientists working in a certain field
of interest. Hence, some segments are supranational (e.g., the multinational firm and the scientists), others may be national (e.g., politics), subnational or even of only local importance.

Each segment has its own <u>'focus'</u>, its own hierarchy of places. The
focal centre for the multinational firm being the location of its corporate Head Quarter(e.g., Eindhoven in the case of Philips), for politics being the national capital (e.g. Bonn) or the supranational capital (Brussels, Washington or Moscow), for scientists the 'leading university'. The focal centre of a segment is not necessarily a high
ranking centre in the national hierarchy of cities; this depends on
the nature of the activities involved (see also Storper 1985, p. 28).

When looking at the level of skills required for certain information
based activities - the knowledge component - we have already noticed
in the product life cycle theory discussion that activities with a
high knowledge component require more face-to-face contacts than activities with a low level of knowledge. Examples of the first are managing functions, examples of the latter are data entry or word processing. Since these face-to-face contacts form an important part of the
segmental network of (exchange of) information, participants who depend on these contacts (especially those who carry out high knowledge
containing activities) will tend to cluster near the focal centre of
this particular network. The higher this dependency on such a network,
the more frequent and intense contacts are required, the higher the
tendency to cluster near the focal centre (for instance, audiovisual
services, or marketing services, etc.) (see Molle and Vianen 1985).

In other words, the <u>'layer'</u> or level of knowledge of the information
based activities determines the degree of dispersal or clustering of
activities around the focal centre of the relevant network. The higher
the knowledge component of certain activities, the more clustering (or

geographic concentration) will occur; the lower the knowledge component, the more dispersal (or geographic decentralisation) is possible.

In this way, proximity to the focal centre of a particular segmental
network could well be an important location factor for users or participants; especially when these participants are geographically concentrated in space, are in a layer of high knowledge activities and/or
cannot fall back on intracorporate networks of information. This is
reflected in the Silicon Valley idea, a hypothesis tested by Kleine
(1982) for the metal sector in Germany.

On the other hand, the possibility exists that for 'new' activities
the focal centre of its network does not yet exist. An hypothesis, put
forward by Storper and Mensch in this book is that since the focal
centres of some networks (e.g., 'industrialists') are dominated by
specific types of activities - smoke stack industries or land properties, - new types of activities abandon these centres to look for
their own centre where they can dominate socially and economically. In
this case, Orange County and again Silicon Valley are examples of
this. In this philosophy, a 'focal centre' of port barons (e.g. Rotterdam) is unlikely to become the focal centre of activities, perceived as 'alien' to the original activities there. Here, segmental
networks assume a connotation of 'social network'.

The extent to which the 'business' oriented network is mixed with the
'social affairs' oriented network depends on the type of activities
and sociocultural habits. For instance, Leonard-Barton (1984) found in
the study on 'face-to-face' contacts of entrepreneurs in Sweden and
the Boston area significant sociocultural differences. Swedish entrepreneurs are less likely to ask an 'outsider' for advice in 'regular'
business decisions than their US counterparts. Furthermore, the Swedes
'did not mix business with their social affairs' and were more oriented towards formal organisations for their information, like the
Chamber of Commerce.

The policy implication of this would be that - when setting up information networks for a specific purpose ('subsets'), of particular importance in the diffusion of technology discussion - we will have to
take the sociocultural component into account, instead of transplant-
ing or copying a 'foreign' system or pattern.

4.2 Telecommuting: 'home work'

Although in the centre of public interest, the dispersing effects of telecommuting are still a matter of guesswork. In theory, we would expect lower knowledge based on activities to be dispersed (geographical decentralisation) to persons doing work at home, along product life cycle patterns.

Apart from the savings on office space, wage differences would be an argument to disperse these activities. Hoever, analogous to the product life cycle mentioned earlier, there is no reason for a geographic decentralisation when a reservoir of (as) cheap labour - e.g., married women - is available in the cities.

Given, however, the lack of organisation of women doing 'homework', we may assume that those areas where employers (or 'principals') manage to bargain for low wages or rates, will receive activities. In fact, this risk of 'exploitation' of these groups is an often heard union argument why they oppose 'homework'.

Further, dispersal of activities depending on telephone and communication networks, requires a certain infrastructure. When the central area has a glassfibre digital communication network, while the peripheral network still works with the 'old fashioned' one, the physical barrier prevents geographic decentralisation or dispersal.

The second type of activity we would expect to decentralise to homework is the 'creativity' type - high knowledge level - activities, where daily face-to-face contacts are not a 'conditio sine qua non', or where satisfactory local support networks exist.

Joanne Pratt (1984) found in a survey among 46 'Home Office Workers', three categories:

1. Clerical women, working full time at home, doing word processing or data entry;
2. Managers - men and women - working only parttime or intermittently at home;
3. Professional men and women including computer programmers and analysts, university professors, research scientists, physicians,

because of the attractive external effects, nowadays the existence of 'internal effects' and the improved transport facilities may imply that the participants of a network are spread over various regions or states. 'Concentration' in economic space does not coincide with 'concentration' in geographic space. Growth poles in economic space do <u>not</u> coincide with a growth growth centre in geographic space. This means that the industrial external effects (the 'localisation effects') are detached from 'urbanisation' effects. While the external effects are internalised to a large extent (intraorganisational scale effects, information, finance), the urbanisation effects (growth of urban centres because of more activities and central services) only take place in those locations where participants of the network operate their activities. When these activities are split up along product life cycle patterns, the urbanisation effect is even more spread over more locations. It is even possible, that - given a high diffusion rate of the participants of the network - the urbanisation effects are hardly noticed and are lost in the statistical 'noise' of general trends.

In other words: <u>the employment effects</u> of a growth pole in economic space are <u>dispersed</u> (over the various regions where participants are located) and <u>'polarised'</u> (along the product life cycle theory). Highly skilled employment will increase in those urban areas where the head offices of participants are, while low(er) skilled employment will increase in those non urban areas where production plants/sites are. The more independent small and medium sized firms and 'new style' non-Tayloristic organisations are involved, the less likely extreme polarisation will occur; here, either the 'filtering down' version applies, or firms move on to a large site nearby.

In order to get more insight into the nature and composition of a 'network', various techniques are available. For instance, the input-output analysis (Gold 1981), although this type of analysis is less geared towards detecting the 'source' of technological change. In this respect Pavitt's (1984) 'taxonomy' of industries, Roobeek's (1984) 'technology web', or Bouliannes' (1982) 'files' (<u>'filieres'</u>) are useful approaches.

Since industries and firms which are part of a growth pole are on the same economic plane but not in the same geographical place, it is more useful to think in terms of industrial complexes, product chains or conglomerates, than in physically clustered industries who do not share anything but being on the same industrial estate. A growth pole should be seen in its economic and functional aspects (Paelinck 1965).

5.   CONCLUSIONS

Economic concentration and growth led to an increase of internal econ- omies of scale. This made geographic concentration (clustering) of industries less necessary, given improved transport facilities. The result of this was an organisational and physical separation of pro- duction activities from managerial activities; the organisation was split up according to 'Tayloristic' principles. Highly skilled labour requiring activities remained in core areas while low skilled labour requiring activities went to peripheral areas and/or LDCs.

Changing demand - from mass produced to small series of custom made goods - and changing perception of the ideal working situation with more autonomy resulted, in conjunction with the new technology of flexible programmable discrete manufacturing in a 'new style' of pro- duction organisation. The more decentralised decision competence of this new organisation means higher skilled jobs in production plants, and a likely return from LDCs and remote peripheral areas to 'interme- diate' (semi) rural areas.

Furthermore, the increasing importance of information based activities meant that the 'focal centre' of a particular segmented network where certain participants depend on, became a possible 'clustering centre' for high knowledge containing activities of the particular network segment.

Areas coinciding with focal centres of certain networks will show an increase in the high knowledge component employment of those skills which are relevant for the specific type of activities linked to those network segments.

Areas not coinciding with focal centres will receive lower skilled employment or, as an exception, high knowledge component activities belonging to a network segment with a supranational focal point (for instance, university or military research).

Clearly, the 'mapping' of networks, based on the exchange of physical goods and formal services, is available and becoming more important, while the mapping of the various segments of information networks (including their specific type of activities, layers of knowledge level, required skills and focal centres) is almost nihil. Given its importance, outlined in this contribution, much more research is needed in this field in order to be able to successfully predict the spatial distribution of employment opportunities, skills and jobs.

REFERENCES

Alexander, K., 'Has progress a future?' Futures, 15.6, December 1983, pp. 441-454.

Altmann, N. and Bechtle, G., Betriebliche Herrschaftsstruktur Industrielle Gesellschaft, 1971.

Andersson, A.E. and Johansson, B., 'Industrial dynamics, product cycles and employment structures', Working Paper of the International Institute for Applied Systems Analysis, Laxenburg, Austria, 1984.

Andriessen, J.E., 'Multinationale ondernemingen', in: Brouwer, M.T. and ter Hart, H.W. (eds), Ondernemen in Nederland, Kluwer, Deventer, 1985, pp. 117-132.

Boulianne, L.M., 'Technological change: firms and region', A case study, in: Maillat D. (ed), Technology: A Key Factor in Regional Development, Georgi, Saint Saphorin, 1982, pp. 39-67.

Chandler, A.D., Strategy and Structure: Chapter in the History of the American Industrial Enterprise, Cambridge, MA, 1973.

Christis, J. e.a., Nationaal Programma Arbeidsonderzoek, Publicatie nr. 6, Projectgroep Techniek, Organisatie, Arbeidsmarkt, Staatsdrukkerij, The Hague, 1980.

Ciciotti, E., 'The incubation hypothesis revisited: the case of the metropolitan area of Milan', Paper, presented at the 24th European Congress of the RSA, Milan, 1984.

McDermott, P., 'Multinational manufacturing firms and regional development: external control in the Scottish electronics industry', Scottish Journal of Political Economy, 26, 1979, pp. 287-306.

Dosi, G., 'Technological paradigms and technological trajectories', in Freeman, C. (ed), 1983, pp. 78-101; also in Research Policy, 1982, II.3 with a more policy oriented character.

Erlandsson, U., 'Contact potentials in the European systems of cities', in Folmer, H. and Oosterhaven, J., Spatial Inequalities and Regional Development, Martinus Nijhoff, Dordrecht, 1979, pp. 93-116.

152

Freeman, C. (ed), Long Waves in the World Economy, Butterworth & Co., Frances Pinter, 1984.

Friedmann, A.L., Industry and Labor Class Struggle at Work and Monopoly Capitalism, Basingstoke, London, 1977.

Galbraith, J.R. and Nathanson, D.A., Strategy Implementation: the Role of Structure and Process, Minnesota, St. Paul, 1978.

Gershuny, J.I., Social Innovation and the Division of Labour, Oxford University Press, Oxford, 1983.

Gold, B., 'Technological diffusion in industry: research needs and shortcomings', Journal of Industrial Economics, 24, 3, 1981, pp. 247-269.

Gudgin, G. and Fothergill, S., 'Geographical variation in the rate of formation of new manufacturing firms', Regional Studies, Vol. 18, No. 3, 1984, pp. 203-206.

Hagedoorn, J., 'Nelson and Winter's contribution to the debate on the relation between technology and economic development', mimeo, (second draft), TNO, Apeldoorn, 1984.

Herzberg, F., Mausner B. and Snyderman, B., The Motivation of Work, John Wiley, New York, 1959.

Holland, S., Capital Versus The Regions, MacMillan, London, 1976.

Hoover, E.M., Regional Economies, Alfred Knopf, New York, 1971, 1975.

Huppes, T., Een Nieuw Ambachtelijk Elan, Stenfert Kroese, Leiden, 1985, Rijksuniversiteit Groningen, 1984.

IATTS, IATTS 633 Project Team, 'The substitution and complementary relationship between traffic and communication', IATTS Research, Vol. 8, 1984, pp. 3-13.

Inglehart, R., The Silent Revolution, Changing values and political styles among Western publics, Princeton University Press, Princeton, NY, 1977.

Johnson, G. and Scholes, K., Exploring Corporate Strategy, London.

Jong, H.W. de, Dynamische Markttheorie (Dynamic Market Theory), Stenfert Kroese, Leiden, 1981.

Kamann, D.J.F., 'Economic impact study of a proposed industrial site at Keenaghan, Carrick-on-Shannon, Co. Leitrim', Working Paper, An Foras Forbartha, Dublin, 1978.

Kamata, S., Japan in the Passing Lane, Counterpoint/Unwin, London, 1984.

Kleine, J., 'Location, firm size and innovativeness', in: Maillat, D. (ed), Technology: A Key Factor for Regional Development, Georgi, Saint Saphorin, 1982, pp. 147-173.

Knickerbocker, Oligopolistic Reaction and Multinational Enterprise, Harvard University Press, Boston, 1973.

Kowalski, J.S., 'Information development poles', Research Memorandum, 8219, University of Amsterdam, Amsterdam, 1982.

Leonard-Barton, D., 'Interpersonal communication patterns among Swedish and Boston area entrepreneurs', Research Policy, No. 13, 1984, pp. 101-114.

Malecki, E.J., 'Corporate organization of R & D and the location of technological activities', Regional Studies, 14, 1980, pp. 219-235.

Mickler, O. e.a., Technik, Arbeitsorganisation und Arbeit. Eine empirische Untersuchung in der automatisierte Produktion, Frankfurt, 1976.

Molle, W.T.M., 'Technological change and regional development in Europe', Papers of the Regional Science Association, Vol. 52, 1983, pp. 23-38.

Molle, W.T.M. and Vianen, J.G., 'De vestigingsplaats van enkele innovatieve bedrijfsgroepen', in Molle, W.T.M. (ed), Innovatie en Regio, Staatsuitgeverij, The Hague, (State Publishing Office), 1985, pp. 77-98.

Myrdal, G., Economic Theory and Underdeveloped Regions, Duckworth, London, 1957.

Nelson, R.R. and Winter, S.G., 'In search of a useful theory of innovation', Research Policy, Vol. 6, 1977, pp. 36-76.

Nijkamp, P., 'Long waves or catastrophes in regional development', Socio-Economic Planning Sciences, 16, 6, 1982, pp. 261-271.

OECD, 'Facing the future. Mastering the probable and managing the unpredictable', Interfutures, OECD, Paris, 1979.

OECD, Information Activities, Electronics and Telecommunications Technologies, ICCP6, Paris, 1981.

Paelinck, J.H.P., 'La Théorie du développement régional polarisé', Cahiers de l'ISEA, Série L, No. 15, 1965, pp. 10-11.

Pavitt, K., 'Sectoral patterns of technical change: Towards a taxonomy and a theory', Research Policy, No. 13, 1984, pp. 343-373.

Perroux, F., 'Note sur la notion pole de croissance', Economie Appliqué, Série D, Vol. 8, 1955.

Pfaff, M. and Hurler, P., 'Employment policy for regional labor markets', Environment and Planning, C1, Government and Policy, 2, 1983, pp. 163-178.

Porat, M.R., Information Economy, Part 1: Definition and Measurement, Washington DC, US Government Printing Office, 1977.

Porter, M.E., Competitive Strategy, Collier, MacMillan, London, 1980.

Pratt, J.H., 'Home teleworking: A study of its pioneers', Technological Forecasting and Social Change 25, 1984, pp. 1-14.

Roobeek, A., 'De relatie tussen technologie en economische ontwikke-
    ling', Research Memorandum 8412, University of Amsterdam, Amster-
    dam, 1984.

Schmookler, J., Invention and Economic Product, Harvard University
    Press, Cambridge, MA, 1966.

Stöhr, W., 'Structural characteristics of peripheral areas: The rele-
    vance of the Stock-in-Trade Variables', Papers of the Regional
    Science Association, No. 49, 1982, pp. 71-84.

Storper, M., 'Essentialism in economic geography: Oligopoly and the
    product cycle', Paper, University of California, Los Angeles,
    1985.

Taylor, M.J. and Hirst, J., 'The restructuring of the Australian trad-
    ing banks', Environment and Planning A, Vol. 16, No. 8, 1984,
    pp. 1055-1078.

Thompson, W., 'Internal and external factors in the development of
    urban economics', in: Perloff, H.S. and Wigo, L., Issues in Urban
    Economics, The Johns Hopkins Press, Washington DC, 1968.

Toffler, A., The Third Wave, Bantam Books, London, 1980.

Vernon, R., 'International investment and international trade in the
    product cycle', Quarterly Journal of Economics, No. 80, 1966,
    pp. 190-207.

Zwart, C.J., 'Innovation, een menselijk vraagstuk', NCR-Handelsblad,
    January 30, 1985.

PART B: ACTUAL TRENDS

SPATIAL DIMENSIONS OF TECHNOLOGICAL DEVELOPMENTS AND EMPLOYMENT EFFECTS
Hans-Jürgen Ewers

1. THE URBAN-RURAL MANUFACTURING SHIFT

The urban-rural manufacturing shift is well documented for the EC as well as for single countries like the UK or the FRG (see Keeble, Owens, Thompson 1982, 1983 for the EC; Fothergill, Gudgin 1982 for the UK; Müller 1983, Peschel 1983 and Hoppen 1979 for the FRG). At the EC level, more than 50 per cent of the total manufacturing job loss suffered by the entire nine-member European Community between 1973 and 1981 was concentrated in the small group of 21 most highly-urbanised regions, as defined by the presence of very large urban agglomerations (over 100,000 inhabitants) and high population densities (Keeble 1984, 3, see Table 1). In the FRG the cores of the five most important agglomerations (Hamburg, Rhein-Ruhr, Rhein-Main, Stuttgart, Munich, see Map 1) lost 22 per cent of the industrial employment between 1962 and 1977 as compared to a 13 per cent loss for the total FRG. In contrast, the 15 peripheral regions of the FRG showed a plus of 1,5 per cent in industrial employment during the same period (Bade 1984,4). As Keeble (1984, 3-5) points out, the urban-rural manufacturing shift is continuous with the level of urbanisation, scale independent (i.e., it applies to smaller areas within particular countries as well as to broad EEC level regions) and can largely not be explained by an industrial structure or industrial overspill type of argument. "By far the dominant process is a markedly greater decline of all existing firms and factories in the cities, both multiplant and single plant, large and small. Equally, rural and small town growth reflects expansion by existing, local firms of all kinds" (Keeble 1984, 5).

TABLE 1

The Urban-Rural Manufacturing Shift
in the European Community

	Total Manufacturing Employment		
	1973 '000s	Change '000s	1973-81 %
Highly Urbanised Regions (21)	11414	-2044	-17.9
Urbanised Regions (23)	10188	- 988	- 9.7
Less Urbanised Regions (32)	7318	- 548	- 7.5
Rural Regions (29)	3838	- 57	- 1.5
Total EEC9 Regions (105)	32758	-3637	-11.1

Source: Keeble 1984, 3.

Several theoretical approaches are offered for the explanation of the urban-rural manufacturing shift (see Keeble 1984). The empirically most promising approach, the constraint location theory, focusses on the impact of factory floor space supply constraints on metropolitan manufacturing. Because of the continuing displacement of labour by machinery as a result of the increased real wage/interest ratio and because of the tendency towards more space intensive technologies. factories located in great cities fall back in their competitiveness vis-a-vis factories in rural locations, where sites for the extension of existing factories are easy to get. Bade (1984, 230-261) extends this argument by interpreting the economic theory of land use in a competitive way. Within the competition for inner city sites those activities will survive which yield the highest profits per square meter ground and therefore allow the highest bid price functions. Dependent on the kind of activity and the centrality of the location, the maximal bids will be different. Because shop floor activities (as compared with tertiary activities in industrial production, for example planning, organising, research and development) are inferior with respect to the profit per square meter ground, they are the first to be pushed out of the cities if prices for sites rise.

This explanatory approach can easily be extended by (and is consistent with) the inclusion of production related costs, which might differ in dependence of the centrality of the location. This applies for example to environmental costs in the widest sense as well as costs caused by absenteeism, unionisation or traffic congestion.

The technical preconditions for the realisation of a <u>functional inter-regional division of labour</u> (i.e., the cities being more specialised in the tertiary functions of the industrial system, the periphery bearing more shop floor characteristics) are the standardisation and the dismantling of production processes into spatially separable partial operations, which - in combination with modern transport and communication technologies - enable producers to allocate partial production processes to those locations where they find cost-minimal combination of labour and capital. But the functional interregional division of labour is by no means restricted (or solely driven) to resp. by large multiplant firms, who try to find the optimal allocation of their activities in their worldwide network of locations. The same phenomenon can be observed even for small single plant firms which show a tendency either to adapt their functional mix to their spatial environment or to find more appropriate locations with respect to their functional mix. At least there is no other explanation available for the observed differences of the functional mix between comparable medium sized firms in agglomerated as compared to rural locations in several studies (for example, Ellwein et al. 1980, Meyer-Krahmer et al. 1984).

The present extent of the interregional functional division of labour in the FRG is well depicted in Diagram 1. The differences of the shares of tertiary activities to total activities along the urban hierarchy are as evident for the manufacturing industry as for the total economy. And there is no doubt that the extent of this functional division of labour has been increasing during the seventies. Using the same data base as Bade (the employment statistics provided by the Social Security records, which reach back until 1976), we find that between 1976 and 1983 the overwhelming part of the manufacturing employment losses in the cores of the agglomerations has been in shop floor activities (see Table 2).

The notion of an increasing functional division of labour between urban and non-urban areas is consistent with the view that the urban cores lost their historic functions as centres of physical production and are in a process of developing into centres of

TABLE 2

Employment Growth 1976-1983 for selected activities[1]
and different area types[2] of the FRG
(first row: absolute figures; second row: % of the 1976 base)

Activities	Area-type	Agglomeration cores	Agglomeration rings	Low density areas	Peripheral areas	Total FRG
1.1 Total Primary and Secondary activities		-252303	-49640	-84675	- 8517	-593135
		-12.7	-3.4	-3.3	-1.0	-5.8
thereof:						
1.2 Shopfloor		-200508	-52944	-77841	-10189	-342481
		-13.8	-4.9	-4.4	-2.0	-7.0
2.1 Total tertiary activities		-24352	233129	282130	122047	604865
		-0.4	9.9	6.9	10.2	4.7
thereof:						
2.2 Research and Development		34792	15244	18338	3709	72089
		18.2	26.6	22.9	22.1	20.9
Total activities		-276656	183489	197455	113530	209730
		-3.7	4.8	3.0	5.7	1.1

Source: Employment statistics 1976, 1983, provided by the social
security records; own calculations.

1) The employment figures for the different activities have been calculated by attributing the occupation figures of the social
security records to activities. For details of this procedure
see Bade 1984.
2) For the delineation of the area types see Map 1.

technical-organisational knowledge with a centralisation of production-oriented tertiary activities (professional services like lawyers,
management consultants and software producers in the widest sense of
the word) and of such technologically complex production activities,
which still require face-to-face contacts , either with consumers of
diversified high-level goods resp. customers of specialised equipment
or with research and development activities and other production-oriented services (see Kasarda 1982, Knight 1982). According to this view

Diagram 1:   **Regional Differences in Functional Economic Structure**
- Share of Total Activities in the Respective Types of Area -
(1981)

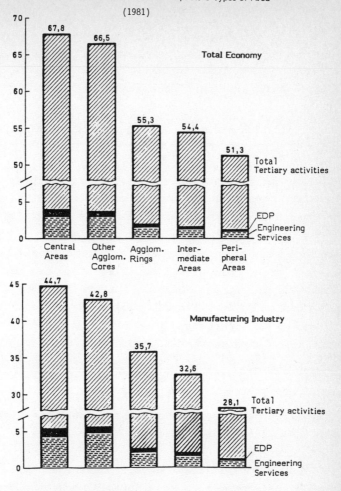

Source : BADE (1984, S.191).

the big cities are the trend setters of a worldwide movement into a
tertiary society. This scenario sees the dynamic industrial cities on
top of a future hierarchy of the industrial system providing the
organisational and technical intelligence for the worldwide industrial
system and is consistent with the observable pattern of the new international division of labour, which moves the production of standardised goods to the newly industrialised countries while leaving the
production of technology and technologically complex goods to the old
industrialised countries. Although one can question the international
part of the scenario vis-a-vis the microelectronic revolution and the

development of highly-automated production systems, which tend to
erode the comparative advantage for production in low-wage countries
(see Ernst 1981), there seems to be little doubt on the irreversibility of the present deindustrialisation trend for the big industrial
cities in Europe as far as traditional shop floor activities are concerned.

2.   IMPLICATIONS OF DIFFERENT EMPLOYMENT GROWTH BY FIRM SIZE AND BY
     PLANT SIZE

Less well documented as compared to the urban-rural manufacturing
shift is the employment shift towards small firms or plants. The main
reason for this lack of empirical evidence is the limited availability
of time series data for small and medium sized firms. The lack of a
representative, non-biased data base for time series of employment
figures by firm or by plant has led to a large debate on the biases
implied in the different data bases (like credit enquiry files, application files for policy programmes, regionally or sectorally selected
firm data), which have been used to show the superiority of small and
medium sized firms with respect to employment creation. It is not necessary to go into detail here (for a survey see Eckart, Stahl, von
Einem 1985). What is striking, however, is the uniformity of the two
results, regardless of the different biases, which might be involved
in the respective data (for summaries of these results see Eckart,
Stahl, von Einem 1985; Ewers, Fritsch, Kleine 1984):

-    There is a uniform indication that particular small firms (up to
     100 employees) contribute considerably more than proportional to
     the net growth of working places and that employment expectations
     decrease with increasing firm size. Where total employment is
     shrinking (as for the UK or the FRG in the 70s), employment gains
     in the group of small firms have been overcompensated by losses
     in the group of large firms. What is not uniform is the critical
     size, up to which the contribution to the net growth of working
     places is more than proportional, as well as the quantity of the
     contribution of small firms to employment creation, although part
     of the existing differences between the studies can be explained
     by the different structure of the firm samples, which have been
     used to derive the results.

-     The shift of employment growth to small firms applies to all sec-
      tors. For industrial manufacturing, one can in addition recognise
      a trend break of the firm size structure at the beginning of the
      70s by the existing macro statistics for the FRG (see Klodt 1980,
      Ewers 1984). While up to 1970 the employment shares of large
      firms in industrial manufacturing grew consistently, they de-
      crease since that. Instead of this, the employment shares of
      firms up to 200 employees are growing, in particular those of the
      smallest firms (for a discussion of the long run macro concentra-
      tion in the UK with a similar result, see Storey 1982, 10ff).

Still under discussion is the   question whether it is primarily the
group of young firms, which contributes most to employment creation.
Although the negative correlation of growth <u>rates</u> and age of the firm
is general wisdom (see Szyperski 1975), this does by no means say that
the youngest firms contribute most to employment growth, because they
have at the same time the highest death rates. Following Birch (1979)
not less than 80 per cent of the total net job growth stems from firms
not older than four years. This result is contradicted by Fothergill
and Gudgin (1979), who find that firms in industrial manufacturing
create less jobs during their first years, but contribute significantly to employment growth during a longer period after foundation. A
part of this divergence might be explained by the fact that Birch had
included the service sector in his sample while Fothergill and Gudgin
argue on the basis of firm data in industrial manufacturing. But there
remains some doubt with respect to a possible bias towards smaller
firms in Birch's sample (see Eckart, von Einem and Stahl 1985, 29).

Another disputable question concerns the contribution to employment
creation by smaller plants belonging to multiplant firms. Having the
results for small firms in mind one expects to find similar employment
creation trends on the plant level also, because most of the small
firms are single plant. In fact there are not only similar trends on
the plant level to be found, but Armington and Odle (1982, 14), using
the same data base as Birch (the credit enquiry files of Dun and Brad-
street), find that <u>plants</u> with up to 100 employees created 78 per cent
of the US net employment growth during the period 1978-1980, while
<u>firms</u> with up to 100 employees accounted for only 39 per cent of net
employment growth. Eckart, von Einem and Stahl (1985, 24) conclude
from this result that beside independent small firms in particular the

medium and large multiplant firms contribute to employment creation. This is clearly a misinterpretation of the findings, because a positive or even more than proportional contribution of the multiplant firms to employment creation must necessarily be visible on the firm level of the analysis, which it is not. If it is not, the evidence presented by Armington and Odle reflects only the sheer fact of a decentralisation of employment within the multiplant sector, while in total losing employment. This explanation is consistent with the urban-rural manufacturing shift described above, if one additionally takes into account the differences in the size structure of the industrial sector between urban and rural locations.

To demonstrate the latter, Table 3 shows the shares of total industrial manufacturing employment of different area types which have been held in 1982 by small plants in the FRG (for the area types, see Maps 1 and 2). It turns out that these shares are lowest in the cores of the agglomerations and highest in two types of areas, which overlap each other and are in general the winners of the urban-rural manufacturing shift - rural areas and peripheral areas. The same contrast shows up, if one compares regions with relatively favourable employment development during the 70s to those with relatively unfavourable employment development. Therefore the notion of an urban-rural manufacturing shift seems to be consistent with the notion of an employment creation shift towards small firms and small plants (for additional evidence, see Fritsch 1984).

TABLE 3

Shares of total industrial manufacturing employment of different
area types held by small plants (FRG, September 1982;
cumulated shares in brackets)

	Share of employment in plants of ... employees			
	up to 19	20-49	50-99	10-199
Total agglomerations	3.6	6.2	7.1	8.8
		(9.8)	(16.9)	(25.7)
Agglomeration cores	3.2	5.3	5.9	7.3
		(8.5)	(14.4)	(21.7)
Agglomeration rings	4.5	8.4	9.8	12.0
		(12.9)	(22.7)	(34.7)
Rural areas	4.2	10.4	10.9	14.1
		(14.6)	(25.5)	(39.6)
Peripheral areas	3.7	10.8	11.4	14.3
		(14.5)	(25.9)	(40.1)
Regions with favourable employment development	3.6	10.9	11.3	14.2
		(14.5)	(25.8)	(40.0)
Regions with unfavourable employment development	4.5	7.2	8.6	10.7
		(11.6)	(20.2)	(30.9)
Total FRG	4.3	8.0	8.9	11.2
		(12.3)	(21.2)	(32.4)

Source: Ewers and Fritsch 1984, 17.

One can only speculate on the reasons which are responsible for the
surprising success of small firms with respect to employment creation
during the 70s. There is no systematic analysis at hand which could
show in detail what happened at the firm level.

One possible explanation for the observed superiority of small firms
might be the technical development which diminished the minimum optimal plant size during the 70s. In particular, the development of
microprocessor technology has contributed (and will contribute) to a
broader use of automation methods in small plants. In addition, the
development of transport and information technology might have

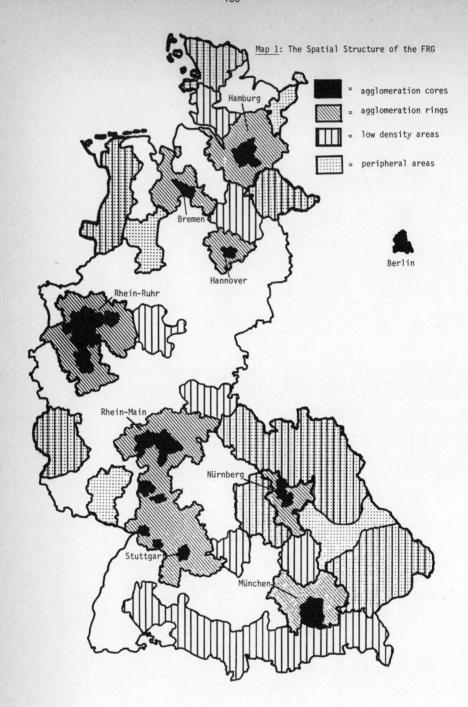

Map 1: The Spatial Structure of the FRG

= agglomeration cores

= agglomeration rings

= low density areas

= peripheral areas

Hamburg

Bremen

Hannover

Berlin

Rhein-Ruhr

Rhein-Main

Nürnberg

Stuttgart

München

Map 2: Regions with favourable (unfavourable) development
of employment in the FRG

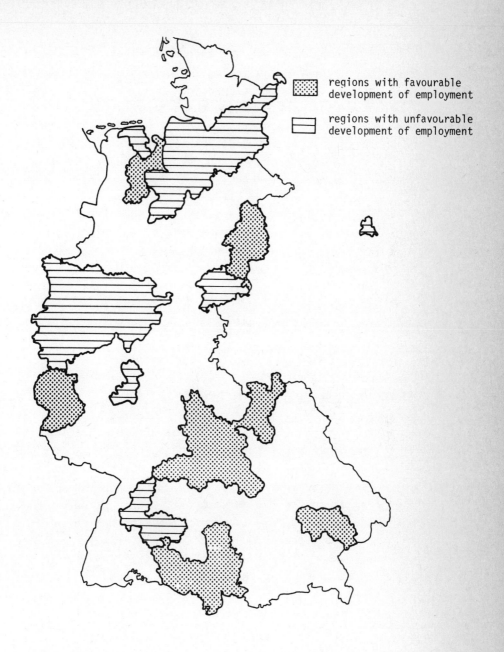

weakened the comparative advantages of large firms in international trade, with a consequence of lower economies of scale on the firm level. However, these factors hardly explain the particular success of the smallest firms.

Another argument could be seen in the popularised notion of small firms being in particular flexible and adaptable to changing economic circumstances. This argument can at least be partly confronted with empirical evidence. Two of the most important changes in the economic environment of industrial growth during the seventies are the erosion of traditional markets for industrial goods by the growing international competition as well as by changes in consumers' tastes and the appearance of new, mainly microprocessor related production technologies. Both forces create a need for innovation, the former on the level of product programmes, the latter on the level of production methods. If the superiority of small firms under the present economic circumstances relies on particular flexibility and adaptability to changing economic circumstances, one should be able to observe a markedly higher innovative performance of small firms. And if this is expected to contribute to the explanation of the (relative) employment gain of rural and peripheral areas, the higher innovativeness of small firms should be independent of the location or even grater in locations outside the agglomerations.

3.   THE IMPACT OF INNOVATION

With respect to innovation, once can draw on growing empirical evidence to discriminate between innovative and non- (or less) innovative firms or between early and late adopters of new technologies. Having said this, I very quickly have to modify the statement with respect to the present context. Although there is much literature on innovation and the diffusion of new technologies in general or either on size effects or on locational effects, only very limited work exists, which allows observation of the bearing of size and of location on innovation at the same time. Most of this work has been done in or in connection with the Centre for Urban and Regional Development Studies at the University of Newcastle Upon Tyne (for a description of the general approach, see Goddard 1980 and Ewers and Wettmann 1980; or the main results, see Oakey, Thwaites and Nash 1980,

1982, Thwaites, Edwards and Gibbs 1982, Kleine 1982, Ewers and Kleine 1983, Rees, Briggs and Hicks 1984). An independent, rather systematic study for the FRG has been recently finished by Meyer-Krahmer et al. 1984).

The reasons for the relative lack of innovation studies allowing a combined analysis of aspatial and spatial characteristics on the plant level become obvious if one considers the methodological problems involved in such studies. One of these problems which has to be overcome in every innovation study is to find a strict measure of innovativeness. If one does not have systematic and representative surveys of significant industrial innovations at hand (like SPRU data covering 1200 important innovations for 55 industries in the UK) and does not want to take input measures of innovative activity because of their various biases (see Meyer-Krahmer et al. 1984, 76-79; Goddard 1980, 12-14), one is forced to do a diffusion study for clearly defined new technologies which represent economically and technically significant leaps in the technical development. Another sheer quantitative (and financial) problem, is the number of cases which is necessary in order to allow a combined quantitative analysis of size and location characteristics.

The main results which are briefly reported below, stem from the diffusion study covering a set of major technical innovations (like computerised numerically controlled machine tools, computer based production planning and design facilities or the utilisation of microprocessors both in manufacturing processes and in products) in the metal working industries of the US, UK and the FRG (see Rees, Briggs and Hicks 1983, Thwaites, Edwards and Gibbs 1982, and Ewers and Kleine 1983). The selection of techniques and industries for study has been done in an interactive way. The techniques were selected on the basis that they introduced fundamental as opposed to incremental change, that they were economically significant, appropriate to a number of industries (which themselves had to be well represented in the most regions of the countries in the study) and had a comparatively recent diffusion pattern. In total, the study covers far more than 3000 plants in the three countries.

In contrast, a recent German study, the result of which remarkably concur with those of the above mentioned international study, mainly uses files for 8200 small and medium sized firms (up to 1000 employees), which took part in a wage subsidy programme for R&D work-ers during the period 1979 to 1981 (see Meyer-Krahmer et al. 1984, 99-101). The authors estimate that they cover 70-80 per cent of all small and medium sized firms in the FRG which conduct R&D. Although using a crude input variable (existence of R&D workers) as proxy for innovative activity, this study can avoid the well known bias of R&D studies towards large firms by its unique data base.

The results of both studies clearly contradict the hypothesis that it is the particular adaptability of the small firm which led to their superiority with respect to employment creation in the seventies, or that the employment success of rural and peripheral regions during the seventies might have something to do with innovation:

-   Single plant enterprises (as compared to multiplants) turned out to be the least adoptive of all establishments. "Their rate of adoption was consistently below that displayed by the lowest status multiplants and those with the least supervisory responsi-bilities in the group. Analysis over time revealed that single plant enterprises have consistently adopted all techniques at a lower level, particularly for microprocessors" (Gibbs and Edwards 1984, 13).

-   Larger (as well as older) plants show consistently higher rates of adoption as compared to smaller (or younger) plants. Plants with on site R&D adopt new technologies at a consistently higher rate than plants without on site R&D.

-   Although the spatial variations in the rate of adoption of new technologies are small, they are however, consistent, rural loca-tions generally displaying lower adoption rates as compared to urban locations. These spatial variations can for the large part be attributed to single plant firms. The same kind of result was found with respect to regional distribution of the innovation potential, as measured by the share of small and medium sized firms with own R&D, in the study by Meyer-Krahmer et al. (1984, 9): While in highly agglomerated areas every fifth firm has its own R&D, in rural areas it is only every tenth.

Admittedly, this empirical evidence concerns only a small part of the spectrum of innovative activities (technical as opposed to non-technical innovation, process as opposed to product innovation, R&D based as opposed to non-R&D based innovation) and it might well be the case that one gets a different picture if other forms of innovation are included. There are for example strong indications for differences in the innovation strategy of small and medium sized firms in rural-peripheral locations as compared to the average (see Meyer-Krahmer et al. 1984, 11; for concurring results see Ellwein et al. 1980). Innovating small and medium sized firms in rural-peripheral areas use less academically trained personnel, tend to rely on own personnel when conducting R&D (instead of recruiting new people) and acquire external knowhow preferably by buying innovative equipment (instead of using external R&D facilities). Nevertheless, the above reported results concur markedly in the results of other, less representative studies (for a survey see Meyer-Krahmer et al. 1984, 23-60). They are univocal in particular with respect to the last mentioned issue of the adoption of innovative equipment, namely the share of small and medium sized firms adopting new technologies being consistently below average in rural areas.

Although not allowing a strict explanation with respect to the determinants of innovative performance, the studies have revealed some factors on the plant and on the firm level which are associated with success in innovation. The poor performance in particular of small, independent single plant firms with respect to the adoption of new technologies can be heavily attributed to the comparatively low ability of this type of firm to overcome bottlenecks with respect to the collection and processing of information on the characteristics of available new technologies and on the needs of the market. The strong correlation between adoption and on site R&D activities even in the case of bought in technical equipment must be interpreted as the expression of the necessity of a systematic monitoring of new technical developments as a precondition for early adoption of new technologies. Into the same direction points the finding that innovative establishments had much more diverse information networks with respect to customers and consultants (Gibbs and Edwards 1984, 18) and significantly higher export quotas (Kleine 1983; for similar results, see Meyer-Krahmer 1984, 12). Larger plants and plants belonging to multiplant organisations seem to overcome this barrier to innovation more easily. Smaller single plant firms tend to have less diversified information networks and do - as the studies reveal - rely more on information sources in their closer local environment.

The latter seems to be one reason for the observed interregional variations of the adoption rates for small single plant firms. Surely the most of these interregional variations have to be attributed to the varying structural characteristics of different area-types for those factors which have a bearing on adoption (industrial structure distribution of R&D activities, size structure). But there remain important locational factors, which further inhibit technological change. Gibbs and Edwards (1984, 21) summarise these locational factors as follows: "The interview survey provided evidence of a number of issues related to this industrial 'milieu', particularly those factors related to the availability and quality of information regarding technology, spatial differentiation in the availability of aid and varying levels of corporate autonomy for establishments belonging to a multiplant enterprise".

4. CONCLUSIONS

To come back to the question at the end of Section 2: what might explain the particular success of small firms in employment creation during the seventies? There is much reason to reject the hypothesis of a superior adaptability of small firms to new economic circumstances, at least with respect to technical change. Instead of this, an adverse hypothesis seems to be more adequate, namely that it is not the particular strength of small firms, but the particular weakness of the large firms vis-a-vis the present conditions of structural change which lets the small firms appear so favourably. There are some arguments which could be put forward in favour of this hypothesis:

-   The new international division of labour affects in particular the mass production of standardised goods and therefore the activities of large plants and firms. Small firms tend to be engaged more in the production of specialities and the supply for market niches as well as for spatially limited markets which are not so strongly affected by international competition.

-   Large firms - because of their stronger engagement in standardised mass production - have (or had at least in the past) - more opportunities to substitute capital for labour.

- Large firms suffer more from the customers' trend to individual, diversified goods.

- Large firms tend to be more strongly affected by environmental regulations as well as by labour market regulations which have been strengthened during the seventies in all European countries.

Under such a view, the urban-rural manufacturing shift does not reflect a specific competitiveness of the rural areas vis-a-vis the ongoing structural change but simply the fact that the larger firms have adapted their employment rigorously to the new economic circumstances, both with respect to the increased bottlenecks for physical production in the urban regions as well as to new competitive pressures. This adaptation process affects in particular the urban areas as traditional locations of the large multiplant firms. But, as the studies on the spatial distribution of innovative activities show, the formation of a new, modernised industrial structure in the same urban areas is already underway, although up till now the positive employment effects caused by innovative firms are not strong enough to compensate for the removal of the obsolete productions. This view opens quite positive aspects for the large industrial cities in general, although one cannot overlook the existing differences in this group, i.e., the great variations with respect to the above mentioned 'industrial milieu', which the old industrial cities offer to small and medium sized firms.

On the other hand, the (relative) gains which have been yielded by the non-urban areas during the seventies might be of short duration. They seem to be more a passive reflection of what has happened in the industrial cores than an expression of active competitive strength. Therefore, the old interregional disparities might be widening again, if policy does not speed up the renewal of the industrial structure of the rural-periphery areas.

For the general policy vis-a-vis the industrial sector as well as for regional policies, these results mean that one cannot trust in the persistence of the present employment trends to small firms and to rural areas. The appropriate starting point for the industrial policy as well as for the regional policy is the set of conditions which enables small firms to take more effectively part in the ongoing technical change. Because the local industrial milieu plays an important role in this set of conditions, this also means that industrial policies should act in a more decentralised manner and stimulate local activities to generate the necessary climate for innovation.

REFERENCES

Armington, C. and Odle, M., 'Small business - how many jobs?' The Brookings Review, 1, 1982, pp. 14-17.

Bade, F.-J., Die funktionale Struktur der Wirtschaft und ihre räumliche Arbeitsteilung, IIM/IP 84-27, Wissenschaftszentrum Berlin, 1984.

Birch, D., The Job Generation Process, MIT Program on Neighbourhood and Regional Change, ms., Cambridge, MA, 1979.

Eckart, W., von Einem, E. and Stahl, K., Dynamik der Beschäftigungsentwicklung: Stand der Forschung, Arbeitspapiere in Wirtschaftstheorie und Stadtökonomie, Universität Dortmund, 1985.

Ellwein, Th. et al., Mittelgrosse Industriebetriebe in unterschiedlichen Regionen, Schriftenreihe 'Raumordnung' des Bundesministers für Raumordnung, Bauwesen und Städtebau 0.6041, Bonn, 1980.

Ernst, D., 'International transfer of technology, technological dependence and underdevelopment: key issues', in: Ernst, D. (ed), The New International Division of Labour, Technology and Underdevelopment, Frankfurt, 1981, pp. 15-76.

Ewers, H.-J., 'Kleine und mittlere Unternehmen als Ansatzpunkt einer beschäftigingsorientierten Strukturpolitik', in: Ewers, H.-J. and Schuster, H. (eds), Probleme der Ordnungs- und Strukturpolitik, Festschrift Seidenfus, Göttingen, 1984, pp. 88-111.

Ewers, H.-J. and Fritsch, M., Zur Bedeutung kleiner und mittler Unternehmen für eine beschäftigungsorientierte Strukturpolitik, Diskussionspapier 93, Wirtsch.-wiss. Dokumentation, TUB, Berlin, 1985.

Ewers, H.-J., Fritsch, M. and Kleine, J., Regionale Entwicklung durch Förderung kleiner und mittlerer Unternehmen, Schriftenreihe des Bundesministers für Raumordnung, Bauwesen und Städtebau, 06.053, Bonn, 1984.

Ewers, H.-J. and Kleine, J., 'The interregional diffusion of new processes in the German mechanical engineering industry', IIM/IP 83-2, Wissenschaftszentrum, Berlin, 1983.

Ewers, H.-J. and Wettmann, R., 'Innovation oriented regional policy', Regional Studies, 14, 1980, pp. 161-180.

Fothergill, S. and Gudgin, G., The Job Generation Process in Britain, Centre for Environmental Studies, Research Series No. 32, London, 1979.

Fothergill, S. and Gudgin, G., Unequal Growth: Urban and Regional Employment Change in the UK, London, 1982.

Fritsch, M., 'Die Arbeitsplatzentwicklung in kleinen und mittleren Betrieben bzw. Unternehmen - Einige empirische Evidenz für die Bundesrepublik Deutschland', Informationen zur Raumentwicklung, 1984, pp. 921-935.

Gibbs, D.C. and Edwards, A., 'The diffusion of new production innovations in British industry', in: Thwaites, A.T. and Oakey, R.P. (eds), The Regional Economic Impact of Technological Change, London, 1984, pp. 132-161.

Goddard, J.B., Industrial Innovation and Regional Economic Development in Britain, Discussion Paper 32, Centre for Urban and Regional Development Studies, University of Newcastle upon Tyne, 1980.

Hoppen, H.-D., Industrieller Strukturwandel, Berlin, 1979.

Kasarda, J.D., 'New urban policies for new urban realities', in: Hellstern, Spreer, Wollmann (eds), Applied Urban Research, Arbeitspapiere, Seminare, Symposien, Heft 2, Bd. 1, Bundesforschungsanstalt für Landeskunde und Raumordnung, Bonn, 1982.

Keeble, D., 'The changing spatial structure of economic activity and metropolitan decline in the United Kingdom', in: Ewers, Goddard and Matzerath (eds), The Future of the Metropolis, De Gruyter, Berlin, 1986 (forthcoming).

Keeble, D., Owens, P.L. and Thompson, C., 'The urban-rural manufacturing shift in the European Community', Urban Studies, 20, 1983, pp. 405-418.

Keeble, D., Owens, P.L. and Thompson, C., Centrality, Peripherality and EEC Regional Development, HMSO, London, 1982.

Kleine, J., 'Location, firm size and innovativeness', in: Maillat, D. (ed), Technology: A Key Factor for Regional Development, Saint-Saphorin, 1982, pp. 147-173.

Klodt, H., 'Kleine und grosse Unternehmen im Strukturwandel - zur Entwicklung der sektoralen Unternehmenskonzentration', Die Weltwirtschaft 1, 1980, pp. 79-99.

Knight, R.V., 'City development in advanced industrial societies', in: Gappert and Knight (eds), Cities in the 21st Century, Urban Affairs Annual Reviews, 23, 1982, pp. 47-68.

Meyer-Krahmer, F. et al., Erfassung regionaler Innovationsdefizite, Schriftenreihe 'Raumordnung' des Bundesministers für Raumordnung, Bauwesen und Städtebau, 06.054, Bonn, 1984.

Müller, J., Sektorale Struktur und Entwicklung der industriellen Beschäftigung in den Regionen der Bundesrepublik Deutschland, Berlin, 1983.

Oakey, R.P., Thwaites, A.T. and Nash, P.A., 'The regional distribution of innovative manufacturing establishments in Britain', Regional Studies 14, 1980, pp. 235-254.

Oakey, R.P., Thwaites, A.T. and Nash, P.A., 'Technological change and regional development: some evidence on regional variations in product and process innovation', Environment and Planning A, 14, 1982, pp. 1073-1086.

Peschel, K., 'Der strukturelle Wandel der Industrie in de Regionen der Bundesrepublik Deutschland 1960 bis 1986', in: Müller, J.H. (ed), Derminanten der räumlichen Entwicklung, Berlin, 1983, pp. 125-172.

Rees, J., Briggs, R. and Hicks, D., New Technology in the American Machinery Industry: Trends and Implications, A study prepared for the Joint Economic Committee, Congress of the United States, Syracuse University and University of Texas at Dallas, 1983.

Storey, D.J., Entrepreneurship and the New Firm, London-Canberra, 1982.

Szperski, N., 'Kritische Punkte der Unternehmensentwicklung', Zeitschrift für betriebwirtschaftliche Forschung, 27, 1975, pp. 366-383.

Thwaites, A.T., Edwards, A. and Gibbs, D., Interregional Diffusion of Production Innovations in Great Britain, Final Report to the Department of Industry and the EEC, Centre for Urban and Regional Development Studies, University of Newcastle upon Tyne, 1982.

THE IMPACT OF INNOVATIONS
ON SERVICE EMPLOYMENT
David Gleave

1. INTRODUCTION

This paper reports some of the findings of two research projects recently completed at The Technical Change Centre, both of which have been concerned with the employment consequences of innovations in the production process. The first investigated the impact of new technology on the labour market and demand for information services in the United Kingdom. The second concerned the impact of office technology on jobs and internal structures of firms. It was executed by collecting primary data, by way of questionnaire survey and indepth interviews.

Although both studies were mainly concerned with subsectors of service employment, top down forecasting methods required more general appraisals of employment change in the economy as a whole and the service sector in particular. The data sets used for the aggregate analysis of labour market restructuring comprised the British Censuses of 1961, 1966, 1971 and 1981 and the biennial Labour Force Surveys of 1975, 1977, 1979 and 1981. At the same time these studies were completed no more recent, secondary data sources were available for analysis. As it was, it proved necessary to analyse the 1981 Census and all the Labour Force Surveys from source data (excluding of course information on individual respondent which would enable their identification). One reason for this was that official data processing had not provided features of labour market dynamics which we considered essential to understanding the processes of efficient matchmaking between labour supply and labour demand. A second reason was that so many changes had occurred in the sectoral and occupational classifications of employment that it proved necessary to return to source material to achieve a consistent classification.

These second difficulties provide an introduction to the question 'what constitutes service employment?' In principle, we aimed to define service employment in a coherent and cohesive fashion which the traditional classifications of primary, secondary and tertiary employment fails to provide. The classification of <u>sectors</u> of employment is primarily concerned with assembling employees into homogeneous groups at the scale of the firm or plant in accordance with the goods and services produced by the firm or plant and independent of the processes used to effect that production. The classification of <u>occupations</u> is primarily concerned with the aggregation of individual workers, irrespective of their sectors of employment, into homogeneous groups according to their principal activity or skill. Yet our findings have shown that the effects of innovation can be so all-embracing that they often have impacts on the nature of specific tasks performed by the worker, such that their aggregation into specific job descriptions is continually changing. The most profound impact of technical change in labour market analysis is that it begs questions about the usefulness of traditional classifications of employment. Consequently, producing a more appropriate classification of employment became a first, major, task.

Barras (1983) has shown, through his analysis of growth and technical change, that great variations in performance occurred between the various service sectors. Restricting his analysis to measures of performance and employment at the peaks of business cycles he showed, for example, that over the period 1960-1979 Financial Services and Professional and Scientific Services increase in the quantity[1] of their output by 4.1 per cent and 3.14 per cent per annum respectively. In contrast, the distributive trades increased the quantity of their output by only 1.84 per cent per annum. Taking a value[2] measure of output, Barras showed that over the same period Professional and Scientific Services increased output by 4.63 per cent per annum and Financial Services by 2.98 per cent per annum. Also in contrast, Transport and Communications increased the value of output by only 2.26 per cent per annum and the Distributive Trades by 1.76 per cent per annum.

The focus of attention of this paper is employment effects. There are no a priori grounds for assuming that the net employment effect of innovation will be either positive or negative. There are theories which suggest that the impact on the processes of production will initially generate reductions due to capital for labour substitution

effects. However, in the longer run, and depending on the price elasticity of demand for goods and services affected by process innovations, reductions in unit output costs can lead to positive employment consequences. Furthermore, the utilisation of innovations in production processes can spawn a wide range of technically related goods and services previously unavailable. This can also lead to increases in employment (see also the contribution by P. Townroe in the present volume).

Notwithstanding the difficulties of predicting the long term consequences of technical change on employment, the detailed sectors within the service sector have exhibited considerable variation in employment change over the period 1960 to 1979. The pattern is similar to that which characterises output growth. Financial Services experienced growth at an average rate of 3.34 per cent per annum whilst Professional and Scientific Services grew on average by 3.22 per cent per annum. In Transport and Communications employment decreased by 0.53 per cent per annum over the nineteen year four cycle period whilst in Distributive Trades it grew by only 0.18 per cent per annum. Furthermore, between the trade cycle employment peak in September 1979 and the trough of August 1983, employment in Financial Services actually increased by 55 thousand workers whilst it declined in all other sectors of the British economy. The above data show unequivocally that the detailed sectors of the service sector are quite heterogeneous with some displaying characteristics more typical of the manufacturing sector! (See Gleave and Sellens 1984). However, the use of crude employment data in measuring changes in labour inputs is problematical. Since 1982 many of the newly created jobs in the British economy have been part time and filled primarily by married females. It is not east to satisfactorily map part time employment into full time equivalent jobs and therefore rates of change in employment must be judged with caution. Nonetheless, employment change provides one of the most reliable sources of data for evaluating structural changes which are taking place within the economy.

An important feature of the long run as well as more recent increases in female employment is that they have tended to occur in occupations traditionally regarded as female employment. These are the areas which are, in theory, susceptible to capital for labour substitutions, particularly within the office working environment. Why has this seemingly not occurred? Is it too early to expect the labour shedding potential of office automation to have yet had a major effect? This question will be examined in the light of employment changes in a variety of new occupation classes which are discussed below. What may be said at this early stage is that a variety of processes operating within the British economy have tended to obfuscate subtle changes occurring in service jobs affected by information and communications technology. For example, macroeconomists in Britain are now revising upwards estimates of the minimum irreducible level of employment but are apparently uncertain why they should do so even though the reason is elementary. Against a backcloth of world recession the manufacturing sector of the British economy have been uncompetitive in the world markets. Those service sectors which do trade in the market place have been more successful in combatting the effects of recession and, therefore, have been better able to maintain high levels of output and employment. Non trading sectors, the public services, have, by and large, been protected from the more serious ravages of world recession. Most jobs in the less competitive manufacturing sectors have been filled by males. Many jobs in the private and public services have been filled by females. Loss of unemployment by a male is almost automatically followed by the unemployment registration. In the case of a married female it is usually followed by withdrawal from the labour market. Consequently, data on unemployment give a poor picture of the sectoral and occupational restructuring of the labour market other than drawing attention to the high number of male jobs being shed in traditional occupations. Increases in part time female employment on the other hand do not lead to reductions in registered unemployment. Within this macroeconomic framework of aggregate restructuring it is hardly surprising that changes related to new technology do not stand out clearly.

To examine some aspects of change due to innovation requires attention being paid to employment rather than unemployment and to a new categorisation of sectors and occupations. This topic is dealt with in the next section. It is followed by analysis of employment change in information industries and occupations and finally by a more detailed analysis of change within the workplace. Finally some policy implications for labour market adjustments are drawn.

2.   A NEW CLASSIFICATION OF EMPLOYMENT BY SECTOR AND OCCUPATION

It is one thing to argue that current, official classifications of employment by occupation and sector are inadequate. It is a far more arduous task to produce an updated classification particularly if the criteria for creating the new classification cannot be spelt out with precision.

In this paper we concentrate on the cluster of innovations most important to understanding changes within service employment that can be broadly described as 'information and communications technologies'. Some of the specific innovations are described in a later section. Here, it is sufficient to say that they embody not only new electronic based equipment, but all capital equipment of varying vintages which is concerned with the gathering, storing, manipulating, retrieving, transferring and disseminating of information. Consequently, certain traditional service sectors, such as domestic services, are excluded from our set of 'sectors-of-interest' while some manufacturing sectors are provisionally included, such as the production of microcomputers.

The classification derived for usage in analysing economic sectors is shown in Appendix I. Conceptually, it relied heavily on the earlier work of Porat (1977) and Rubin and Taylor (1981) which was modified to take account of the broad classification of ITAP (1983). Details of the method are to be found in Gleave, Angell and Woolley (1985). The classification identified four major groups, two drawing from manufacturing, and two from services described as the Goods Enabling, Goods Content, Service Enabling and Service Content groups. For the purposes of this paper the two manufacturing groups are excluded from further consideration except where data aggregates made this impossible.

The classification of occupations clustered around the handling of information leant even more heavily on the pioneer work of Porat (1977) and also on Debons et al., (1980). The resulting classes of information occupations comprised the following:

    Scientific and Technical Workers
    Private Information Services
    Educators
    Public Information Disseminators
    Communications Workers
    Information Gatherers
    Search and Coordination Specialists

Planning and Control Workers
Information Processors
Machine Operators
Telecommunications Workers

3.   CHANGES IN SERVICE EMPLOYMENT: PAST TRENDS, FUTURE PROSPECTS

In this section, past trends in employment in various categories of service work are examined. This will be followed by a discussion of a relationship of these changes to technical change and a brief outline of future prospects.

The previous section identified four groups of 'information sector' employment of which two, the Service Enabling Group and the Service Content group lie within the service sector. Employment within these groups of industries can be described as being within information oc- cupations and within non information occupations. In addition there are two other subgroups of interest. These are workers in other infor- mation groups in information occupations and workers in non informa- tion groups in information occupations. (See Figure 1)

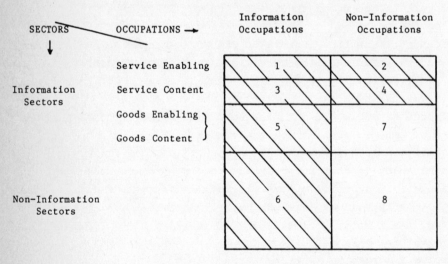

Figure 1   Sectoral and Occupational Representation of 'Service' Jobs

Analysis of Census data for 1961, 1966, 1971 and 1981 shows that em- ployment in these information related service subgroups increased in each intercensal period, irrespective of trade cycle fluctuations.

This is a remarkable trend compared with employment in the economy as a whole. Total employment according to the Census increased only between 1961 and 1966. Thereafter, it recorded a decline in each successive Census (although not in all intercensal years).

In aggregate employment terms, the most important of the six subgroups was employment in information occupations in the non information related sectors (primarily manufacturing). This accounted for 3.073 million jobs in 1961 and increased to 3.308 million jobs by 1981. However, although important in numerical terms, this subgroup did not increase its percentage share of total employment very dramatically. It accounted for 13.71 per cent of all jobs in 1961 and 14.43 per cent in 1981, a percentage increase of only 1.26 per cent.

These two subgroups which accounted for the most radical increases in percentage of total employment were both in the Service Content group of sectors. Information Occupations in this group (subgroup three) increased in numerical terms from 1.854 million jobs to 2.905 million jobs. In percentage terms, this was from 7.94 per cent of the total to 12.67 per cent. Non information occupations in this service group increased numerically from 1.248 million jobs to 2.110 million; or from 5.35 per cent of the total to 9.21 per cent.

Although changes in the underlying classifications make these data somewhat unreliable, the general trend is clear. In contrast, jobs in the non service sector part of the economy (and excluding non information occupations in the Goods Enabling and Goods Content groups) declined from 67.99 per cent of the total to 55.68 per cent in just twenty years. The full data set is shown in Table 1.

Returning briefly to the original four major information groups mentioned above (and including non information as well as information occupations), the following regular pattern of employment change occurred over the twenty year period of analysis. Service Content employment grew fastest overall, followed by Service Enabling employment. Next came Goods Content employment followed by Goods Enabling. All four major groups performed more effectively in employment terms than the residual sectors although over the decade 1971-1981, when manufacturing employment in the UK recorded a significant loss of jobs, both the 'Goods' groups exhibited employment decline.

What happened over the same period to employment in the detailed information occupation subgroups? The introduction stated that, despite
the capital for labour substitution <u>potential</u> of information technology, increases in female employment show that, to date, this has not
occurred. Does a more detailed analysis of employment growth in the
information related occupations confirm this?

TABLE 1

Percentage of Employment in Various Subgroups
of the British Economy 1961-1981

		1961	1966	1971	1981
1.	Service Enabling, Information Occupations	1.37	1.50	1.59	1.66
2.	Service Enabling, Non-Information Occupations	0.15	0.18	0.17	0.28
3.	Service Content, Information Occupations	7.94	8.64	9.89	12.67
4.	Service Content, Non-Information Occupations	5.35	6.52	7.94	9.21
5.	Other Information Sectors, Information Occupations	4.03	4.46	5.18	6.06
6.	Non-Information Sectors, Information Occupations	13.17	13.04	13.88	14.43
7+8.	All Other Jobs	67.99	65.66	61.33	55.68
	Total, percentage	100.00	100.00	100.00	100.00
	Total, million jobs	23.34	24.17	23.73	22.92

In 1961 there were 6.187 million workers employed in the information
occupations in the UK, a total which increased to 7.981 million by

1981. However, within this total considerable occupational restructuring occurred. (The term restructuring should not be understood here to
mean the direct substitution of one type of worker by another - it
simply refers to differential rates of occupational growth.)

All occupations except Telecommunications workers experienced absolute
growth in employment terms and even amongst this group decline was
limited to three thousand jobs. However, the fastest rates of growth
were not concentrated in those occupations traditionally regarded as
areas of female employment.

The largest single group, Information Processors, which includes typists, secretaries, word processor operators and clerks, employed 3.242
million workers in 1961 in all sectors. By 1981 the total had only
increased to 3.294 million. The greatest overall levels of employment
increase occurred amongst Planning and Control workers. This group
includes middle and senior management in all sectors together with
middle and senior ranking Civil Servants. In 1961 employment in these
occupations totalled 0.704 million workers; by 1981 this had increased
to 1.480 million. Yet this is regarded by experts in office automation
to be the occupation group most susceptible to labour substitution
especially within the ranks of middle managers.

Another group which experienced considerable increases in employment
was Scientific and Technical workers. In 1961 0.250 million were in
employment. By 1981 this increased to 0.480 million. Other groups experiencing similar rates of increased employment opportunities were
Communications workers (advertising, public relations, authors, jour-
nalists, etc.) and Information Gatherers (estimators, valuers, asses-
sors, surveyors, etc.). Can these changes be ascribed to technical
change or do they simply reflect gross expansion and over manning in
the public sector?

To what extent can the changes reported above be ascribed to innovation? How has technical change contributed to restructuring within the
labour market? In truth these questions cannot be answered directly
from aggregate analysis. In general, firms employing the most
up-to-date production technologies are best able to minimise their
unit output costs and thereby remain potentially competitive within
the international market place. However, overall performance and profitability of firms depends on much more than reducing unit output

costs. If the products being brought to the market place are not price elastic in demand, cost reductions are not a major consideration. If the marketing of products in demand is ineffective then quality and costs become irrelevant. More succinctly, the utilisation of the most up-to-date production technologies are a necessary but not a sufficient condition for achieving international competitiveness. This is particularly the case with manufactured goods. The failure of British companies in this regard is well documented. Sayer and Morgan (1984) show how the British Electronics Industry has captured a declining share of a growing world market for goods in information and communications technologies. Sciberras and Payne (1985) have shown similarly that British industry's share of world machine tools production declined from 8 per cent to 3 per cent over the period 1965 to 1972. At the same time, the Japanese increased their share of output from 4 per cent to 17 per cent. The declining performance of British manufacturing industry was traced directly to the failure to innovate and seize new opportunities provided by microelectronic based control mechanisms.

It can reasonably be concluded that failure to innovate, particularly in widely traded goods, leads to loss of markets and loss of jobs. Innovation in the processes of production may also lead to loss of jobs in the short run, but the Japanese experience shows that making rapid inroads into world markets, particularly when they are growing leads, in the longer run, to increased employment opportunities.

To conclude that a failure to innovate leads to a loss of markets and jobs is one thing. Are the growth of markets and increases in employment necessarily indicative of high rates of innovation? Within the British economy, the sectors which have grown the fastest have been in what is often described as 'business services'. There is no evidence that this has been achieved by increased competitiveness or by penetrating world markets with new services. There is, however, evidence that these sectors have been early adopters of information and communication technology. However, this is more likely to be because they have been relatively profitable and, therefore, able to invest in new technology. The evidence does not suggest that their performance has been a consequence of adopting new technology. The adoption of new technology provides the opportunity for these sectors to remain competitive in the future. But, the question remains, how did they achieve growth and competitiveness in the first place? One factor which must not be forgotten is that most companies in the business services sectors trade internally within the British economy (notwithstanding the contributions of 'invisibles' to the balance of payments). They have been operating in a market place which is less price resistant than that of most of its international competitors. Furthermore, in some of these markets, such as banking services, high profitability in the recent past may be partially a consequence of oligopolistic behaviour.

This still does not draw a clear picture of the linkages between innovation, competitiveness and jobs. To do this it is necessary to examine th detailed behaviour of firms.

4. OFFICE TECHNOLOGY: ITS IMPACT IN THE WORKPLACE

The findings reported in this section are again restricted to one area of process innovation and their impact on service occupations rather than the service sector. Nonetheless, they shed some light on the nature of the adoption process and its impact on employment.

One clear feature which emerges from the study from which these findings are taken is that the full ramifications of office automation take many years to be felt. Although primary reasons for automation can be identified, many of the knock-on effects were not anticipated at the time of implementation.

A questionnaire was circulated to organisations in the UK and US[3] which inquired about office technology available on site and its date of acquisition (or replacement). Other questions investigated the prime reasons for acquisition, the nature of the decision taking process, the impact on the geographical organisation of work, departmental structure, levels of responsibility and impact on staffing. The questionnaire was sent to firms in all sectors of economic activity.

Office technology was defined specifically in terms of identifiable pieces of equipment. These included: electric and electronic typewriters, word processors, dictation machines and systems, copying and storage mechanisms, hi-tech printers, computers and terminals of all types and communications systems.

Certain types of equipment were regarded as essential to the execution of the office function and possessed by almost all respondents in both countries. Not surprisingly these included typewriters or word processors of one form or another, dictation machines and photocopiers. Access to different forms of computing equipment was not as high as might be expected, ranging from 40 per cent access to mainframe computers in the US to 80 per cent access to microcomputers in the UK. The uptake of more recently available 'equipment' such as local area networks and laser printers was generally low (less than 20 per cent of the sample).

How had the access to new technology affected business performance? Why was it acquired? In both the UK and the US the primary reason stated for acquiring information technology was to improve efficiency followed by the desire to improve quality. General cost reductions were the third most important reason for acquisition. Reduction in either staffing levels or the rate of expansion was only mentioned as being the fourth most important reason out of a list of eight. The similarity between stated priorities in both the UK and the US could not be ascribed to the ordering of options on the questionnaire (a well known problem in survey work). It is of interest to not that the desire to generate new customer services was not regarded as being important in either the US or the UK.

What impact has office technology had on the geographic organisation of work? In the UK, 56 per cent of organisation said it had no effect whatsoever. Just under a quarter of organisations said there was a reorganisation of offices within the site and/or changes in the architecture of the site (office refurbishment). Only 11 per cent of British organisations suggested that the acquisition of new technology had led to changes in the type of activities carried out on their particular sites run by the organisations.

In contrast, only 39 per cent of US organisations said there had been no effects. Over a quarter stated that reorganisation of offices and/or changes of architecture had occurred. More importantly, the same proportion said there had been changes in the activities carried out on the sites and 8.1 per cent that it had led to changes in the number of sites operated. In both the US and the UK new technology had not resulted in staff working regularly off-site.

How does the acquisition of new technology influence job responsibilities? Again, in the UK over half the sample said it had no effect. Less than 40 per cent of respondents in the US stated this to be the case. Changes in areas of responsibility was stated to be the second most frequent consequence. This occurred in 30 per cent of US organisations but only 20 per cent of those in the UK. Also in the US there were higher incidences of decentralisation of decision taking, devolution of responsibility to more junior staff and elimination of some grades of management than in the UK. Only in the case of centralisation in decision taking did the UK outrank the US.

This suggests that American organisations have been more positive in seizing the full range of possibilities provided by office technology. They appear more adaptive than British firms in not only implementing changes to organisational structure and the range of activities which occur on site but also in changing the job descriptions and areas of responsibility of staff. British organisation do not, in general, appear to be aware of the broad range of opportunities for restructuring their service functions provided by the new technology. Interviews with organisations suggests this may be to do with power structures. In particular, there is often conflict concerning the areas of responsibility of data processing managers and office services managers. Rather than restructure a broad range of activities within the organisations so that the potential of the technology is fully realised there is a tendency to simply replace manually executed tasks by machine execution.

Both the questionnaire survey and the interview evidence suggest that in the US the decision to adopt office automation is made strategically. At the same time, issues regarding corporate structure and organisation are also considered. This is less likely to be the case in the UK, reflecting a more entrenched and conservative attitude to business practice in Britain.

What effect has new technology had on levels of employment in different types of service jobs? Aggregate analysis showed employment growth to have occurred in all six subgroups employing service workers. Is this trend also occurring in individual firms with office technology?

In general, the US and the UK responses suggested that the technology was having a neutral effect. It will be recalled from the aggregate analysis that Information Processors, the female dominated occupations including typists, etc., experienced relatively <u>slow</u> growth compared with other information occupations. This is born out from the results of the questionnaire analysis. In both the US and the UK, the only groups experiencing <u>small</u> net job loss due to the technology were typists, secretaries and clerks. Although most respondents reported 'no effects' there was a net loss of jobs in these occupations and in other cases the technology prevented increases which would otherwise have occurred. In other occupations, most notably computer programmers, operations researchers and technical and professional staff, there was an excess of job creation over job loss. Even in these cases the most predominant consequence was no effect.

In the case of managers the 'no effect' response was so overwhelming that the whole idea of employment consequences of new technology appears absurd. In the UK, this category accounted for 86 per cent of responses; in the US for 81 per cent. The full responses are shown in Table 2.

TABLE 2

Effects of Office Technology of Staffing Levels

Percentage Responses

	UK RESPONSES				US RESPONSES			
	Job loss	Prevented Increase	No effect	Job Increase	Job loss	Prevented Increase	No effect	Job Increase
Typists etc.	27.2	29.8	39.7	33.1	8.9	29.5	46.4	15.2
Secretaries	12.3	21.1	65.8	0.9	14.2	21.2	61.9	2.7
Clerks	34.5	22.1	42.5	0.9	16.9	19.8	56.6	6.6
Admin. support	15.3	19.5	55.1	10.2	7.5	15.0	64.5	13.1
Technical, Prof.	1.8	13.4	63.4	21.4	2.9	13.5	59.6	24.0
Programmers	3.0	5.0	56.4	35.6	4.3	4.3	59.6	31.9
OR systems An.	2.1	5.3	58.9	33.7	1.1	3.4	68.2	27.3
Data processors	9.4	3.1	56.3	31.3	4.2	3.1	59.4	33.3
Managers	2.8	2.8	86.0	8.4	2.0	4.0	81.0	13.0

5.   <u>CONCLUSIONS AND POLICY IMPLICATIONS</u>

Drawing together the findings of both the more aggregate analysis of employment data and those from the questionnaire survey there is some evidence that the process innovations facilitated by office automation may lead to job loss in certain occupations. For example, slow overall employment growth in secretarial jobs was <u>not</u> found in the firms adopting office automation. In contrast, rapid overall growth in technical jobs was mirrored in the findings of the questionnaire survey. The two analyses still prevent a clear distinction being made between the employments effects of growth in product (service) demand and the impacts of process innovation on the quality of labour required to service that growth. More detailed microeconomic studies are required which take account of either the quantity or value growth in output of firms adopting office automation (information) technology. This is also necessary in order to analyse more precisely the substitution processes of capital for labour, not only in a sectoral but also in a functional context.

The detailed analysis of changes in the workplace tends to confirm the occupation restructuring observed in the analysis of aggregate data. Will this trend continue? As mentioned above, there is a belief amongst experts in the office automation business that many layers of middle management can be removed through the adoption of office automation. This belief is, itself, based on the assumption that senior managers will, in taking decisions, be users of office technology themselves. Interviews with senior managers suggest that in the majority of cases this is not their wish. A majority recognises the importance of adapting to the new technology but most managers fail to realise its full potential. Many also consider it to be equipment which has no direct impact in their strategic decision taking. Hence the finding that in most firms the adoption has no impact on staffing levels of managers.

Managers in the US appear more open to the additional advantages that can be reaped from reorganising their workplace to optimally utilise the potential of the technology. This tendency is not so apparent amongst many British managers. Consequently, the implications for policy in the UK are rather dismal. How can national policy bring pressure to bear on individual entrepreneurs and managers to shed their conservative business practices and be more dynamic in the utilisation of new technology? However, they are seemingly less dynamic and imaginative in changing their methods of office practice after having acquired new equipment. Adoption must be followed up by adaptation throughout the workforce if full benefits are to accrue in terms of increased productivity. This need not necessarily result in reductions in employment.

NOTES

1. The quantity measure is based on sectoral indices of output at constant factor cost, combined using current price shares of each sector in GDP.

2. The value measure is based on the deflated value of GDP by sector.

3. Response rates to the questionnaire survey were generally low, 19 per cent in the UK and 18 per cent in the US. They were highest from firms in the business services sector (36 per cent UK, 38 per cent US) where the uptake of office automation is known to be greatest. This probably means that firms' propensity to respond is a function of the rates of adoption. Although low response rates make it dangerous to generalise across the economy those questionnaires returned (254) make it possible to accurately trace the employment effects of adoption in the responsive firms.

193

APPENDIX 1

Categorisation of Information Industries using the British SIC at the MLH
and Activity levels

GOODS ENABLING	1958 SIC MLH No.	1968 SIC MLH No.	1980 SIC[1] Activity No.
Office Machinery	338	338	3301
Watches and Clocks	352	352	3740
Photographic and Document copying equipment	]351 (also	351	3733
Surgical instruments and appliances	]part 364)	353	3720, 3731
Scientific and Industrial Instruments	]	354	3732, 3710, 3442
Telegraph and Telephone Apparatus etc	363	363	3441
Radio and Electronic Components		364	]3453, 3444
Broadcast receiving and Sound reproducing equipment	364	365	]3452, 3454]see note 2
Electronic Computers		366	] 3302
Radio, radar and electronic Capital goods		367	]3433, 3443
Paper and Board	481	481	4710
Manufactured Stationery	483/3[3]	483	4723
Miscellaneous Stationers' Goods	495	495	4953
GOODS CONTENTS			
Printing, Publishing of newspapers	] 486	485	4751
Printing, Publishing of periodicals	]	486	4752
Printing, Publishing of Books	]	489	4753
Other Printing, publishing, book-binding, engraving, etc	] 489		4754
SERVICE ENABLING			
Postal Services	707	708	7901
Telecommunications			7902
SERVICE CONTENT (see note 2)			
Cinemas, theatres, radio etc	881	881	9711, 9741, 9760, (part 4930)
Insurance	]	860	8200, 8320
Banking and bill discounting	] 860	861	]8310 8140
Other Financial Institutions	]-860/4	862	] 8150

SERVICE CONTENT	1958 SIC MLH No	1968 SIC MLH No	1980 SIC[1] Activity No
Advertising and Market Research	]	864	8380
Other Business Services	]	865	8395 8394
Central Offices not allocable	] 899	866	8396
elsewhere	]		
Other Services		899	9611, 9631, 9690 (part 4930)
Accountancy Services	871	871	8360
Educational Services	872	872	9310, 9320, 9330
Legal Services	873	873	8350
Medical and dental Services	874	874	9510, 9520, 9530, 9540, 9550
Research and Development Services	]	876	9400
Other Professional and Scientific	] 879	879	8370, 9560
Services	]		
National Government Service	901	901	9770, 9111,
Local Government Service	906	906	9120, 9130, 9140, 9150, 9190

Notes to Table

1. The 1980 SIC has a very different structure compared to
    the previous SICs and the coding system is based on 4
    rather than 3 digit numbers.

2. The correspondence between the 1968 MLHs and 1980 Activ-
    ities as listed in the table are not exact but this is
    compensated for by the fact that although parts of an
    MLH may fall into different activities both activities
    will be under the same broad category (i.e. goods enab-
    ling/service content etc). Hence combined Activities
    3452, 3453, 3443, 3444, 3433, 3302 and 3454 correspond
    to MLHs (1968) 364, 365, 366 and 367. Similarly with
    all the Service Content industries.

3. In a few cases in the 1958 classification it is necess-
    ary to go below the MLH to its sub-divisions. This is
    only possible where data is published at this lower
    level in the Census as is the case with those sub-div-
    isions shown in the table.

    There were some minor alterations to the definition of
    some of the MLHs when reclassification took place in
    1965. In most cases reallocations affecting the MLHs
    listed in the above table were to other MLHs within the
    same broad category as was the case with differences
    betwen MLHs and Activities (see note 2 above). Hence
    the reallocations will have a negligible effect on our
    results.

195

Details of the differences between the 1958 and 1968
classificaion may be found in Fothergill and Gudgin (1976),
Appendix 8. Details of the differences between the 1965 and
1980 SIC may be foud in "Standard Industrial Classification
Revised 1980: Reconciliation with Standard Industrial
Classification 1968" available from the Central Statistics
Office.

The following industries, separated in only the 1980 SIC are
excluded from the study for reasons of consistencey (see
Appendix 8).

2552	Printing Ink
3275/4 and 3276	Printing and Paper making machinery
8440	House and Estate Agents
8500	Owning and dealing in Real Estate
530	Retail Distribution of Books, Stationery and Office Supplies.

REFERENCES

Barras, R., Growth and Technical Change in the UK Service Sector, Report TCCR-83-015, Technical Change Centre, London, 1984.

Debons, et al., Manpower Requirement in Scientific and Technical Communication; An Occupational Survey of Information Professions, The University of Pittsburgh, Pittsburgh, PA, 1980.

Gleave, D., Angell, C. and Woolley, K., 'Structural change within the information profession: a scenario of the 1990s', Aslilb Proceedings, Vol. 37, No. 2, 1985, pp. 99-133.

Gleave, D. and Sellens, R., An Investigation into British Labour Processes, Environment and Planning Committee Paper No. 3, Economic and Social Research Council, London, 1984.

ITAP, Making a Business of Information, the Information Technology Advisory Panel, HMSO, London, 1983.

Porat, M.U., The Information Economy, US Department of Commerce and the Office of Telecommunications,, Washington DC, 1977.

Rubin, M. and Taylor, E., 'The US information sector and GNP: an input-output study', Information Processes and Management, Vol. 17, No. 4, 1981, pp. 163-194.

Sayer, A. and Morgan, K., The Electronics Industry and Regional Developments in Britain, paper presented to ESRC/CURDS Workshop on Technological Change, Small Firms and Employment, University of Newcastle upon Tyne, 1984.

Sciberras, E. and Payne, B.D., Technical Change and International Competitiveness, Longmans, London, 19

THE DE-INDUSTRIALISATION OF THE
FEDERAL REPUBLIC OF GERMANY AND
ITS SPATIAL IMPLICATIONS
Franz-Josef Bade

1.   THE SERVICE ECONOMY

1.1 Sectoral Perspective

Since the work of Fisher (1952), Clark (1940), Fourastie (1954) and
others it was widely accepted that in the long run, the leading industrial countries evolve into a post-industrial society dominated by the
service sector. As pilot example, the US economy is often mentioned:
in 1982 more than two thirds of total GNP are produced in the service
sector while the share of manufacturing industries has steadily decreased during the last decades.

In some recent papers, however, the hypothesis of the secular decline
of the manufacturing sector is seriously put in question (e.g. Lawrence 1983). Firstly, it is shown that over time there is strong positive correlation between the growth in GNP and the increase of industrial production. Furthermore, in the last 15 years production as well
as employment in the US manufacturing industry has <u>absolutely</u> grown.
In addition, the US growth rate was even higher than in France, the
United Kingdom or West Germany which obviously does not correspond
very highly with the postulated hypothesis that countries of higher
economic development levels should demonstrate less or no increase in
the secondary sector.

Regarding the FRG, some further contradictory peculiarities can be
observed. On the one hand, a clear shift towards services has occurred. However, in an international comparison, the FRG has one of
the highest share of manufacturing sector; correspondingly, the share
of the service sector is one of the lowest, although the German economy is generally regarded as relatively developed.

Furthermore, like the USA and in spite of the high industrialisation
no absolute decrease of the industrial production could be observed in

the last decades. And, again similar to the USA, there is a strong
correlation between industrial and total economic growth. The strongest shift towards services did not happen in times of strong economic
growth as is theoretically supposed, but in the years of stagnation or
even recession after 1973.

Table 1:   **The Development of Sectoral Structure
in Selected Industrialized Countries**
- Share of sector in % of total GNP -

Secondary Sector[1]

	1965	1970	1975	1980
Federal Republic of Germany	50.3	51.3	49.1	48.0
USA	34.2	32.2	30.6	30.6
Sweden	39.4	40.4	39.4	37.4
France	37.0	40.4	40.5	38.6
Great Britain	39.7	40.3	38.0	34.1
Italy	39.4	42.4	40.4	42.3
Japan	33.4	40.3	39.8	43.4

Tertiary Sector[2]

	1965	1970	1975	1980
Federal Republic of Germany	44.4	44.0	46.7	48.4
USA	59.2	61.6	63.7	64.0
Sweden	53.1	53.1	54.9	57.5
France	53.4	51.8	53.2	55.6
Great Britain	55.1	55.1	57.8	58.9
Italy	50.5	49.5	52.2	51.1
Japan	56.3	53.0	54.5	52.5

1) Energy, Mining, Manufacturing, Construction, 2) Trade, Transport,
Finance, Public and Other Services.
Source: FRANZMEYER (1983, p. 72).

But even then, it is not justified to interpret the structural change
as a general industrial decline: within the manufacturing sector considerable intrasectoral differences can be observed which clearly exceed the deviations between the secondary and tertiary sector as a
whole. Some branches of the manufacturing industry (such as vehicle
construction or the office machines industry) have attained growth
rates in value added which are as high as these attained by the most
successful services, such as the credit and insurance institutes or

the miscellaneous services which comprise traditional services such as cleaning or restaurants on the one hand and newer services such as consultancies or research laboratories on the other.

Table 2:   **The Sectoral Structure of Gross Value Added**[1]
in the FRG

	Sectoral Share in %			Annual Change Rate in %		
	1960	1973	1984	60-73	73-84	60-84
Agriculture	6.1	3.0	2.1	+3.2	+2.8	+2.9
Secondary sector[2] thereof:	52.6	48.8	42.4	+8.4	+4.8	+6.7
- Plastics	0.4	0.7	0.8	+14.0	+6.8	+10.6
- Office machines, EDP	0.3	0.6	0.7	+15.1	+8.1	+11.9
- Road Vehicles	2.5	3.3	3.8	+11.2	+7.6	+9.5
- Aviation	0.1	0.2	0.2	+16.6	+7.5	+12.4
Tertiary sector[3] thereof:	41.4	48.2	55.5	+10.3	+7.5	+9.0
- Credit and Insurance	2.5	3.9	6.5	+12.7	+11.3	+12.1
- Miscellaneaous Services	7.3	9.9	13.6	+11.6	+9.3	+10.5
Total Gross Value Added	287.4	882.9	1 707.2	+9.0	+6.2	+7.7

1) In actual prices; 2) Energy, Mining, Manufacturing, Construction; 3) Trade, Transport, Finance, Public and Other Services.

Source: Federal Statistical Office; System of National Accounts.

1.2 Functional Perspective

Apparently, the FRG seems to be still far away from a service society. However, this impression is strongly influenced by the kind of structural perspective which is focussed on the <u>output</u> of production. Sectorally seen, the service character of an economy is judged according to the shares of goods resp. services in its total domestic production.

There are a lot of various and heterogeneous factors which may influence the demand for domestic products and services in a nonuniform direction. For example, a rise of domestic demand for services is not reflected in the production output structure if at the same time, the export of domestic goods increases, as is shown by the example of Japan in Table 1.

As the changes of the output structure offers a quite diffuse picture, the evolution into a service society is much more evident if a functional perspective is chosen. Already suggested by Fourastie (1954), this perspective concentrates on the kind of labour input and on the process of production. Analysing the kind of activity performed by the employed persons - no matter which product is finally produced - and, thus, taking tertiary functions instead of tertiary products as the starting point, the transformation of the industrialised countries into a service society can be detected much more clearly.

In the FRG more than two thirds of total employment (64%) were involved in a service activity in 1982; almost one third (30%) were employed in production and the remainder (6%) were engaged in agriculture. This distribution of activities is, as shown by diagram 1, the result of a continuous process of development. The further one goes back in time, the smaller is the share of services in comparison with production activities. In 1950, the proportions were roughly equally large and in 1939 more people were actually engaged in production (39%) than in services (34%).

In comparison to the sectoral structure, however, it is not only the steadiness and the extent of the change in the functional structure of activities which is of significance, since in the end the tendency to move towards a services society can also be seen from the sectoral structure of employment. Much more significant is the homogeneity with which the structure of activities has been developing.

Looking at the output of production it was shown that considerable differences in growth rates existed within both manufacturing and service sectors. Some of the manufacturing branches managed to attain growth rates similar to those achieved by the strongest of services. Differentiated by functions, however, the variations within the large areas of activities are considerably smaller. On the one hand, there is scarcely a single tertiary activity which has not increased its employment (provided it is not replaced by another tertiary activity). On the other hand, with few exceptions, practically all of the secondary activities have contracted.

Thus, the service functions are the clear winners in the change in
economic structure. During the last few decades, activities have
switched more and more from manufacturing to services functions in all
sectoral branches of the economy. There is no industry in which the
share of people employed in production has not decreased and in which
the share of tertiary activities has not increased over the course of
time. Thus, even in the construction sector, which traditionally has
the largest share of production, production activities fell from 88 to
75% between 1961 and 1982, whilst, for example, the share of production-oriented services, i.e., technical and administrative services
increased from 7 to 17% in the manufacturing industry production activities actually fell from 67 to 58%. If the decline were to continue
at the present rate (which of course, is a speculation), then in the
year 2000, more than half of all people employed in the manufacturing
industry would be engaged in activities other than production.

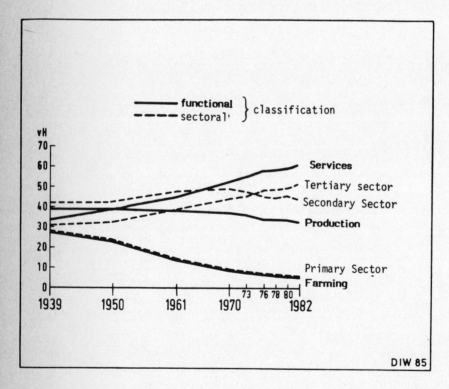

Diagram 1.   Long-term development frends in structural change (percen-
             tage shares of functional and sectoral classes in total
             employment)
Source: Federal Bureau of Statistics; calculations by the author
             (1939-1970 census; 1973-1982: microcensus)

Table 3: **The Functional Structure by Sectors**

- Employment share of selected functions
as percentage of sectoral total employment in the resp. year; resp. total employment = 100% -

Sectoral Branch		Share of functions in %					Total Employment in 1,000
		Miners Production	Technical Services	Administrat. Services	Trade	Health & Social Services	
Energy,	1961	73.5	6.7	7.9	1.7	0.3	722
Mining	1970	64.8	10.6	12.9	1.8	0.4	551
	1982	58.7	14.2	15.4	1.3	0.4	508
Manufac-	1961	67.1	4.7	12.0	2.5	0.1	9 905
turing	1970	61.5	7.4	15.5	4.4	0.2	10 117
Industry	1982	57.7	9.1	17.2	4.4	0.3	8 460
Construc-	1961	88.0	2.4	4.4	0.2	0.0	2 178
tion	1970	82.0	4.2	7.3	0.8	0.0	2 319
	1982	75.1	5.8	11.7	1.3	0.1	1 929
Trade	1961	6.7	0.6	17.3	54.9	0.7	3 344
	1970	9.8	1.0	24.8	50.3	1.0	3 348
	1982	9.2	1.3	26.2	49.6	1.5	3 356
Transport,	1961	14.0	3.9	19.7	3.2	0.1	1 464
Communi-	1970	14.9	3.8	23.2	5.5	0.2	1 407
cation	1982	13.9	5.5	28.1	5.1	0.4	1 470
Finance,	1961	0.7	0.4	89.8	3.3	0.0	411
Insurance	1970	1.0	0.7	90.7	2.1	0.2	597
	1982	0.7	0.1	89.8	3.2	0.3	749
Miscel-	1961	7.7	4.1	15.5	2.8	33.9	2 960
laneous	1970	6.3	5.1	18.1	4.0	39.4	3 438
Services	1982	4.3	4.9	20.5	2.5	42.9	4 552
Public and	1961	7.3	4.7	43.8	1.0	5.3	1 993
Non- Market	1970	7.7	4.8	38.2	0.4	5.0	2 521
Services	1982	6.7	5.1	39.8	0.6	10.1	3 167
Total	1961	37.5	3.3	14.8	8.6	4.3	26 426
Sectors	1970	35.6	4.9	19.2	9.1	5.8	26 560
	1982	29.6	5.7	23.2	9.0	9.2	25 572

Source: The shares of functions are based on the census of 1961 and 1970 as well as on the microcensus 1982; the absolute figures of total employment are taken from the System of National Accounts.

1.3   The Growth of Production-Oriented Services

What is so surprising about the uniformity with which services have grown in each sector, is that fact that the increase of services cannot only be explained by the growth of person and consumer oriented services (which is the reason for the differing results between the functional and the sectoral perspective). These functions are mostly offered by service enterprises and public organisations; therefore, sectoral and functional changes are closely related in those cases.

By way of contrast, production oriented services such as administrative and technical services are faced with economic developments which differ widely among the various sectors. Unlike the more consumer oriented services, the production oriented services are rather uniformly spread out amongst the sectoral branches (see Table 4). Managerial and technical services, for example, occur not only in the regulation and control of production in manufacturing industry, but are also required in the service sector - in connection with the introduction of EDP in credit institutes or in insurance firms, for instance.

Table 4:   The Sectoral Concentration of Selected Functions
- GINI-Coefficients -

Functions	1961	1970	1982
Miners, Production	0.42	0.40	0.41
Technical Services	0.29	0.30	0.29
Administrative Services	0.25	0.22	0.21
Trade	0.46	0.37	0.37
Health and Social Services	0.60	0.57	0.65

In the FRG in 1982 almost one third of total administrative services (measured in terms of employment) were performed in goods producing firms which belong to the industries energy, mining, manufacturing and construction. With regard to technical services, their share is still higher. Two thirds of total technical services can be found in these sectors. By way of contrast, only 15% is the corresponding share of the sector 'Miscellaneous services', hence, of those firms which can be primarily considered as external suppliers of technical services.

Frequently, production oriented services are regarded as complementary to the proper production activities. As the volume of the latter directly depends on the demand for the actual final product, the growth of the production oriented services within a sectoral branch should at the very least, without wishing to assume a limitational production function, reflect the overall growth of the sectoral branch.

Actually, however, such a dependency has not occurred. Even in those economic groups in which total employment has fallen (in some cases considerably), the production oriented services have increased not only relatively, but also in absolute terms. Between 1961 and 1982 total employment in manufacturing industry, for example, fell by 1.4 million persons. In contrast, its production oriented services increased by more than half a million people while the production activities themselves diminished by more than 1.8 million. The development in other contracting branches, energy, mining or construction took a similar course: without the gains in the production oriented services the process of contraction would have been far more obvious.

In order to observe the development of individual functions within their sectoral environment in more detail, correlation analysis was done on the basis of 62 sectoral branches (thereof 32 within the manufacturing industry) and of 23 functions (thereof 5 for production activities). The data sources are the social security statistics covering the years 1976 till 1983. As only insured people are recorded, most of the independent employers or civil servants are not included.

With regard to production activities the results conform to the expectations. More than 80% of the sectoral variations of the change rate of production activities are 'explained' by the sectoral differences in total employment change. In respect of services, however, - leaving out store and transport activities - the dependence on the sectoral development is less strong and not significant for many functions. Among others, the hierarchical level of function seems to play a role. Executive services, for example, are less cyclical than total administrative services. Similarly, for research and development absolutely no relationship could be detected ($r^2 = 0.02$), whilst for total technical services at least more correlation with the sectoral growth rate exist ($r^2 = 0.32$).

1.4 The Economic Importance of Production Oriented Services

There are various and complementary reasons which help to understand the independence of production oriented services from the total employment growth rate. For example, in stagnating or declining industries, which are exposed to a strong international competition it is often observed that domestic firms stop the production of goods little by little and buy the products from the former competitors. Thus, they change more and more to trading companies whereas statistically they are still classified as industrial firms.

Beyond this more statistical argument, production oriented services are also less dependent on the global development as they seem to have an important influence on the competitiveness of a firm. In order to stand up to the increased competition, there are only two possible (but not exclusive) strategies. Either the firm tries to elude the rivals by new products or the old product has to be produced cheaper. For both strategies there exist a lot of variants, but with regard to the production oriented services, they altogether show common consequences. The strategy of price competition requires comparative cost advantages which in general can only be achieved by more efficient production processes and more capital input. Both are not conceivable without adequate production oriented services such as the permanent analysis, planning and control of the production process. Just as unequivocal are the consequences for the activity structure of the firm, if the strategy of product innovation is chosen. Apart from isolated cases, it is hardly probably that new and profit promising products can be found without intensive marketing and R&D activities; the more so as the competitors have also increased their research activities so that the chance of discovering new ideas without systematic analysis gets rather unlikely. Even the strategy of the 'fast second' (e.g., IBM) would not be very successful for a firm if it does not have the necessary activities to analyse and to avoid the technical and commercial weakness of the innovator.

Thus, certain production oriented services seem to become necessary (but of course not sufficient) preconditions for the economic success of a firm. There is a long and famous list of authors, e.g.,

Schumpeter, who stress the importance of R&D for the competitiveness of firms. However, if empirical findings are given, they are often based on a small sample of firms so that the representativeness of the results is questionable. Therefore, aggregated industrial analyses have an important task. For, if the supposed influence of production oriented services is representative for the majority of firms, its impact must be reflected in the aggregate also.

In fact, the empirical analysis of 29 industrial groups of the manufacturing sector brings forward unequivocal results. (In order to use data of the System of National Accounts the 32 industries of the social security statistics are condensed to 29 groups.) If the growth of an industrial group between 1976 and 1983 is related to the share of certain functions in its total activities 1976, then, above all, there is a strong positive relation to the technical services, especially to research and development as well as to EDP, marketing and consulting. Furthermore, the correlation increases essentially if sectoral growth is not measured in terms of employment, but in terms of value added ($r^2 = 0.39$ for employment, 0.54 for value added in actual prices and 0.69 for value added in prices of 1976).

Certainly, the relatively high degree of correlation is also produced by the two leading industries office machines and aviation. But even if these two industries are excluded from the analysis, there remains an evident relationship between the growth of an industry and its intensity of production oriented services ($r^2 = 0.54$). Interestingly, contrary to expectations, the share of production activities only reveals a weak relation (which was supposed to be negative). Thus, at least on the aggregate statistical level, the relative volume of production is of no importance. The more important question is whether, among the service activities, those functions are represented on above average which are necessary preconditions for the competitiveness of firms (see Diagram 2).

206

Diagram 2:

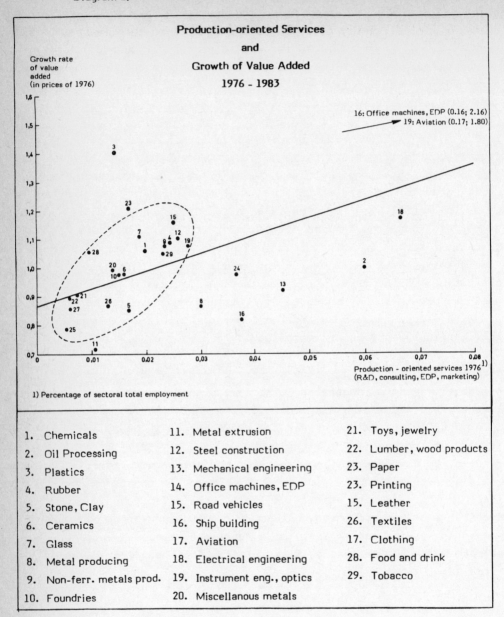

Production-oriented Services
and
Growth of Value Added
1976 - 1983

Growth rate
of value
added
(in prices of 1976)

16: Office machines, EDP (0.16; 2.16)
19: Aviation (0.17; 1.80)

Production - oriented services 1976 [1]
(R&D, consulting, EDP, marketing)

1) Percentage of sectoral total employment

1. Chemicals	11. Metal extrusion	21. Toys, jewelry
2. Oil Processing	12. Steel construction	22. Lumber, wood products
3. Plastics	13. Mechanical engineering	23. Paper
4. Rubber	14. Office machines, EDP	23. Printing
5. Stone, Clay	15. Road vehicles	15. Leather
6. Ceramics	16. Ship building	26. Textiles
7. Glass	17. Aviation	17. Clothing
8. Metal producing	18. Electrical engineering	28. Food and drink
9. Non-ferr. metals prod.	19. Instrument eng., optics	29. Tobacco
10. Foundries	20. Miscellanous metals	

2. REGIONAL DIFFERENCES IN THE SERVICE DEVELOPMENT

2.1 Employment Decline in Metropolitan Areas

While the rise of production oriented service proceeds uniformly beyond all sectoral boundaries, the evolution into a service economy
largely varies among the regions of the FRG. Among all types of areas,
the large metropolitan areas - such as the cores of the agglomerations
Hamburg, Rhein-Ruhr, Rhein-Neckar, Stuttgart and München, sometimes
also called central or metropolitan areas - have been experiencing the
strongest change of functional structure.

At a first sight, the employment changes of these cities seem to contradict. For, the cores of agglomerations have had a particularly high
loss of employment in the last two decades.

Table 5:

Employment Changes in The Agglomerations of The F R G 1961 bis 1983

Agglomeration[2]	Employ-ment 1983 in '000s		Change rate[1] of regional percentage of total employment in the FRG		
	Core	Ring	Core	Ring	total
Hamburg	728.2	268.8	-17.4	+41.9	-6.9
Bremen	233.9	209.2	-15.4	+10.6	-4.9
Hannover	284.8	109.2	-14.8	+24.4	-6.6
Rhein-Ruhr	2 341.1	1 357.2	-16.9	-5.2	-13.0
- Ruhr	993.3	724.6	-25.6	-13.5	-20.4
- Rhein	1 347.8	632.6	-9.0	+6.4	-4.8
Rhein-Main	902.9	481.6	+8.3	+13.5	+10.1
Rhein-Neckar	348.1	225.6	-2.9	+12.4	+2.6
Karlsruhe	193.0	166.0	-4.3	+28.4	+8.5
Stuttgart	349.9	789.0	-10.0	+26.0	+12.2
München	725.9	290.0	+19.8	+20.9	+20.1
Nürnberg	358.5	127.1	+2.5	+9.2	+4.2
Berlin	699.7	-	-22.9	-	-22.9
All agglomerations	7 166.0	4 023.8	-8.7	+10.7	-3.5
Intermediate areas	6 831.3				+3.8
Peripheral areas	2 119.9				+7.5
Total FRG	20 141.0				

1) The shares are estimated on the basis of the Census 1961
and the Social Security Statistics 1983.
2) See map 1.

In the sixties, the spatial deconcentration process was mainly restricted to the redistribution of new additional working places. While
total employment in the FRG increased, most of the new jobs were created outside the agglomeration cores in their rings, in the intermediate or in the periphery; with the result that the intermediate and the
peripheral areas could strengthen their industrial base.

208

Map 1: **Employment Shares of Agglomeration Cores 1961 - 1983**

- percentage of total employment in the FRG -

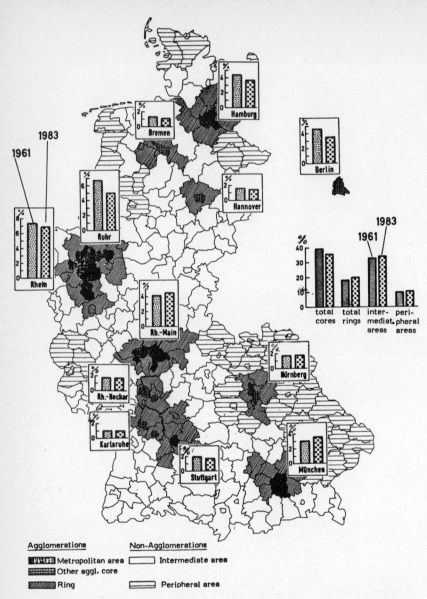

Agglomerations   Non-Agglomerations

▓▓▓ Metropolitan area   ☐ Intermediate area
▒▒▒ Other aggl. core
╱╱╱ Ring   ☰ Peripheral area

Since the early seventies, however, the expansion of employment has
stopped so that the redistribution potential of new working places has
sharply decreased. Yet, due to regionally differing loss rates the
deconcentration process is still going on: in the core areas jobs are
given up earlier and more frequently than in the rings of or outside

of the agglomerations. Particularly concerned are those cores which, in addition, have an unfavourable sectoral structure, such as the area of Ruhr, Bremen, Berlin and partly Hamburg. But even Stuttgart, a core area of strong industrial base, has experienced a large reduction of jobs in the last decade.

2.2 Changes in Functional Structure

Beyond the first impression, however, the loss of jobs within the cities is not only a particularly strong contraction process. At the same time, it is also a process of functional change by which the large metropolitan centres concentrate their activities more and more on dispositive and communicative activities, since the reduction of working places applies primarily to the production activities.

Most of these jobs are exposed to the pressure of international competition. In addition, their use of space is relatively intensive. Consequently, related to one unit of space, they can only achieve low profits, if at all. Thus, they have a rather weak position in intensive process of selection which is taking place in the agglomerations, especially in the metropolitan areas. The enormous rise of rents observed in the agglomeration cores during the last decades leads to the understanding that the more profitable activities are suitable to survive inside the agglomeration cores.

As the abovementioned social security statistics are available on the level of 'Kreise' (districts), the selection process can be observed in more detail for the years 1976 to 1983. During this period, employment in the agglomeration cores decreased by 277,000, or as percentage, by 3.7%. If only the reduction of production activities is considered, the loss in this functional group alone is of nearly the same size, namely 269,000. Thus, their loss amounts to 3.6 of the total employment in 1976, although in the core areas only less than one third (31%) of total employed persons were involved in production activities (cf. Table A1 in the Annex). Outside the cores, in the rings of agglomeration and in the intermediate areas the loss due to the reduction of production activities was only 1% of total jobs in 1976, whereas in the peripheral areas only 1,000 production jobs were closed, that means less than 0.1% of total employment in 1976.

Among the metropolitan areas especially the so called old industrial- ised region of Ruhr was concerned by a strong decrease of production. Because of its less favourable sectoral structure this could be ex- pected. However, the weak competitiveness of the industries in the Ruhr centre has not only affected the production area, but the whole regional economy. Although the decrease in production amounts to near- ly 8% of total employment, which, by far, means the biggest loss among all other agglomeration cores, the total reduction was even -13%. Thus, other functions, especially the consumer oriented functions like commercial or boarding services, but also store and transport activi- ties have decreased. Even total production oriented services, i.e., the sum of technical and administrative services as well as of con- sulting, EDP and marketing, have been reduced. Certainly, the loss is restricted to the administrative area, and here more to the lower and middle levels. But the technical and the other production oriented services, too, made only a relatively small contribution to additional employment. Among the other metropolitan areas, a similar decrease of production oriented services can only be observed in Berlin, where the loss in those functions even amounts to 3% of total employment in 1976.

In comparison, the other metropolitan areas, especially the regions of Rhine-Main, Stuttgart and Munich, increased their production oriented services so far, that the loss of production activities could be part- ly equalised, partly more than compensated. At the top is Munich, where the production decline (-1%) is far exceeded by the increase of production oriented services (+5%).

The development outside the metropolitan areas surprises insofar as it contradicts certain hypotheses which postulate that most of the dis- positive and communicative functions have strong locational preferenc- es for areas of high density because of their information potential and their contact facilities. Actually, at least in the FRG, the less congested and more peripheral areas could increase their production oriented services by and large. On average, the contribution to total employment in these regions was even higher (+3% of total employment in 1976) than in all cores of agglomeration (+1%) or than in the metropolitan areas without the Ruhr region (+2%).

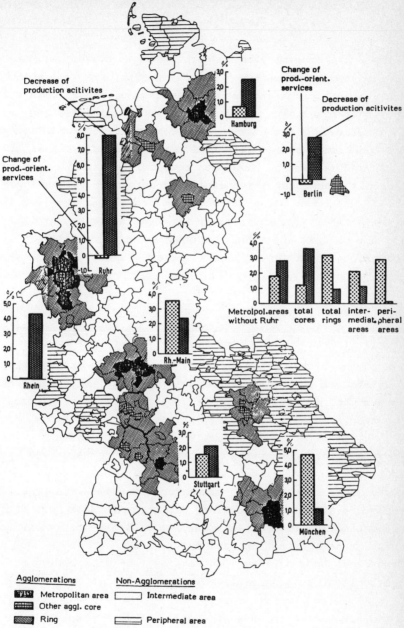

Map 2: Functional Components of Change in The Metropolitan Areas
- Absolute loss of production activities resp.
absolute change of production- oriented services 1976 - 1983
as percentages of regional total employment 1976 -

With regard to the traditional regional disparities in economic potential between central and peripheral areas this development surely
calls for a positive judgement. Yet, there are two important points to

be taken into account. First, in areas outside the agglomerations the gains in employment primarily concentrate on those functions which are usually carried out on a lower level of organisational hierarchy: among all additional jobs of administrative services in the peripheral areas (+21% of regional total employment in 1976) only 7% were executive functions (+1.5% of regional total employment in 1986). In the agglomeration cores, the relationship is just reverse. Here, the number of new jobs in executive functions was higher (+0.9%) than the total increase in administrative services (+0.5%). It follows that the jobs of lower hierarchical levels must have diminished. An extreme example is Stuttgart where an increase of 1,100 persons in executive functions is opposed to an overall reduction in total administrative services by 2,700 persons.

A similar influence of hierarchical level could be observed in the group of technical services. In the agglomeration cores three of four persons (77%) who were additionally engaged in technical services do research and development. In the peripheral area the corresponding share only amounts to 30%. In contrast, even in the Ruhr area, the worst among all metropolitan areas, more than every second additionally employed person (56%) was involved in R&D.

The second point which should be mentioned is the regional difference in the intensity of structural change. It was demonstrated that the increase of production oriented services was relatively high outside the agglomeration cores. On the other hand, the decrease of production activities has to be taken into account also in order to estimate the overall effect of structural change. While the production loss in the metropolitan areas was extremely large, it was rather small outside the agglomerations and can even be neglected in the peripheral areas. Consequently, both developments taken together, the change of functional structure towards production oriented services was stronger inside the agglomerations cores, especially within the metropolitan areas, than outside the agglomerations.

2.3 The Functional Structure of Regions

As a whole, the regionally varying degree of change actually results in a clear functional division of labour between locations in and outside the agglomeration cores. In 1983 more than every third employed person (37%) in the agglomeration cores was engaged in production oriented services. If only the metropolitan areas (without the Ruhr

region) are considered, the share even rises to 40%, that is almost
double the percentage in the peripheral regions (22%), which, in turn,
does not differ very much from the share of production oriented services in the intermediate regions (25%) or even from the corresponding
percentage in the agglomeration rings (27%; cf. Map 3 and Table A.2)
in the Annex).

Map 3:   The Functional Structure of Metropolitan Areas 1983

- Functional groups as percentage of regional total employment 1983 -

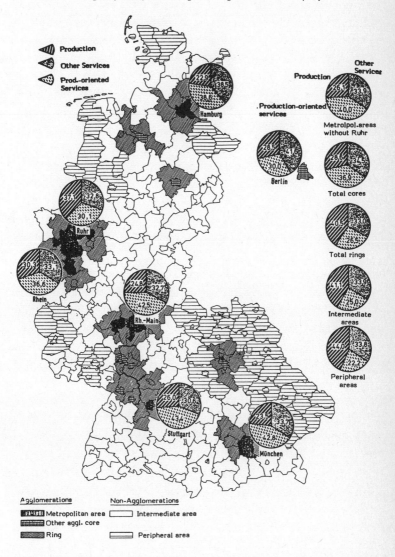

With respect to production activities the relationship between metropolitan and peripheral areas is just the opposite since the regional

shares of the remaining, mostly person and consumer oriented services are rather identical (35% in the cores, 34% in the periphery). In the agglomeration cores only every third to fourth employed person(29%) is engaged in production - in the metropolitan areas even only every fifth (22%) - whereas it is almost every second 44%) in the peripheral locations. Comparing the differences between the type of areas, the strongest break is between cores and rings of agglomeration, whereas the increase of production share from ring to intermediate and, finally, to peripheral areas is rather low (which is quite similar to the regional differences in production oriented services, but, of course, with reversed premises). The functional division of labour between the regions in the FRG is the more marked, the higher the hierarchical level of the functions. 46% of total technical services in the FRG are performed in the agglomeration cores, in respect of R&D the share is 54%. Considering the metropolitan areas (without the Ruhr) 26% of total technical services in the FRG are located there, but 32% of total R&D. In the same way, the share of the latter areas is higher in the case of executive services than with regard to total administrative services.

Instead of the regional distribution of functions, in Diagram 3, the regional degree of specialisation is used in order to demonstrate the functional division of labour in the FRG. For example, 3.2% of total employed people in the cores are involved in R&D (cf. Table A.2 in the Annex). In Diagram 3, this percentage is expressed in terms of the corresponding FRG average: since in the Federal Republic as a whole, 2.1% of total employment is engaged in R&D, Diagram 3 shows the value 152.4% for the agglomeration cores with regard to R&D. Likewise, the peripheral areas only attain 47.6% of the Federal average, as only 1% of their total employment is involved in R&D.

Diagram 3 reveals that not only the hierarchical, but also the educational level has an influence on the degree of regional specialisation (whereby the combination of functional and educational levels may indicate differences in functions which cannot be realised by only using the statistical definition of functions). Among all functions shown in Diagram 3 the regional concentration on agglomeration cores is the highest in the case of persons who are engaged in R&D as well as being graduates. Thus, the share of these persons in regional total employment shows the strongest centre periphery decline.

Diagram 3:   **Centre-Periphery-Decline in The Functional Structure**
- Selected functions as percentage of regional total employment;
regional percentages in terms of the FRG average percentage -

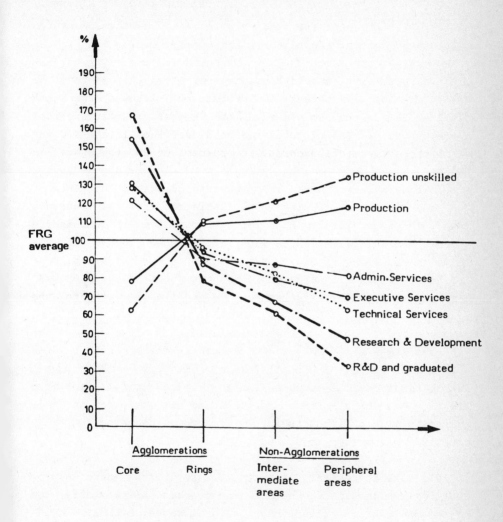

To analyse the reasons why such a strong regional specialisation of
higher-level functions has happened is beyond the scope of this paper.

Among others, one important development, i.e., the selection process within the metropolitan areas has already been indicated above. Furthermore, the importance of the sectoral structure of an area should be shortly mentioned at least. In fact, the specialisation of metropolitan areas on higher-level production oriented services is also supported by their sectoral structure: service sectors or manufacturing industries of high service intensity, e.g., the chemical industry, are largely represented in the metropolitan areas.

However, the sectoral structure of regions, or reversely regarded, the regional distribution of sectors cannot be the decisive influence since the centre periphery decline exists in each sectoral group more or less intensively. Whether it is the clothing or the leather industry or the electrical or the mechanical engineering, in each group of the manufacturing industry the centrally located plants have a higher degree of production oriented services than the establishments in the rings of or outside the agglomerations. Consequently, the regional distribution of sectors is only of limited importance for explaining the functional specialisation of regions. Rather, the location of sectors itself appears to be a result of those forces - among other factors, of course - which are responsible for the functional differences in the economic specialisation of regions.

3.   CONCLUDING REMARKS

Although only first results could be reported - the empirical investigation is just beginning - the analytical concept proposed in this paper delivers promising insights into the structural changes of the economy and its spatial implications.

Firstly, leaving aside regional aspects, the functional differentiation of activities reveals the general tendencies of structural and technological changes more clearly than an exclusively sectoral classification. For example it facilitates recognition of the consequences for the future kinds of occupations and the estimation of future requirements of qualifications.

Furthermore, in respect to innovation research it stresses the importance of research and development as well as of other (less technical) production services for the competitiveness of firms, insofar as it suggests that proficient products are not the cause, but a symptom of successful firms. The primary reason for the competitiveness of firms lies in their capability to develop new products and production procedures superior to their competitors. The results indicate that own activities in research and development, strategic planning, marketing or EDP appear to be an urgent essential for such a capacity.

In comparison, a sectoral approach by analysing the prospects of selected products is much more insecure. Obviously, to prognosticate the future success of products is extremely difficult and uncertain for policy makers. Thus, instead of promoting the production of some products by, for example, capital subsidies, policy measures which strengthen the general capacity for innovation and structural adaptation by stimulating the firm's own activities in research and development and other production services, appear much more promising.

Secondly, on the regional level, the functional differentiation of activities helps to understand the process of regional change. It is especially a valuable concept for revealing the structure and the development of the spatial division of labour. For example, the optimistic evaluation of recent tendencies of decentralisation are to be relativised when functional aspects are additionally taken into account.

It is true that the areas outside the large agglomerations could increase their employment, even regardless of which function (or sector) is considered. However, the speed of the deglomeration process is much lower for production oriented services of higher hierarchical as well as educational level. On the other side, less valued activities, like production and storage, have been extensively disclosed in the highly congested centres. Thus, in summary, the specialisation of the metropolitan areas on higher valued production services has still risen in recent years.

It is not possible to evaluate all regional consequences in detail which are generated by this functional division of labour between the central and the peripheral areas of the FRG. One effect, however, is rather obvious: the agglomerations Ruhr and Berlin (as well as Bremen which was not particularly analysed in this paper) have to be regarded as the main losers in the changes of the spatial division of labour. On the one hand, they have experienced all the negative trends which

also happened in the other metropolitan areas, i.e., a strong loss of
activities. On the other hand, however, the loss has not been restricted to the less valued services, but has also included important
production and consumer oriented services. Thus, there has happened a
change for the worse not only in quantitative, but also in qualitative
terms.

In the other metropolitan areas, especially in Munich, Stuttgart and
in the Rhein-Main core, the quantitative loss was at least partly compensated by an amelioration of the functional structure of jobs.
Finally, the areas in the rings and outside the agglomerations could
profit by a net increase in jobs whereby the amount of additional
higher valued jobs, however, was relatively low.

REFERENCES

Clark, Colin, The Conditions of Economic Progress, London, 1940.

Fisher, A.G.B., 'A note on tertiary production', Economic Journal 62,
    1952, pp. 820-825.

Fourastie, J., Die grosse Hoffnung des zwanzigsten Jahrhunderts,
    Cologne, 1954.

Lawrence, R.Z., 'Is trade deindustrializing America?' Brookings
    Papers, 1983, pp. 129-171.

Franzmeyer, F., 'Zum Wandel der volkswirtschaftlichen Produktions-
    struktur im internationalen Vergleich', DIW-Wochenbericht 6/83,
    1983, pp. 69-76.

Annex A.1

Changes in the Functional Structure of Metropolitan Areas
1976 - 1983

Area [1]	Total employment 1976 in '000s	Absolute change of selected functions as per mille of regional total employment 1976								
		Production functions	Technical services total	thereof: R & D	Production - oriented services / Admin. services total	thereof: executive services	Consulting, EDP, marketing	Commercial services	Health and educational services	Domestic, boarding a. other services
All cores of agglomerations	7 442.7	-36.1	+6.1	+4.7	+0.5	+0.9	+5.4	-0.3	+14.4	-14.2
thereof:										
- Hamburg	753.0	-25.2	+4.4	+2.5	-2.8	+0.4	+6.1	-0.2	+13.1	-10.1
- Rhein-Ruhr	2 570.4	-58.8	+2.2	+2.4	-5.8	-0.2	+2.9	-3.7	+12.3	-22.0
= Ruhr	1 138.3	-79.1	+3.9	+2.2	-6.9	-0.6	+1.4	-7.2	+12.1	-30.1
= Rhein	1 431.8	-42.7	+0.8	+2.4	-5.0	+0.0	+4.1	-1.0	+12.5	-15.5
- Rhein-Main	889.3	-23.7	+10.9	+6.2	+16.0	+2.7	+8.7	+5.6	+12.9	-8.8
- Stuttgart	357.2	-20.9	+12.3	+11.1	-4.5	+3.1	+7.4	-2.8	+11.0	-12.7
- München	688.6	-10.9	+13.7	+11.6	+21.0	+3.6	+12.3	+11.6	+15.8	-5.1
- Berlin (West)	729.7	-28.1	+0.6	+1.7	-7.1	+1.2	+3.8	-6.6	+21.0	-11.7
All rings of agglomerations	3 840,9	-9.5	+7.8	+4.0	+20.4	+2.0	+3.7	+11.7	+21.7	-5.9
Intermediate areas	6 633,2	-11.3	+6.9	+2.8	+14.8	+1.1	+2.9	+8.8	+21.3	-7.1
Peripheral areas	2 006.3	-0.7	+6.1	+1.8	+20.6	+1.5	+2.5	+12.8	+22.3	-3.5
Total FRG	19 923.2	-19.1	+6.7	+3.6	+11.1	+1.2	+3.9	+6.4	+18.9	-9.2

1) See map 1.

Annex A.2   The Functional Structure of Metropolitan Areas 1983

Area 1)	Total employment 1976 in '000s	Share of selected functions as percentage of regional total employment 1983 resp. total employment = 100%								
		Production functions	Technical services total	thereof: R & D	Production - oriented services Admin. services total	thereof: executive services	Consulting, EDP, marketing	Commercial services	Health and educational services	Domestic, boarding a. other services
All cores of agglomerations	7 166,0	28,6	8,7	3,2	25,1	2,6	3,1	9,4	7,7	8,4
thereof:										
- Hamburg	728,2	22,9	6,6	2,4	28,3	3,1	3,7	11,1	7,6	9,3
- Rhein-Ruhr	2 341,1	33,2	8,7	2,7	22,7	2,5	2,5	9,2	7,2	7,4
= Ruhr	993,3	37,1	9,1	2,4	19,1	2,0	1,8	8,8	7,7	7,3
= Rhein	1 347,8	30,3	8,4	2,7	25,3	2,8	3,0	9,6	6,9	7,4
- Rhein-Main	902,9	24,8	9,1	3,4	29,6	3,3	3,8	9,4	6,8	8,1
- Stuttgart	349,9	26,0	10,6	4,4	28,7	3,1	4,1	8,1	6,7	7,6
- München	725,9	23,5	10,2	4,7	27,9	3,0	4,7	9,3	7,4	9,1
- Berlin (West)	699,7	28,5	6,2	2,3	21,3	2,0	2,5	9,0	11,6	11,7
All rings of agglomeration	4 023,8	40,5	6,5	1,8	18,6	1,9	1,5	8,8	7,6	7,3
Intermediate areas	6 831,3	41,2	5,6	1,4	18,0	1,6	1,4	8,6	8,2	8,3
Periphera areas	2 119,9	44,0	4,3	1,0	16,8	1,4	1,1	8,5	7,5	8,6
Total FRG	20 141,0	36,9	6,7	2,1	20,5	2,0	2,0	8,9	7,8	8,2

1) See Map 1.

SPATIAL DIMENSIONS OF INNOVATION
AND EMPLOYMENT: SOME DUTCH RESULTS
Els Hoogteijling, Jan Willem Gunning
and Peter Nijkamp

1.   INTRODUCTION

Innovations in the industrial sector are the outgrowth of technology
dynamics. In recent years, technology impact assessment has become an
important and intriguing research issue. The conditions for and - more
importantly - the consequences of technological development have also
been given much attention in economic analysis, particularly because
it is widely believed among economists that structural economic changes and technology growth are two closely intertwined phenomena (see
also Klein 1978). Consequently, technology research has received increasing attention from the side of economists.

In a series of studies, attention has been drawn to the intricate relationship between technological progress and economic dynamics (see
among others Clark et al. 1981, Forrester 1977, Kleinknecht 1983,
Mensch 1979). Clearly, this relationship has many aspects. In a recent
study on the economics of technological development, Stoneman (1983)
distinguished three major aspects, viz. the generation of new technology, its diffusion pattern and its socioeconomic impacts.

It is clear that each of these aspects has important links to employment. For instance, the availability of a skilled labour pool may provide a stimulus for technological innovation (the 'breeding place'
hypothesis, e.g.); innovation diffusion may - either in a hierarchical
filtering down process or in a multiple nuclei process - generate new
jobs in other industrial branches or in other regions; new technological developments may be labour saving (implying a negative impact on
employment) or labour using (due to direct or indirect multiplier effects).

Usually, technological innovations are not uniformly spread over all
sectors of the economy - and consequently not uniformly over all regions of a spatial system, but usually concentrated in a limited

number of key sectors - and consequently only in a specific region (or set of regions) offering a favourable locational profile for innovative activities in a certain sector. Thus, it is evident that cities or regions in a spatial system represent a geographical projection of technological developments in various industrial branches. As different locational profiles in different regions lead to variations in spatial industrial specialisation, the pertaining employment effects exhibit also a strong urban or regional dimension (see also Aydalot 1984 and Gillespie 1983). Thus, to a large extent, one may consider regional labour dynamics as a projection of sectoral technology shifts.

In the case of a uniform dispersion of structural economic changes and technological innovations, all regions of a spatial system would follow the national trajectory of technological and economic developments and/or fluctuations. However, as explained before, the unequal locational profiles of diverse regions may cause spatial imbalances in technology adoption and - consequently - in labour market effects. This is illustrated in Figure 1 exhibiting some spatial developments in The Netherlands (see Nijkamp 1982), where the symbols C, D and P stand respectively for the industrialised central provinces, the intermediate (halfway) provinces, and the northern peripheral provinces.

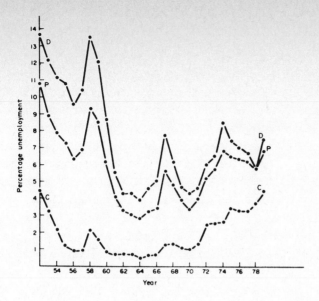

Figure 1. Evolution of unemployment in various Dutch regions
        (1952 - 1979).

The foregoing remarks have indicated the existence of close links between technological innovation, employment, and urban or regional development. In Section 2, a selection of some relevant literature on
the interaction between technological innovation and employment will
be reviewed in more detail, while next in Section 3, the spatial dimensions of technology development and labour market will be described
briefly. Section 4 will then present some general findings from a case
study in The Netherlands among industrial firms, followed by a presentation of empirical results on the regional aspects of technological
innovation and unemployment in The Netherlands in Section 5.

2.   TECHNOLOGICAL INNOVATION AND EMPLOYMENT: SOME VIEWPOINTS

In the context of the present paper, innovation will be regarded as a
process of research, development, application and exploitation of a
new (as yet not commercially implemented) technology. Innovation is
regarded as one of the key factors inducing industrial dynamics and
assuring survival in a competitive system. Lack of innovation (or of
diffusion or adoption of innovation) may lead to unstable economic
growth, with serious repercussions for the labour market. On the other

hand, an uncoordinated introduction of new technologies may lead to various imbalances on the labour market, due to structural changes in the (qualitative) composition of labour demand.

Popular discussions on the employment effects of innovations often centre around the question whether the adoption of a particular innovation will reduce total employment in the long run. This question is to some extent misguided: any innovation makes an increase in employment possible, and if this potential is not realised, usually market rigidities rather than the innovation itself are to be blamed. In a sense, the fear that jobs will be lost is either irrational - and there is indeed often a Luddite streak in the debate - or it is based on a confusion of gross and net employment effects; a failure to realise that the loss of particular kinds of existing jobs will be offset by the creation of new types of jobs, in either a quantitative or a qualitative sense.

The reasons for the coexistence of conflicting views in the academic literature are rather diverse. Many economists involved in theoretical or applied research on technological innovation and employment continue to be influenced by the growth theory literature of the 1950s and 1960s. This manifests itself in four ways. First, the effects and not the causes of innovations are studied. Technical progress is assumed to be exogenous in the analysis and is usually (and conveniently) also assumed to proceed smoothly. One implication of this approach is that innovations cannot cause unbalanced growth. Consequently, some of the adjustment problems are assumed away. Secondly, there is little or no attention for the process of diffusion and adoption of an innovation, since growth theory focusses on the long run so that short or medium term socioeconomic or spatial frictions inherent in the introduction of a new technology are ignored. Thirdly, the nature of a product or of a production process is considered as fixed so that life cycle effects (with large impacts on locational patterns and on the labour market) are ignored. Finally, markets are usually (implicitly) assumed to be perfect. This is particularly important in the case of the labour market. An innovation typically implies a change in the skill composition and in the geographical distribution of employment. If geographical mobility and skill acquisition is hampered by market rigidities then imbalances will arise, unemployment may result and the process of diffusion may even grind to a halt.

Some of the more recent literature differs from this traditional (and strongly macroeconomically oriented) approach on all four counts. There is indeed a growing awareness of the strict limitations inherent in conventional approaches. An example is the work of Freeman et al. (1982). They emphasise that technical change does <u>not</u> occur <u>smoothly</u> over time, stress the <u>interrelatedness</u> of innovations, (e.g. the followup innovations in the diffusion process of a major innovation) and they analyse the <u>life cycle</u> of an innovation rather than just the end result. In the early phase of the diffusion process the new technology is not yet standardised. In this phase employment growth can be rapid. Maturity is reached when the market begins to be saturated and when the production process becomes standardised. Economies of scale then become important, the process becomes more capital intensive and the innovation generates less additional employment. Freeman et al. also introduced factor market rigidities and thereby the possibility that excess capacity (in declining industries) and labour shortages (especially in new sectors, for new skills) can coexist.

The 'evolutionary' model of Nelson and Winter (1984) provides a second example. Their work is based on a microeconomic analysis of decision making within firms. This gives results which differ from those in the traditional approach because decision rules can vary between firms and also over time. A firm can change its decision rule in response to external developments, so that e.g. diffusion can be modelled as imitating the behaviour of an early innovator. The work of Nelson and Winter, like that of Freeman et al. has many aspects which place it in the tradition of Schumpeter.

What matters in the present context is, first, the emphasis in the recent literature on differences between locations and skills in the employment effects of innovations (and on the way such differences can be reinforced by market imperfections); secondly, the increased attention to new behavioural, 'bottom up' approaches; and thirdly, and most importantly, the recognition that employment effects in the short run and in the long run can be very different.

3. SPATIAL ASPECTS OF TECHNOLOGICAL DEVELOPMENTS AND LABOUR MARKETS

Technological innovation has a significant impact on the efficiency of a spatial system and hence on its labour market development. In the present section particular attention will be paid to the complex triangle of technological progress, employment and regional or urban development.

In the past decade, various studies have been made on this triangle, with a particular view of explaining the backgrounds of structural spatial dynamics in Western societies. We will give here a concise overview of this triangular relationship.

A first interesting analysis of spatial dynamics in the context of Schumpeterian innovation concepts was provided by Thomas (1972) who made an attempt at identifying American urban fluctuations due to urban immigration. These migration movements were codetermined by technological and economic growth of these cities and exerted a significant effect on the labour market (particularly in the construction, building and housing sector). By demonstrating the existence of a relationship between economic growth, technology, employment and urban evolution, Thomas was able to provide a plausible basis for the validity of the 'urban waves' concept in US cities before World War II. After World War II such waves could no longer be identified due to restrictions on immigration.

A second author who has provided a substantial analysis of growth patterns of (mainly industrial regions), is Pred (1977). Industrial growth and population growth have - via the labour market - a mutually reinforcing effect upon each other, caused by cumulative and circular feedback processes in a competitive spatial system. Economic base multipliers and agglomeration economies induce urban dynamics, which is in turn favoured by technological progress. Therefore, in a spatial context, diffusion and adoption of innovation is of crucial importance for urban and regional growth. Pred has illustrated his theory on the basis of the industrial evolution and urban and regional dynamics in Western Europe (inter alia by studying the spatial interaction and communication patterns based on a geographical multiple nuclei structure).

Another interesting contribution has been provided by Jacobs (1977), who explains urban cyclical processes from the diversity of functions (for instance, living, working, shopping, recreation) in a city. She uses the notion of an optimal urban diversity which is composed of four elements: 1) a wide variety of functions (including employment opportunities), 2) a variable age structure of buildings, 3) accessibility of urban facilities, and 4) an appropriate concentration of urban population. Lack of diversity undermines urban dynamics and may cause a downward spiral movement of cities. On the other hand, over attractiveness of a city (leading inter alia to congestion, environmental decay and unrestricted land use competition) may cause a self-destruction of the diversity in a competitive urban system.

A transfer of the product cycle concept to urban systems has been made by Norton (1979), who studied city life cycles in the US. In his view, particularly the older cities are suffering from stagnation and decline due to their compact layout, the urban segregation and its related dual labour market, and the inadequate tax base (due to the flight to suburbs by wealthier people). Furthermore, older cities are mainly based on the nineteenth century industrialisation. New cities are more spacious, less segregated and have a more satisfactory tax base. Due to a structural economic and technological change from the primary and secondary sector to the tertiary and quaternary sector, older cities were unable to compete with the flexibility and innovation potential offered by new cities and suburbs. Consequently, structural changes in the labour markets in a spatial system are dependent on the position of a city in the urban life cycle.

Finally, Allen et al (1981) have developed a set of models of spatial settlements and structures as dynamic self-organising systems. In these (mainly theoretical) models spatial systems are analysed as dynamic, nonlinear entities, based on principles of dynamic self-organisation of cities and regions. Various components of a spatial system could be included, such as transportation, housing, employment, social overhead capital, R & D etc. Spatial and economic self-structuring processes could be generated by establishing links to decision making, behavioural spatial patterns and hierarchical interactions. By stimulating next spatial development patterns, the economic resurgence and the spatial dynamics (including cyclical processes) could be imitated. In the simulation experiments, especially the interactions between employment, residential patterns, the tertiary sector, and transportation and communication were taken into account. The model itself was based on rather simple nonlinear dynamic relationships including attractiveness and bottleneck factors.

Two interesting conclusions can be drawn from these contributions. First, there is a wide variety of theoretical models for analysing the spatial dimensions of innovation and employment. Secondly, despite these variations all these studies have demonstrated that technology is a major driving force, in one way or another, for spatial economic dynamics and hence for the dynamics of urban and regional labour markets.

The relationship between locational conditions and technological innovation deserve a closer examination. In the literature on urban and regional productivity analysis it is often suggested that large scale industrial concentrations and city size favour innovative ability due to a higher efficiency potential, more business diversification and an appropriate breeding ground for technological innovation (see among others, Carlino 1977, Kawashima 1981, and Nelson and Winter 1977). Malecki (1979) however, has shown that the innovative potential of traditional large agglomerations is declining relative to medium sized cities. Apparently, innovative activity is also suffering from diseconomies of scale (see also Sveikauskas 1979), so that congestion phenomena may have a negative impact on the location of innovative jobs. Several authors have even claimed that urban growth patterns in Western countries exhibit a 'clean break with the past' (e.g., Vining and Kontuly 1977), although this reversal of past trends has been questioned by others (see Gordon 1982).

The abovementioned issues also play a crucial role in recent discussions on the locational and employment profile of innovative high-tech industries. Here also, contrasting views are expressed by various authors. The locational pattern of the high-tech sector - an extremely dynamic and mobile sector - appears to be a source of much confusion.

The relationship between locational quality (or the location profile) and the presence of technology intensive activities (measured on the basis of R & D efforts, innovations, number of highly skilled employees or any other relevant indicator) is a research issue which is of utmost importance in an effective regional development strategy (see among others McQuaid and Langridge 1984, Rogers and Larsen 1984, Doody and Munzer 1981, and Hall and Markusen 1983).

The locational aspects of the high technology sector have especially been investigated by Premus (1984), who used the following attributes for characterising this sector: a high labour intensity regarding highly skilled employment, a strong science based product design and implementation, and a large amount of R & D expenditures. In this framework, the following locational aspects of high technology (including the labour market aspects) may be mentioned (see also Levy 1983, Oakey 1982, and Thwaites 1982):

- a strong orientation towards information, as far as it is available in research institutes and educational centres (including job hopping);
- the availability of a highly qualified labour force (also acting as a keep factor for mobile employees);
- the quality of the housing and labour market (in terms of environmental attractiveness);
- the presence of various financial incentives (tax systems, venture capital, etc.).

In this context, a cross-country comparison of the evolution of the high-tech sector and of its geographical dispersion is fraught with difficulties, as the spatial scale of countries and the size of the sectors involved may be totally different. For instance, many states in the USA are larger than The Netherlands as a whole, so that cross comparisons have to be undertaken with caution. In any case, it turns out that the high-tech sector in many countries is exhibiting a dual spatial pattern, viz. a concentration of head offices etc. near larger agglomerations marked by scale advantages and a dispersion of production activities towards less central areas.

Thus the labour market developments associated with the evolution of new technologies may be extremely unstable and deserve more profound attention (see also the contribution of Bouman and Verhoef on the spatial employment pattern of the high-tech industry in The Netherlands, published in the present volume).

These remarks indicate once more that there is an intricate (though not always an easily identifiable) mutual relationship between innovative activities and local and regional employment dimensions. Consequently, more substantial insight into this relationship has to be gathered from empirical research. This will be the subject of the next sections.

4. GENERAL RESULTS FROM AN INDUSTRIAL ENQUIRY IN THE NETHERLANDS

The present authors have been involved in a recently completed extensive Dutch study on 'Innovation and the Labour Market'. As part of
this study a postal survey was conducted which covered a sample of
1000 Dutch firms in both the industrial and service sectors. In the
questionnaire the term 'innovation' was precisely described. A clear
distinction was made between product, process and combined innovations
(in the industrial sectors), while for the tertiary sector - by means
of a list of examples - the type of innovation to be reported on by
the firms was included. The questionnaire, which was sent out early in
1984, contained a large series of questions on innovation, R & D,
bottlenecks, institutional measures, etc. and also a subset of questions about the number of innovations adopted by the firm in the preceding two years and about changes in employment and sales. The response rate was 30 per cent; 295 usable questionnaires were returned.
This is disappointingly low (although conceivable, given the fact
that employment issues are regarded as delicate items in an enquiry).
An analysis of variables (e.g., size in terms of employment), which
were known for all firms (whether they responded or not), fortunately
revealed however, no evidence that the responding firms formed a
biased subset of the sample.

We present some of the results in Tables 1 - 5. Given the space available, only a very small subset of the results can be presented here.
The reader is referred to Hoogteijling (1985) for more details. Table
1 shows that 60 per cent of industrial firms adopted at least one innovation in 1982 or 1983 and, more importantly, that there are large
intersectoral differences, e.g., only 40 per cent of firms in the textile, leather and wool industries were involved in innovation. It is
interesting to observe that no clear relation between growth of sales
and innovation activity emerges at the level of firms. While Table 2
indicates that firms which adopted three or more innovations in the
two year period are disproportionately represented (as one would expect) in the group of rapidly growing firms, this difference turned
out not to be statistically significant. Similarly, and contrary to
what is often suggested, there is no clear relation between innovation
and changes in employment at the firm level. Table 3 shows that the
distribution of employment changes over firms does not differ appre-
ciably between innovating and non innovating firms. This negative evidence must be treated with some caution. First, because a firm which

231

has gone out of business because of its failure to innovate cannot be part of the sample. Secondly, because some of the innovations will have been adopted too recently to affect a firm's total employment, especially if the firm had 'hoarded labour' during the recession years. While Tables 2 and 3 indicate that there is no clear link between innovation activities and the growth of output or of employment, Table 4 shows that not even sales and employment are positively related. More than half of the growing firms (excluding those which expanded their sales by more than 10 per cent per year) continued to shed labour.

Firms were also asked about their reasons for adopting an innovation. Almost 60 per cent of the respondents indicated that a reduction of the wage bill was an important objective. In 56 per cent of those firms employment fell in 1982 and 1983 (panel a of Table 5). One out of three firms indicated that a more extreme objective (avoiding contraction of closing of the firm) played an important role and of those firms 60 per cent reduced their workforce in the two year period (panel b of Table 5).[1]

TABLE 1

Percentage of Firms by Activity and Number of Innovations

ISIC-code	Description	Number of Innovations (1982-1983)				
		none	1 or 2	more than 2	total %	number absolute
31	food manufacturing	37	24	39	100	38
32,33	textile, leather & wood industries	61	12	27	100	33
34	paper & printing industries	49	33	19	100	43
35,36	chemical and non-metallic industries	30	32	38	100	47
37, 38, 39	metal, machinery & other manufacturing	36	29	35	100	134
3	total manufacturing	40	27	33	100	295

TABLE 2

Percentages of Firms by Number of Innovations
and Growth of Output

Number of innovations	Growth of output (average 1982-1983)				
	less than 0%	0-10 %	more than 10%	total %	number (absolute)
none	22	54	25	100	97
1 or 2	24	56	21	100	63
more than 2	18	43	39	100	88

TABLE 3

Percentage of Firms by Number of Innovation and Growth of Employment

Number of innovations	Growth of employment (average 1982-1983)				
	less than 0%	0-5 %	more than 5%	total %	number (absolute)
none	46	34	20	100	109
1 or 2	48	36	16	100	77
more than 2	49	24	27	100	98

While interesting, the interpretation of these results is not
straightforward. On the one hand, the innovations may be seen as the
cause of the loss of employment: the firm is practising 'triage', destroying some jobs in order to save the remaining ones. On the other
hand, the results may be seen as supporting the 'trigger hypothesis: if
a firm's innovation activity is triggered by the fall in employment,
innovations are adopted to arrest and reverse a declining trend.

TABLE 4
Percentages of Firms by Growth of Output and of Employment

Growth of output (average 1982-1983)	Growth of employment (average 1982-1983)				
	less than 0 %	0-5 %	more than 5%	total %	number (absolute)
less than 0 %	69	25	6	100	51
0-10 %	54	31	15	100	120
more than 10%	16	35	49	100	68

TABLE 5
Innovating   Firms   by Reason of Innovation
and Growth of Employment

a. reduction of wage bill

	Growth of Employment (average 1982-1983)				
	less than 0 %	0-5%	more than 5 %	total %	number (absolute)
not an important motive	42	29	29	100	65
important motive	56	27	17	100	93

$$(\chi_2^2 = 4.16; \ s = .13)$$

b. to avert a contraction or closing down of the firm

	less than 0 %	0-5%	more than 5 %	total %	number (absolute)
not an important motive	43	33	24	100	107
important motive	60	23	17	100	53

$$(\chi_2^2 = 4.29; \ s = .12)$$

5. <u>SPATIAL ASPECTS OF INNOVATION AND EMPLOYMENT IN THE NETHERLANDS</u>

In this section attention will be focussed on the specific regional
dimensions of the interrelationships of innovation and employment.
Table 6 represents some results for enterprises by region and type of
innovation. In contrast to the commonly held belief (based on the incubator hypothesis) that the innovative climate is more favourable in
large cities, which have a relatively large supply of educational and
knowledge centres, a dense communication network, and a   concentration
of industries and R & D services, the innovative activity in the three
major cities (Amsterdam, Rotterdam and The Hague) is less than in the
remaining part of the country. This supports the view that the innovative potential of large cities and traditional areas are no longer
able to compete with more flexible new cities and recently (re)indus-
trialised areas with a modern infrastructure.

R & D activities in the Randstad,[2] however, do not systematically
differ from R & D activities in other areas in The Netherlands (see
Table 8). This suggests that though R & D favours in   general

innovation, specific regional aspects also play a crucial role; the empirical evidence in The Netherlands indicates that R & D is more effective in the Northern, Southern and Eastern regions than in the Randstad.

This hypothesis is supported by Table 7. It shows a threeway contingency table of enterprises by region, R & D behaviour and innovations. In order to prevent too low values of cell frequencies, and to provide a clear interpretation, the sample has been subdivided into two areas; the Randstad and the rest of The Netherlands. Table 7 has been further analysed with a loglinear model for contingency tables.[3]

The outcomes for the successive variants of the model are given below.

basic model:	λ	df	$\chi^2.95(df)$
(REGION).(R&D).(INNOVATIONS)	116.3	12	21.0
extensions of the basic model	$\Delta\lambda$	Δdf	$\chi^2.95(\Delta df)$
(REGION.R&D).(INNOVATIONS)	.9	2	5.99
(R&D.INNOVATIONS).(REGION)	100.1	4	9.49
(INNOVATIONS.REGION).(R&D)	9.9	2	5.99

Clearly, the independence of the separate variables could not be accepted, so that the first order interaction effects between region, R & D behaviour, and innovations, and between region and innovations added new significant information. This supports the suggestion by the previous tables that:

1) there is a close interrelationship between R & D activity and innovative activity;
2) given the interrelationship, the areas outside the Randstad favour innovation more than the Randstad itself;
3) there is hardly any relationship between region and R & D behaviour.

TABLE 6
Enterprises by Region and Type of Innovation

Type of Innovation (1982-1983)

region	none %	1 or 2 %	more than 2 %	total %	number (absolute)
North	40	33	28	100	43
East	38	20	42	100	65
South-East	40	26	34	100	58
South-West	39	19	42	100	31
Middle	29	25	46	100	30
Rotterdam	43	37	20	100	30
The Hague	48	24	29	100	21
Amsterdam	43	48	9	100	23

TABLE 7
Enterprises by Region, R & D Behaviour and
Number of Innovations

	Randstad			Outside of Randstad		
	none	1 or 2	more than 2	none	1 or 2	more than 2
no R & D	22	9	1	69	22	17
informal R&D	6	8	2	7	18	14
R&D department	5	10	11	8	14	52

TABLE 8
Enterprises by Region and R & D Behaviour

Region	no R&D %	R&D Behaviour informal R&D %	R&D department %
North	58	11	30
East	49	15	35
South-East	52	17	31
South-West	42	26	32
Middle	33	25	42
Rotterdam	40	27	33
The Hague	38	14	48
Amsterdam	52	22	26

Tables 9 and 10 show enterprises by region and, respectively, growth
of output and growth of employment. Economic developments have been
much more unfavourable in the three major cities than in the rest of
the country. Thus, it can be argued that the economic and infrastructural climate in the Randstad has a negative impact on both innovative
potential, output growth and growth of employment.

Tables 11, 12 and 13 take a closer look at the relationship between
innovation, output and employment. We explore here in particular

whether the increase in unemployment and the relatively low growth of output are due to lack of innovation, or whether there exists a common underlying factor which has a negative impact on both employment and output in the Randstad, and a positive influence on other parts of The Netherlands. Again, we are using a loglinear model.

The basic model for the interrelationship of innovation, output growth and region is given by:

basic model:	λ	df	$\chi^2_{.95}(df)$
(REGION).(INNOVATIONS).(OUTPUT)	36.51	12	21.03
extensions of the basic model:	$\Delta\lambda$	Δdf	$\chi^2_{.95}(\Delta df)$
(REGION.INNOVATIONS).(OUTPUT)	8.11	2	5.99
(INNOVATIONS.OUTPUT).(REGION)	8.98	4	9.49
(OUTPUT.REGION).(INNOVATIONS)	11.46	2	5.99

The interaction terms (OUTPUT.REGION) and (REGION.INNOVATIONS) are both accepted, while the interaction of innovations and output is rejected by the χ^2-test. This confirms the thesis that:

1) conditions in areas outside the Randstad favour both innovative activities and growth of output;
2) given 1), there exists no significant relationship between the number of innovations and growth of output.

The relationship between innovation, growth of employment and region is analysed by the following model:

basic model:	λ	df	$\chi^2_{.95}(df)$
(REGION).(INNOVATIONS).(EMPLOYMENT)	25.45	12	21.03
extensions of the basic model:	$\Delta\lambda$	Δdf	$\chi^2_{.95}(\Delta df)$
(REGION.INNOVATIONS).(EMPLOYMENT)	7.66	2	5.99
(INNOVATIONS.EMPLOYMENT).(REGION)	5.98	4	9.49
(EMPLOYMENT.REGION).(INNOVATIONS)	8.23	2	5.99

It can be concluded from the model that:

1) conditions in areas outside the Randstad favour both innovative activities and growth of employment;

2)   given 1), there is no significant relationship between number of
      innovations and employment growth.

Thus, the relationship between the variables location, number of innovations and employment growth is analogous to the relation between
region, number of innovations and growth of employment.

The cross tabulation of region, output growth and growth of employment
is given in Table 13. A first inspection of Table 13 shows that there
is a rather strong relationship between growth of output and growth of
employment in areas outside the Randstad, and that the same relationship is much weaker in the Randstad itself. The relations are formally
analysed by the loglinear model.

basic model:	λ	df	$\chi^2_{.95}(df)$
(REGION).(OUTPUT).(EMPLOYMENT)	74.57	12	21.03
extensions of the basic model:	$\Delta\lambda$	Δ df	$\chi^2_{.95}(\Delta df)$
(REGION.OUTPUT).(EMPLOYMENT)	5.78	2	5.99
(OUTPUT.EMPLOYMENT).(REGION)	52.68	4	9.49
(EMPLOYMENT.REGION).(OUTPUT)	10.42	2	5.99

This gives support to the view that

1)   there is a close interrelation between growth of output and
      growth of employment;
2)   given the interrelation between output and employment, employment
      evolves more favourably in areas outside the Randstad;
3)   given 1) and 2), the relationship between location and output
      growth is of minor importance, and adds no significant informa-
      tion.

TABLE 9
Enterprises by Region and Growth of Output

region	Growth of output (average 1982-1983)		
	less than 0%	0-10 %	more than 10%
North	14	51	35
East	21	45	34
South-East	11	62	28
South-West	24	48	28
Middle	22	44	33
Rotterdam	30	57	13
The Hague	33	39	28
Amsterdam	33	50	17

TABLE 10
Enterprises by Employment (average 1982-1983)

region	Growth of employment (average 1982-1983)		
	less than 0%	0-5 %	more than 5%
North	37	29	34
East	49	31	20
South-East	45	32	23
South-West	37	43	20
Middle	39	30	30
Rotterdam	57	29	14
The Hague	76	14	9
Amsterdam	55	36	9

TABLE 11
Enterprises by Region, Number of Innovations
and Growth of Output

number of innovations	Randstad growth of output:			Outside of Randstad growth of output:		
	less than 0%	0-10%	more than 10%	less than 0%	0-10%	more than 10%
none	10	16	2	11	36	22
1 or 2	5	8	5	10	27	8
more than 2	4	5	4	12	33	30

TABLE 12
Enterprises by Region, Number of Innovations
and Growth of Employment

number innovations	Randstad growth of employment:			Outside of Randstad growth of employment:		
	less than 5%	0-5%	more than 5%	less than 0%	0-5%	more than 5%
none	19	9	4	31	28	18
1 or 2	13	8	4	24	29	8
more than 2	12	2	0	34	20	25

TABLE 13
Enterprises by Region, Growth of Output
and Growth of Employment

growth of output	Randstad growth of employment:			Outside of Randstad growth of employment:		
	less than 0%	0-5%	more than 5%	less than 0%	0-5%	more than 5%
less than 0%	13	3	2	22	10	1
0-10%	17	9	2	48	28	16
more than 10%	6	3	2	5	21	31

6.   CONCLUSIONS

The recent literature on the interactions between technological innovations and employment, reviewed in Section 2, has abandoned the earlier macroeconomic approach. As a result, differences between sectors, between locations and between skills in the employment effects of innovations have received more attention. The importance of firm level studies of innovating behaviour has been recognised and, finally the fact that the effect of innovations on employment may change both quantitatively and qualitatively over time, has come to be appreciated.

The data presented for The Netherlands confirm firstly the existence of large intersectoral differences in the adoption of innovation. Secondly, they contradict the 'incubator hypothesis': firms located outside the main urban areas of The Netherlands are not less innovative. Finally, at the level of firms, there is no simple, positive relation between innovation and employment growth.

This last result is consistent with the findings on the motivation of firms for innovations. In many cases, innovations are adopted because the firm experiences (or expects) a fall in sales. Adoption of innovations may then well be associated with a reduction in the workforce, even if the effect on employment is positive in the long run. There is a second reason why cross section analyses may underestimate the positive effect on employment of technological innovation: many of the effects may occur elsewhere in the economy, in the supplying firm, rather than in the innovating firm itself. This suggests the importance of indepth, microlevel studies of particular sectors or innovations, preferably over a longer period than the two year interval considered in our study.

Finally, our results indicate the importance of incorporating spatial dimensions in studies of employment and innovations.

NOTES

1) In Table 5, x_n^2 denotes the value of the x^2 variable (with n degrees of freedom). If x is x^2 distribution then $s = \int_{x_n^2}^{\infty} f(x)$ x is the probability that a value xt at least as high as x_n^2 is found when the variables are in fact independent, i.e. the probability that the hypothesis of independent effects is wrongly rejected. Hence in Table 5, this probability is 13 per cent and 12 per cent respectively.

2) Randstad (Rimcity) is the common name for the urbanised Western area of The Netherlands enclosed by Rotterdam, The Hague, Utrecht, Haarlem and Amsterdam.

3) If the variables X, Y and Z in the threeway contingency table are independently distributed, the expected cell frequencies Fijk can be written in a loglinear model:
log Fijk = $\mu + \mu_1(i) + \mu_2(j) + \mu_3(k)$, where μ is the mean of the logarithm of expected cell frequencies, and μ_1, μ_2 and μ_3 are the deviations from the overall mean logarithm frequencies of group i of variable X, group j of variable Y and group k of variable Z. Denoting actual frequencies by fijk, the hypothesis of independency can be tested with the likelihood ratio $\lambda = 2 \sum_{ijk} \log$ (fijk/Fijk) which is asymptotically x^2-distributed.

In the contingency tables, the log likelihood ratio λ and the degrees of freedom (df) are shown, together with the critical value $\chi^2_{.95}$ (df) for a 95 per cent confidence interval. Hence if λ is equal to this critical value then the probability of wrongly rejecting the hypothesis of independence is 5 per cent (i.e., the variable s defined in footnote 1 then equals 0.05). Similarly, for the extensions of the basic model, the increase of in the log likelihood is denoted by $\Delta\lambda$, the increase in the degrees of freedom as Δdf and the critical value of λ as $\chi^2_{.95}(\Delta$df). Hence in the first table we accept the first extension (since 8.11 exceeds 5.99), but we reject the second one (since 8.98 is less than 9.49).

If this hypothesis is rejected, the model is augmented with one or more of the interaction effects $\mu_{12}(ij)$, $\mu_{23}(jk)$ and $\mu_{31}(ki)$. If the augmented model is also rejected, the second-order interaction term $\mu_{123}(ijk)$ has to be added, in which case the model becomes saturated (marked by zero degrees of freedom).

REFERENCES

Allen et al., Models of Urban Settlements and Structure of Dynamic Self-Organizing Systems, US Department of Transportation, Washington, DC, 1981.

Aydalot, Ph. (ed), 'Crise et Espace', Economica, Paris, 1984.

Carlino, G.A., Economies of Scale in Manufacturing Location, Kluwer Nijhoff, Boston, 1977.

Clark et al., 'Long waves and technological developments in the 20th century', in: Petzina, D. and Van Room, G. (eds), Konjunktur, Krise, Gesellschaft, Klett-Cotta, Stuttgart, 1981, pp. 132-179.

Doody, E.J. and Munzer, H.B., High Technology Employment in Massachusetts and Selected States, Massachusetts Division of Employment Security, Boston, 1981.

Forrester, J.W., 'Growth cycles', De Economist, Vol. 125, no. 4, 1977, pp. 525-534.

Freeman, C. et al., Unemployment and Technical Innovation, Frances Pinter, London, 1982.

Gillespie, A. (ed), Technological Change and Regional Development, Pion, London, 1983.

Gordon, P., 'Deconcentration without a "Clean Break"', in: Kawashima T. and Korcelli, P. (eds), Spatial Patterns and Trends, International Institute for Applied Systems Analysis, Laxemburg, Austria, 1982, pp. 193-202.

Hall, P. and Markusen, A., Technology Innovation and Regional Economic Development, Berkeley, 1983.

Hoogteijling, E., 'Innovatie en Arbeidsmarkt', Organisatie Strategisch Arbeidsmarktonderzoek, The Hague, 1985.

Jacobs, J., The Death and Life of Great American Cities, Vintage Books, New York, 1977.

Kawashima, T., 'Urban optimality', in: Nijkamp P. and Rietveld, P. (eds), Cities in Transition, Sijthoff and Noordhoff, Alphen aan Den Rijn, 1981, pp. 141-156.

Klein, B., Economic Dynamics, Oxford University Press, Oxford, 1978.

Kleinknecht, A., Innovation Patterns in Crisis and Prosperity, PhD Dissertation, Department of Economics, Free University, Amsterdam, 1984.

Levy, J.M., Economic and Social Factors Influencing Future Industrial Land Use in the US, International Workshop, Canada, 1983.

Malecki, E.J., 'Locational trends in R&D by large US corporations', Economic Geography, Vol. 55, 1965-1977, pp. 309-323.

McQuaid, R.W. and Langridge, R.J., Defining High Technology, Paper British Regional Science Meetings, Canterbury, 1984.

Mensch, G., Stalemate in Technology, Ballinger, Cambridge, 1979.

Nelson, R.R. and Winter, S.G., 'In search of useful theory of innovation', Research Policy, Vol. 6, 1977, pp. 36-76.

Nelson, R.R. and Winter, S.G., 'Neoclassical vs. evolutionary theories of economic growth: critique and prospectus', Economic Journal, Vol. 84, 1974, pp. 886-905.

Norton, R.D., City Life Cycles and American Urban Policy, Academic Press, New York, 1979.

Nijkamp, P., 'Long waves or catastrophes in regional development', Socio-Economic Planning Sciences, Vol. 16, No. 6, 1982, pp. 261-271.

Oakey, R.P., 'Technological change and regional development: a note on policy implications', Area, Vol. 11, 1982, pp. 340-344.

Pred, A.R., City-Systems in Advanced Economies: Past Growth, Present Processes and Future Development Options, Hutchinson, London, 1977.

Premus, R., Location of High Technology Firms and Regional Economic Development, Staff Study Joint Economic Committee, US Congress, Washington, 1982.

Rogers, E.M. and Larsen, J.K., Silicon Valley Fever Growth of High Technology Culture, New York, 1983.

Stoneman, P., The Economic Analysis of Technological Change, Oxford University Press, Oxford, 1983.

Sveikauskas, L., 'Inter-urban differences in the innovative nature of production', Journal of Urban Economics, Vol. 6, 1979, pp. 216-227.

Thomas, B., Migration and Urban Development, Methuen, London, 1972.

Thwaites, A.T., 'Some evidence of regional variations in the introduction and differentiation of industrial products within British industry', Regional Studies, Vol. 16, No. 5, 1982, pp. 371-381.

Vining, D.R. and Kontuly, T., 'Population dispersal from major metropolitan regions', International Regional Science Review, Vol. 3, 1977, pp. 143-156.

TECHNOLOGICAL CHANGE AND EMPLOYMENT PATTERNS:
THE GREEK CASE
Maria Giaoutzi

1.   INTRODUCTION

Technological change during the last years has been widely accepted as
one of the main forces towards economic progress in periods of stagnation and structural change (Nelson and Winter 1982). On the other hand
though, it may comprise an important long term determinant of the persistence of regional economic disparities (Thwaites 1978, Stöhr 1984,
Tödling 1984, Oakey 1983).

Support for the above issues has been supplied by a number of scholars
and as such has given rise to other questions which among others, are
related to the impact of innovation diffusion processes (long term or
short term, direct or indirect) upon the employment patterns of the
regions.

The importance attached to the knowledge of the intricate relationships between technological change and employment by policy makers is
gaining ground quite rapidly as the socioeconomic and spatial impact
of technological change increases.

How should the problem of job replacement in the traditional sectors
be faced in the short run? What is the type of employment pool which
gives rise to certain innovative behaviour? How will a certain regional employment market respond to certain goals of regional development?
Some questions similar to those presented above are likely to arise in
the problem solving process of policy making.

The main effort of this paper will be to explore the ways technological change may effect the employment patterns of the regions. In this
context, the Greek case will also be used as a reference framework for
further empirical conclusions.

2.   TECHNOLOGICAL CHANGE AND EMPLOYMENT: SOME INTERACTIONS

The recent streams of literature in the area of technological change - which to a great extent can be placed to the traditions of Schumpeter - deal in most cases with the impact of technological change upon employment in a rather tangential manner.

Most of the difficulty in exploring thoroughly the above relationship mainly stems - as Thwaites puts it - from the difficulty in separating this effect from all the other changes taking place at the same time, internal and external to the establishment (Thwaites 1983).

The intention of this paper to approach the above relationship will first make its way through some considerations of the double nature of employment in its role as factor involved in the regional innovation patterns: in the first place, as a cause of certain differences in regional innovation rates and potential, while in the second place, as an actor in itself, undergoing changes within a wider interplay of demand and supply forces.

Therefore, employment will be approached either in respect to its structure and in this context is considered as one of the main locational factors of technological change, or in respect to its nature, where other sides such as skill range and skill orientation come to the fore. In the following section, from a number of research findings, we will see the impact of technological change upon employment from various angles.

In the work of many scholars, we find that technological change takes place unevenly through space (Thwaites 1978, Thwaites et al. 1981). Product and process innovations, in their spatial bias, exhibit varying patterns of occurrence. Process innovations on the one hand, appear independently of a central or peripheral location, but are negatively related to employment creation (Thwaites 1978, Oakey et al. 1982, Thwaites 1983). Product innovations on the other hand, vary considerably in space according to a core periphery pattern (Oakey et al. 1982) and have positive effects upon employment for 'direct' and 'indirect' production employment (Thwaites 1983).

The above pattern conforms rather consistently with the product life cycle hypothesis (Vernon 1966, Hirsch 1967) where the employment effects in economic space (Perroux 1955) are dispersed in line with the state of the cycle. So, in the early phase of a product life cycle, critical input requirements of skilled personnel, external economies and venture capital will be available in the core locations. But in the mature phase, characterised by large firms, standardised production and increased competition, a peripheral and often non-metropolitan location is favoured for cheaper land and labour. As a result, product innovations and 'in situ' process innovations tend to be located in the core region with a counterbalancing effect upon each other in terms of employment.

Some indication of the above trend is given in Planque's work (Planque 1982) where he measures the concentration of innovative activities and educated workers in the central area of Paris, and finds a reversal of this trend for the period after 1974 (see also Aydalot 1984).

By drawing from the product life cycle hypothesis, industrialisation in peripheral regions usually takes place by large industrial plants which are led out of the core areas by certain diseconomies of scale. This implies creation of jobs in these areas mainly for lower skilled or unskilled workers.

Large multiplant corporations though, operate rather differently from domestic small and medium sized firms. Ewers and Wettman in their classical work have identified 'barriers to innovation' - both within particular regions and within corporate structures - which they consider as important bottleneck factors in regional development and argue for a specifically 'innovation oriented' regional policy (Ewers and Wettman 1980). Regional policy in most cases has overlooked the above barriers. Along this line, Thwaites has criticised regional policy on the basis of attracting in peripheral areas indifferently capital intensive industries upon 'imported' technology with an inferior employment growth record (Thwaites 1978). He also criticised the fact that the provision of regional development grants for rationalisation and new investment in process technologies which aims at enhancing long term competitiveness may lead to labour displacement in the short run (Thwaites 1980, Martin and Hodge 1983, Oakey 1983).

Motives and impacts though of product, process, institutional and managerial innovations may be quite different and are closely related to the phase in a product life cycle as well as the implied locational requirements of a firm (Nijkamp 1985).

Crum and Gudgin find significant regional disparities also in the spatial distribution of non-production manufacturing employment (technical, administrative and clerical staff) which vary considerably between the Greater London Area and Wales (Crum and Gudgin 1978). They also show the persistence of disparities despite regional policies which somehow supports Thwaites' criticisms mentioned above (Thwaites 1978), and come to decide that very little is explicable in this context by means of industrial structure. Instead, differences in industrial productivity between central and peripheral areas as well as the tendency that exists within corporate organisations to locate branch plants in the periphery, while headquarters and R&D at the core, is more important (Crum and Gudgin 1978).

Goddard, in the same context, also shows that this tendency to concentrate headquarters of firms in London is increasing despite improving communications (Goddard and Smith 1978) with all the implied consequences on employment structures of the periphery.

But what do all the above patterns imply for the 'nature' of the employment? And by 'nature' is meant to be the level and range of the skill of the workforce, which is affected by the type of tuning of the organisation of the work to the demands posed and patterns established by the new technologies. The 'nature' of employment in this context also consists of the main locational factors of the firm as it is closely related to the organisational aspects of the product life cycle theory as well as to the perspectives of the 'future developments' mainly of information technology.

In another line of thought, but within the same context, Andersson and Johansson refer to various levels of 'knowledge'. They try to find ways of classifying the range of skills and so they give 'information' (or data) as the most elementary level of knowledge; 'ordered information' as the next highest level of knowledge; 'competence' as the type of knowledge which is embedded in the patterns of social and physical entities and can be subdivided into 'instrument oriented' competence, 'sector specific' competence, and 'region specific' competence. Finally, they give 'creativity' as the highest level of knowledge which refers to the ability of the person to order and regroup information in an original manner and consists of the synthesis of all the above levels of knowledge (Andersson and Johansson 1984). The impact of technological change upon the qualitative transformations of the work organisation develops in a rather dynamic context since varying combinations of the overlapping economic sociocultural and physical spaces of each area create different 'impact outputs' upon the supply and demand patterns of this organisation. These can be reflected either as 'upgrading' or as 'downgrading' effects or in parallel with the previous two as 'polarisation' effects in the words of Taylor and Hirst (see Taylor and Hirst 1984).

In some recent work by Goddard (see Goddard et al. 1985), it is very clearly shown, for example, that process innovations may have a de-skilling effect and could also result in labour displacement.

David Gleave on the other hand, in his recent work on the impact of new technology upon the labour market, claims that he fails to draw a clear picture of the linkages between innovation competitiveness and jobs unless somebody examines the detailed behaviour of the firms (Gleave and Sellens 1984).

The following section of the paper draws from the Greek experience and makes some efforts to identify patterns vis a vis of the existing research findings in the same area.

3.   EMPIRICAL RESULTS FROM SOME GREEK REGIONS

Empirical evidence to study the patterns in the study area will mainly draw from an enquiry into innovation diffusion held in the area of Northern Greece (see Giaoutzi 1985c).

The study area includes the two main regions of Macedonia and Thrace where a wide range of development cases can be found having at the one end, the industrialised area of Thessaloniki (second urban/industrial centre of the country). The survey, for the purpose of the above study of 1187 firms, resulted in 57.3 per cent response rate (n = 680).

3.1 In the first place, some characteristics of the industrial structure of the area include the age of the firms (see Tables 1 and 2),

the size of the firms (Table 3), type of ownership, as well as location of headquarters (Tables 4 and 5).

TABLE 1
Establishment of Firms within the Study Area

Date of Establishment	Core %	No. of Firms Periphery %
- 1919	2.6	-
1920 - 1929	4.4	-
1930 - 1939	4.0	-
1940 - 1949	3.9	0.1
1950 - 1954	4.6	0.5
1955 - 1959	5.2	0.9
1960 - 1964	11.7	3.8
1965 - 1969	13.8	6.2
1970 - 1974	20.9	16.2
1975 - 1979	22.5	12.5
1980	2.4	14.9
1981	3.4	14.0
1982	0.6	13.7
1983	-	11.3
1984	-	5.5
	100	100

Source: ICAP Hellas 1984.

The above table shows a high rate of creation for the core region for
the period 1970-1979 and also a high rate for the periphery but at a
lower pace for 1970-1982. Both imply a rather high number of young
firms. Unfortunately, data on firm closures are not available.

Table 2 which follows, reveals some of the remnants of the old industrial structures in the area (e.g. N. Kavalas).

The most prevalent size of firms in the area is the small and medium
sized (10-15) (see Table 3). Large firms are mainly located in the
periphery (see N. Dramas, Kavalas, Kozanis, Pierrias, Pellas, Chalki-
dikis, Xanthis and Rodopis) which of course,rather consistently conforms to the product life cycle hypothesis where cheaper land and
labour attract standardised production of a large scale at the periphery.

As to the type of ownership of the firms in the area, we find multiplants of foreign ownership being to a great extent, located in the
core area (see Table 4).

TABLE 2

Date of Establishment of Firms

Nomos	before	1920	1950	1951	1952	1953	1954	1955	1956	1957	1958	1959	1960	1961	1962	1963	1964	1965	1966	1967	1968	1969	1970	1971	1972	1973	1974	1975	1976	1977	1978	1979	1980	1981	1982	1983
1. N. Thessaloniki	-	-	11	-	9	4	2	4	8	3	5	6	9	17	17	15	21	8	11	16	14	19	20	29	19	27	42	20	25	21	19	16	15	4	-	-
2. N. Dzamas	-	2	1	-	-	-	1	1	-	-	-	1	-	1	-	-	-	1	-	-	-	3	-	1	1	1	2	3	-	2	2	2	-	-	-	-
3. N. Imathias	1	6	-	1	1	1	2	-	1	2	-	-	2	3	2	3	2	1	-	4	2	2	6	3	8	4	8	7	8	4	-	3	2	1	-	-
4..N. Kavalas	-	15	-	-	1	1	2	2	1	1	2	-	2	3	1	2	2	2	1	-	2	2	1	-	5	3	5	3	2	3	4	2	1	-	-	-
5. N. Kastorias	-	-	-	-	-	-	-	1	1	-	1	-	1	2	1	1	1	1	1	1	1	1	1	2	2	1	1	-	4	-	2	-	3	-	-	-
6. N. Kilkis	-	2	-	-	-	-	-	-	-	-	-	-	-	-	-	-	-	-	1	-	-	2	2	1	5	8	-	4	3	2	6	4	2	2	-	-
7. N. Kozanis	-	1	-	-	1	-	-	1	-	-	2	-	1	1	1	1	1	1	1	1	5	1	1	2	-	5	2	1	1	1	1	-	1	-	1	-
8. N. Pellas	-	-	-	-	-	-	-	1	-	-	2	-	1	1	1	2	1	1	1	-	5	2	7	2	2	-	2	1	1	3	2	-	1	-	-	-
9. N. Pierrias	-	1	-	-	2	-	-	1	-	-	-	-	1	1	1	1	-	1	1	1	1	1	-	2	4	5	1	2	1	1	1	-	1	1	-	-
10.N. Serres	-	3	-	1	-	1	-	1	-	-	-	-	2	1	1	1	-	1	1	1	2	1	1	5	1	1	1	3	2	1	3	5	6	1	-	-
11.N. Florinas	-	2	-	-	-	-	-	-	-	-	-	-	2	1	1	1	-	1	-	1	1	1	1	1	2	1	1	1	2	2	1	1	1	-	-	-
12.N. Chalkidikis	-	2	1	-	-	-	-	1	-	-	-	2	2	-	-	1	-	1	1	1	1	1	1	1	1	2	2	2	2	2	2	-	1	-	-	-
13.N. Evros	-	1	1	-	-	1	-	1	-	-	-	-	-	-	-	1	1	1	-	-	1	1	-	1	1	1	6	2	2	1	1	2	1	1	-	-
14.N. Xanthis	-	2	-	-	-	-	1	2	-	-	-	-	1	-	-	-	1	1	-	1	1	5	1	2	9	4	1	8	8	5	1	2	2	1	1	-
15.N. Rodopis	-	-	1	-	-	-	-	-	-	-	-	-	1	-	-	1	1	1	1	1	1	-	1	1	2	2	-	3	3	3	1	3	1	1	1	-

Source: ICAP Hellas 1984

251

TABLE 3

Size of Firms

	No. Firms per nomos	0-9 No.	0-9 % per nomos	10-49 No.	10-49 % per nomos	50-99 No.	50-99 % per nomos	100-199 No.	100-199 % per nomos	200-499 No.	200-499 % per nomos	500- No.	500- % per nomos
Nomos Thessaloniki*	688	22	11.9	352	51.2	121	17.6	68	9.8	40	5.8	25	3.6
" Dzamas	22	3	13.6	11	50.0	2	9.0	2	9.0	1	4.5	3	13.6
" Imathias	90	7	7.7	40	44.4	26	28.8	6	6.7	6	6.7	5	5.5
" Lavalas	76	1	1.3	28	36.8	13	17.1	15	19.7	16	21.0	3	3.9
" Kastorias	23	3	13.0	12	52.2	5	21.7	1	4.3	2	8.7	–	–
" Kilkis	44	3	6.8	19	43.8	12	27.2	6	13.6	4	9.0	–	–
" Kozanis	19	1	5.3	12	63.1	1	5.2	–	–	3	15.7	2	10.5
" Pellas	37	4	10.8	11	29.7	11	29.7	5	13.5	4	10.8	2	5.4
" Pierrias	25	2	8.0	11	44.0	4	16.0	8	32.0	–	–	–	–
" Serres	62	9	14.5	23	37.0	19	30.6	6	9.7	2	3.2	3	4.8
" Florinas	18	1	5.5	13	72.2	3	16.6	1	5.5	–	–	–	–
" Chalkidikis	16	1	6.3	7	43.7	3	18.7	3	18.7	1	6.25	2	6.3
" Evros	24	–	–	14	58.3	6	25.0	2	8.3	2	8.3	–	–
" Xanthis	67	7	10.4	30	44.7	10	14.9	13	19.4	7	10.4	–	–
" Rodopis	21	3	14.2	8	38.0	6	28.5	3	14.2	1	4.8	–	–
(N = 1254)	1232	127	–	591	–	242	–	139	–	89	–	44	–

Source: ICAP Hellas 1984

* Nine tobacco firms are omitted due to high seasonal employment.

TABLE 4

Type of Ownership

Region	no.of firms	Multiplant		Indigenous Ownership		Foreign Ownership	
		no.	%	no.	%	no.	%
N. Thessaloniki	718	69	52.3	39	51.3	30	53.3
N. Dzamas	22	3	2.3	2	2.6	1	1.8
N. Imathias	94	11	8.3	7	9.2	4	7.1
N. Kavalas	63	10	7.6	9	11.8	1	1.8
N. Kastorias	23	1	0.7	1	1.3	-	-
N. Kilkis	46	8	6.1	6	7.8	2	3.6
N. Kozanis	18	1	0.7	1	1.4	-	-
N. Pellas	37	7	5.3	2	2.6	5	8.9
N. Pierrias	26	4	3.1	2	2.6	2	3.6
N. Serres	53	8	6.1	5	6.5	3	5.4
N. Florinas	18	-	-	-	-	-	-
N. Chalkidikis	17	6	4.5	2	2.8	4	7.1
N. Evros	24	2	1.5	-	-	-	3.6
N. Xanthis	61	2	1.5	-	-	2	3.6
N. Rodopis	21	-	-	-	-	-	-
N = 1254	1254	132	100	76	57.6	56	42.4

Table 5 on the headquarters plant location of firms shows on the one
hand a great deal of the periphery's headquarters located either in
Thessaloniki or in Athens, but also a great deal of the Thessaloniki
firms' headquarters located in Athens.

TABLE 5
Office Plant Location of Firms

Office plant location

Region	Office plant same address		Office within core/Thess.		Plant within N.office Athens	
	no.	%	no.	%	no.	%
N. Thessaloniki	472	55.7	227	77.2	51	44.7
N. Dzamas	19	2.2	-	-	3	2.6
N. Imathias	68	8.0	16	5.4	10	8.7
N. Kavalas	56	6.6	1	0.3	6	5.2
N. Kastorias	13	1.5	1	0.3	-	-
N. Kilkis	14	1.6	24	8.2	2	1.7
N. Kozanis	15	1.7	-	-	3	2.6
N. Pellas	23	2.7	6	2.0	8	7.0
N. Pierrias	20	2.4	4	1.4	2	1.7
N. Serres	44	5.2	6	2.0	4	3.5
N. Florina	13	1.5	-	-	5	4.3
N. Chalkidikis	7	0.8	6	2.0	5	3.5
N. Evros	22	2.6	1	0.3	1	0.8
N. Xanthis	43	5.0	2	0.6	6	5.2
N. Rodopis	17	2.0	-	-	4	3.5
(N = 1254)	846	67.5	294	23.5	114	9.0

Source: ICAP Hellas 1984

3.2 For the demarcation of the new technology sector, the selective sector approach has been employed which identifies as such firms which are characterised by a higher degree of use of new technology activities (see Nijkamp 1985).

In line with the above approach, the new technology sector includes: basic metals, textiles and food processing from the resource oriented sectors while electronics, machinery and plastics from the skill oriented sector (see Table 6).

TABLE 6
Characteristics of Technologically Advanced Sectors

Sectors	Technology Rating		Stability		Total
	Sectoral	Average	Sectoral	Average	Employed
Basic metals	1.11		0.37		10.000
Textiles	0.97	0.96	0.20	0.25	50.000
Food Processing	0.85		0.19		36.000
Electronics	0.87		0.33		4.000
Machinery	0.70	0.72	0.32	0.33	7.000
Plastics	0.62		0.35		8.000

Source: Scoumal and Kazis (1984).

In the context of the new technology sector, Table 7 shows a higher concentration of the new technology resource oriented firms within the periphery while the greater part belongs to routine (or standardised) activities. The core region on the other hand, concentrates a higher percentage of new technology skill oriented firms and a considerably higher percentage of non-routine activities.

TABLE 7
Types of Firms within the New Tech Sector

Type of firm / Type of Region	Resource Oriented firms %	Skill Oriented firms %	Routine		Non-routine	
			Res.	Skill	Res.	Skill
Core	53.1	46.9	35.6	24.6	17.5	22.3
Periphery	83.1	16.8	62.7	11.6	20.5	5.2

3.3 Large multinational corporations have been given a separate consideration within the study context since as it shows from a previous study, they comprise most of the technologically advanced sectors of the Greek economy (see Giaoutzi 1985d). In their locational preferences they exhibit a pattern of concentrating in the core area (see Table 8). Non-routine activities of this type of firm concentrate also, to a great extent, in the core region, mainly attracted by factors as agglomeration advantages, availability of skilled and professional labour, residential environment, quality of life with emphasis on sociocultural aspects (see Table 8 and Giaoutzi 1985b).

Routine activities on the other hand, to a large extent, are located in the periphery, mainly attracted by low cost labour, and some need for geographical accessibility. The rest of the their locational factors do not exhibit any pattern considerably different from the traditional location factors.

TABLE 8

Establishment of MNCs within the Study Area

Year	Core	Periph.	Year	Core	Periph.	Year	Core	Periph.
1920	1	-	1955	-	-	1961	-	-
1950	-	-	1956	-	-	1962	2	-
1951	-	-	1957	-	-	1963	3	-
1952	1	-	1958	-	-	1964	3	-
1953	1	-	1959	1	-	1965	1	-
1954	-	-	1960	-	-	1966	1	-
1967	1	-	1973	1	5	1979	1	-
1968	1	1	1974	4	1	1980	1	1
1969	1	-	1975	2	-	1981	1	-
1970	-	-	1976	2	1	1982	1	-
1971	-	-	1977	1	-	1983	-	-
1972	2	1	1978	1	1	1984	-	-

Source: ICAP Hellas 1984

Regarding non-routine activities, the above results are in agreement with previous research findings which hold that the locational preferences of the technical personnel play an important role in the location decision of R&D (see Oakey 1981, 1983), or that residential environment becomes a major locational motive for new technology firms (Brotchie et al. 1985).

Concerning routine activities, the results of the study are also consistent with previous findings which show routine activities locate either in small towns of peripheral areas or in low wage third world countries (see Bluestone and Harrison 1982).

TABLE 9

Type of Activity of MNCs with the Study Area

Type of Activity Type of Region	Routine	Non-Routine
Core	54.2	45.8
Periphery	75.4	24.6

Source: ICAP Hellas 1984.

4. TECHNOLOGICAL CHANGE AND EMPLOYMENT

But what might the above industrial structure and location patterns really imply for the employment patterns of the region?

It is really difficult to trace the direct links as Thwaites puts it in a previous chapter (Thwaites 1983), since the impact of technologi-cal change on the economic performance of the regions depends rather on each area's integrated breeding place function (see Dieperink et al. 1985), than on favourable locational or infrastructural conditions alone. The production environment in the region appears somehow to play the most important role (viz. presence or not of academic re-search institutes, the institutional or political willingness, and effective cooperation between the private and public sector, venture capital, etc.) (see Dieperink et al. 1985).

The patterns of innovative activity in the area in the first place conform to previous research findings where product innovations appear at a much higher rate in the core region (viz. Thessaloniki) while process innovations appear independently of a central or peripheral location (see Table 10).

TABLE 10

Number of Innovations since 1.1.1980

Innovations	Product		Process	
Regions	no.	%	no.	%
1. N. Thessaloniki	105	42.1	38	15.3
2. N. Dzamas	8	3.2	14	4.9
3. N. Imathias	26	10.4	33	11.6
4. N. Kavalas	10	4.0	20	7.0
5. N. Kastorias	2	0.8	15	5.3
6. N. Kilkis	25	10.0	20	7.0
7. N. Kozanis	8	3.2	12	4.2
8. N. Pellas	10	4.0	20	7.0
9. N. Pierrias	5	2.0	10	3.5
10.N. Serres	10	4.0	22	7.7
11.N. Florinas	-	-	13	4.6
12.N. Chalkidikis	15	6.0	29	10.2
13.N. Evros	-	-	8	2.8
14.N. Xanthis	15	6.0	28	9.9
15.N. Rodopis	-	-	11	3.9
	249	46.8	283	53.2

N = 532

Empirical evidence on the production environment and intraindustry links in the study area finds strong links for the core region of most of the technology firms with university and research centres outside the country. The latter is the case for both domestic as well as foreign ownership firms. Domestic firms also exhibit some links with universities within or outside the region. Cooperation between private and public sectors (e.g. contract research) is very low for both domestic and foreign ownership firms. For the periphery on the other hand, the study finds strong links with university and research centres abroad while relatively weaker links than those the firms in the core areas have with universities or firms within Greece. The above findings weld well with the differences in the innovative rates of the various regions (see Giaoutzi 1985). Important reasons restraining innovative activity in the study area were mainly mentioned: financial reasons, lack of technical expertise, organisational problems, as well as 'no need for innovation'. In their spatial bias in the core area, the limited access to financial resources appears as a main barrier, while in the periphery, the lack of technical expertise and the issue of limited financial resources (see Table 11).

TABLE 11

Reasons Restraining Information 1980-1985

Reasons Regions	Total %	Financial reasons	Lack of technical expertise	Organisa- tional problems	No need for innovation
Core	100	33.3	26.9	3.8	37.0
Periphery	100	30.7	46.1	-	23.0

As to the impact of technological change upon employment, a number of firms (M = 39) were interviewed both in the core region and the periphery. From a rough estimation, higher positive effects were found on employment by product innovations.

Table 12 below shows that no negative impact exists upon employment apart from some sectors in the periphery (food industry) with high seasonal employment rates.

Despite the results of Table 12, which in many cases mostly show some positive impact, generalisations are hard to be drawn due to the interrelatedness of all the changes taking place in a firm, externally as well as internallyto a firm. In this context, some emphasis on long run patterns of sectoral 'innovation trajectories', which would separate the implied effects upon employment for each type of adopted innovation, parallel to rationalisation aspects, could be an intersting research approach which might shed some more light on the future perspectives of this rather delicate research issue.

TABLE 12

Impact of Innovations upon Employment 1980-1985

Sectors	Core					Periphery				
	very positive	positive	less positive	none	negative	very positive	positive	less positive	none	negative
20 Food industry	-	-	-	4.5	-	5.9	23.5	-	11.7	5.9
21 Beverages	-	-	-	-	-	-	5.9	-	5.9	-
22 Tobacco	-	-	-	-	-	-	-	-	-	-
23 Textiles	-	9.0	-	-	-	-	-	-	-	-
24 Clothing and Footwear	-	4.5	9.0	9.0	-	-	-	-	5.9	-
25 Wood and cork	-	-	-	-	-	-	-	-	-	-
26 Furniture	-	-	-	4.5	-	-	-	-	-	-
27 Paper industry	-	-	-	-	-	-	-	-	-	-
28 Printing and Publishing	-	-	-	-	-	-	-	-	-	-
29 Leather	-	-	-	-	-	-	-	-	5.9	-
30 Rubber and plastic products	4.5	-	4.5	4.5	-	-	5.9	-	-	-
31 Chemicals	-	4.5	-	-	-	-	-	-	5.9	-
32 Products Petroleum and Coal	-	9.0	-	-	-	-	-	-	-	-
33 Nonmetallic mineral products	-	-	-	-	-	-	-	5.9	-	-
34 Basic metal Industries	-	4.5	-	-	-	-	-	-	-	-
35 Metal products	-	-	-	4.5	-	-	-	-	-	-
36 Machinery (non electrical)	9.0	-	-	-	-	5.9	-	-	-	-
37 Electrical supplies	4.5	-	4.5	-	-	-	17.6	-	-	-
38 transport and communication equipment	-	-	-	4.5	-	-	-	-	-	-
39 Miscellaneous manufacturing	-	-	-	-	-	-	-	-	-	-

REFERENCES

Andersson, A.E. and Johansson, B., Industrial dynamics, product cycles and employment structure, Working Paper of the International Institute for Applied Systems Analysis, Laxenburg, Austrial, 1984.

Aydalot, P., 'The reversal of spatial trends in French industry since 1974', in: Lambooy, J.G. (ed), New Spatial Dynamics and Economic Crisis, Finn Publishers, 1984.

Bluestone, B. and Harrison, B., The Deindustrialisation of America, Basic Books, New York, 1982.

Brotchie, J., Newton, P., Hall, P. and Nijkamp, P. (eds), The Future of Urban Form, Croom Helm, London, 1985.

Crum, R. and Gudgin, G., New Production Activities in UK Manufacturing Industry, Brussels, EEC, 1978.

Davelaar, E.J. and Nijkamp, P., The urban incubator hypothesis: old wine in new bottles?, Research Memorandum, Department of Economics, Free University, Amsterdam, 1985.

Dieperink, E.J. and Nijkamp, P., Innovation and regional policy in a spatial context, Paper presented at the conference on 'The Role of Time in Regional Development', Tbilisi, May 1985.

Dosi, G., 'Technological paradigms and technological trajectories', in: Freeman, C (ed), Long Waves in the World Economy, Butterworth Co., Frances Pinter, 1983.

Ewers, H.J. and Wettmann, R.W., 'Innovation oriented regional policy', Regional Studies, 14, 1980, pp. 161-179.

Frost, M. and Spence, N., 'Policy responses to urban and regional economic change in Britain', Geographical Journal, 147, 3, 1981, pp. 321-439.

Giaoutzi, M., Sectoral versus regional patterns of technological development, Paper presented at the conference, 'Technologies nouvelles: condition de renouveau de regions en crise?' by ASRDLF and SRBII, 1985a.

Giaoutzi, M., Locational aspects of technological development within a development context, Paper presented at the 25th conference of RSA in Budapest, August 1985b.

Giaoutzi, M., Technological Change and Regional Development in Greece (in Greek), Centre of Planning and Economic Research (KEPE), Athens, 1985c (forthcoming).

Giaoutzi, M, 'Factors affecting the capacity of technological change: the case of LD countries', Papers of the Regional Science Association, Vol. 58, 1985d (forthcoming).

Gleave, D. and Sellens, R., 'An investigation into British labour processes', Environment and Planning Committee, Paper no. 3, Economic and Social Research Council, London, 1984.

Goddard, J.B. and Smith, I.J., 'Changes in corporate control in the British urban system 1972-77', Environment and Planning A, 10, 1978m pp. 1073-1084.

Goddard, J.B., Gillespie, A.E., Robinson, A.E. and Thwaites, A.T., 'New information technology and regional development', in: Oakey, R. and Thwaites, A.T. (eds), Technological Change and Regional Development, Frances Pinter, London, 1985.

Hirsch, S., Location of Industry and International Competitiveness, Oxford University Press, 1967.

Martin, R.L. and Hodge, J.S.C., 'The reconstruction of British regional policy: the crisis of conventional practice', Environment and Planning, C, 1,2, 1983.

Nelson, R.R. and Winter, S.G., An Evolutionary Theory of Economic Change, Harvard University Press, Cambridge, MA, 1982.

Nijkamp, P., New technology and regional development, Paper presented at the conference on 'Long Term Fluctuations in Economic Growth', Weimar, June 1985.

Oakey, R.P., High Technology Industry and Industrial Location, Gower, Aldershot, 1981.

Oakey, R.P., 'New technology, government policy and regional manufacturing employment', Area, 15, 1, 1983, pp. 61-65.

Oakey, R.P., Thwaites, A.T. and Nash, P.A., 'Technological change and regional development: some evidence on regional variations in product and process innovation', Environment and Planning A, 14, 1982, pp. 1073-1088.

Perroux, F., 'Nole sur la notion pole de croissance', Economie Appliqué, Vol. 8, 1955.

Planque, P., 'Towards a decentralised innovative organisation', in: Maillat, D (ed), Technology: A Key Factor for Regional Development, St. Saphorin, Georgi, 1982.

Stöhr, W., Industrial structural change and regional development strategies: towards a conceptual framework, Paper presented at the symposium on 'Regional Processes/Policies and the Changing International Division of Labour', Vienna, August 1984, IIR-Discussion Paper no. 21.

Stoneman, P., The Economic Analysis of Technological Change, Oxford University Press, Oxford, 1985.

Taylor, M.J. and Hirst, J., 'The restructuring of the Austrian trading banks', Environment and Planning A, Vol. 16, 8, 1984.

Thwaites, A.T., 'Technological change, mobile plants and regional development', Regional Studies, 12, 1978, pp. 445-461.

Thwaites, A.T., 'The employment implications of technological change in a regional context', in: Gillespie, A. (ed), Technological Change and Regional Development, Pion, London, 1983.

Thwaites, A.T., Oakey, R.P. and Nash, P., Industrial innovation and regional development, CURDS, Final Report to the DOE, Vol. 2, 1981.

Tödling, F., 'Organisational characteristics of plants in core and peripheral regions in Austria', Regional Studies, 18, 1984, pp. 397-411.

Vernon, R., 'International investment and international trade in the product cycle', Quarterly Journal of Economics, 80, 1966, pp. 190-207.

SEGMENTATION THEORIES AND MANPOWER POLICY
IN DUTCH CITIES
Jan G. Lambooy and Chris van der Vegt

1. INTRODUCTION

In this paper we will deal with the application of labour market policies in an urban environment. If the hypothesis of segmentation of
labour markets is true, it would affect the outcome of manpower policies. The structure of the unemployed with regard to age, sex and
skills is, of course, not the exact replica of the entire labour market, but it is not unlikely that segmentation should have some relation
to the results of policies.

In our study we have made an evaluation of certain labour market instruments applied to unemployed in Rotterdam. Our research method and
the selection of the research population is based on the hypothesis of
segmentation. A basic problem is the comparable relevance of segmentation and job deficiency as causes for unemployment. Job deficiency can
be seen as a structural problem in a period of economic stagnation
linked to the impact of an intensive technological development. Conventional economic theory argues that this job deficiency can be
solved by changes in the factors prices, i.e., lower real wages
(Casson 1982), or by boosting demand by a Keynesian public works policy, most probably with a concomitantly higher inflation. If segmentation is relevant, alternative measures should be taken, for instance,
education and urban renewal.

Cities and regions do not possess many instruments to directly influence the creation of jobs. The increased general unemployment rate has
not only hit many weak regions, but - unexpectedly - also the big cities. In previous recessions, those cities showed a strong resistance
to the rise of unemployment caused by a business cycle (in the case of
the Great Depression, however, the cities were hit severely by the
crisis). More in particular, the inner city areas are showing high
concentrations of unemployed people (Lambooy 1984, Valkenburg and Ter
Huurne 1983).

The policy question is whether national, regional and urban government can attack this social and economic problem. The first reactions were based on Keynesian short term instruments. Recognition of the more structural character of this crisis came relatively late. Policy instruments were in general of the Keynesian type or oriented towards the manpower side. Only quite recently the orientation has become directed more towards the restructuring of the economic basis by attracting new high technology industries and by stimulating small businesses. The latter approach is a long term supply side policy, which is probably the best kind of attack to the structural problems, but with a main problem remaining unsolved: it takes time. The question of what to do about the present high unemployment remains unsolved. Is the relevant socioeconomic group just a 'lost generation'? Is it possible to help the unemployed by an effective manpower policy? And, with regard to the typical urban problems: do we have to emphasise a 'people oriented', or an 'areas oriented' approach?

In the United States an important theoretical development has been the attention of the theory of segmented labour markets with a main focus of interest on the 'ghetto economy' (Piore 1971, Gordon 1972, Harrison 1974), with special interest for the black population. These studies have stressed the cumulative character of unemployment, bad housing, poverty and low education.

In England, the first study on the special characteristics of urban unemployment was carried out by Metcalfe (1975) and by Metcalfe and Richardson (1976). Metcalfe observed strong differences in unemployment rates within metropolitan areas: '... there is unfortunately little agreement on the causes of these unemployment differentials and, by implication, on policies to alleviate the hardship resulting from unemployment'. In this study, Metcalfe observed that differences in education was one of the best indicators for the explanation. Manpower training policies thus were regarded as one of the most effective means to help those unemployed. It has to be noted, however, that Metcalfe made his investigation in a period of sound general economic conditions, with a strong job deficiency.

The Lambeth Group has analysed the worsening situation for the inner cities of large agglomerations (Needham 1982). Their conclusion was that area specific policies were needed, because of the cumulative effects of unemployment, poverty, bad housing, and insufficient

educational facilities. The approach to alleviate unemployment had to
be combined with urban renewal programmes.

This conclusion has been attacked by Cheshire. He argued that the negative characteristics of the concentration areas were the effect, and
not the cause of unemployment. The main cause - he argued - remains
the job deficiency, not only in the inner cities, but also in the metropolitan regions in general (Cheshire 1979, 1981).

Another attack has been published more recently by Sim (1984), who
argues that many peripheral housing estates, for example, in Glasgow
and Liverpool, show similar bad characteristics when compared to many
other inner city areas. He concludes: 'It would seem, therefore, from
the evidence so far available, that outer states are not only areas of
disadvantage, but are disadvantages further in terms of government
policy'. And further on he states: 'Although programmes aimed specifically at inner areas can, of course, help those areas, they are all
too often treating the symptoms of economic decline rather than the
cause'.

2.   UNEMPLOYMENT AND THE THEORY OF THE SEGMENTED LABOUR MARKET

Unemployment in The Netherlands has risen from less than two per cent
in 1970, to six per cent in 1980; was doubled in the next two years,
and has increased to 17,5 per cent in 1983; in 1984 it fell back
slightly, to about 14 per cent.

Conventional macroeconomic policies and substantial programmes of public works have not been able to stop the slow, but persistent growth
of the unemployment rate during the 1970s. As in the second half of
the decade unemployment as well as unfilled vacancies increased, the
problem was at last considered - at least partly - as a structural
one. Public works were discontinued and training programmes, wage subsidies in the private sector and public service employment became important instruments of labour market policies. These seemed to be well
suited to cope with structural unemployment in some occupations, in
some regions, or for some categories of workers, where a stimulation
of overall demand would not help. These policies are applied each
year to 60,000 - 70,000 workers and cost over Dfl. 600 million per
year.

A typical situation of structural unemployment exists in the large cities; not for the bigger urban regions as a whole. Comparison of unemployment rates in the Amsterdam and Rotterdam metropolitan regions with the average for The Netherlands as a whole, however, does not reveal this; the inner areas of the agglomerations display very high percentages. The rates for many parts of these regions are 50 per cent higher than unemployment rates in the Western provinces as a whole. In the older parts of the cities, very high unemployment rates are found, up to a 40 per cent level.

This development is not new. In the US, the problem of the urban unemployment is extensively studied by those authors who formulated the 'Dual Labour Market Theory' (Gordon 1972, Piore 1971). They observed the parallel existence of a strong demand for labour of certain kinds, and a shortage of jobs for others. The latter could remain unemployed, even in a high growth economy, because of their personal characteristics (for instance, being black, female, or unskilled). A duality exists between a 'primary segment' - the low paid, low qualified persons. And another duality has been observed, being the duality between the 'internal' and 'external job market'. The first is the mechanism in which priority is given to members of a labour union or to those already working in the firm or in the department. This is an impediment for a high mobility on the labour market and may lead to protectionism against better qualified people.

One specific observation concerned the spatial clustering in certain residential districts, mostly with dilapidated dwellings. A typical example was mentioned, being the 'black ghettos' such as Harlem in New York.

The causality between unemployment and the spatial clustering can be two sided and cumulative. Living in an area with unemployment and poverty does not motivate younger people to work hard at school, especially if they possess exactly those characteristics that make their parents so unattractive in the labour market. Because they stay unemployed, they remain poor and have to look for cheap houses in comparable areas. The causality also works in the other direction: because they live in these bad areas, employers will not select them for good jobs. So their only chance is low paid work, part time jobs and unemployment.

This situation pervades their lives. Being classified as such people means a certain life style, a low class education, and a mistrust in social and economic structures. In this theory, this segment is called the 'secondary segment' of the labour market. Auletta (1982) has coined the concept of 'urban underclass' for this group. Wilson (1983) has analysed the situation of great and increasing poverty of this group, mostly consisting of blacks and Hispanics, in American cities.

The dual labour market theory is already widely known. Therefore it is not necessary to dwell extensively with it, nor with its many criticisms. The main criticism concerns the duality itself. The existence of 'segments' on the labour market is quite generally accepted, but duality is usually considered to be too strong a simplification.

The duality mentioned is one on the supply side of the labour market and is related to the selection based on the characteristics of people. The other duality - the one between the internal and external labour markets - is linked with the position within firms. Only a small part of the externals can be internalised, in particular those with a good education.

Both forms of duality are, of course, much too simplified concepts, because firms and institutions are more differentiated than those two categories indicate. It is especially difficult to use this duality if small business is integrated within the study. In that category of firms, other relations and processes often prevail.

Still a third kind of simplistic duality has been postulated, viz. that there are two kinds of firms. The first one being large, mostly capital intensive firms that are able to pay good wages, and the second one being small, often labour intensive firms, that pay low wages and where job security is low.

Of course, the segmentation is much more complicated than has been accepted in the 'dual labour market theory'. Nevertheless, a certain segmentation of the labour market cannot be denied. For our research project, it has been a stimulating starting point, because of the opportunities it offered to develop hypotheses about the behaviour of certain categories of unemployed. Segmentation does not necessarily have to be a structural and permanent barrier. It may be changed by an effective set of measures, directed towards areas and towards the relevant categories of people.

One lesson to be learned from the theory of the segmented labour market, however, is that unemployment is often <u>involuntary</u>, not related to wages, but rather to personal and social characteristics. Lower wages do not always function as an instrument to clear the markets. The selection by employers of the best qualified persons becomes more severe in a period of crisis and rapid technological change. Demand deficiency and selection based on personal characteristics then go hand in hand.

A related approach to the selection process has been developed by Thurow (1975, 1983). He conveys the idea of a queue of jobs. The employer offers a certain number of jobs with well described characteristics. Unemployed, or those people trying to improve their position, are queueing for the jobs in supply. The best jobs have a long waiting list, but if the supply of good jobs is low, the applicants continue their search for jobs with a lower position. The lowest paid jobs will have the competition of unskilled, low skilled and the rest filtering down from the higher positions. The allocation process is not that of the simple price quantity type, but is mixed up with segmentations of jobs and of people applying for the jobs.

If one investigates the labour market from that point of view, it is not without sense to accept other 'distorting' factors as well, for instance, the influence of labour unions and government regulations (Storper and Walker 1983, Pfriem 1979). In this paper, we will limit ourselves to the 'simple segmentation' approach, in order to evaluate measures in an urban labour market. It may be stressed, however, that the economic theory of the labour market is as yet far from complete. Thurow (1983) even writes about the 'Sargasso sea' of economics, wherein the wrecks of economic theory are buried.

Economic growth is the necessary precondition for promoting new firms and new jobs. In the meantime, it will remain necessary to improve job chances for the unemployed. An efficient manpower policy, however, is very difficult to implement in times of crisis and of restructuring the economy. Many unemployed do not believe in a better future, even if they should be better skilled.

During the period 1980-83, a large research project was set up by the Ministry of Social Affairs and Employment in The Netherlands. The intention was to get a clearer picture of the size and geographical distribution of the unemployed in the following five cities of the three Western provinces: Amsterdam, Rotterdam, The Hague, Utrecht and Leiden. Three research institutes participated in this project. The present authors were involved (as chairman of the coordinating committee and as researcher of the Foundation for Economic Research (SEO) respectively). The SEO part was oriented mainly towards the measurement of the effectiveness of manpower programmes.

In the following sections we will discuss some of the problems and the main results of this part of the study. The two remaining parts were focussed on the statistical description and the analysis of the differentiation of the supply side.

3.   TRAINING PROGRAMMES AND JOB CREATION POLICIES

In this section and the following, we shall deal in more detail with training programmes and job creation policies. Training and job creation programmes by the central government have not been designed for specific regions or cities; they are part of a nation wide policy, targeted at certain groups. However, it has been easy to allocate a larger part of the related budget in favour of depressed areas, and later on (1981) to the large cities.

Although we distinguish between training programmes and job creation policies on the one hand, and job creation by means of wage subsidies for the private as well as for the public sector on the other, these manpower policies have a lot in common. If the employer gets a subsidy for formal training of new personnel, or if he receives a temporary subsidy in the wage costs of an additional employee, in either case the subsidy functions as a (temporary) reduction of the wage costs. For public service employment, the temporary subsidy is 100 per cent of the wage costs, the difference with training and job creation programmes being mainly that the job is temporary also, whereas in the latter case, the job is - in theory - permanent.[1] Training programmes are originally designed for a more efficient allocation of labour. As there are at present hardly any occupations left where an excess demand exists, these programmes nowadays mainly upgrade labour.

Wage subsidies are generally advocated for their supposedly positive effect on (total) employment. Because of a scale effect (lower costs and larger output) and a substitution effect (lower labour costs and more labour intensive production processes), employment increases and unemployment decreases. If the subsidies are temporary and marginal, or if they are applied to the gross flow into employment (as is the case in The Netherlands), these effects will be very modest indeed. Moreover, if they are targeted at disadvantaged groups, another, not intended effect may occur: a subsidised worker, instead of the more productive one, may fulfil a vacancy. Such a displacement effect is accepted, however, The goal of manpower policy is not only to be efficient, but also to promote a just allocation of labour. Public service employment in this respect is the last opportunity for the hard core unemployed, if a training programme or wage subsidy in the private sector does not succeed. Although we have acquired additional employment in this case, the primary aim is to provide a temporary job (for 6 months or a year), and working experience that will enable the workers to find a normal job.

In order to be effective instruments for application in the urban labour market, these policies have to be attuned to the specific employment conditions within the large agglomerations, especially to those of the areas that have been most severely hit by poverty and unemployment.

4.   THE UNEMPLOYMENT SITUATION; THE CASE OF ROTTERDAM

We have taken Rotterdam as a case study and we have investigated the effectiveness of instruments for the year 1979. This analysis is based on a study by the SEO, which examined the effects of training and job creation in that area.[2]

In Rotterdam, unemployment has risen from 1.4 per cent in 1971 to 7 per cent in 1979; it has increased to about 25 per cent in 1984. The situation has deteriorated so rapidly, that what in 1979 was considered to be a very high rate of unemployment, may now, with hindsight be labelled as only a very moderate level.

As we know, the increase in unemployment has particularly hit categories such as the young, women, immigrants and the low skilled workers.

This is also true for Rotterdam, as may be seen from Table 1. Their weak position in the labour market, however, is not so much the result of the duration of unemployment (at least in 1979), as of a high rate of turnover. In other words: these categories have a high probability of becoming unemployed, but also of finding another job within a relatively reasonable period of time. It may be stressed that if manpower policies are targeted at groups with more than the usual amount of problems in getting a job, the most relevant groups are old workers and skilled workers, not the categories with high unemployment rates as such. An exception may be made for workers from Surinam, who have a high turnover and a long average period of unemployment, resulting in a very high unemployment rate. The problem of other weak categories on the labour market, however, is not so much getting a job, but rather keeping a job.

TABLE 1

Estimates of Unemployment by Categories: Rate, Inflow and Duration in 1979 in the Rotterdam Area

Category		Rate (% dep. labour force)	Inflow (% dep. labour force)	Average duration (months)
AGE:	15-24	11	24	5
	25-49	6	10	7
	50-64	5	3	19
SEX:	Male	6	11	7
	Female	6	16	7
ORIGIN:	Surinam	31	36	10
	Mediterranean	13	53	3
	Dutch + Others	6	8	8
EDUCATION:	Only primary school	15	31	6
	More than primary school	3	4	10
AREA:	Low income	13	21	7
	Other	6	11	7
TOTAL AVERAGE:		7	12	7

Source: SEO 1983.

A closer analysis of the figure in Table 1 would reveal that women have a higher unemployment rate than men, because the female labour force is, on an average, much younger. Within the same age groups. there is not much difference between the sexes. The higher unemployment rate among women would disappear - at least statistically - if not so many young people would be unemployed.

The classification according to country of origin might also be somewhat misleading. Migrant workers from the Mediterranean countries are unskilled and do not show much difference in labour market behaviour when compared with Dutch unskilled workers. Their being unskilled is the main factor for explaining the restriction in their employment possibilities to the casual and low wage jobs. This characteristic is a problem common to Dutch and foreign unskilled workers.

As these unskilled labourers are over-represented in the low income areas of the city, with relatively bad housing conditions, unemployment rates are high in these areas; in some of them even much higher than the average of 13 per cent.

5.   SELECTION AND PARTICIPATION

When looking at unemployment rates of 3 per cent for the skilled, and of 15 per cent for the unskilled (i.e., those who completed primary schooling only), the appropriate policy to attack unemployment of the disadvantaged seems to be training. This conclusion holds true only if we look at the policy directed towards the supply side of the labour market. Such a policy would, as one may assume after analysing the figures of Table 1, lead to a considerable extension of average job duration and therefore to a decrease in the unemployment rate. Indeed, most applicants for manpower policy participate in a training programme; in Rotterdam even up to 70 per cent. More than half of all unemployed school leavers in 1979 in Rotterdam obtained a subsidy training-annex-job and about 2 per cent of all other workers that became unemployed that year were involved in training-on-the-job or in some institutional setup. If, however, according to the judgement of the mediator at the Labour Exchange, training is not the appropriate tool to improve the position on the labour market of a worker, the first alternative is a wage subsidy in the private sector. In 1979, several kinds of wage subsidies existed, most of them with selected criteria based on duration of unemployment and age. Wage subsidies were also given to the disabled and to migrant workers from Surinam. The subsidies either consisted of a fixed amount in guilders, or of a percentage of wage costs. In all cases, they were set up with the explicit goal of providing permanent jobs. Participation rates were about 1 per cent of the target population[3] for each kind of subsidy. Comparable percentages may be found for the two programmes of public service employment with selection criteria based on unemployment for at least six months or a year.

Because the various populations overlap, one should compare the total number of participants with the gross flow into unemployment plus the existing stock of unemployed at the beginning of the year. This leads to a participation rate of 11 per cent and without the training programme for school leavers of 4 per cent.

Of greater interest, however, is an investigation into the representation of the categories of workers who have been identified as disadvantaged on the labour market. Table 2 shows that the young are well represented, with 25 per cent, but also that no other categories of workers with high unemployment rates are really mentioned. The selection is biased towards the male, the Dutch, the better skilled and the workers who do not live in low income areas. Most striking is the selection of 35 per cent of all eligible workers with medium or higher education and of 3 per cent of those with only primary schooling. The participation rate of workers from the Mediterranean countries accounts for only 1 per cent.

There are three main explanations for these results:

1) Formal selection criteria are based on the duration of unemployment or are targeted on workers with more than the usual amount of problems in getting a job. Wage subsidies and public service employment therefore are more easily applied to the old and the better skilled with a relatively long average duration of unemployment (compare Table 1).

2) Employers in the private sector are not really interested in temporary wage subsidies for the advantages. They want a qualified worker for the job and they prefer the subsidised applicant to the equally qualified, non subsidised applicant. The skilled worker - whether or not subsidised - is preferred to the unskilled.

3) Although no formal selection rules exist for participation in training programmes, a selection does take place at the Labour Exchange, because of a limited budget. In order to spend this budget as efficient as possible, the selection is in favour of

the best 'students'. Migrant workers from the Mediterranean countries are extra handicapped, because of language problems.[4]

TABLE 2

Selected Workers in Per Cents of the Target Population
by Age, Sex, etc.

AGE:	15-24	25
	25-49	3
	49-64	4
SEX:	Male	12
	Female	8
ORIGIN:	Surinam	7
	Mediterranean	1
	Dutch and others	15
EDUCATION:	Primary school	3
	Medium and higher	35
AREA:	Low income	5
	Other	13
TOTAL AVERAGE:		11

Source: SEO 1983.

6. EFFECTS ON LABOUR MARKET BEHAVIOUR

Effects of participation in manpower policies on labour market performance are not easily evaluated. Labour market conditions may deteriorate after participation - as they did, and drastically so - and obscure positive effects. One should also like to compare the effects of different policies: are training programmes more effective than public service employment programmes? This question cannot be answered by comparing unemployment rates of participants after application. These rates will also be different, because of differences in qualifications of the workers selected.

In order to be able to solve these problems, labour market behaviour has been analysed with a longitudinal model, specifying intensities of transition from one position on the labour market to another, or from one 'state' to another. When distinguishing the states 'job' (1), 'another job' (2), and 'unemployed' (3), the speed of transition between states may be explained by variables such as sex, age, skill, etc. and by time-dependent variables as a proxy of changing labour market conditions in general and of participation in one of the programmes (a dummy variable). Formally: $q_{ij} = \exp(\beta_{ij} X + \gamma_{ij} U(t))$, in which q_{ij} = intensity of transition from state i to j;

X = a vector of time-independent variables;

$U(t)$ = a vector of time-dependent variables; and

β_{ij} and γ_{ij} are vectors of parameters.

From $\dfrac{1}{q_{12} + q_{13}}$, we find the expected job duration, and from $\dfrac{1}{q_{31}}$ we find the expected unemployment duration.[5]

Before dealing with the estimated effects of the programmes, we present in Table 3 a simulation of the model for various categories of workers, i.e., estimated unemployment rates in 1979 after participation in a programme. Workers selected for a training programme appear to have lower unemployment rates than those selected for a wage subsidy, whereas those who were employed in the public service have the highest unemployment rates.

TABLE 3

Estimated Unemployment Rates in 1979 After Application
of Manpower Policies

Category	Training	Wage Subsidy	Public Service unemployment
1. Reference group*	4	10	21
2. Young	5	9	18
3. Female	9	9	14
4. Low skilled	7	18	32
5. Migrant worker	8	24	15
6. Often unemployed	11	28	36
7. Long unemployed	9	17	48
8. Programme not finished	24	36	9

Source: SEO 1983.

* 1. Dutch male of average age and average school education in years, not more than four times unemployed in the last ten years with an average duration of less than a year, who did not leave the programme before its termination,

2. As 1, but one times the standard deviation in years younger'

3. As 1, but female,

4. As 1, but one times the standard deviation in years of school education less,

5. As 1, but from Surinam or a Mediterranean country,

6. As 1, but more often unemployed,

7.   As 1, but with a longer average duration of unemployment,
8.   As 1, but leaving the programme before its end.

As we have pointed out, this also is the ranking according to which selection for the different types of manpower policy takes place. So the application of the policies does not overcome these differences in labour market performance. This conclusion can also be drawn from a comparison of the figures in Table 3 and Table 1. For many categories of workers, unemployment figures are still very high, indicating that if the policies do have a positive effect, it cannot possibly be a strong one. Moreover, if we stimulate the model for 1981 (in which year the labour market conditions were worse), unemployment rates become much higher. The selected workers are vulnerable to a situation of a large excess supply of labour.

There are also some categories of workers with rather low unemployment rates after participation in a programme, especially those who followed a training programme. This, however, is mainly the result of a prior selection of the best workers, i.e., workers who did have a relatively good labour market performance anyhow. The conclusion is based on the effect of average job duration of the implemented policy, as given in Table 4. Extension of job duration is not the only criterion for measuring effectiveness of manpower policies, but it probably is the most important one. As might be concluded from Table 4, job duration is more extended with public service employment and wage subsidies, than with training programmes. The majority of participants in the training programmes - young Dutch males, not unskilled - does not seem to benefit from the training.

Older workers do not benefit from any policy at all. A possible explanation for this phenomenon is that they lost their job specification 'human capital' after becoming unemployed and that no programmes can replace this. Very positive effects of public service employment are found for women and migrant workers. Their relatively low unemployment rates, compared with those of other participants of public service employment programmes (Table 3) are explained by this. There seems to be some evidence that getting working experience, possibly in a new field of activity, opens better perspectives on steady jobs for some categories of workers, than may be achieved by formal training.

TABLE 4

Estimated Multipliers of Expected Job Duration for

Different Categories of Workers

Categories	Training	Wage Subsidy	Public Service Employment
1. Male, Dutch, age < 35	1	1.3	2.3
2. Male, Dutch, age ≥ 35	0.2	0.9	0.6
3. Female, Dutch, age < 35	1.5	2.4	3.4
4. Male, immigrant, age < 35	1.6	0.7	3.9

Source: SEO 1983.

7. CONCLUSIONS

Our case study was part of a broader project aiming at acquiring a better understanding of the specificity of the urban unemployment situation. In the other parts of the project, the attention was focussed on the description and analysis of the specific conditions of unemployment in the urban renewal parts of the large agglomerations.

The final results may be summarised with the general remark that the urban labour market shows a segmentation, but not as strict a one as is predicted by the dual labour market theory. The partition between segments is related rather to education and skills than to factors that have been emphasised by the theory mentioned. A correlation of employers' selection behaviour and the place of residence, could not be proven. Probably the American mechanism is quite different from the Dutch process of selection.

Manpower policies have a great flexibility in application as well as in setup. They can be targeted at various groups of workers with employment problems. In our case study, they have also shown positive effects on the employment of disadvantaged workers. These effects, however, are modest. Perhaps we should not expect that, by participation in training programmes and job creation policies, the disadvantaged worker will change into an 'average worker'. Being disadvantaged on the labour market is caused by several factors, only one or two of which are affected by these policies. If we accept this restriction, they have the potential of being rather effective. A main problem seems to be the targeting and the selection of workers.

Local and regional authorities often do not possess the financial and institutional instruments to create jobs in a period of high unemployment. Macroeconomic theory has not explicitly paid attention to the local and regional level of the economic system. Even regional economics has not yet developed a fully grown theory of job creation on this spatial scale. It has specialised in the analysis and description of interregional differences, in growth pole theories, and - more recently - in the transfer of technology. These and other theories contain elements that can possibly be of use for the construction of new approaches, specifically when linked with the local and regional job creation programmes.

We have found that labour market conditions in 1979 were particularly unfavourable for the young and the unskilled, because of high rates of turnover. The situation therefore demanded selection criteria based on the frequency of unemployment, and not based on the duration of unemployment. By doing the latter, a bias was introduced towards the skilled, instead of towards the unskilled. An alternative policy in a period of downswing might be to introduce a selective integral wage subsidy, instead of a marginal one. To prevent payoffs would seem to be a more direct approach than to stimulate regaining jobs.

As 70 per cent of the unemployed in Rotterdam were unskilled, one should have high expectations from training. These expectations did not show results however. Existing training programmes in 1979 were not well suited to the completely unskilled, in particular to the immigrant workers. Most of the workers that were selected, hardly improved their unfavourable position on the labour market. Therefore, training programmes should be designed for the unskilled. However, formal training is not the only possibility; getting work experience appears to be an effective alternative. If we should want to intensify manpower policies, this might be done in the private sector, in about the same way in which public service employment is organised, viz. a temporary subsidy to get some work experience. Such programmes are still in an experimental state in The Netherlands.

NOTES

1. For a more detailed comparison of various forms of wage subsidies, see e.g., Daniel S. Hamermesh, Subsidies for jobs in the private sector, in: J.L. Palmer (ed), Creating jobs: public

employment programs and wage subsidies. The Brookings Institution, 1978.

2. Further details are to be found in C. van der Vegt, C.H.M. Lutz, W.C.G.M. van Paridon and G. Ridder. De toepassing van arbeidsvoorzieningsmaatregelen op de grootstedelijke arbeidsmarkt, SEO, 1983.

3. All workers are eligible at the beginning of the year and during the year.

4. After 1979, special training programmes were arranged for these migrant workers.

5. This part of the analysis in the research project of SEO is due to G. Ridder; see especially C. van der Vegt et al., 1983, Appendix D.

6. Estimates of changes in average duration of unemployment were biased due to the below average duration of unemployment before application of the programme.

<u>REFERENCES</u>

Auletta, K., The Urban Underclass, Random House, New York 1982.

Casson, M., Economics of Unemployment, London, 1982.

Cheshire, P., 'Inner areas as spatial labour markets', Urban Studies, Vol. 16 and Vol. 18, respectively, 1979, 1981.

Gordon, D., Theories of Poverty and Underdevelopment, Lexington, 1972.

Harrison, B., 'Ghetto employment and model cities program', Journal of Political Economy, Vol. 82, No. 2, 1974, pp. 353-371.

Haveman, R.H. and Palmer, J.L. (eds), 'Job for disadvantaged workers: the economics of employment subsidies', The Brookings Institution, 1982.

Kopits, G.F., 'Wage subsidies and employment: an analysis of the French experience', International Monetary Fund Staff Papers, 1978, pp. 494-527.

Lambooy, J.G., 'Stedelijke werkloosheid', Regionale Raad voor de Arbeidsmarkt, Werkloosheid in de grote steden, Den Haag, 1984, pp. 8-24.

Metcalfe, D., 'Urban unemployment in England', Economic Journal, Vol. 85, 1975, pp. 578-589.

Metcalfe, R. and Richardson, R., 'Unemployment in London', in: Worswich, G.D.N. (ed), The Concept and Measurement of Involuntary Unemployment, London 1976.

Needham, B., 'Inner areas as spatial labour markets', Urban Studies, Vol. 18, 1981.

Palmer, J.L., 'Creating jobs: public employment programs and wage subsidies', The Brookings Institute, 1978.

Pfriem, H., Konkurrierende Arbeitsmarkttheorien; neoklassische, duale und radikale Ansätze, Campus Verlag, Frankfurt, 1979.

Piore, M.J., 'The dual labour market', in: Gordon, D.M. (ed), Problems in Political Economy, Lexington, 1971.

Reich, M., Gordon, D. and Edwards, R., 'A theory of labour market segmentation', American Economic Review, 1973, pp. 359-365.

Sim, D., 'Urban deprivation: not just the inner city', Area, Vol. 16, No. 4, 1984, pp. 299-306.

Storper, M. and Walker, R., 'The theory of labour and the theory of location', International Journal of Urban and Regional Research, Vol. 7, No. 1, 1983.

Thurow, L., Generating Inequality, Basic Books, New York, 1975.

Thurow, L., Dangerous Currents, Oxford University Press, New York/London, 1983.

Valkenburg, F. and Ter Huurne, A., Werkloosheid in Oude Stadswijken, IVA, Tilburg, 1983.

Vegt, C. van der, Lutz, C.H.M., Paridon, W.C.G.M. van and Ridder, G., De toepassing van arbeidsvoorzieningsmaatregelen op de grootstedelijke arbeidsmarkt, Stichting voor Economische Onderzoek, Amsterdam, 1983.

Werneke, D., 'Job creation programmes: the United States experience', International Labour Review, 1976, pp. 43-59.

Wilson, W.H., 'Inner city dislocation', Society, Vol. 21, 1983, pp. 80-86.

LOCAL ENTREPRENEURIAL INITIATIVES
AND CENTRAL GOVERNMENT
Ad J. Hendriks

1. INTRODUCTION

Local initiatives undertaken by entrepreneurs require a wide variety
of actions. To conduct a business enterprise implies first of all
scanning the market for chances. The next thing is to accurately identify the ensuring problems, to look for and to find solutions and - on
that basis - to act. Consequently, to conduct a business means to be
informed and to permanently gather information. Developments within
the company must be monitored on the basis of continuous records of
the turnover, the clients, the staff, the cost factors, etc. Besides,
there must be external information on the competitors, developments
within the various levels of government, the objectives of trade
unions, and so forth. It is also essential to be information well
ahead of sudden events. A monetary crisis is a case in point, but so
are abrupt changes with customers or licence issuing government agencies.

One of those unexpected surprises are technological innovations
achieved at short notice in a certain branch of activity or activity
column. Such technological innovations may imply promises as well as
threats for an organisation. Therefore, the question how to respond is
in order. An entrepreneur has to explore all feasible possibilities
and to face the question what to do in order to benefit from the opportunities offered. Business enterprise does not only require innovation, but also use of information. Systematic information treatment is
part of the modern company's scientific management. Frequently, this
is one of the weaker points of a starter for obvious reasons: to reserve productive work time for a general orientation and information
gathering is only to a limited extent possible for a starter.

This can be illustrated by means of an empirical investigation among
recently established small scale companies in one of the Dutch cities.
Out of 82 newly started firms which were recently investigated by

Projektburo Stimulans in Utrecht, 47 were most urgently in need of general orientation.[1] In another context, it turned out that when instruction meetings were organised about conducting one's own business in the Dutch province of Noord-Brabant, the need for general orientation again proved to be overwhelming. For the latter research project, questionnaires were sent to 382 visitors of instruction meetings, of which 141 were completed and returned. One question was why the respondents had applied for instruction. The percentage distribution of the answers is given in Table 1.

TABLE 1

Results of a Questionnaire

Motives for applying for instruction	Town			
	Eindhoven %	Tilburg %	Den Bosch %	Oss %
- Already had a business and desired more information	15	12	20	8
- Was planning own business shortly	28	12	20	14
- Wanted to know more about 'setting up one's own' before actually starting own business	48	66	50	87
- Was interested in new business because of being unemployed or going to lose job	30	20	20	60
- Professional interest	9	10	10	-

From the survey, out of those present at the instruction meetings an average of 22 per cent was soon going to start his own business. The large majority of the visitors, namely an average of 55 per cent, consisted of people who wanted more information so that they might start their own business. For approximately 30 per cent of the participants, current or future (threats of) job redundancy played a role. In the meantime, confronted with unemployment, many municipal authorities in The Netherlands encourage people to start their own business.

2. LOCAL INITIATIVES

According to the 'Atlas of local initiatives in the Netherlands 1983',[2] the notion of 'local initiatives' refers to 'all activities, projects, schemes, institutions and organisation initiated and developed on the regional or local level for the purpose of stimulating employment and activity in the area'. Essentially, the initiatives must spring off from the local community and be developed in close cooperation. In 'Publikatieblad van de Europese Gemeenschappen' (Information Bulletin of the European Communities) of March 12, 1984, local employment initiatives are defined as 'those initiatives that have been taken on the local level - often on the basis of cooperation of individuals, action groups, social partners and local and regional authorities - for the specific purpose of providing additional permanent employment by creating new small scale companies'. Initiative - cooperation - employment are in both descriptions cites here as essential elements of local regional dynamics. These dynamics differ from one region to another, and in this Bulletin the European Commission identifies a number of factors responsible for the differences, such as: local expertise, natural resources, renewable energy sources, town renewal schemes, creation of small companies. Differences in regional conditions may cause a large variety in local initiatives.

The Netherlands constitute a small part of the European Community, but the Atlas of local initiatives 1983 - and even more that of 1984 - shows tremendous regional variety of local initiatives. By analysing the editions of 1983 and 1984 of the Atlas of Local Initiatives, the development of local initiatives in The Netherlands could be examined (see Table 2). The development expressed in the figures is somewhat imprecise because some information was provided for 1984 but not for 1983.

TABLE 2

Local Initiatives in The Netherlands, 1983 and 1984

Category	1983	1984
Business consultants	36	100
Business centres	78	168
Export promotion	-	24
Financing	35	88
Innovation bureaus	21	40
Management courses	29	93
Business manifestations	19	33
	218	546

Within a year, the number of local initiatives has apparently doubled. The fast growing figures with respect to business centres are particularly interesting. Business centres are multifirm buildings with common facilities such as a canteen, a reception desk and office equipment. The advantages of business centres for starting firms are evident. The presence of a manager in a centre provides additional possibilities of guidance. Such managers/advisors appeared to have the following functions:

1. allround advice can be given, for instance on correspondence, archives, VAT handling, government licenses, debitor and staff matters,
2. entrepreneurs may jointly contract part time accountants and tax consultants,
3. the manager-advisor knows in some detail the conditions under which the entrepreneur works, which makes adequate recruitment of external advisors possible,
4. starting entrepreneurs thus become more amenable to helping one another by exchanging experience and advice.

On the other hand, in recent years also some doubts have been raised on the benefits of the fast increasing number of business centres.[3] Business centres can drastically disturb the relations between supply and demand on the market of business buildings in a region, in particular if their realisation is stimulated by substantial subsidies. Proper agreements have to be made to avoid conflicts between the government, banks, investors and entrepreneurs, but hasty procedures often neglect this issue. Moreover, the cost of aspects of settling in a business centre appear of particular importance to small entrepreneurs, which underlines the desirability of a project wise approach, preceded by a feasibility study.

Rauwenhoff (Directorate-General, Philips of The Netherlands) is reported to have stated:

> 'The stimulation philosophy of Philips in this matter can be summarised as follows: As the largest private employer in The Netherlands and in view of its dependence on an adequately functioning network of large and small suppliers, the company thinks that supporting small scale activity is a good way to help make our economy sound.'(4)

In May 1983 the Stichting Kleinschalige Bedrijvigheid (Foundation for Small Scale Enterprise) was founded in Valkenswaard by Philips Nederland BV and the Nederlandsche Middenstandsbank (Dutch Tradesmen's

Bank), for the purpose of helping innovative young entrepreneurs on the right track. Philips would account for technological support, the Nederlandsche Middenstandsbank for financial and administrative aid. In February 1984 the activities actually started. By the end of 1984, 55 projects had been taken on, 19 of them have become companies, 16 have been refuted, and the remaining 20 are still being examined.

3.   THE POLICY OF CENTRAL GOVERNMENT ON STARTING A SMALL SCALE BUSINESS

Observing the new interest in private enterprise and aware of the related problems, The Ministry of Economic Affairs in 1981 decided to issue a memorandum on relevant policy aspects. In that socalled Starters' Memorandum, the Ministry argued that new forms of new entrepreneurships were favourable for employment and for the economy. That does not mean, however, that the government considers starting forms the most important solution to problems of economy and employment. In view of the present economic recession the government wishes to stimulate in particular new businesses that offer prospects of expansion and hence of creating employment. The government's policy is:

1.   to discourage new enterprise in branches with a (threat of) overcapacity; the Memorandum mentions as such various branches of retail trade. Discouragement can be effectuated by information, by withholding income support and state credit guarantees from initiatives lacking market prospects, and by strict application of the Company Settlement Act;

2.   to stimulate the creation of promising new businesses (for instance innovative ones) by removing unnecessary obstacles and offering to such starters the greatest possible chance of survival. Stimulation can be effectuated, among other things, by good information, state guarantees on credits, income support, provision of accommodation at a reasonable price and according fiscal facilities for starting entrepreneurs.

The Minister described his policy as follows: 'At the same time it should be emphasised that the special attention which the government gives to new enterprises should not be taken from existing small companies. To lead starters by the hand is not the government's task:

they, like other entrepreneurs, are responsible for their companies' dealings.'

4. <u>SPECIFIC ASSISTANCE: INFORMATION, ADVICE AND GUIDANCE</u>

In the Starters' Memorandum, the central government explicitly states that it is not for the lower authorities to open all kinds of windows for business information: that would only obscure the information structure; it would be less transparent, and moreover, the local levels often lack expertise. Parliament, discussing the Memorandum, agreed with the view that, apart from financial and material support, new entrepreneurs are in need of information, advice and guidance. In its letter of May 30, 1984, the Ministry explains the principles of its relevant policy. Its primary concern is to stimulate that (potential) starters are able to draw up their own plan of enterprise. Most new entrepreneurs used to have a normal job and have not been brought up to entrepreneurship; lacking business knowledge, they tend to apply to various agencies with their questions and problems. To help them, the Ministry wishes to design a strategy suited to their needs by establishing organisations that fit their functional background, knowledge and experience best. To that end, a coordinated approach at the regional level is pleaded for, because a multitude of initiatives and activities tends to lower the efficiency and quality of the information and advice given to new entrepreneurs. Accordingly, the Ministry wants to favour: a well accessible first contact addresses to be established in the region; avoidance of overlaps; a transparent structure; high quality facilities.

For a coordinated regional approach, the Ministry suggests the following policy: providing general information for new entrepreneurs; organising orientation days or courses for new entrepreneurs; coordination or harmonisation of separate regional or local initiatives and activities concerned with those starting business; a good consultancy framework geared to the problems of individual beginning entrepreneurs.

To provide general information is primarily seen as a task of the Chambers of Commerce. Collective information meetings for starting entrepreneurs are often suggested in order to give them insight into the various aspects of entrepreneurship and the qualifications needed

(for instance, an entrepreneurs' certificate for legal establishment).
'Such a collective approach can mark the beginning of the road along
which serious starters, working on their plans of enterprise, are put
in contact with the appropriate agencies', according to the Ministry.

The Ministry also stresses the need for starters to be well informed
of the requirements of independent entrepreneurship and the elements
that should form part of a plan of the enterprise. To that end, courses are organised in various regions, in which the marketing and financing aspects of the business to be set up are considered in relation to the plan of enterprise to be drafted. To apply for participation in such courses, candidates usually have to submit a plan of enterprise, to be judged by a selection committee. For the selection,
the following criteria were used: applicants must have the intention
to start their own business in the foreseeable future; the plan must
offer market prospects; starters must already have made their plan to
some extent concrete, that is to say, have taken some steps towards
its realisation; the subjects to be treated in the course must be relevant to the plan's bottlenecks.

One positive result emerging from the evaluation of the instruction
course for starters organised in these regions was that the high demands
made on the market prospects and feasibility of the plans submitted
have led to a high proportion of the new entrepreneurs indeed starting
their own business at the end of the course. However, if the selection
of candidates has convinced some of them that they had better abandon
their plans for a business on their own, this may also be regarded as
a positive result of the selection.

Many agencies have taken it upon themselves to develop activities in
the interest of interested new entrepreneurs. To achieve a consistent
regional structure, it is necessary - in the view of the Minister of
Economic Affairs - for those agencies to coordinate their activities.
'The Chamber of Commerce offers a good platform for such coordination,
and therefore that body is the obvious one to convene regional organisations of businessmen and regional and local authorities, for a collective attempt to inventory and coordinate the initiatives taken for
instruction, advice and guidance to would-be entrepreneurs.'

After the stage of general orientation, the new entrepreneur enters a
new stage of substantiating his ideas in a plan of enterprise. The

Ministry recognises that many beginners find it difficult to design a realistic plan. Nevertheless, the Ministry takes a reticent attitude as to the degree of advice and guidance to be given to would-be entrepreneurs: as far as possible they must themselves collect the necessary data and draw up the plans, for in that way 'they learn the most and find out for themselves what it takes to be an independent businessman'. The Ministry points at - mostly unsubsidised - orientation courses and other courses in plan preparation. On the other hand, the Ministry is sympathetic to socalled secondee-system, by which ex-managers guide new entrepreneurs, once they have actually set up in business. This system has for some years been applied to good effect in the United Kingdom (Local Initiatives, UK).

A final quotation concerns the role of municipalities in this context. 'To our mind, the task of municipalities is to create adequate conditions in fields where they have an authority of their own (licences, accommodation) and to give information about the municipal policy and municipal rules with respect to business enterprise.'

5.   CONCLUSION

From the foregoing reflections, it has become clear that socioeconomic policy is highly centralised with hardly a responsibility left to local and regional authorities. Local initiatives to give business information and advice and to set up municipal starting funds do not have support from the central government, fearing inexpert action, legal discrepancies and thwarting of its own structural policy. The proliferation of local initiatives has caused tensions between the central and lower governments, which are seriously hampering the coordination of all policy instruments for the benefit of those wanting to start a new business in the various regions or municipalities.

NOTES

1.   '82 companies', T. de Jong et al., September 1984.

2.   'Atlas van Lokale Initiatieven in Nederland' (Atlas of local initiatives in The Netherlands), L. Verhoef et al., Bunnik, Tilburg, 1983 and 1984.

3. See 'Advies oprichting en functioneren van bedrijvencentra (Advice about the foundation and functioning of business centres). Raad voor het Midden- en Kleinbedrijf, The Hague 1984.

4. In M. van 't Hoff et al., 'Groot helpt klein' (Large helps Small), Tilburg, 1983, p. 25.

REFERENCES

Bannock, G., The Smaller Business in Britain and Germany, London, 1976.

Bannock, G., The Economics of Small Firms, Oxford, 1981.

Birch, D.L., The Job Generation Process, MIT, Cambridge, MA, 1979.

Boekema, F., Verhoef, L., 'Lokale initiatieven, theorie en praktijk', (Local initiatives, theory and practice', Deventer, 1984.

Bos, et. al., Small and Medium-sized Enterprises Coping with their Environment, Tilburg, 1983.

Broeder, A.L. den, 'Over kleine zelfstandigen', (On small enterprises), Kroniek Ambachten en MKB, Vol. 35, No. 2, 1981, pp. 78-85.

Department of Economic Affairs, 'Beleid inzake het starten van een eigen bedrijf', (Government policy regarding the foundation of small enterprises), Tweede Kamer, 17.554, The Hague.

Huppes, T., 'Een nieuw ambachtelijk elan', (A new spirit among tradesmen), Leiden, 1985.

Raad voor het Midden- Kleinbedrijf, 'Advies oprichting en functioneren van bedrijvencentra', (Advice about the foundation and function of business centres), The Hague, 1984.

Rothwell, R. and Zegveld, W., Innovation and the small and medium sized firm , London, 1982.

Shapero, A., The entrepreneur, the small firm and possible policies , Limmerick, Ireland, 1980.

Verhoef, L. et al., 'Atlas van lokale initiatieven in Nederland', (Atlas of local initiatives in The Netherlands), Stichting Economisch Instituut, Tilburg, 1983.

Wagner, G.A. et al., 'Een nieuw industrieel elan', (A new industrial spirit), Deventer, 1984.

Wever, E., Nieuwe bedrijven in Nederland , (New enterprises in The Netherlands), Assen, 1984.

Zeil, P.H., 'National Government and the small and medium sized enterprises', Department of Economic Affairs, The Hague, 1983.

HIGH-TECHNOLOGY AND EMPLOYMENT :
SOME INFORMATION ON THE NETHERLANDS
Huub Bouman and Bram Verhoef

1.   INTRODUCTION

During the years of massive industrial job losses, one branch of industry was characterised by very high growth rates. This explains the
great interest of researchers and policy makers in the high-tech sector. High-technolgy is generally considered a shortcut to
reindustrialisation. But does the high-tech sector live up to its
promises? A lot of research has been done on the developments in the
US. Focal points were areas like the Silicon Valley, the Greater
Boston Area and the Research Triangle. However, after years of reports
about astonishing growth rates of firms which had been founded by
young, unconventional entrepreneurs, recent press releases have been
less optimistic.

This article will make an attempt at assessing the contribution of
high-tech industries in revitalising the Dutch economy. The first part
of this contribution addresses itself to the factors influencing the
location of the high-tech sector. The second part is concerned with
the generation of employment and implications for the labour market.

Before assessing this contribution, however, it is most important to
know what high-tech really is. The main reason for this is that otherwise government policies run the risk of being based on what has been
called a vague advertising slogan, used to describe anything from cars
to computers (McQuaid 1984).

Literature and export opinion do not provide us with an exact and generally accepted definition of the sector. This is rather surprising
considering that high-tech is frequently seen as the 'Third Revolution', a revolution which can be characterised by key works such as
electronics, automation, communication and information. It will however be clear that the term 'high-tech' stands for some of the new

developments in the economies of industrialised countries in recent years.

The various ways in which researchers have attempted to define the sector reveal that key criteria for identifying high-tech activities are: a high proportion of personnel involved in research and development activities, high growth rates, expanding markets and product innovations.

In technology research nowadays, a division of the economy into high, intermediate and low-technology sectors is quite commonly employed. Knowledge intensity is the criterion by which these sectors can be distinguished. In a special issue of Business Week, June 1981, entitled 'America's restructured economy', a division into five sectors is presented: an old line industries, agriculture, energy, services and high-technology.

The central problem with the above mentioned classifications and with definitions of high-tech in particular, is that they are generally not compatible with existing standard industrial classifications. In the research project on which this article is based, an attempt has been made to link the concept of high-technology to the Dutch SIC.

2.   TECHNOLOGY, INNOVATION AND ECONOMIC DEVELOPMENT

Technology can be described as the formal and systematic entity of knowledge and skills needed to realised and control complex production techniques and processes (de Smidt 1981). Technology, and as a consequence, innovations, are not randomly dispersed and are not coincidental. They are the result of explicit and motivated decision of enterprises with respect to products and processes (Malecki 1983). The innovative capacity of a firm depends heavily on its R&D expenditures. Together with investments in general, this expenditure is an important indication of the growth potential of an enterprise. In The Netherlands, research expenditure shows a strong concentration. The five largest firms account for approximately 70 per cent of total expenditure, involving about 80 per cent of the employment in R&D (Wijers 1985).

Technology and innovation can also be linked to macroeconomic developments. Schumpeter introduced the idea of technological revolution as a motor of the long waves of Kondratieff. From this point of view, economic growth is set in motion by the introduction of basic innovations.

Schumpeter related the outburst of innovative activity on the part of entrepreneurs to important technological changes (e.g. steam railway transportation, electricity and the private car). In recent discussions about long waves, the idea of clustered innovations is revived with the aid of the 'product life-cycle' and the theory of the multiplier accelerator (Lambooy et al. 1983). One should, however, bear in mind that the assumption that innovations are not introduced continuously cannot hold good unless a distinction is made between product and process innovations (de Jong and Terhorst 1983). Process innovations imply cost reductions and/or quality improvements and can in principle be introduced continuously. In fact, it is only the product innovations that are characterised by noncontinuous introduction.

In this survey, product innovation is considered to be the distinguishing factor in operationalising the high-tech sector. Next, a set of four-digit SIC categories have been selected which can be assumed to represent the sector. This leads to a choice of activities which are characterised by new products, regardless of the nature of the production process. This sometimes leads to a paradox in cases where high-tech firms with low-tech production techniques are included, while more standardised products which can be manufactured by very sophisticated production methods are not taken into consideration (Map 1). We admit that linking the high-tech concept to SIC categories does not provide an exact definition. Nonetheless, it offers the possibility for quantitative research and mapping.

3. HIGH-TECHNOLOGY IN THE NETHERLANDS: A CONCENTRATED PATTERN

On the basis of the four-digit SIC categories, 1287 plants were selected. These plants showed a strong concentration in larger cities and, as consequence, in the Randstad, Holland which occupies the western central part of the country. (Figure 1). More than 57 per cent of the high-tech plants are located in the three Randstad provinces, while another 12.4 per cent are located in the southern province of North-Brabant. The remaining seven provinces account for just over 30 per cent of the total number of high-tech plants. This concentration is far stronger than might be expected on the basis of the unequal distribution of population and industrial activities in The Netherlands.

When high-tech plants are classified according to types of urbanisation of their location, a strong preference for larger urban centres surrounding suburban municipalities is revealed.

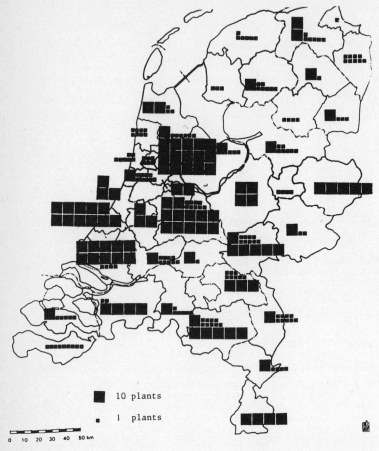

■ 10 plants

▪ 1 plants

0 10 20 30 40 50 km

Map 1.   Number of high tech plants per COROP region.

Another form of concentration emerges when the average number of employees per plant is examined. High-tech plants on the average have a larger number of employees than other industries. Most striking in the high-tech sector is underrepresentation of the one-man firm as well as the very large proportion of small firms employing one to give workers. One other phenomenon to which attention should be drawn is the presence of a small number of very large firms (Philips, Fokker, Océ, IBM and Siemens).

4.   LOCATION FACTORS OF HIGH-TECH INDUSTRIES

The locational pattern of plants is influenced by many and diverse factors. One structuring element, however, is the spatial scale at which the location factors are operational. Some factors influence the choice of country (e.g. language, life-styles and interest rates). Other factors are of important on the interregional level (e.g. availability of labour, while others are operational on the local level. An example of the last category is the availability of suitable sites for location (Premus 1982).

In the Dutch situation, our research addresses itself to those factors which are supposed to influence interregional dispersion. This implies that supply of sites and the level of local taxes need not be taken into consideration. Despite the fact that high-tech is very hard to operationalise, several locational factors are mentioned in the literature. Sometimes they are traditional, sometimes relative new. It is generally assumed that traditional location factors are of limited importance to the high-tech sector.

Often these firms are considered footloose as regards markets, sources of raw materials and transport (Premus 1982). Despite the apparent confusion in the literature, some factors are mentioned more than once. The factor which the majority of authors consider most important is the availability of highly skilled labour (among others Levy 1983). Others qualify this by pointing out that in the course of time, more unskilled labour will be required (Berry 1983). A second factor often mentioned is the proximity to research institutes and centres of knowledge and knowhow (Thwaites 1982, Levy 1983, Premus 1982). Obviously, there is a relationship between this factor and the former.

Amenity is the third factor frequently mentioned in the literature. The fourth is the availability of 'venture capital', a type of high risk capital provision, characterised by greater involvement of the supplier of capital in the enterprise (Rothwell 1982). From the literature it may be concluded that availability of highly skilled labour is the most important factor, closely followed by proximity to knowledge centres. Venture capital and amenity are also very important but play a less decisive role that the first two factors.

5. PROFILES: DEMAND AND SUPPLY CONFRONTED

Given the four locational requirements and the order of importance as set out above, the supply side was investigated. Several indicators were used to operationalise the locational requirements found in the literature. The availability of highly skilled labour was approximated by assess the educational level of the active population of the provinces. In this approximation advanced technical education and exact sciences were considered most important. The factor proximity to research institutes and centres of knowledge and knowhow was operationalised by measuring the distance to these centres and institutes. In total 22 such locations were distinguished.

The third factor, amenity, was considered equivalent to a sociocultural indicator containing five variables: the provision of sports facilities, natural amenities, monuments, cinemas and music and theatre performances, all divided by the resident population of the area in question.

The number of providers of venture capital was used to determine the supply of that location factor per province.

Next, the four location factors were accorded a certain weighting factor, dependent upon their importance in the literature. This set of weighting factors was found to be quite insensitive to variation of their values.

Finally, this supply profile, derived from the operationalised location factors mentioned above, was confronted with the actual distribution pointed out earlier. Comparing the two showed that overall tendencies corresponded, but that the residual variance quite systematically pointed to the degree of urbanisation as a major location factor. Indeed, the introduction of this factor (by simply considering the population densities) as a very prominent influence (considerably raised the level of correspondence between the normative location profile and the actual dispersion pattern of high-tech plants. Further research demonstrated that the availability of venture capital did not exert a significant influence on the interregional level. The same is true of amenity, which is probably operational at the subregional level, as may be deduced from the preference of high-tech plants for urban and suburban environments.

An interesting hypothesis in this respect is that diffusion of high-tech plants first took place in accordance with the urban hierarchy all over the country, and subsequently radiated out of these larger centres to suburban locations. If this hypothesis survives testing, the second stage in the diffusion process would be amenity-based.

Concluding, it may be posed that the spatial distribution of high-tech plants in The Netherlands can be explained by three processes: orientation towards larger urban centres, pools of highly skilled labour, and sources of information and knowledge.

6.   HIGH-TECH EMPLOYMENT GENERATION BETWEEN 1975 AND 1985

In the group of smaller high-tech firms (less than 1000 employees) employment rose by 47.2 per cent between 1975 and 1980. In the next five-year period, this figure levelled of to 28.9 per cent. On the basis of the small number of vacancies at this moment, it may be concluded that a stage of stabilisation has been reached. The five large firms (Philips, Fokker, Océ, IBM and Siemens) seem to have been greatly influenced by the world recession. Employment levels within these firms remained stable or dropped. For Philips, the employment decline was a continuation of a ten-year trend. In the case of other firms, like Fokker and Siemens, an employment decline was a break point in a long era of expansion. With all three firms, people laid off were mostly older than 57.5 years.

The upswing in economic activity in 1984 has greatly increased employment in the major five high-tech firms. At the moment, each of the corporations has several hundred vacancies. This significantly increased demand is partly due to the employment stops of the 'bad years'. It is generally assumed that demand will not rise further, but will level off at the present high level.

This demand is strongly oriented toward people with a high level of education in the technical and exact sciences. As representatives of those corporations put it, some firms are in the middle of a transformation phase from a production to a knowhow type of firm. This is illustrated by Philips. Between 1977 and 1979, 14 per cent of the employees fitted into the category highly educated. By 1985 this proportion is expected to reach 49 per cent. Despite the apparent risk in forecasting employment development, it would appear that the demand for unskilled personnel with these firms will remain low for several years to come.

In the American semiconductor industry, several authors found a bifurcated employment structure. The labour force was dominated by a fairly large group of highly skilled and highly paid specialists and a large group of assembly line workers with very minimal qualifications. This phenomenon has been termed the 'vanishing middle'.

In the research on which this paper is based, no evidence was found of such a bifurcation in the Dutch high-tech sector. The sudden increase in demand for the aforementioned highly educated staff is not matched by an equally significant rise in supply. The labour market for these employees shows clear signs of scarcity. This leads to significant increases in salaries, especially in small firms which are not inhibited by rigid salary structures.

This situation is even expected to deteriorate because of the smaller cohorts of students now entering the relevant university faculties. It is expected that the greatest problems will arise after 1989. In order that the growth of the high-tech sector not be obstructed, some personnel managers set out to attract more women to information courses intended to promote the choice of this branch of study.

7. REGIONAL LABOUR MARKETS

Within the labour market as a whole, a number of geographical levels of scale can be distinguished. The site of these submarkets is highly dependent upon the educational level of the people concerned.

In the Dutch situation, four levels can be distinguished:
-   local: unskilled production workers (where married women
                   are concerned sometimes even very local)
-   regional: medium-skilled

-    national   highly skilled and university graduates
-    international: university graduates

These levels of scale can greatly influence the market mechanism for specific categories of employees. Besides categories of highly educated people, some categories of medium skilled personnel are also becoming scarce. This demand is often geographically concentrated, which leads to spatially concentrated shortages. Because of the regional scale of the labour market, the odd situation may occur that surpluses and shortages coexist in the same area.

8. CONCLUSION

The Dutch high-tech sector has proved to be far from immune to the world recession. The smaller firms showed a clear decline of growth rates between 1980 and 1985. Some of the larger firms even showed declining employment levels. The present situation would seem to indicate better prospects for the large firms considering the far higher percentages of vacancies. This trend may be expected to continue for some time since R&D expenditures in high-tech products are very high. Smaller firms have the best opportunities for development in very specific market niches. Taking advantage of these niches calls for a high degree of specialisation. As regards the high technological and financial barriers to entering the high-tech sector, the formation of new firms in the computer services offers better prospects.

REFERENCES

Berry, B., 'Is a broom hi-tech?' Iron Age, Vol. 13, April 1983, pp. 47-63.

Bouman, H., Thuis, Th.J.F. and Verhoef, A., High-Tech in Nederland, Utrecht, 1985.

Business Week, Special Issue, 'America's restructured economy', June 1981.

Duijn, J.J. van and Lambooy, J.G., Technological Innovation and Regional Economic Growth: a Meso Economic Analysis, University of Amsterdam, Amsterdam, 1982.

Jong, M. de and Terhorst, P., Innovaties en Ruimtelijke Concentratie, University of Amsterdam, Amsterdam, 1983.

Lambooy, J.G., Duijn, J.J. van and Paelinck, J.H.P., Rapport Inzake Het Regionaal Sociaal-Economisch Beleid en Het Ruimtelijk Beleid, SER/RARO, The Hague, 1983.

Levy, J.M., Economic and Social Factors Influencing Industrial Land Use in the US, International Workshop, Canada, 1983.

Malecki, E.J., 'Technology and regional development', International Regional Science Review, Vol. 8, No. 2, 1983, pp. 89-125.

Premus, R., Location of High-Technology Firms and Regional Economic Development, OESO, Paris, 1982.

McQuaid, R.W. and Langridge, R.J., Defining High Technology, Cambridge, 1984.

Rothwell, R., 'The role of technology in industrial change: implications for regional policy', Regional Studies, Vol. 16, No. 5, 1982, pp. 361-369.

Smidt, M. de, 'Innovatie, industriebeleid en regionale ontwikkeling', Geografisch Tijdschrift, 15, No. 3, 1981, pp. 228-238.

Thwaites, A.T., 'Some evidence of regional variations in the introduction and differentiation of industrial products within British industry', Regional Studies, Vol. 16, No. 5, 1982, pp. 371-381.

Wijers, G.J., 'Technologie en economische ontwikkeling', ESB, 69, No. 3444, 1985, pp. 176-181.

PART C: MODELLING

ADAPTIVE ECONOMISING, TECHNOLOGICAL CHANGE AND THE DEMAND
FOR LABOUR IN DISEQUILIBRIUM
Richard H. Day and Kenneth A. Hanson

1. INTRODUCTION

Technological change as incorporated into an economy through capital
investment has a bearing on the organisation of production and the
derived demand for labour. A widely held view is that innovation is
the main spring of economic growth. We see this in the business cycle
theory of Schumpeter (1934) and the capital dynamics of Hicks (1977).
Both attempt to discover how an innovative impulse works itself out in
a multisector economy in which there is generated a dynamic feedback
process. An innovation influences the productivity and demand for
labour and the distribution of income between wages and profits which
has a feedback effect on investment by firms, and hence, future demand
for labour. In a multisector economy where a structural shift in the
demand for labour may arise, Hicks suggested that an 'innovative impulse may have drastic and possibly unacceptable effects on distribution' and that the prospects of convergence from one full employment
equilibrium to another 'looks poor' (Hicks 1977, pp. 190-195, Ch. 2).

Similarly, Malinvaud (1982, 1984) has suggested that wage and profit
adjustments do not provide adequate incentives for capital investment
to maintain full employment over the long run. Instead, he argues, a
complex macro dynamic process arises out of the economising behaviour
of agents interacting in the labour, capital and product markets. The
stability of this process cannot be taken for granted. There is a need
to assess the institutional structure of labour and capital markets,
and to determine how the disequilibrium adjustment processes of agents
in these markets respond to innovative impulses in capital technology
over the medium to long term.

For such disequilibrium analysis, new representations of the economic
system, other than the neoclassical-classical aggregate models based
on assumed stability of market feedback adjustment processes, are required. As Koopmans observed 'until we succeed in specifying fruitful

assumptions for the behaviour in an uncertain and changing economic environment, we shall continue to be groping for the proper tools of reasoning' (1957, p. 183). Clower and Leijonhufvud suggest that 'what we need is a theory capable of describing system behaviour as a temporal process, in or out of equilibrium, which requires a prior account of how trade is organised in the system and of how business and household units behave when the system is not in equilibrium and is predicated on how trade is organised' (1975, p. 183).

To analyse labour market aspects of long term industrial development what we need, then, is a new modelling framework. This paper describes such a framework, or more correctly part of such a framework based upon principles of adaptive economising in disequilibrium. It is applied to a firm's production-investment planning problem to illustrate how short run and medium run developments in labour demand are related to capital investment and technological change. The framework will be completed when various submodels of this kind are linked in a network of intersectoral and urban-regional flows. Then it will be possible to study in detail how important macroeconomic problems are generated by microeconomic forces in a way called for by Malinvaud and by Clower and Leijonhufvud.

2.   THE DYNAMIC ECONOMY

An economy is comprised of a set of agents consisting of households, firms in different industrial sectors, financial intermediaries, and government, all interacting on markets for commodities, labour and financial services. Each market is a process which coordinates plans and mediates transactions among agents, through legal institutional rules. With agents making plans for activities and transactions into the uncertain future, using imperfect information, the plans of agents may be inconsistent, and hence transactions will be constrained and markets in disequilibrium. Under conditions of imperfect coordination, disequilibrium mechanisms such as rationing schemes, inventory-order backlog adjustment, and the use of credit and maintenance of liquidity, provide the means of mediating transactions and maintaining agency-economy viability. With feedback information from transacting in disequilibrium, agents use an adaptive planning procedure. The adaptive economising behaviour of agents, transacting on markets in disequilibrium, and the market process of coordinating plans and mediating transactions are the microfoundations to the aggregate dynamics of an economy.

At the beginning of each elemental period (week, month, quarter, year), a state of technology, resource availability, social organisation, and individual preference prevails, and, of course, a history of past consumption, production and technological practice has occurred. On the basis of all this the various agents make their plans, modifying or retaining old plans, or drawing up altogether new ones, and carry out actions based on part on these plans but also on mechanisms and adjustment rules that lead to viable activity when plans cannot be carried out.

The next period the situation has changed. Resources have been depleted, capital may have been augmented, prices and other indexes of value and wealth will be modified and so on. The system is poised for a new round of planning and action.

Observed over a sequence of periods, the economy will exhibit a history of specific activities that were and were not pursued, of specific technologies and resources that were and were not utilised, of specific constraints that were or were not binding. At each point in time choices are available. Once the agents decide among them and implement their plans, the current state and its successor are connected by more or less precise relationships that determine the flow of goods and services, the accumulation of goods, the decumulation of resources and so on. In this way, the unfolding of economic events comes to be governed by dynamic structure.

When in the course of this process the consumption and/or production activities actually utilised change, or the constraints actually impinging on choice and actions switch, we observe a change in dynamic structure. Some variables that appeared relevant will no longer appear so; other variables that once seemed of no importance at all will not appear to play an active role in development; some technologies may be abandoned, different ones taking their place; some resources once available in plenty and perhaps thought of as free goods, now become scarce and attain great value in exchange; still other resources once crucial in the production transformation are abandoned, perhaps before they are exhausted, again becoming valueless.

In the short run and in the small, one will see individuals and organisations occasionally change what they do and how they do it. Viewed in the aggregate, waves of growth or decline in productivity and fluctuation in output and value will occur, and in the long run, various 'epochs' or 'ages' will appear, dominated by characteristic activities and resources. In general the economy's technological regimes will switch; its consumption and production patterns will change: its structure and behavioural pattern will evolve.

We want to consider economising behaviour in this dynamic context.

3.   ADAPTIVE ECONOMISING

Economising involves the allocation of scarce resources according to a criterion such as profit, sales utility, or more generally, preferences. It involves doing the best one can in production or consumption or both, where 'best' is clearly defined. How is economising to be represented?

The answer depends in an essential way on the preconceived notion of the complexity of change occurring in the economic-environment and the cognitive capacity of agents. Research in cognitive psychology, see Simon(1978), suggests that the complexity of change and the limited cognitive capacity of agents, bounds the rationality of economic agents. Prior to this research in psychology, Keynes was perceptive enough to recognise that, in regards to orthodox theory, 'the hypothesis of a calculable future leads to a wrong interpretation of the principles of behaviour which the need for action compels us to take' (Keynes 1937, p. 222).

In an historical process where the emergence of novelty is the main spring of economic growth and the complexity of change is a reason for cautious, behavioural rules of thumb, prevalent in most firm planning procedures, it seems appropriate to assume that agents are boundedly rational. This is to claim they have limited foresight and computational ability, that errors in expectations is the rule and not the exception, and that a sequential process of short term planning with behavioural rules of adjustment to market-environment feedback is characteristics of planning procedures.

Economic activities planned at the beginning of a given period are to be undertaken immediately or in future periods. The choice among alternative activities and the determination of activity levels are constrained by technology - the set of available and perceived opportunities (the state of the art) - and by resource availabilities and financial constraints. At any given time these constraining factors and the degree of their limitedness circumscribe the individual's opportunities within a feasible region of activity levels.

Associated with each constraining factor or influence is a constraint function that determines how the various activities are restricted by that factor and a limitation coefficient that describes how limiting the particular constraint is. The latter are inherited from the last and are fixed for the time being. Their effective limitedness, however, can be reduced by the choice of certain activities. Machine capacities inherited from the past can be augmented by the purchase of new machines. The supply of money available for investment can be augmented by borrowing. However, investment in a given year is limited by reinvestment funds, and borrowing is limited by lenders' credit rationing rules. Hence choices that reduce the effective restriction on other activities in any one year are in their turn bounded by limitations of their own. Adaptation in response to feedback from past decisions and the external environment has the effect of modifying the feasible region from one period to the next. For a given period it is fixed.

Faced with uncertainty as they contemplate change from existing patterns of behaviour, decision makers usually limit the consideration of alternatives to a local search of those in a neighbourhood of current practice. The willingness to depart from current practice, that is, the extent of the region searched may depend on experience and on the behaviour of other agents. Thus, adaptation to current economic opportunity may be more or less flexible. The set of alternatives that may be considered at a given time is called the zone of flexible response. Such zones depend on experience and imitation. This dependence means that economising is more or less cautious and the degree of flexibility changes in response to feedback.

Finally, the choice within the constraints determined by technology, resource availability and by the willingness to be flexible in responding to opportunity is directed by various goals perhaps arranged to some (perhaps temporary) hierarchy or priority order. A first goal dominates comparison of alternatives until a satisfactory solution is obtained according to this goal; then a less important goal is used to choose among the alternatives satisfying the higher order goal, and so on, until a single choice is reached.

To summarise, adaptive economising involves optimising a sequence of simplified, constrained choice problems according to a hierarchy of objectives in which choice is restricted not only by objective resource constraints but also by subjective constraints that have the effect of confining behaviour to a region of flexible response in the neighbourhood of current, operating conditions. The constraints and objectives are adjusted period to period in response to experience and to feedback from the environment.

4.   RECURSIVE PROGRAMMING MODELS

The mathematical analogue of adaptive economising is the recursive programming model. Such models provide a formal, computationally convenient means for representing boundedly rational planning. While such models can incorporate farsighted planning over a finite (or infinite) horizon they distinguish explicitly between the agents approximate and imperfect knowledge of the environment from its true structure. By embedding the model of adaptive economising in a model of the 'true' environment, it is possible to perform simulation experiments of a modelled representation of a real time process. See Figure 1.

The solution of such a model involves the values of the various activities from period to period. Typically, solutions involve nonlinear dynamics exhibiting changing modes of behaviour, nonperiodic fluctuations and sensitivity to perturbations in initial conditions and parameter values. In addition, they exhibit changing sets of utilised activities and tight constraints. When these sets switch the variables and equations governing the evolution of the system switch, in effect bringing in a different set of causal structures and feedback loops.

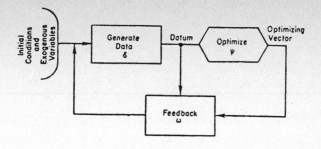

a.   The recursive programming model

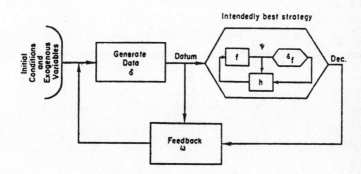

b.   Recursive strategic programming model of intendedly
      optimal behaviour (rolling plans of planning revision)

Figure 1 Recursive programming models, from Day and Cigno (1978)

These structures are called phase structures. A given model may contain a single regime or a very large set of potential phases. The result is not only an endogenous theory of changing modes, as in any nonlinear dynamic system, but also an endogenous theory of structural evolution based on explicit economising behaviour.

The demand for any particular resource, including labour, is derived in such a model from the various production and investment activity levels which depend on all of the constraints and objective function coefficients; these in turn depend on the past activity levels and past states of the environment. In this way, one derives a dynamic demand for inputs that incorporates technological change as well as the usual economic variables.

5. APPLICATIONS

Various authors have constructed an tested recursive programming models of agricultural and industrial development. See Day and Cigno (1978) and Day and Singh (1977). In an early example, Day (1967), one of us showed how investment in new technology influenced the utilisation of labour in agriculture and patterns of rural-urban migration. In essence the process involved a labour market disequilibrium induced by labour saving technology and which precipitated intersectoral flows of people.

Analogous results could be derived from the industrial models described in Day and Cigno (1978, Ch. 4). In these models the structure of production is represented by sets of activities that make possible alternative production processes.

The path from 'primary' inputs to 'final' product usually involves a sequence of conversions which constitute a production process, a series of discrete steps during each of which a given task is performed. A task performed by a specific transformer or machine is an operation. The transformers use various inputs such as labour, fuel, lubricants, etc. The output of the operation is an intermediate good ready for the next task or final good ready for storage or sale and shipment. The use of an operation in a given time period is an activity - Koopmans'

'elemental atom of technology', its intensity is the activity level.
These activity levels are the fundamental decision variables of the
economic unit. A collection of alternative activities for producing a
given intermediate product or final good is a stage of production.
Most industries involve a variety of such production stages. Assuming
linearity of each activity (Koopman 1951) the input-output structure
is represented by vectors of input-output coefficients, and the sequence of activities by a technology matrix. Although individual activities possess fixed technical coefficients, alternative activities
for given tasks allow for substitution and complementarity in the use
of industry resources.

Innovations in production technology are accommodated by introducing
new production and investment activities. New investment activities
may represent construction of capacity in the new technology or conversion of existing capital equipment. Both categories represent
capital-embodied technological change. Disembodied technological
change, which leads to a gradual modification of technical coefficients, requires periodic updating of the input-output matrix. Diffusion of a given technique is described endogenously so that the entire
model explains its dominance or lack of dominance over competing techniques.

Production planning is viewed as passing through four stages. First,
data concerning input-output structures, production goals, input supplies, behavioural rules, production rules, and annual investment
charges are formulated. Second, feasible production goals are determined. Third, production-investment activity levels are planned that
minimise production and investment costs, where the latter are determined by a cashflow, payback criterion. Fourth, given estimated expanded capacity, estimated actual production is performed at minimum
variable cost leading to a final model estimate of production activity
levels.

The heart of the model is the third stage in which investment levels
are determined. Investment is motivated by two distinct considerations: (i) capacity expansion to meet anticipated sales and (ii) replacement of existing plant and equipment by technologically superior
alternative capital goods to lower production costs. Because of this
second consideration excess capacity can be generated even in the face
of stable or declining demand for final production for, as long as an

investment will 'pay for itself' by reducing production costs to pay back the sacrificed capital in a sufficient period of time (the pay-back period), investment will occur.

However, the rate of investment in our models is constrained, first by adjustment bounds that reflect hedging against uncertainties, second by adoption constraints that reflect learning, and third by abandonment constraints that reflect inertia in departing from established practice. These constraints determine the zone of flexible response to current economic opportunity. Because of these constraints and because of the behavioural feedback relations, investment may continue in obsolescent capacity until the willing expansion in new technology increases enough. Likewise, abandonment of obsolescent or obsolete technology may be limited by this reluctance to 'plunge' into the latest techniques, as well as by an inherent inertia in the planning process. Because the model incorporates all these considerations, it will generate capital capacity trajectories with overlapping, wavelike appearances. Indeed, for a given capital good, the phase diagram of capacity would appear like that shown in Figure 2, where it is assumed that the sales forecast is constant over time. If the good is profitable, it follows the adaptation constraint for a time, until the adjustment rule becomes tight.

Eventually, as capacity expands in superior techniques, capacity change will fall within the shaded area, perhaps increasing for a time, then declining and finally, declining at a maximal rate determined by depreciation or the production abandonment constraints.

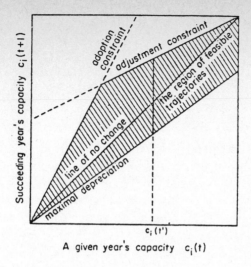

Figure 2 Phase diagram for an individual capital good within a constrained sales forecast. The trajectory of capacity must lie
within the convex, shaded region.

Source: Day and Nelson (1973)

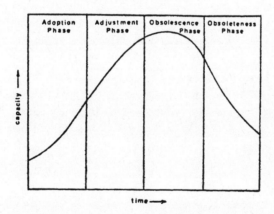

Figure 3 A typical capital good trajectory generated by one of the
RP models.

Source: Day and Nelson (1973)

Our models thus simulate the nonlinear patterns of diffusion, the su-
perimposed waves of 'creative destruction' so characteristic of industrial development. Indeed, such patterns have been observed so often
that they have been called 'the Law of Industrial Growth' (Schmookler
1965). And idealised history generated by one of our models is shown

in Figure 3 which approximates the path of US open hearth steel capacity since the turn of the century.

Generally speaking, when one technology is replacing another, when the old one has become obsolescent or obsolete, the demand for inputs will change, even if production levels are constant, because the different technologies have different input requirements. Typically, the demand for some grades of labour will decline so much that even if demand is increasing for labour with other skills and qualifications the aggregate effect is an overall reduction in employment. This is why a growth in output or a growth in leisure must usually accompany technological development if full employment is maintained.

6. A NEW RP MODEL EMPHASISING FINANCIAL FLOWS

There are several dimensions of firm behaviour which these earlier models of industrial development did not elaborate upon. First, is the financial-budgetting procedures used by firms to acquire new capital and maintain an adequate cash flow on a year to year basis. A second limitation involves construction lead times and the specification of cost coefficients in the investment planning criterion. As inflation and rising prices for primary materials and labour occurs, the inclusion of factor prices escalation in the cost coefficients may influence the current choice of technology. Third, due to the potential for errors in expectations, and, hence current period plans, it is necessary to consider the use of disequilibrium butter stock mechanisms and rules of adjustment behaviour.

The second author is now developing a new RP model that accommodates these three considerations. The central features are represented in Figures 4 and 5.

The general planning sequence of the firm, see Figure 5, is embedded into the market environment feedback process of Figure 4, providing a modelled representation of a real time process. With this a recursive programming model, the dynamics of an agent environment feedback process can be simulated.

313

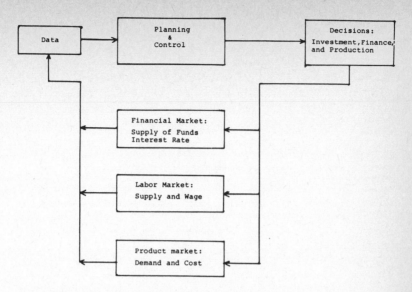

Figure 4   Adaptive economising model of a firm with market feedback.

Rather than going into the details of model structure, a simple illustration of how the choice of technology depends on anticipated factor prices and the financial situation of the firm.

Assume a firm has a given stock of financial and physical capital and confronts a growing demand. The firm has a choice of investing two types of technology, one capital intensive and the other fuel-labour intensive. Assume the capital intensive technology has the lower levelised annual cost but requires a larger amount of external funding. Assume at first the firm's financial position is below debt capacity. As demand grows and more debt is issued, the firm may reach its debt capacity requiring a more expensive source of financing. This comprises a switch in the phase of activity. Whether a shift to the fuel-labour intensive technology is the optimal investment strategy given the switch in financial policy can be determined from a phase switching rule as derived from the Kuhn-Tucker conditions. The phase switching rule in terms of the cost coefficients for the two technologies and the cost of financing before and after the switch is

$$\alpha_1 \leq \frac{CP_1 - CP_2}{CK_1 - CK_2} \leq \alpha_2$$

314

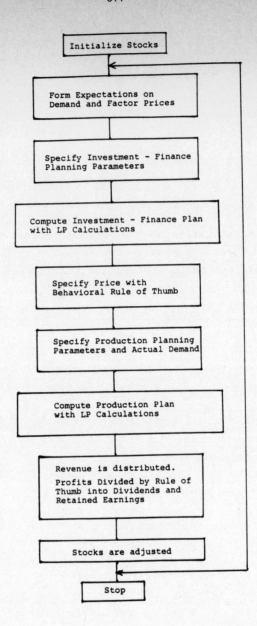

Figure 5. Firm investment-production planning model

where

(CP$_1$, CK$_1$) :   fuel-labour intensive production and capital cost coefficients

(CP$_2$, CK$_2$) :   capital intensive production and capital cost coefficients

α_1, α_2 :   parameters which depend on the cost of financing before and after the phase switch, respectively, and a common economic life of the technologies.

When this inequality holds then the optimal investment strategy is to shift from capital intensive to fuel-labour intensive technology when the phase shifts to more expensive external financing. With these parameters changing from period to period due to changing expectations on prices the impact of a change in the cost of financing will vary. For instance, if the expected wage rate is higher, then cP$_1$ will increase relative to cP$_2$. If a technological change in the capital intensive technology occurs reducing cost then cK$_2$ will decrease relative to cK$_1$. A change in the cost of financing will effect α_1 and α_2. From period to period, the choice of capital technology may change in response to market feedback and innovation, leading to complex dynamics of derived labour demand. Through if - then simulation experiments a more elaborate picture of the potential for labour demand dynamics may be illustrated.

7.   MARKETS IN DISEQUILIBRIUM

Equilibrium is a powerful assumption in economic analysis allowing considerable simplification in the representation of economic phenomena. Setting supply equal to demand is a mathematical convenience, but can we just assume equilibrium? Certainly considerable insight has been gained by doing so. But as suggested in the correspondence principle, 'for an equilibrium analysis, one must show not only stability but also rapid convergence, otherwise the study of transient behaviour, where the processes of adjustment are determined endogenously by the behaviour of agents and the way markets are organised, is of paramount importance' (Fisher 1983, p. 11; also Samuelson 1948).

With errors in expectations the plans of agents need not be consistent in the markets, and, hence there is unanticipated market feedback and spillover effects among markets, stimulating disequilibrium adjustment behaviour. This potential for disequilibrium is reinforced by the bounded rationality of agents, who, having limited foresight are not able to balance adequately the short run and long run implications of behaviour. Thus, what appears to be optimal in the short run may have a disequilibrating impact in the long run.

In this section we discuss how to extend the adaptive economising model of firm planning and adjustment behaviour to one which captures the essential ingredients of disequilibrium. A firm's capital investment and demand response to labour and capital finance market feedback provides a good example for investigating how the dynamics of adjustment to exogenous technological change need not lead to an equilibrium.

Firm investment and production plans, and derived labour demand, need not be consistent with labour supply and supply of financial funds, given real wages and the rate of interest, leading to excess supply or demand. Traditional equilibrium theories assume stability of the excess supply and demand adjustment processes which may well be valid for the implicitly assumed institutional structure of markets and agent response (Fisher 1983).

Under existing institutional structure of markets and the bounded rationality of agents, there is no a priori grounds for assuming stability. Supply, demand, and price adjustments in the different markets need not be consistent in the sense of converging to a full employment equilibrium. The wage-profit distribution and the feedback effect on capital expansion, and hence future labour demand need not be consistent with labour supply, leaving the economy in a dynamic disequilibrium adjustment process, where they may arise a disequilibrium unemployment above and beyond frictional or search levels.

For instance, elements of real market situations involve real wages and labour supply which are predominantly determined by such forces, autonomous to the economic process, as demographic trends and social-cultural aspirations for real relative income (Malinvaud 1982, 1984, Hicks 1977, Kaldor 1966). Consequently, demand and supply need not be equal to existing real wages. Similarly the required rate of return and the supply of funds in the financial market will not be consistent with the profit rate from capital expansion necessary to provide adequate jobs given the supply of labour.

In developing a disequilibrium approach to economic analysis, it is of interest to take a closer look at how the firm market feedback process has evolved as a self-organising system, endogenously modifying the institutional structure of resource allocation. Two factors instigating such structural change are technological and organisational innovation.

The changing capital technology, new energy supplies, and modes of transportation of the early 1900s permitted high volume production, mass marketing, and standardisation of product price and quality which has promoted change in the internal structure of firms and the forms of contractual arrangements for transactions. Most noticeable have been horizontal and vertical integration of production (Williamson 1982, Hicks 1977). With boundedly rational management, organisational innovation was necessary to govern the growing modern corporation. One outcome is the multidivision with a hierarchical planning and budgeting procedure.

As these developments were occurring in the organisation of production, labour market institutions were changing as well. Trade unions were rising in power, promoting the share of labour in the division of income. Change in financial markets also occurred as the limited liability of firm owners altered the procedure of financing capital. A conflict between wages and profits did not arise until the 1970s when the growth in productivity declined.

Given the structure of the modern firm and markets, several new elements must be introduced into the adaptive economising representation of firm behaviour and market feedback, relative to the temporary equilibrium framework for a disequilibrium perspective.

First, a distinction between plans and realised activities must be made, for there will be errors in expectations, and a given plan may not be practicable. The firm will therefore devise disequilibrium mechanisms to buffer the impact of these discrepancies. For instance, there is a precautionary maintenance of such buffer stocks as inventory-order backlog on the commodity market and working capital-financial liquidity on the financial market.

Second, there is a feedback response to a maladjustment of stocks and flows. Due to unrealised plans the firm will initiate an adjustment process. Flexprice and fixprice adjustments are two extreme, pure cases, suggested by Hicks and considered in the literature. According to various factors, such as industrial structure, demand elasticity, inventory cost, and production technology, a firm will use some combination of price, production, and inventory-order backlog adjustment rules on the commodity markets, the use of which will also depend on the state of the macroeconomy. The use of these different adjustment rules will have different implications for labour demand which is derived from production activities.

Third, a more detailed representation of the internal structure and planning process of a firm is necessary. A natural division in firm structure is based on the length of planning horizon. First there is the planning of production and factor demand given capital stocks. Second is the planning of capital investment which will involve a planning horizon long enough to account for construction lead times and economic life or repayment period of capital. A third department serves as a controlling agency using a financial-budgetting procedure.

A final element in need of consideration is the contractual arrangements for transactions. In recognition that agreements are incomplete and there is pressure to maintain ongoing relations, the nature of contracts will have built-in flexibility over what transactions are promised at what price and over what period of time. These factors may be incorporated into the constrain set on the firm (Williamson 1981).

Currently the details of a firm model with these disequilibrium features is being developed. Once completed it will be possible to distinguish different types of firm-sectors and experiment with the dynamics of multisector interactions with transactions in disequilibrium. Upon introducing labour saving technological change in one sector it will be possible to simulate the impact on derived labour demand.

8.   A FINAL COMMENT

We have summarised some models of adaptive economising and have described how they can shed light on embodied technological change and the derived demand for labour. We have also proposed a more general framework for a multisectoral model of adaptive economising in intermarket disequilibrium. Such studies are by nature more complicated than models of optimal intertemporal equilibrium and contain more structural ingredients than conventional econometric models of labour demand based on production function and equilibrium assumptions about productivity, profits and wages. Consequently, they are more costly in research and computational input and post special problems for analysis and interpretations.

Because of these modelling costs it is doubtful if the adaptive economics approach could replace conventional methodology. It is probable that we must continue to rely on the powerfully simplifying assumptions of economic equilibrium and econometric technique. Nonetheless, it seems to us that far more research effort should be directed to the adaptive economics approach which, though more complicated, allows for incorporation of strategic details of production technology and of real economic behaviour. Without attention to those strategic details it seems doubtful to us that a real understanding of how labour markets and, indeed, the economy as a whole work over time. And without this improved understanding it seems unlikely that better policies for enhancing human welfare can be developed for the rampant 'creative destruction' of evolving market economies.

REFERENCES

Clower, R. and Leijonhufvud, A., 'The coordination of economic activities: a Keynesian perspective', American Economic Review, 65 (2), 1975, pp. 182-187.

Day, R.H., 'The economics of technological change and the demise of the share cropper', American Economic Review, 57, 1967, pp. 427-450.

Day, R.H., 'Disequilibrium economic dynamics: a post-Schumpeterian contribution', Journal of Economic Behaviour and Organization, 5 (1), 1984, pp. 57-76.

Day, R.H. and Cigno, A., Modelling Economic Change: The Recursive Programming Approach, North-Holland Publ. Co., Amsterdam, 1978.

Day, R.H. and Nelson, T.R., 'A class of dynamic models for describing and projecting industrial development', Journal of Economics, 1, 1973, pp. 155-190.

Day, R.H. and Singh, I.I., Economics as an Adaptive Process, Cambridge University Press, New York, 1977.

Fisher, F.M., Disequilibrium Foundations of Equilibrium Economics, Cambridge University Press, New York, 1983.

Hicks, J.R., Economic Perspectives: Further Essays on Money and Growth, Clarendon Press, Oxford, 1977.

Kaldor, N., 'Inflation and recession in the world economy', Economic Journal, 86, 1976, pp. 703-714.

Keynes, J.M., 'The general theory of employment', Quarterly Journal of Economics, 51, 1937, pp. 209-223.

Koopmans, T.C. (ed), Activity Analysis of Production and Allocation, John Wiley and Sons, New York, 1951.

Koopmans, T.C., Three Essays on the State of Economic Science, McGraw Hill, New York, 1957.

Malinvaud, E., 'Wages and unemployment', Economic Journal, 92, 1982, pp. 1-12.

Malinvaud, E., Mass Unemployment, Basil Blackwell, Oxford, 1984.

Samuelson, P., The Theory of Economic Development, Harvard University Press, Cambridge, MA, 1947.

Schmookler, T., 'Technological change and the law of industrial growth', in: Alderson, W., Terpstra, V. and Shapiro, S.T. (eds), Patents and Progress, Homewood Press, Irwin, 1965.

Schumpeter, J., The Theory of Economic Development, Harvard University Press, Cambridge, MA, 1934.

Simon, H.A., 'On the behavioral and rational foundations of economic dynamics', Journal of Economic Behavior and Organization, 5 (1), 1984, pp. 35-55.

Simon, H.A., 'On how to decide what to do', Bell Journal of Economics, 9 (2), 1978, pp. 494-507.

Williamson, O.E., 'The modern corporation: origins, evolution, attributes', Journal of Economic Literature, 19, 1981, pp. 1537-1568.

ON THE INCONGRUOUS SPATIAL EMPLOYMENT DYNAMICS
Dimitrios S. Dendrinos[1]

1. INTRODUCTION

The rationale for this paper lies in two sources: one is the ubiqui-
tous experience surrounding intra and international labour and capital
movements; the other is a purely analytical finding, namely that fluid
convection dynamics and the dynamics involved in spatial input factor
mobility are to a certain degree equivalent from a methodological
viewpoint. Both factors will be addressed next, in turn.

a. The Spatial Mobility of Labour Demanded

Large scale spatial movements of the two mobile input factors in production, namely labour and capital, have been recorded in the post
World War II era. Capital movements from the more developed regions
towards the less developed ones have been widely reported in the popular press, as well as in the scientific literature. This capital flow
particularly from the US, Japan and Western Europe towards the Third
World has been quite pronounced and its causes and effects debated
during the last decade. Third World nations' indebtedness and the rise
of the multinationals are central events to this recent phenomenon. A
host of factors, too many and not all quite clear, are involved. They
are related to economic, geographical, political, sociological, military and other variables.

Among the very complex set of factors affecting this movement from an
economic standpoint, has been the behaviour of the profit rate differentials in the manufacturing sectors recorded over this period between
the more developed economies (that of the US and Western Europe in
particular) and the less developed nations of Latin America, South and
South-East Asia. Apparently, interregional differentials in the expected rates of return on capital in international capital markets
produce a spatial as well as temporal portfolio of diverse investment
opportunities. However, capital mobility is only one of the broader

spatial dynamics in the production process, the other being labour
mobility.

Finance capital movements have been accompanied by the reallocation of
a portion of the manufacturing job demanded pool from the more to the
less developed nations and regions. Employment related to the automobile parts, engines and assembly manufacturing, steel and steel mill
products manufacturing, and chemicals manufacturing (all quite capital
intensive) has been reallocating from the US to nations like Mexico,
Brazil and those in the Far East. More broadly, the bulk of the pool
of increases in jobs demanded in these manufacturing categories has
been moving from the more to the less developed nations.

Contrary to the way the price of capital is determined in both less
and more developed nations, the price of the less mobile of the two
input factors in production, labour, does not reflect in less developed nations its marginal productivity. Rather, it is determined in
markets where chronic excess supply of labour conditions prevail.

Thus, differentials in capital productivity is one element in the mobility of jobs demanded particularly for the capital intensive manufacturing firms already mentioned. In fact, the regional differentials
in capital productivity may not even be favourable. It is the other
factors, namely wage rate regional differentials, that may be the de-
termining one. Consequently, input factors' differentials in prices
must be viewed in conjunction with the input factor proportions employed by various manufacturing sectors at various locations under
various technologies. In a capsule, the wage rate differentials may be
large enough to offset the capital intensity characterising production
in these sectors. Given wide wage rate differentials, the stock of
labour demanded in low wage regions increases, whereas, it declines
for higher wage ones.

This spatial movement is by no means confined to inter-national markets for employment in manufacturing. Similar intra-national spatial
labour and capital mobility patterns have been very much in evidence
over the past forty years or so. A case in point is the recent spatial
shift in the total employment demanded pool for various manufacturing
and nonmanufacturing sectors from the Northern and North-central regions of the US to the Southern and Western ones.

b.   The Spatial Mobility of Labour Supplied

Parallel to the above response of labour demanded stocks to positive
wage differentials (i.e., the inflow of employment opportunities made
available to lower wage rate regions from higher wage rate ones),
there has been a counterflow of population migration from low wage
rate regions to higher wage rate ones. Expectations for employment
seem to be formed by positive wage rate differentials, particularly
when these wage rates are weighted by the prevailing unemployment
rates at the origin and the destination.

This has been evidenced by the relatively large scale migration of
population from Central and South America into the US and Canada, as
well as migration from the Far East (particularly the Philippines and
Malaysia) into North America. Similar forces have been present in
labour movements from Africa, Southern Europe and Asia into Northern
and Western Europe.

As in the movements of labour demanded, spatial shifts in labour supplied are also recorded in intranational environments, again exemplified by the continued migration of the domestic and recently arrived
foreign pool from the South to the Northern parts of the US. Although
these two opposite in direction forces found in interregional labour
flows have been previously studied in the economic, sociological and
regional science literature in isolation, their combined effect has
not been carefully examined.

In a previous paper, Dendrinos (1982) outlined the interregional economic theory of spatial labour and capital mobility in a neoclassical
framework where both factor prices were determined by their marginal
product valuation. The paper analysed the dynamic stability of the
interregional factor mobility and provided the conditions for stable
and/or unstable dynamics, cycles, multiplicity of equilibria and bifurcations expected to occur under a variety of technological conditions.

This paper takes a different view by assuming disequilibrium dynamics
in the demand for and supply of labour spatial functions. It is a more
realistic framework in view of the evidence characterising labour dynamics among developed and developing nations. It asks then the following broad question: where do the incongruous regional mobility

forces lead in the long term? Institutional barriers notwithstanding, one might expect, from conventional international trade economics of arbitrage behaviour, that is, movement will tend to equalise wages among the various regions: as wage rates increase in less developed countries they decrease in more developed ones. Consequently, migration flows in labour demand and supply will tend to converge to an equilibrium as their volume decreases in both directions following a decline in spatial wage rate.

It turns out that this is only a part, indeed a very simplistic one, of a much more complex picture. The qualitative dynamic features of this spatial incongruity hide an extraordinary variety of performance, the full gamut of which has not been previously explored. This paper is an attempt to set a simple dynamic model within the framework of which this phenomenon its qualitative features can be analysed through numerical simulations. In doing so, one may obtain an indication of the, possibly chaotic, movements of populations and employment stocks among the regions of the globe.

Some interesting questions one can ask in spatial labour mobility dynamics are the following: are labour migration movements quite local, meaning do they occur in very specific ranges of the model's parameters space, or do they occupy a wide range in that space? And are they expected to last for short time periods (i.e., are they unstable), or over the long haul (making them stable events)?

c. Fluid Convection

The above observations highlight one of the motivating factors for this paper. There is another motivating factor, as already mentioned, which connects these spatial flows to fluid convection dynamics. This is more fully addressed next.

When fluids are exposed to temperature differentials (as for example a mass of fluid cells when warmed from below and cooled from above) convection results, as for example events modelled by meteorologists. The resulting complex outcomes of model simulations are then linked to unpredictable events associated with, for example, the weather or any other similar physical system. Normally, one state variable is identified with the horizontal temperature variation, another with the vertical temperature variation, and finally a third state variable measures the rate of convection. It turns out that spatial mobility in stocks of labour demanded (one variable), as labour supplied (another variable) share a lot in common with such a convection process defined in three dimensions. The role of temperature is played by the wage rate differentials (the third variable).

2. THE SIMPLE NO LIMITS TO GROWTH MODEL

Assume a relatively less developed region in which there is an internal population growth rate, which (for mere simplicity) will be assumed to equal the rate of growth of the region's labour force supply. At the same time, the region is assumed to be open so that outmigration of labour to other regions is possible. This outmigration of labour is due to current returns to labour differentials between this region and the background prevailing (perceived) one. Consequently,

$$\frac{dx(t)}{dt} = \alpha x(t) - \beta(\bar{w} - w(t)) \, , \qquad \alpha, \, \beta, \, \bar{w} > 0 \qquad\qquad 1.1$$

where α is the internal growth rate in the supply of labour, $\bar{w}$ is the background perceived return to labour, $w(t)$ is the region's perceived return to labour, and β is a response (speed) parameter. The greater the perceived difference in the return to labour between the background and the region, the greater the outmigration of labour from the region. In case $\bar{w} < w$ of course, labour supply will be flowing into the region from its (background) environment. The return to labour must include the prevailing wage rate (r) and the employment rate (e):

$$w(t) = r(t) \, e(t); \quad \bar{w} = \bar{r} \, \bar{e} \qquad\qquad 1.2$$

where, for purposes of simplicity the background return to labour is assumed to be a (fixed) known constant (designated by bars).

Demand for labour in the region is due to two factors: labour demanded for domestic product (the output of which is to be either locally consumed or exported); and labour demanded from foreign owned production (with its output again being either locally consumed or exported). As already argued, the latter is due to significant returns to labour differentials between the region in question and the background environment. So:

$$\frac{dy(t)}{dt} = \gamma(\bar{\bar{w}} - w(t)) + \delta y(t) \quad , \quad \gamma, \bar{\bar{w}}, \delta > 0 \qquad 1.3$$

where γ is a response (inmigration rate) of foreign production to wage rate differential parameters; $\bar{\bar{w}}$ is a wage rate (determined by the background prevailing returns to labour) below which foreign capital will commence flowing into the region; equivalently, domestically owned production will outmigrate when $\bar{\bar{w}} < w$. Parameter δ is a rate of change in labour demanded from domestically induced production. Parameter $\bar{w}$ in general is not equal to $\bar{\bar{w}}$ since labour and capital respond differently to returns to labour differentials depending on their respective opportunity costs. For simplicity hereon, the return to labour will be referred to as the wage rate.

Finally, the region-background interaction closes with a response of wages to excess demand/supply conditions in the region's labour market:

$$\frac{dw(t)}{dt} = \varepsilon(y(t) - x(t)) \quad , \quad \varepsilon > 0 \qquad 1.4$$

where is a speed of adjustment parameter. If demand for labour exceeds supply, the return to labour must increase, whereas it must decline otherwise. All parameters, naturally depict relative technology present in the production process within the region and the (background) environment. The above is a system of three simultaneous, ordinary, differential equations describing the regional labour kinetics, as a function of returns to labour differentials between a local area (region) operating within a broader (background) environment.

a.   Discussion

The above system bears some resemblance to the Lorenz (1963) model of three-dimensional atmospheric turbulence:

$$\dot{x} = \sigma(y - x) \qquad 1.5$$

$$\dot{y} = rx - y - xz \qquad 1.6$$

$$\dot{z} = xy - bz \qquad 1.7$$

discussed extensively by C. Sparrow (1982) among others. Not much will
be added here on this system. The variables x, a, z are the three
state variables, whereas σ, r, b are the model's (input) parameters over the range of which the behaviour of x, y, z can be analysed.
Note that the Lorenz model has three parameters, a number equal to the
state variables, thus it is the most efficient model specification for
a three dimensional state space.

The regional employment model has three state variables, but seven
parameters. In fact, as it will be seen later, only four parameters
matter, but its efficiency is still lower than the Lorenz model.

Although the variable definitions differ, certain qualitative features
of the two models are the same: although locally (i.e., from a detail
standpoint) the simulations produce different configurations in the
various areas of the parameters space, from an overall perspective
there are similar (and possibly unpredictable) attractors present.
Both systems are dissipative. For some parameter values, the trajectories tend to converge towards periodic orbits, although such orbits
may not be well defined. In the case of the Lorenz system, chaotic
attractors are present. Whether or not identical attractors are
present in the regional labour dynamics model is not clear. There are
two major differences between the two systems: in the Lorenz system
the origin is a repulsor; as it will be seen later, in the regional
system the origin can be attractor, implying that extinction is feasible in sociospatial systems. In the Lorenz system x would be either
positive or negative. It can only be positive in the labour model.

The Lorenz model has been studied extensively, so that the most interesting parts of its behaviour in the parameter space have been examined. However, since three (or higher dimensional) nonlinear systems
of differential equations are not well understood, there might be
areas in the parameter space where unexpectedly interesting behaviour
may exist. Similar is the case with the regional employment dynamics.

What is shown next, is an analysis of the qualitative behaviour of the
regional dynamics system for certain parameter values. It must be kept
in mind that the results are not exhaustive. They may also not be the
outcome of the intrinsic dynamics found in (1.1), (1.3), (1,4), but
instead the results of the numerical integration algorithms of the

Runge-Kutta subroutine used in the simulation. Much more research is required.

b.   Analysis of the simple labour migration model

The stationary points of the dynamic system are:

$$\dot{x} = 0 \quad x^* = a(\bar{w} - w^*) \; , \; a = \frac{\beta}{\alpha} > 0 \qquad\qquad 1.8$$

$$\dot{y} = 0 \quad x^* = b(w^* - \bar{w}) \; , \; b = \frac{\delta}{\gamma} > 0 \qquad\qquad 1.9$$

$$\dot{w} = 0 \quad y^* = x^*. \qquad\qquad 1.10$$

They imply, from an economic standpoint that the labour market has an equilibrium (where $x^* = y^*$); and that $\underset{=}{w} < w^* < \bar{w}$, meaning that the wage rate at which foreign investment will start flowing in must be below the equilibrium wage rate, which in turn must be below the background rate for outmigration of labour. Is this equilibrium stable? To answer this one must solve the system, and this can be done analytically in this case. The details are given in Appendix A. The system has one real eigenvalue ($\lambda_1 = 1.4656$) and two conjugate complex ones ($\lambda_2 = -.204 + .928i$, $\lambda_3 = -.204 - .928i$).

The conclusion from the fact there is one real and two complex eigenvalues is that the three state variables' dynamics are oscillatory; since the real parts of the conjugate eigenvalues are negative the oscillatory behaviour is a sink. Finally, since the real eigenvalue is positive, it is concluded that the three variables grow exponentially. Consequently, the equilibrium solution is unstable. These properties characterise globally the behaviour of the system.

The substance of the above analysis is that the exponential growth in labour supply strongly drives the system over time. The equalising force of wage differentials is weak, relative to the exponential growth of the labour force supplied stock. It is also evident that the three variables' dynamics are given by, see Hirsch and Smale (1974, p. 139):

$$x(t) = C_{11}e^{1.46} + e^{-.204t}(C_{12}\cos .928t + C_{13}\sin .928t) \qquad 1.11$$

$$y(t) = C_{21}e^{1.46} + e^{-.204t}(C_{22}\cos .928t + C_{23}\sin .928t) \qquad 1.12$$

$$w(t) = C_{31}e^{1.46} + e^{-.204t}(C_{32}\cos .928t + C_{33}\sin .928t) \qquad 1.13$$

where $C_{ij}(i,j=1,2,3)$ are constants associated with the starting values, $x(0)$, $y(0)$, $w(0)$ and the speed of motion at $t=0$.

An interesting aspect of the above model is the dynamic behaviour of the three variables when compared pairwise; each pairwise connection stabilises over time. This is immediately obvious from the condition:

$$\frac{x(t)}{y(t)} \approx \frac{C_{11}}{C_{21}} \quad \text{when } t \to T \gg 0 \qquad\qquad 1.14$$

which says that over the very long run the ratio of the labour supply to labour demand tends asymptotically to a constant determined by the original perturbation.[2]

The origin is not a stationary point. Note that the condition $\bar{\bar{w}} < w^* < \bar{w}$ is satisfied for all a,b values if $\bar{\bar{w}} < \bar{w}$. In this simple model, there are no chaotic (turbulent) regimes in the parameter space. This is due to the fact that the exponential growth in labour supply is overwhelming the local (and weak) effects of wage differentials.

3. THE LIMITS TO GROWTH MODEL

In this version of the theoretical model it is assumed that there are limits as to how much the population of a developing nation can grow; these limits are due to a carrying capacity constraint associated with the developing nation's land and other natural resource availability within the broader regional environment. In the ecological literature this carrying capacity is attributed to friction, Hirsch and Smale

(1974, p. 257). In the regional economic literature this limit is due to net negative external economies of population agglomeration.

According to the above, the concentration of the labour (population) supply stock obeys now the following differential equation:

$$\dot{x} = \alpha x - \beta(\bar{w} - w) - \zeta x^2, \quad \zeta > 0 .$$ (2.1)

Parameter α's unit is (percent per unit time); β's is (population per unit time, per one unit of wage difference); and ζ's unit is (per cent per unit time, per capita). Scaling this differential equation, by dividing both sides by α, one obtains:

$$\frac{\dot{x}}{\alpha} = x - \frac{\beta}{\alpha}(\bar{w} - w) - \frac{\zeta}{\alpha} x^2$$ (2.2)

so that all terms express labour. By substituting the new positive parameters, $a = \beta/\alpha$ (population per unit of wages difference), and $b = \zeta/\alpha$ (per cent per capita) one has:

$$\frac{\dot{x}}{\alpha} = x - a(\bar{w} - w) - bx^2$$ (2.3)

where a is an outmigration coefficient, and b is a friction per capita coefficient. The change in the accumulation of the stock has been scaled by its natural growth rate, α.

The rest of the system is not altered. Parameter $c = \gamma/\delta$ is an inmigration of labour demanded opportunities (jobs) per unit of labour demanded for domestic production per capita, so that the accumulation of labour demanded stock has been scaled by the demand for labour per capital in the nation, δ:

$$\frac{\dot{y}}{\delta} = c(\bar{w} - w) + x .$$ (2.4)

Finally, the wage response to excess demand for or supply of labour conditions remains unchanged, appropriately scaled:

$$\frac{\dot{w}}{\varepsilon} = y - x .$$ (2.5)

The dynamic system of the three simultaneous, ordinary, linear, differential equations is at rest when:

$$\dot{x} = 0 \rightarrow x^* - a(\bar{w} - w^*) - bx^{*2} = 0 \qquad \qquad 2.6$$

$$\dot{y} = 0 \rightarrow c(\bar{\bar{w}} - w^*) + x^* = 0 \; ; \; w^* > \bar{\bar{w}} \qquad \qquad 2.7$$

$$\dot{w} = 0 \rightarrow y^* = x^*. \qquad \qquad 2.8$$

This is a five parameter system with three state variables. Its stationary points are:

$$x^*_{1,2} = y^*_{1,2} = \frac{1 + \frac{a}{c} \mp \sqrt{(1 + \frac{a}{c})^2 - 4ba(\bar{w} - \bar{\bar{w}})}}{2b} \qquad \qquad 2.9$$

$$w^*_{1,2} = \bar{\bar{w}} + \frac{x^*_{1,2}}{c} . \qquad \qquad 2.10$$

For these two sets of equilibria, to be referred to as $E_1(x^*_1, y^*_1, w^*_1)$ and $E_2(x^*_2, y^*_2, w_2)$, to be real, the following condition must hold:

$$(1 + \frac{a}{c})^2 \geq 4abd \qquad \qquad 2.11$$

$$d = \bar{w} - \bar{\bar{w}} . \qquad \qquad 2.12$$

If condition (2.11) holds as equality, then $E_1 = E_2$, so that the equilibria are identical. The fraction a/c is the out- to inmigration coefficients ratio; the difference d (which could be in the general case either negative or positive) must be positive from an economic standpoint. The product (abd) identifies a negative force working against growth (outmigration, friction, wage differences). Condition (2.11) points to some upper bounds that must hold for the equilibrium to exist subject to (2.12). By employing d > 0, the system becomes a four parameter, three state variables one, thus containing one more parameter than the initial Lorenz system.

Do the E_1 and E_2 equilibria exist, and are they stable (i.e., in which region of the parameter space are they stable)? and finally, what are their qualitative features? To address these questions must again must look at the analytical properties of the characteristic polynomial. In this case to answer the questions on global/local stability/instability and nature of the equilibria in the universe of the four parameter space one must resort to numerical simulations. Following are certain results obtained for the following parameter values:

$$a = 5 \qquad x(0) = 100 \qquad \alpha = .1$$
$$b = .005 \qquad y(0) = 50 \qquad \delta = .1$$
$$c = 20 \qquad w(0) = 1.5 \qquad \varepsilon = .001$$
$$d = 15 \qquad \bar{w} = 16$$
$$\bar{\bar{w}} = 1$$

For these parameters values (identifying conditions close to the aggregate macro-indicators of the Mexican economy, where x,y are in millions, and w's in US $ 1,000) the two equilibria are:

$$E_1 \rightarrow x_1^* = y_1^* = 150 , \quad w_1^* = 8.5 \qquad \text{(stable, spiral sink)}$$

$$E_2 \rightarrow x_2^* = y_2^* = 100 , \quad w_2^* = 6 \qquad \text{(unstable, spiral source)} .$$

The discriminant of the system (see Appendix B, condition B.16) is negative for these values; thus, one eigenvalue is real, the other two being complex conjugate. Thus, the system's behaviour is oscillatory. Whether or not these equilibria are stable requires numerical simulation, which seems to indicate stable behaviour in E_1 and unstable in E_2. This implies that the real part of the eigenvalues near E_1 are all negative, whereas some (or all) are positive near E_2. For the parameter values reported in the main text E_1 and E_2 collapse to a single equilibrium when $\bar{w} = 16.625$. Numerical simulations indicate that under these conditions x and y tend to zero (i.e., the region becomes extinct).

Further numerical experimentations is needed to locate the thresholds in parameter values where all eigenvalues' real part is positive in both E_1 and E_2. Then the question is where do the dynamic trajectories go? Since the origin can be an attractor (from the positive part of the x,y space), extinction may be the outcome. Were it possible (for some parameter or a modification of the model for the origin to be a repulsor), then one could replicate the qualitative features of the

Lorenz model in regional employment dynamics. This is left to future
research.

4.   <u>CONCLUSIONS</u>

In this simple labour migration model, the classical approach was revisited. It was demonstrated that the picture is much more complex
than previously thought. An equivalence between labour movements and
fluid convection was uncovered. In view of the analytical statement of
the problem, its simulation, and the original substantive concern it
is concluded that the migration of populations movements can result in
unpredictable events of either a local or global nature, of short or
long term duration. At present, the events surrounding the US-Mexican
migration patterns, seen through rough qualitative simulations, seem
to be locally stable and of no 'cyclonic' nature meaning of large
scale, long term nature. Whether this will continue is not clear, depending on fluctuations in the model's parameters induced from (exogenous) environmental changes.

<u>NOTES</u>

1.   The author wishes to thank Michael Sonis for very helpful com-
      ments and suggestions, and his Research Assistant Jemsheed Metha
      for the computer work. Partial funding from the National Science
      Foundation is gratefully acknowledged.

2.   I am grateful to Michael Sonis for pointing this out to me.

<u>REFERENCES</u>

Archbold, J.W., Algebra, Pitman and Sons, 1958.

Dendrinos, D.S., 'On the dynamic stability of interurban/regional
      labour and capital movements', Journal of Regional Science,
      Vol. 22, No. 4, pp. 529-540.

Hirsch, M.W. and Smale, S., Differential Equations, Dynamical Systems
      and Linear Algebra, Academic Press, New York, 1974.

Lorenz, E.N., 'Deterministic non-periodic flows', Journal of Atmo-
      spheric Sciences, Vol. 20, pp. 130-141.

Meserve, B.E., Fundamental Concepts of Algebra, Addison-Wesley, 1953.

Sparrow, C., The Lorenz Equations: Bifurcations, Chaos, and Strange Attractors, Vol. 41, Springer Verlag, Berlin, 1982.

APPENDIX A
Solution for the Simple Labour Migration Model

The dynamics of the stationary point $(\frac{ab(\bar{w}-\bar{\bar{w}})}{a+b}$, $\frac{ab(\bar{w}-\bar{\bar{w}})}{a+b}$, $\frac{a\bar{w}+b\bar{\bar{w}}}{a+b})$ are given by the linearised flow near it, obtained by the eigenvalues of the characteristic polynomial:

$$M = \begin{bmatrix} \frac{\partial \dot{x}}{\partial x}\Big|_* & \frac{\partial \dot{x}}{\partial y}\Big|_* & \frac{\partial \dot{x}}{\partial w}\Big|_* \\[2mm] \frac{\partial \dot{y}}{\partial x}\Big|_* & \frac{\partial \dot{y}}{\partial y}\Big|_* & \frac{\partial \dot{y}}{\partial w}\Big|_* \\[2mm] \frac{\partial \dot{w}}{\partial x}\Big|_* & \frac{\partial \dot{w}}{\partial y}\Big|_* & \frac{\partial \dot{w}}{\partial w}\Big|_* \end{bmatrix} = \begin{bmatrix} 1 & 0 & a \\ b & 0 & -1 \\ -1 & 1 & 0 \end{bmatrix} \qquad \text{A.1}$$

of the, appropriately scaled, transformed dynamic system:

$$\dot{x} = x - a(\bar{w} - w) \qquad \text{A.2}$$

$$\dot{y} = \bar{\bar{w}} - w + bx \qquad \text{A.3}$$

$$\dot{w} = y - x \qquad \text{A.4}$$

of four parameters and three state variables. The eigenvalues of M are obtained from:

$$(1 - \lambda)\,\lambda^2 + 1 = 0 \rightarrow \lambda^3 - \lambda^2 - 1 = 0 \ . \qquad \text{A.5}$$

To find whether the three eigenvalues are all real or they contain a complex conjugate pair of roots, one has to construct the transformed third degree equation:

$$f(x) = a_0 x^3 + 3a_1 x^2 + 3a_2 x + a_3 = 0 \qquad \text{A.6}$$

with a discriminant D:

$$D = -27\,(a_0^2\, a_3^2 - 6a_0 a_1 a_2 a_3 + 4a_0 a_2^3 - 3a_1^2\, a_2^2 + 4a_1^3 a_3) \qquad \text{A.7}$$

and find its sign. For the case at hand, from the characteristic polynomial:

$$a_0 = 1, \ a_1 = \frac{1}{3}, \ a_2 = 0, \ a_3 = -1 \qquad \text{A.8}$$

so that: D = -31 < 0. Consequently, only one eigenvalue is real, the other two being complex conjugate. In order to compute the three roots, one has to reduce the original polynomial $\lambda^3 - \lambda^2 - 1 = 0$ to its equivalent:

$$\mu^3 - \frac{1}{3}\mu - \frac{29}{27} = 0 \qquad \text{A.9}$$

where $\mu = \lambda - \frac{1}{3}$.

From the theory of cubic equations, see for example Meserve (1953), the Cardan formulae for the roots of the cubic are given from:

$$u^3 = -\frac{q}{2} + \sqrt{(\frac{q}{2})^2 + (\frac{p}{3})^3} = A \qquad \text{A.10}$$

$$v^3 = -\frac{q}{2} - \sqrt{(\frac{q}{2})^2 + (\frac{p}{3})^3} = B \qquad \text{A.11}$$

where, in this case provide:

$$p = -\frac{29}{27} \qquad q = -\frac{1}{3}$$

and the roots μ_1, μ_2, μ_3 are given by:

$$\mu_1 = u_1 + v_1$$

$$\mu_2 = u_2 + v_2 = \omega^3\sqrt{A} + \omega^2 \sqrt[3]{B}$$

$$\mu_3 = u_3 + v_3 = \omega^2 \sqrt[3]{A} + \omega \sqrt[3]{B}$$

where u_1, u_2, u_3, and v_1, v_2, v_3 are the roots of A, B. In this case, A = 1.0728, B = .00128, so that the real root is $\mu_1 = 1.1323$ and correspondingly $\lambda_1 = 1.4656 > 0$. Thus, the real root of the characteristic polynomial is positive. The two conjugate roots are:

$$\mu_2 = (-\tfrac{1}{2} + i\,\tfrac{\sqrt{3}}{2})\,(1.0728) + (-\tfrac{1}{2} - i\,\tfrac{\sqrt{3}}{2})\,(.00128) \qquad \text{A.15}$$

$$\mu_3 = (-\tfrac{1}{2} - i\,\tfrac{\sqrt{3}}{2})\,(1.0728) + (-\tfrac{1}{2} + i\,\tfrac{\sqrt{3}}{2})\,(.00128) \qquad \text{A.16}$$

which in turn gives:

$$\lambda_2 = -.204 + .928i \qquad\qquad \text{A.17}$$

$$\lambda_3 = -.204 - .928i \qquad\qquad \text{A.18}$$

so that the real part of the complex configurate eigenvalues is negative.

APPENDIX B
Properties of the Limits to Growth Model

From the Jacobian of the linearised system near the two equilibrium points, $M_{1,2}$:

$$M_{1,2} = \begin{bmatrix} \frac{\partial \dot{x}}{\partial x} = 1 - 2bx^*_{1,2} & \frac{\partial \dot{x}}{\partial y} = 0 & \frac{\partial \dot{x}}{\partial w} = a \\[2mm] \frac{\partial \dot{y}}{\partial x} = 1 & \frac{\partial \dot{y}}{\partial y} = 0 & \frac{\partial \dot{y}}{\partial w} = -c \\[2mm] \frac{\partial \dot{w}}{\partial x} = -1 & \frac{\partial \dot{w}}{\partial y} = 1 & \frac{\partial \dot{w}}{\partial w} = 0 \end{bmatrix} \qquad \text{B.1}$$

one obtains the characteristic polynomial:

$$(1 - 2bx^*_{1,2} - \lambda)\lambda^2 + c(1 - 2bx^*_{1,2}) = 0 \ . \qquad \text{B.2}$$

Designate as:

$$k_{1,2} = 1 - 2bx^*_{1,2} = -\,(\tfrac{a}{c} \mp \sqrt{(1 + \tfrac{a}{c})^2 - 4abd} \qquad \text{B.3}$$

then, (B.2) becomes:

$$\lambda^3 - k_{1,2}\lambda^2 - ck_{1,2} = 0 \ . \qquad \text{B.4}$$

the third degree equation (B.4) has the following reduced form at the two equilibria:

$$E_1: \mu_1^3 - \frac{k_1^2}{3}\mu_1 - \frac{2k_1^3}{27} - ck_1 = 0 \qquad\qquad \text{B.5.1}$$

$$E_2: \mu_2^3 - \frac{k_2^2}{3}\mu_2 - \frac{2k_2^3}{27} - ck_2 = 0 \qquad\qquad \text{B.5.2}$$

where:

$$\lambda_{1,2} = \mu_{1,2} + \frac{k_{1,2}^2}{3} \qquad\qquad \text{B.6}$$

These two reduced systems will be revisited when the two sets of eigenvalues are to be computed.

From the conditions (B.4) one obtains their corresponding discriminants, $D_{1,2}$ along similar lines as in the simple model:

$$D_{1,2} = -27ck_{1,2}\ (ck_{1,2} - 4)\ . \qquad\qquad \text{B.7}$$

When $ck_{1,2} < 4$ then $D_{1,2} > 0$ and all three roots of (B.4) are real; if $ck_{1,2} = 4$ then $D_{1,2} = 0$ then two of the three real roots are equal; finally, if $ck_{1,2} > 4$ then $D_{1,2} < 0$ and equation (B.4) has one real root and two complex, conjugate ones. The condition for existence of these real roots is that the wage difference (d) be such that:

$$E_1: c(- \frac{a}{c} - \sqrt{(1 + \frac{a}{c})^2 - 4abd})\ < 4 \qquad\qquad \text{B.8.1}$$

$$E_2: c(- \frac{a}{c} + \sqrt{(1 + \frac{a}{c})^2 - 4abd})\ > 4\ . \qquad\qquad \text{B.8.2}$$

For the equilibrium E_1 condition (B.8.1) always holds; in the case of E_2 condition (B.8.2) holds if:

$$d > (4 + \frac{2}{c} (2 + a)) (1 - \frac{4}{c})\ /\ 4ab\ . \qquad\qquad \text{B.9}$$

In the case of very high inmigration coefficient c, the above becomes: $d > 1/ab$, requiring the wage differentials $(\bar{w} - \underline{w})$ to be inversely related to the outmigration and negative externalities coefficients.

To compute the values of the three eigenvalues for E_1 and E_2 one has to go back to the reduced systems (B.5.1, 2), which can be written as:

$$E_1: \ \mu_1^3 + p_1\mu_1 + q_1 = 0 \qquad\qquad\qquad\qquad \text{B.10.1}$$

$$E_2: \ \mu_2^3 + p_2\mu_2 + q_2 = 0 \qquad\qquad\qquad\qquad \text{B.10.2}$$

where:

$$p_{1,2} = -\frac{k_{1,2}^2}{3} \ , \quad q_{1,2} = -\left(\frac{2k_{1,2}^3}{27} + ck_{1,2}\right) \ . \qquad\qquad \text{B.11}$$

Using Cardan's formulae one obtains, as in the simple model:

$$u^3 = -\frac{q}{2} + \sqrt{\left(\frac{q}{2}\right)^2 + \left(\frac{p}{3}\right)^3} = A \qquad\qquad \text{B.12.1}$$

$$v^3 = -\frac{q}{2} - \sqrt{\left(\frac{q}{2}\right)^2 + \left(\frac{p}{3}\right)^3} = B \qquad\qquad \text{B.12.2}$$

$$\mu_1(1) = u_1 + v_1 = \sqrt[3]{A} + \sqrt[3]{B} \qquad\qquad\qquad \text{B.13.1}$$

$$\mu_1(2) = u_2 + v_2 = \omega^3 \sqrt{A} + \omega^2 \sqrt[3]{B} \qquad\qquad \text{B.13.2}$$

$$\mu_1(3) = u_3 + v_3 = \omega^2 \sqrt[3]{A} + \omega^3 \sqrt{B} \ . \qquad\qquad \text{B.13.3}$$

The above give:

$$u_1^3 = \frac{2k_1^3}{27} + ck_1 + \sqrt{\left(\frac{2k_1^3}{27} + ck_1\right)^2 - \left(\frac{k_1^2}{3}\right)^3} = A \qquad \text{B.14.1}$$

$$v_1^3 = \frac{2k_1^3}{27} + ck_1 - \sqrt{\left(\frac{2k_1^3}{27} + ck_1\right)^2 - \left(\frac{k_1^2}{3}\right)^3} = B \qquad \text{B.14.2}$$

The square root part of u_1^3 and v_1^3 can be negative, positive or zero:

$$\left(\frac{2k_1^3}{27} + ck_1\right)^2 \ > < \ \left(\frac{k_1^2}{3}\right)^3 \ . \qquad\qquad\qquad \text{B.15}$$

This discriminant is positive if: $k_1^2 > 7.772c$; whereas, it is zero if: $k_1^2 = 7.772c$; and is negative if: $k_1^2 < 7.772c$. Negativity implies at E_1:

$$\left(- \left(\frac{a}{c} + \sqrt{\left(1 + \frac{a}{c}\right)^2 - 4abd}\right)\right)^2 < 7.772c \ . \qquad\qquad \text{B.16}$$

To obtain the ranges in parameter values where the real parts of the eigenvalues become positive (destabilising the stationary points) one must resort to numerical simulations. It must be noted, that it is possible for u_1^3 and v_1^3 to be imaginery numbers depending on conditions (B.15).

A STOCHASTIC THEORY FOR RESIDENTIAL AND LABOUR MOBILITY INCLUDING TRAVEL NETWORKS
Günter Haag

1. INTRODUCTION

Regional labour market conditions depend in a complex manner on the decisions of <u>individuals</u> on the supply side and firms on the demand side of the market. Changes in social and technological conditions have a profound impact on the structure and mechanism of these labour markets. The individuals must decide whether to quit or retain their present jobs, to search for new employment, perhaps in another region, and/or to search for a new residential location which increases their utility. Firms must set desired employment levels and determine the number of job opportunities in the different regions, taking into account the market conditions. This highly complex interactions between the labour market and the housing market require an adequate explanation of the nature of the decisions made by the different decision makers. The theory of job search (Rogerson 1983, Lippman and McCall 1976) and residential search (Clark 1983) is concerned with optimal behaviour of individuals who want to maximise their utility. Optimal policies for firms is concerned with maximising profits (Mortensen 1970, Eaton and Watts 1977).

Innovations can be seen as the main spring of economic growth (Mensch 1975). According to the business cycle theory of Schumpeter (1934) and its dynamic modelling (Mensch et al. 1985) an innovative impulse is generated in the socioeconomic system via a dynamic feedback. Innovations influence the productivity and demand for labour and change the investment shares of firms (expansionary via rationalising investment) and bias the decision behaviour of investors on all socioeconomic levels. Therefore there is a strong interaction between regional growth or decline and the embedding of appropriate innovations into the production process.

This contribution has several objectives. Since the spatial aspects of the residential and labour mobility processes are crucial for a better understanding of regional growth or decline, a dynamic spatial structure is introduced. Now it seems to be risky to assume equilibrium conditions for the markets. Therefore a dynamic description is preferred. The inherent fluctuations of the decision process require a stochastic description. We introduce fluctuations via a master equation approach. Since this framework has already been introduced into the social sciences by Weidlich and Haag 1983, we describe only briefly the more general and formal framework and go straight forward to the more aggregate level of the meanvalue equation.

2.   THE INDIVIDUAL TRANSITION PROBABILITIES FOR THE SEARCH PROCESS

We subdivide the system into L nonoverlapping regions. Moreover, the whole population is supposed to be made of workers, unemployed people and a kind of background population. Being pedagogical, we start with a more simplified version and drop more and more assumptions later on. Changes in both residence and workplace are taken into account, and commuting costs are introduced explicitly. The housing stock and workplaces are differentiated by zones or regions only, with no further sectoral disaggregation. A further simplification will be introduced by dropping moving costs from the model, as they are in any case negligible compared to other costs and benefits (cf. Leonardi 1984).

In the following we introduce the convention that all exogenous variables of the model are denoted by capital letters, and all endogenous variables by small letters. The basic definitions are: $n_{ij}(t)$ is the number of people living in region i and working in region j, at time t. Therefore, the number of people living in i and working somewhere is

$$n_i(t) = \sum_{j=1}^{L} n_{ij}(t) \; , \tag{1}$$

and the number of people working in zone j, at time t

$$w_j(t) = \sum_{i=1}^{L} n_{ij}(t) \; . \tag{2}$$

The total number of working people is

$$n(t) = \sum_{i=1}^{L} n_i(t) = \sum_{j=1}^{L} w_j(t) \; . \tag{3}$$

The following variables are exogenous: $N_i(t)$, the number of people living in i and searching for a job (fraction of the total population in i); $M_i(t)$, the number of housing units in i (scaled on $N_i(t)$ (or in other words, the housing stock in i); $W_i(t)$, the number of job opportunities in i; $R_i(t)$, the rent or price level in i; $Y_i(t)$, the income in zone i. Then, by definition, $(N_i(t) - n_i(t))$ equals the number of unemployed people in i; $(W_i(t) - w_i(t)) = 0_i(t)$ the number of open positions in i; and $(M_i(t) - n_i(t))$ the number of vacant dwellings in i.

We introduce the socioconfiguration

$$\underset{\sim}{n}(t)=\{n_{11}(t),n_{12}(t),\ldots,n_{1L}(t),n_{21}(t),n_{22}(t),\ldots,n_{ij}(t),\ldots n_{LL}(t)\}$$

which describes a possible realisation of a flow pattern in an abstract configuration space S

$$\underset{\sim}{n}(t)\,\epsilon\,S$$

Due to decision processes of individuals changing their residential location of their place of work, the actual socioconfiguration changes in the course of time. The number of transitions (in configuration space) due to a 'migration process' from a state living in k, working in l to a state living in i, working in j is proportional to $n_{kl}(t)$ times on individual transition probability (rate) $P_{ij,kl}(\underset{\sim}{n})$ for a transition $(k,l) \to (i,j)$. Thus,

$$w_{ij,kl}(\underset{\sim}{n}+\underset{\sim}{k};\underset{\sim}{n}) = \begin{array}{l} n_{kl}(t) \cdot P_{ij,kl}(\underset{\sim}{n}) \\ \text{for } \underset{\sim}{k} = (\ldots0\ldots1_{ij}\ldots0\ldots(-1)_{kl}\ldots0\ldots) \\ 0 \text{ for all other combinations} \end{array} \qquad (4)$$

The equation of motion is the master equation for the probability $P(\underset{\sim}{n};t)$ to find the socioconfiguriation $\underset{\sim}{n}$ to be realised at time t:

$$\frac{dP(\underset{\sim}{n};t)}{dt} = \sum_{\substack{i,j \\ k,l}}^{L} w_{ij,kl}(\underset{\sim}{n};\underset{\sim}{n}+\underset{\sim}{k})P(\underset{\sim}{n}+\underset{\sim}{k}) - \sum_{\substack{i,j \\ k,l}}^{L} w_{ij,kl}(\underset{\sim}{n}+\underset{\sim}{k};\underset{\sim}{n})P(\underset{\sim}{n}) \qquad (5)$$

In order to obtain explicit results, the individual transition proba-bilities describing residential and labour mobility have to be mod-elled.

We consider in this contribution the residential and labour market on a more spatially disaggregated level. The utility of an individual depends on commuting costs and also on the living conditions in both the residential zone and the employment zone. It seems to be reason-able to introduce the following individual transition probability (in relation to the configuration $\underset{\sim}{n}$)

$$P_{ij,kl}(\underset{\sim}{n}) = e^{v_{ij}(\underset{\sim}{n})-v_{kl}(\underset{\sim}{n})} \delta_{ij,kl} \tag{6}$$

for a changing from living in k and working in l to living in i and working in j, $(k,l) \rightarrow (i,j)$ where $v_{ij}(\underset{\sim}{n})$ is the utility of an individ-ual for living in i and working in j. Moreover the utilities $v_{ij}(\underset{\sim}{n})$ have two subscripts (for place of residence and place of work) since they measure the competition for housing and/or labour in different zones. The $\delta_{ij,kl} > 0$ are coefficients which describe the correspond-ing mobilities for this migration process.

To obtain further insights, it is useful to split the utilities v_{ij} into two parts:

$$v_{ij}(\underset{\sim}{n}) = u_{ij}(\underset{\sim}{n}) - \beta c_{ij} , \quad i,j=1,\ldots L \tag{7}$$

where $c_{ij} \geq 0$ are the commuting costs per unit time between zone i and zone j. The intrazonal costs c_{ii} refer to the mean commuting costs for living and working in the same region or zone. On a daily basis, it can be assumed that

$$c_{ij} = c_{ji} . \tag{8}$$

The deterrence parameter $\beta > 0$ describes the influence of the commut-ing costs on the utility as judged by an individual. It should be men-tioned in this section we do not distinguish between different routes of travel from the zone of residence to the zone of work or between different travel modes. These restrictions will be dropped in Section 8 below.

The $u_{ij}(\underset{\sim}{n})$ is that part of the utility for an individual living in i, working in j, at time t which is independent of commuting costs. Therefore, it is reasonable to assume that $u_{ij}(\underset{\sim}{n})$ depends on two parts

$$u_{ij}(\underset{\sim}{n}) = U_i(\underset{\sim}{n}) + V_j(\underset{\sim}{n}) , \qquad (9)$$

where $U_i(\underset{\sim}{n})$ is the utility of living in zone i, and $V_j(n)$ the utility of working in j. Without loss of generality we can scale the utility u_{ij} so that

$$\sum_{i,j=1}^{L} u_{ij}(n) = 0 . \qquad (10)$$

At each time, two types of choices are now possible for an individual: changing residence of changing job (and it is also possible to change nothing, of course). We assume the time interval is sufficiently short to exclude the joint occurrence of both types of events.

Then the coefficients $\delta_{ij,kl}$ can be defined as:

$$\delta_{ij,kl} = \begin{cases} \nu, & \text{for } (k,l) \rightarrow (i,l) \\ \nu, & \text{for } (k,l) \rightarrow (l,l) \\ \rho, & \text{for } (k,l) \rightarrow (k,j) \\ \rho, & \text{for } (k,l) \rightarrow (k,k) \\ 0, & \text{for all other combinations} \end{cases} \qquad (11)$$

The parameter ν describes housing mobility, the parameter ρ labour mobility. In general, these mobilities will be different $\rho \neq \nu$. Figure 1 then depicts the basic events taken into account in this joint model

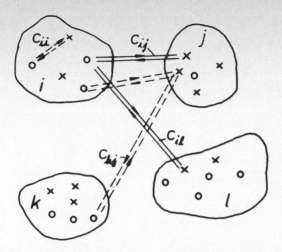

Figure 1   The basic events taken into account in the joint model. The
o,x corresponds to places of living and working,
respectively.

3.   THE MEANVALUE EQUATIONS

Insertion of (4), (6) in (5) yields the explicit form of the master
equation for the joint model of residential and labour mobility. The
corresponding exact meanvalue equations can be obtained   straightforwardly (Haag and Weidlich 1984):

$$\dot{\bar{n}}_{ij}(t) = \sum_{k=1}^{L} \overline{w_{ij,kl}(\underset{\sim}{n})} - \sum_{k,l}^{L} \overline{w_{kl,ij}(\underset{\sim}{n})} \; , \tag{12}$$

$$i,j = 1,2,\ldots,L$$

Using again the (unessential) assumption that $\overline{f(\underset{\sim}{n})} \approx f(\underset{\sim}{\bar{n}})$, the closed
set of approximate meanvalue equations reads

$$\dot{\bar{n}}_{ij}(t) = \sum_{k,l}^{L} p_{ij,ik}(\underset{\sim}{\bar{n}}) \cdot \bar{n}_{ik} - \sum_{k=l}^{L} p_{ik,ij}(\underset{\sim}{\bar{n}}) \cdot \bar{n}_{ij}$$

$$+ \sum_{k=1}^{L} p_{ij,kj}(\underset{\sim}{\bar{n}}) \cdot \bar{n}_{kj} - \sum_{k=1}^{L} p_{kj,ij}(\underset{\sim}{\bar{n}}) n_{ij}, \tag{13}$$

$$i,j = 1,\ldots,L$$

where the first line describes labour mobility and the second line
housing mobility. In general (13) will be a nonlinear system of L^2
coupled differential equations. With (6) substituted in (13) the more
detailed version of the meanvalue equations is obtained:

$$\dot{n}_{ij}(t) = \rho(t)\{\sum_{k=1}^{L} e^{v_{ij}-v_{ik}}\bar{n}_{ik} - \sum_{k=1}^{L} e^{v_{ik}-v_{ij}}\bar{n}_{ij}\}$$

$$+ \nu(t)\{\sum_{k=1}^{L} e^{v_{ij}-v_{kj}}\cdot\bar{n}_{kj} - \sum_{k=1}^{L} e^{v_{kj}-v_{ij}}\cdot\bar{n}_{ij}\}\ . \tag{14}$$

It is worthwhile to emphasise that the utility of an individual for living in one zone and working in another zone explicitly appears in (14). Since, according to (7), commuting costs c_{ij} and the evaluation of housing and working conditions u_{ij} appear in v_{ij}, the structure of (14) is still very general.

We insert (7), (9) in (14):

$$\dot{n}_{ij}(t) = \rho(t)\sum_{k=1}^{L} e^{-\beta(c_{ij}-c_{ik})}\cdot e^{V_j(\bar{\underset{\sim}{n}})-V_k(\bar{\underset{\sim}{n}})}\cdot\bar{n}_{ik} \qquad \text{labour mobility}$$

$$- \rho(t)\sum_{k=1}^{L} e^{-\beta(c_{ik}-c_{ij})}\cdot e^{V_k(\bar{\underset{\sim}{n}})-V_j(\bar{\underset{\sim}{n}})}\cdot\bar{n}_i$$

$$+ \nu(t)\sum_{k=1}^{L} e^{-\beta(c_{ij}-c_{kj})}\cdot e^{U_i(\bar{\underset{\sim}{n}})-U_k(\bar{\underset{\sim}{n}})}\cdot\bar{n}_{kj} \qquad \text{housing mobility}$$

$$- \nu(t)\sum_{k=1}^{L} e^{-\beta(c_{kj}-c_{ij})}\cdot e^{U_k(\bar{\underset{\sim}{n}})-U_i(\bar{\underset{\sim}{n}})}\cdot\bar{n}_{ij}$$

$$i,j=1,2,\ldots,L \tag{15}$$

In (15) the commuting costs appear explicitly, thus introducing a relationship among housing, workplaces and transport in a dynamic framework. Moreover, accessibilities have two subscripts, (for place of residence and place of work) while potential utilities $U_i(n)$, $V_j(n)$ each have one subscript (for the place of residence in the case of the housing market, for the place of work in the case of the labour market). $(U_i(n) - U_k(n))$ measures the competition for housing and $(V_j(n) - V_k(n))$ the competition for workplaces in différent zones. The potential utilities U_i, V_j characterise the attraction of each zone with respect to socioeconomic preferences of the individual.

4. THE DEPENDENCE OF UTILITIES ON KEY FACTORS

So far we have been rather general and we were not concerned with the (exogenous and endogenous) variables which determine the functional shape of the potential utilities $U_i(\underset{\sim}{n})$, $V_i(\underset{\sim}{n})$. We will demonstrate later (Section 7) how exogenous variables introduced as a first step can be made endogenous in a second step.

We assume that the utility u_{ij} is a function of the (endogenous) state variables n_{ij} and a set of other relevant (exogenous) socioeconomic and/or technological variables. Then we can expand $u_{ij}(\underset{\sim}{n})$ into a Taylor series and take into account terms up to first order. This procedure yields:

$$u_{ij}(\underset{\sim}{n}) = \delta_i - \alpha_1(N_i - n_i) + \alpha_2(M_i - n_i) - \alpha_3 P_i + \alpha_4(W_j - w_j) + \alpha_5 Y_j + C \qquad (16)$$

The first term, δ_i , describes the natural preference for zone i. Social factors like the desire to stay in one's birthplace are part of δ_i, but also factors such as accessibility to shops (in the first step), schools available and retail activities. It is further assumed, that unemployment $(N_i - n_i)$ in the residential area reduces the attractivity of that zone. The residential attractivity U_i is assumed to depend also on the number of vacant dwellings in i and the price level (rents) in zone i. On the other hand, we expect that income Y_j and the number of open positions $(W_j - w_j)$ are crucial components of the attractivity V_j of the place of work.

An innovative impulse can be created by a clustering of <u>basic innovations</u> (Mensch 1975). These clustering processes of innovations may be one of the main forces leading to long waves in the economic development (Bianchi et al. 1983). In general, these clustering trends are both temporal and spatial events. Spatial clustering processes may lead to growth pools and growth centres in the economic system. A spatial and temporal innovation impulse diffuses through the spatial system and penetrates the multisector economy. The labour market, the distribution of income between wages and profits, the attractivity of a residential area and the service sector are influenced by such an event. Therefore, innovations contribute to exogenous variations on almost all variables of the utility v_{ij}.

Since the amounts and signs of the trends parameters $\{\alpha_i, \delta_i\}$ are determined explicitly by the estimation procedure, the weights of the different variables can be tested. The constant C is fixed by (10). Is further convenient to scale the preference parameter according to

$$\sum_{i=1}^{L} \delta_i = 0 \ . \tag{17}$$

Then

$$u_{ij}(\underset{\sim}{n}) = U_i(\underset{\sim}{n}) + V_j(\underset{\sim}{n}) \tag{13}$$

with

$$U_i(\underset{\sim}{n}) = \delta_i - \alpha_1 [(N_i - n_i) - \frac{1}{L}(N-n)] + \alpha_2 [(M_i - n_i) - \frac{1}{L}(M-n)] + \alpha_3 (p_i - \bar{p})$$

$$V_i(\underset{\sim}{n}) = \alpha_4 [(W_j - w_j)] - \frac{1}{L}(W-w) + \alpha_5 (Y_j - \bar{Y}) \ , \tag{19}$$

where

$$\bar{P} = \frac{1}{L} \sum_{i=1}^{L} P_i \ , \quad \bar{Y} = \frac{1}{L} \sum_{i=1}^{L} Y_i \ . \tag{20}$$

Therefore the following relations hold:

$$\sum_{i,j}^{L} u_{ij}(\underset{\sim}{n}) = 0 \ ; \quad \sum_{i=1}^{L} U_i(\underset{\sim}{n}) = 0 \ ; \quad \sum_{j=1}^{L} V_j(\underset{\sim}{n}) = 0 \ . \tag{21}$$

The equations (19) with (15) complete our construction of a joint dynamic model for residential and labour mobility. Since we are dealing with a highly nonlinear system we can expect phase transitions in a synergetic sense (Weidlich and Haag 1985, Nijkamp and Schubert 1983). Therefore a variety of stationary points (attractors) may occur. Our model describes the dynamics of commuting trips in a spatial system and a natural question to be asked is to what extent the steady solution is related to the known static trip distribution models.

5. THE EXACT STATIONARY SOLUTION

In order to explore this problem, let us consider the static version of (14)

$$
0 = \rho \{ \sum_{k=1}^{L} e^{\hat{v}_{ij} - \hat{v}_{ik}} . \hat{n}_{ik} - \sum_{k=1}^{L} e^{\hat{v}_{ik} - \hat{v}_{ij}} . \hat{n}_{ij} \} +
$$

$$
+ \nu \{ \sum_{k=1}^{L} e^{\hat{v}_{ij} - \hat{v}_{kj}} . \hat{n}_{kj} - \sum_{k=2}^{L} e^{\hat{v}_{kj} - \hat{v}_{ij}} . \hat{n}_{ij} \} ,
$$
for i,j=1,...,L
(22)

where $\underline{\hat{n}}$, $\underline{\hat{v}}$ denote the stationary value of $\underline{n}$, $\underline{v}$ respectively. Of course, the residential mobility parameter ν and the labour mobility parameter ρ are non zero.

It can easily be seen, by substitution of (23) into (22), that the exact stationary trip distribution fulfils the nonlinear system of transcendental equations

$$
\hat{n}_{ij} = C . e^{2\hat{v}_{ij}(\underline{\hat{n}})} , \quad i,j=1,...,L
$$
(23)

where C is determined by (3). This yields the very general and interesting result

$$
\hat{n}_{ij} = \hat{n} . \frac{e^{2\hat{v}_{ij}(\underline{\hat{n}})}}{\sum_{k,l=1}^{L} e^{2\hat{v}_{kl}(\underline{\hat{n}})}} , \quad i,j=1,...,L
$$
(24)

with

$$
\hat{n} = \sum_{i,j}^{L} \hat{n}_{ij} .
$$

Therefore, the stationary trip distribution $\hat{n}_{ij}$ (24) depends on the utility of an individual $\hat{v}_{ij}$ to live in i and to work in j. Since this result is obtained without making use of any assumption concerning the functional shape and the set of variables introduced, (24) is rather general.

The commuting costs c_{ij} appear via (7) explicitly in the stationary solution

$$\hat{n}_{ij} = \hat{n} \cdot \frac{e^{2(\hat{u}_{ij}(\underset{\sim}{\hat{n}})-\beta c_{ij})}}{\sum\limits_{k,1}^{L} e^{2(\hat{u}_{kl}(\underset{\sim}{\hat{n}})-\beta c_{kl})}} \quad , \quad i,j=1\ldots,L \quad , \tag{25}$$

thus introducing a relationship among housing, workplaces and transport. The residential mobility ν and the labour mobility ρ do not enter the stationary solution.

In our more specific model $\hat{u}_{ij}$ has to be replaced by (18), (19). The result (25) is different from a standard demand model. The interactions between housing and workplace is mediated by the utility $\hat{u}_{ij}(\hat{n})$ for the pair of origin destination zones and the commuting costs. (25) is a nontrivial system of L^2 coupled transcendental equations for the L^2 stationary values of $\hat{n}_{ij}$. From the mathematical point of view a variety of critical points is possible if the utility is a function of the state variable. The basins of the attractors determine which solution will finally $(t \to \infty)$ be realised.

6. ESTIMATION OF THE PARAMETERS

The theoretical transition probabilities (4), (6) can be compared with the corresponding empirical quantities $w_{ij,ik}^{(e)}(t), w_{ij,kj}^{(e)}(t)$ using regression analysis

$$w_{ij,ik}^{(e)}(t) = \rho n_{ik}^{(e)} e^{v_{ij}-v_{ik}} \quad ; \quad w_{ik,ij}^{(e)}(t) = \rho n_{ij}^{(e)} e^{v_{ik}-v_{ij}} \tag{26}$$

and

$$w_{ij,kj}^{(e)}(t) = \nu n_{kj}^{(e)} e^{v_{ij}-v_{kj}} \quad ; \quad w_{kj,ij}^{(e)}(t) = \nu n_{ij}^{(e)} e^{v_{kj}-v_{ij}} \quad . \tag{27}$$

In Haag and Weidlich (1983), we discussed in detail the regression analysis of this kind of model. Therefore, we describe the estimation procedure only briefly here. Consider the product of (26) and (27) and then we obtain for the labour mobility $\rho(t)$

$$\rho(t) = \frac{1}{L^2(L-1)} \sum_{\substack{i,j,k \\ i \neq k}}^{L} \sqrt{\frac{w_{ij,ik}^{(e)}(t)w_{ik,ij}^{(e)}(t)}{n_{ik}^{(e)} \cdot n_{ij}^{(e)}}} \tag{28}$$

and similarly for the housing mobility $\nu(t)$

$$\nu(t) = \frac{1}{L^2(L-1)} \sum_{\substack{i,j,k \\ i \neq k}}^{L} \sqrt{\frac{w_{ij,kj}^{(e)}(t)w_{kj,ij}^{(e)}(t)}{n_{kj}^{(e)} \cdot n_{ij}^{(e)}}} \tag{29}$$

These results are independent of the v_{ij}.

By considering the quotient of (26) and (27) we obtain the over determined set of equations

$$r_{ij,ik} = v_{ij} - v_{ik} , \quad i,j,k = 1, \ldots, L, \quad j \neq k$$
$$r_{ij,kj} = v_{ij} - v_{kj} , \quad i,j,k = 1, \ldots, L, \quad i \neq k \tag{30}$$

where

$$r_{ij,ik} = \frac{1}{2} \ln \frac{w_{ij,ik}^{(e)}(t) \ n_{ij}^{(e)}}{w_{ik,ij}^{(e)}(t) \cdot n_{ik}^{(e)}}$$
$$r_{ij,kj} = \frac{1}{2} \ln \frac{w_{ij,kj}^{(e)}(t) \ n_{ij}^{(e)}}{w_{kj,ij}^{(e)}(t) \ n_{kj}^{(e)}} \tag{31}$$

and

$$v_{ij} = - \beta c_{ij} + U_i + V_j . \tag{32}$$

We can, however, choose an optimal set of attractivities for residence
U_i and workplace V_j by minimising the least square deviations of the
functional

$$F_t[\underset{\sim}{U},\underset{\sim}{V}] =: \frac{1}{L^2(L-1)} \sum_{\substack{i,j,k \\ j \neq k}}^{L} \{[r_{ij,ik} - (-\beta(c_{ij}-c_{ik})+(V_j-V_k))]\}^2$$

$$+ [r_{ji,ki} - (-\beta(c_{ji}-c_{ki})+(U_j-U_k))]^2\} \tag{33}$$

We introduce the abbreviations

$$R_{jk} = \frac{1}{L} \sum_{i=1}^{L} r_{ij,ik} \quad ; \quad S_{jk} = \frac{1}{L} \sum_{i=1}^{L} r_{ji,ki}$$

and
$$\tag{34}$$

$$C_j = \frac{1}{L} \sum_{i=1}^{L} c_{ij}$$

and obtain

$$F_t[\underset{\sim}{U},\underset{\sim}{V}] =: \frac{1}{L(L-1)} \sum_{\substack{j,k=1 \\ j \neq k}}^{L} \{[R_{jk} - (-\beta(C_j-C_k)+(V_j-V_k))]^2$$

$$+ [S_{jk} - (-\beta(C_j-C_k)+(U_j-U_k))]^2\} \tag{35}$$

The optimal set of attractivities $\{\underset{\sim}{U}, \underset{\sim}{V}\}$ is found by setting the derivatives (35 to zero):

$$\frac{\partial F_t}{\partial U_i} = 0 \quad ; \quad \frac{\partial F_t}{\partial V_i} = 0 \quad ; \quad i = 1,2,\ldots, L \, . \tag{36}$$

This yields the attractivity of the place of residence (potential utility)

$$U_i(t) = \frac{1}{L} \sum_{j \neq i}^{L} S_{ij} - \beta(\bar{C}-C_i) \tag{37}$$

and for the attractivity of the place of work (potential utility)

$$V_i(t) = \frac{1}{L} \sum_{j \neq i}^{L} R_{ij} - \beta(\bar{C}-C_i) \tag{38}$$

where

$$\bar{C} = \frac{1}{L} \sum_{i=1}^{L} C_i \, . \tag{39}$$

This yields a very robust estimation of the utilities for living in i and working in j, or in other words for U_i, V_j, i, j = 1,2,..., L. The trend parameters in the origin destination utility v_{ij}, namely $\beta, \alpha_1, ..., \alpha_5$ can be determined by an optimal spatial correlation. We therefore drop this part because of its simplicity.

This model does not lose its validity or applicability is instead of (16) - (18) the utility functions $v_{ij}(n)$ are modelled in a different manner. This is one of the fundamental points of this mind of model building. Different input factors to $v_{ij}(n)$ can therefore be tested and the key factors of the joint model for residential and labour mobility can be determined. By insertion of the estimated parameters into the dynamic systems of equations (15), the model can be used for forecasting purposes. The equilibrium solution can also be obtained by (25).

7.   HOW EXOGENOUS VARIABLES BECOME ENDOGENOUS VARIABLES

Although the model outlined here so far is still lacking some realistic features, the method is quite general and the model can easily be generalised in several respects, for example, we introduced a set of exogenous variables and the problem to be solved is, in effect how to make them endogenous. It is an advantage of this method, that the fundamental structure of the equations ((4) - (6), (12) - (14), (24)) remain unchanged even if we change the character of the variables. We have to add to the dynamic equations (12) - (14) the more general version of the utilities $v_{ij}(n)$, together with the additional dynamic equations for the new endogenously treated variables.

For illustrative purposes, we show how the exogenous variable M_i, which describes the housing stock in region or zone i, can be made endogenous, or in our notation

$$M_i \rightarrow m_i(t) \tag{40}$$

We consider the dynamic system (15) with (19). In (19) we replace according to (40) the exogenous housing stock variable M_i by the endogenous variable $m_i(t)$. Then we add the meanvalue equations of the housing stock to the dynamic system. This procedure and other extensions will be described in detail in an IRES publication (1985). By comparing computer simulations of the model with observed data we can decide whether this is an improvement or not. Other exogenous variables such as prices or number of job opportunities can be transformed into endogenous variables in the same way.

8. DYNAMIC THEORY OF TRAVEL NETWORKS AND RESIDENTIAL LOCATION MARKETS AND LABOUR MOBILITY

In treating the problem of travel network, it is normally assumed that the travel networks and the residential location market are in equilibrium (Anas 1984, Wilson 1983). In the framework of the dynamic master equation approach we derived a joint model for residential and labour mobility. The output of our model yields as one main result predictions of the mean number of trips (or flows) between residence in zone i and workplace in zone j, namely $\bar{n}_{ij}(t)$. The number of trips may also be split into different routes and/or modes. Then $\bar{n}_{ij}^{(\gamma)}(t)$ is the mean number of trips of people living in zone i and working in zone j, at time t using route and/or travel mode γ. Of course, each of the available routes between an origin destination pair will carry some traffic, even though these route costs can vary greatly among them. Since the mean number of trips between i and j is the sum over all contributions from different routes (see Figure 2).

$$\bar{n}_{ij}(t) = \sum_{\gamma} \bar{n}_{ij}^{(\gamma)}(t) .$$ (41)

The utilities of the commuters $v_{ij}^{(\gamma)}(n)$ are functions of travel time, travel costs, the rent of housing, income at workplace in j, and other attributes of the route of travel, the zone of residence and the zone of workplace.

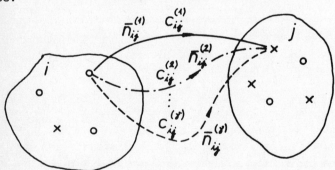

Figure 2 Several different routes between zone i and zone j, distinguished by aggregate travel costs $c_{ij}^{(\gamma)}$.

All attributes of the route of travel γ are assumed to merge into the aggregate travel costs $c_{ij}^{(\gamma)}$.

$$c_{ij}^{(\gamma)} = f(\text{travel time, travel costs, travel risk}). \qquad (42)$$

A possible decomposition of $c_{ij}^{(\gamma)}$ is described in (Anas 1984). Then for each mode under consideration, we can derive the corresponding set of meanvalue equations:

$$\dot{\bar{n}}_{ij}^{(\gamma)}(t) = \rho(t)\sum_{\gamma'}\sum_{\substack{k=1 \\ k\neq j}}^{L}\{e^{v_{ij}^{(\gamma)}-v_{ik}^{(\gamma')}}\cdot\bar{n}_{ik}^{(\gamma')}-e^{v_{ik}^{(\gamma')}-v_{ij}^{(\gamma)}}\cdot\bar{n}_{ij}^{(\gamma)}\}$$

$$(43)$$

$$+ \nu(t)\sum_{\gamma'}\sum_{\substack{k=1 \\ k\neq j}}^{L}\{e^{v_{ij}^{(\gamma)}-v_{kj}^{(\gamma')}}\cdot\bar{n}_{kj}^{(\gamma')}-e^{v_{kj}^{(\gamma')}-v_{ij}^{(\gamma)}}\cdot\bar{n}_{ij}^{(\gamma)}\}$$

$$i,j = 1,2,\ldots,L$$
$$\gamma,\gamma' \varepsilon \Omega_{ij}$$

with

$$v_{ij}^{(\gamma)} = -\beta c_{ij}^{(\gamma)} + u_{ij}(\underset{\sim}{n}) \qquad (44)$$

This set of equations must be solved simultaneously. This kind of generalisation of our model does not create any difficulties in principle. The flows are distributed among the routes available for travel between each origin destination pair. The positivity of all variables is always guaranteed.

9. THE STATIONARY SOLUTION OF TRAVEL NETWORKS, RESIDENTIAL LOCATION AND LABOUR MARKETS

By substitution of a generalisation of (23)

$$\hat{n}_{ij}^{(\gamma)} = C.e^{2\hat{v}_{ij}^{(\gamma)}(\hat{n})} \qquad (45)$$

into (43), it can be proved that (45) is the exact stationary solution. The constant C is determined by normalisation. This finally yields

$$\hat{n}_{ij}^{(\gamma)} = \hat{n} \cdot \frac{e^{2[\hat{n}_{ij}(\hat{\underset{\sim}{n}}) - \beta c_{ij}^{(\gamma)}]}}{\sum\limits_{\gamma' k, l} \sum e^{2[\hat{u}_{kl}(\hat{\underset{\sim}{n}}) - \beta c_{kl}^{(\gamma')}]}} \tag{46}$$

where

$$\hat{n} = \sum\limits_{\gamma}^{L} \sum\limits_{i,j} \hat{n}_{ij}^{(\gamma)}. \tag{47}$$

The stationary trip distribution $\hat{n}_{ij}^{(\gamma)}$ (46) of mode γ, depends on the utility $\hat{u}_{ij}(\hat{\underset{\sim}{n}})$, to live in i and work in j and on the aggregate travel costs $c_{ij}^{(\gamma)}$. Equation (46) can be seen as a logit model. But, it is worthwhile to emphasise that the result of (46) coincides with the stationary points of the meanvalue equations (43) and with the extremal values of the stationary probability distribution as well.

Therefore, assumptions concerning the distribution function of the random utility part, as used in random utility theory (Leonardi 1984), are not needed. But since our model based on the master equation approach ends up with the <u>same structure of the stationary solution</u> as random utility theory, it seems to be justified to interpret $v_{ij}(\underset{\sim}{n})$ as a utility function <u>even</u> if our system would be <u>out</u> of equilibrium. This may imply that within this model the special choice of the individual transition probabilities are therefore in the same sense equivalent to the assumption of a Gumbel or Weibull distribution used in random utility theory. In this sense, random utility theory is embedded.

This model can be used in regional planning to treat a variety of questions, for example, what will happen if a new mode is introduced between i and j assuming that the 'travel costs' are about 30% less than the alternative connections. The new mode leads to an additional choice possibility in the travel network. By a simulation of this travel network the optimal path of a new route as well as its 'capacity' can be obtained with respect to several strategies.

ACKNOWLEDGEMENT

It is a pleasure to thank my friends W. Weidlich and G. Leonardi for many helpful discussions. This work has been supported by IRES and VW-foundation.

REFERENCES

Anas, A., 'The combined equilibrium of travel networks and residential location markets', Contribution to the Metropolitan Study: II, IIASA, Collaboration Paper, 1984.

Clark, W.A. and Smith, T.R., 'Housing market search behaviour and expected utility theory', Environment and Planning A, 14, 1982, pp. 681-698, pp. 717-737.

Clark, W.A., 'Structures for research on the dynamics of residential search', in: Griffith, D.A. and Lea, A.C. (eds), Evolving Geographical Structures, Martinus Nijhoff, The Hague, 1983, pp. 372-397.

Eaton, B. and Watts, M., 'Wage dispersion, job vacancies and job search in equilibrium', Econometrica, 44, 1977, pp. 23-25.

Haag, G. and Weidlich, W., 'A stochastic theory of interregional migration', Geographical Analysis, 16, 1983, pp. 331-357.

Leonardi, G., 'A choice-theoretical framework for household mobility and extensions', Research Report, IIASA, Laxenburg, Austria, 1984.

Lippman, S. and McCall, J., 'The economics of job search: a survey', Economic Inquiry', 34, 1976, pp. 155-189.

Mensch, G., 'Das Technologische Patt', Frankfurt, 1975.

Mensch, G., Haag, G. and Weidlich, W., 'The Schumpeter Clock', Ballinger, Cambridge, 1985 (forthcoming).

Mortensen, D., 'Job matching under imperfect information', in: Ashenfelter, O. and Blum, J., Evaluating the Labour Market Effects of Social Program, Princeton University Press, Princeton, 1973, pp. 194-231.

Nijkamp, P. and Schubert, U., 'Structural change in urban systems', Contribution to the Metropolitan Study, Research Report 1983-5, IIASA, Laxenburg, Austria, 1983.

Rogerson, P., 'The effects of job search and competition on unemployment and vacancies in regional labour markets', in: Griffith, D.A. and Lea, C.A., Evolving Geographic Structures, Martinus Nijhoff, The Hague, 1983.

Weidlich, W. and Haag, G., Concepts and Models of a Quantitative Sociology: The Dynamics of Interacting Populations, Springer, Heidelberg, New York, 1983.

Weidlich, W. and Haag, G., 'A dynamic phase transition model for spatial agglomeration processes', 1985.

Wilson, A.G., 'Location theory: a unified approach', Working Paper 355, School of Geography, University of Leeds, 1983.

TECHNOLOGICAL CHANGE AND LABOUR MIGRATION
IN A GENERAL SPATIAL INTERACTION SYSTEM
Peter Nijkamp and Jacques Poot

1.   INTRODUCTION

It has been indicated in recent publications that technological change
and spatial reallocation of employment are two closely connected phenomena (see, among others, Malecki and Varaiya 1986). The US 'sunbelt
drift' is a good illustration of such technological-spatial dynamics.

We observe that technological change does not exhibit a smooth time
trajectory and, for example, the long wave literature points to a
space-time clustering of innovations which fuel economic growth (e.g.,
Kleinknecht 1985). Irrespective of the question whether such waves are
in some way self-generating, the intricate interaction of innovation
and economic growth produces periods of rapid change through innovation diffusion, regional specialisation or differentiation, and the
reallocation of mobile productive resources.

A major but as yet unresolved problem is under which conditions a new
spatial equilibrium will emerge, after a reallocation of production
factors, whereby equilibrium is defined as a steady-state configuration of economic activity over space. The present paper provides an
analytical contribution to a key aspect of this problem: the distribution of employment. The framework for analysis results from a general
theory of movement (or a generalised spatial interaction model).

Central to the discussion on spatial labour market impacts of new
technologies is the breeding place hypothesis, which states that large
agglomerations offer an enormous potential for the generation and
adoption of new ideas and technological innovations due to their strategic place in a spatial network (external linkages) and their syner-
gistic scale economies inside the system (internal or nodal linkages).
Traditionally, such innovations were seen as self-reinforcing. Through
cumulative causation, the largest agglomeration would be growing fastest and be the most innovative (e.g., Myrdal 1957).

However, it is also a well known fact that such 'growth poles' exceeding beyond a critical saturation level may suffer from diseconomies caused by capacity limitations and congestion. Thus a flexible adjustment pattern of agglomerations to technological changes has to take place between a <u>minimum threshold level</u> for agglomeration forces to be operative, and <u>critical bottleneck level</u> determined by the production capacity of an agglomeration.

Given the limits to growth of an agglomeration, its locational and employment profile may set boundaries for new technological innovations as well. For there is a continuous diffusion of innovations, principally through supply and demand linkages, competition and communication (see the review by Malecki 1983), but such diffusion may generate new 'breeding grounds' where the locational and employment profiles have become more favourable than in the original growth pole. Such developments are likely to lead to a perturbation in the socio-economic situation of the latter.

It is assumed in the present paper that the spatial distribution of employment, through differentials in economic growth, can ultimately be associated with technology which has a <u>push-pull</u> effect on all agglomerations (or regions) in a spatial system. The <u>push</u> effect of technology means that beyond a critical level economic activities (and thus also employment) will be driven out of the initial agglomeration to other regions. Two factors are mainly responsible for this push effect, viz.

- <u>congestion</u>, which can be broadly interpreted as representing both an intrinsic push resulting from a decline in the quality of life, environmental pollution, increasing criminality rates, etc. and an intrinsic push caused by technologically induced labour market disequilibrium (through wage and structural rigidity). The congestion factor will be denoted by an index variable c, which is a function of measurable indicators.
- <u>competitiveness</u> of other regional labour markets, which may be related inter alia to differences in rates of return on human capital (thus representing the opportunity cost of not migrating), employment prospects and non-wage utility yielding locational attributes. This 'repulsiveness' factor will be denoted by an index variable d, to be specified below in Section 2.

The pull effect of technology is exerted by places acting as 'attractors' of new activities, and hence, of employment. Two different factors which favour this pull effect are distinguished here, viz.

- intrinsic pull through favourable labour market conditions and the presence of public facilities, reflected in educational facilities, sociocultural and medical provisions, social overhead capital, infrastructure, etc. This factor will be denoted by an index variable p which can be evaluated as a function of measurable characteristics of an agglomeration.

- attractiveness of the labour market compared to all potential labour markets in the spatial system at hand both in terms of labour market conditions itself and the quality of life. This factor is represented by an index variable a, which will be defined below. Clearly, both push and pull factors have a significant effect on the spatial interaction and allocation patterns of activities, and hence, of jobs. The foregoing remarks are briefly summarised in Figure 1.

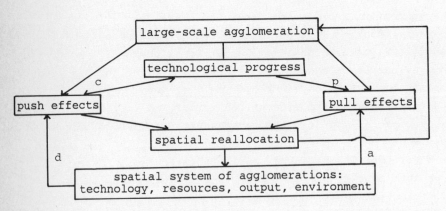

Figure 1. A schematic representation of the breeding place concept in a spatial system.

The main question is now how spatial interaction effects are intertwined with structural changes in the technological and socioeconomic conditions of the system at hand. In order to provide an analytical framework for a spatial equilibrium analysis of the movements of people, in Section 2 a brief introduction will be given to a general theory of movement which provides a rich platform for a profound analysis of spatial interaction and equilibrium processes.

2.   A GENERAL THEORY OF MOVEMENT

In this section the regional implications of spatial interdependencies associated with the impact pattern from Figure 1 will be analysed by using as a starting point a theory of movement developed by Alonso (1978), which has the potential of providing a unifying framework for all kinds of spatial interaction phenomena.

Alonso's theory defines a family of spatial interaction models which can be shown to encompass a wide variety of popular spatial interaction models such as gravity and entropy models. Further contributions to this theory of movement - both extensions and applications - can be found in Anselin (1982), Anselin and Isard (1979), Fisch (1981), Hua (1980), Ledent (1980, 1981), Porell (1982), Porell and Hua (1981), Tabuchi (1984), and Poot (1984). In the present paper only a brief presentation of Alonso's model and a dynamic extension will be given; full details can be found in Nijkamp and Poot (1985). Despite the generality of the Alonso model, it has also some severe restrictions, viz. the assumption of a closed system, the absence of feedback loops and the reliance on short run equilibrium. In the following presentation, we will describe a dynamic version of Alonso's model which includes also feedback loops.

Assume a system composed of R regions indicated by indices r and s (r, s = 1, ..., R). A flow of job migrants from r to s during period (t, t+1) is represented as $m_{rs}(t)$. The elements $m_{rs}(t)$ are included in a spatial flow matrix M(t). The number of job migrants leaving region r (i.e., total outmigration) is - according to the push effects in Figure 1 - functionally determined (in a multiplicative form) as:

$$m_{r.}(t) = \sum_{s=1}^{R} m_{rs}(t)$$
$$= \delta_r(t) \, c_r(t) \, d_r(t)^{\gamma_r} \tag{1}$$

where $\delta_r(t)$ represents the impact of external effects (e.g., pull effects from outside the spatial system), and where $c_r(t)$ and $d_r(t)$ have already been defined before.

In a similar way the inmigration into region s can be determined as follows:

$$m_{.s}(t) = \sum_{r=1}^{R} m_{rs}(t)$$
$$= \varepsilon_s(t)\ p_s(t)\ a_s(t)^{\mu_s} \tag{2}$$

where $\varepsilon_s(t)$ represents again external forces inducing inmigration to regions, and where $p_s(t)$ and $a_s(t)$ have already been defined in Figure 1.

The variables $d_r(t)$ and $a_s(t)$ are called <u>systematic</u> variables, since they represent the influence of the spatial system on the focus region r.

Next, the total push effect exerted by region r can be represented by the following push <u>indicator</u> (see Anselin and Isard 1979):

$$\bar{c}_r(t) = m_{r.}(t)/d_r(t) \tag{3}$$

while analogously the following pull <u>indicator</u> for regions s can be defined as:

$$\bar{p}_s(t) = m_{.s}(t)/a_s(t) \tag{4}$$

Now it is assumed that the flow of job migrants between region r and s satisfies a gravity model, implying that labour force migration is proportional to the push indicator, the pull indicator, and a distance friction function $f_{rs}(t)$ between region r and s, i.e.,

$$m_{rs}(t) = \alpha(t)\ \bar{c}_r(t)\ \bar{p}_s(t) f_{rs}(t) \tag{5}$$

where $\alpha(t)$ is the well known cross section proportionality constant.

In order to assure internal consistency of this model in terms of additivity conditions, the systematic variables have to satisfy:

$$d_r(t) = \alpha(t) \sum_{s=1}^{R} \bar{p}_s(t) f_{rs}(t) \tag{6}$$

and

$$a_s(t) = \alpha(t) \sum_{r=1}^{R} \bar{c}_r(t) f_{rs}(t) \tag{7}$$

Thus the systematic variables are essentially weighted averages of the push and pull indicators. It is clear that this system can only be solved in a recursive way, while a unique solution exists if the following scaling condition is introduced:

$$\prod_{r=1}^{R} d_r(t) = \prod_{s=1}^{R} a_s(t) = 1$$

The solution procedure for the systemic variables is essentially equivalent to a bi-proportional adjustment procedure, so that the systemic variables act in fact as the well known balancing factors in gravity and entropy models.

It can easily be shown that the model presented above is a general case of popular specific spatial interaction models (including gravity and entropy models). For instance, if $\gamma_r = \mu_s = 1$ for all r and s, the conventional single-equation gravity model is obtained. If $\gamma_r = \mu_s = 1$ for all r and s, the conventional single-equation gravity model is obtained. If $\gamma_s = \mu_s = 0$, the doubly constrained trip distribution model can be found by setting $\mu_s = 1$.
The foregoing model reflects a spatial interaction process including movements of people due to structural changes (technological changes, e.g.) on the labour market.

3. PROPERTIES OF THE GENERAL MODEL

The proportion of workers in the labour force of region r that migrates to s can be written as:

$$\frac{m_{rs}(t)}{l_r(t)} = \pi_{rs}(t) \frac{m_{r.}(t)}{l_r(t)} \tag{8}$$

where $l_r(t)$ is the labour force in region r, and where π_{rs} is the probability that a migrant from r moves to s, i.e.,

$$\pi_{rs}(t) = \frac{m_{rs}(t)}{m_{r.}(t)} \tag{9}$$

This can be expressed in the Alonso model in terms of equations (1) and (5) by

$$\pi_{rs}(t) = \alpha(t) \frac{\bar{p}_s(t)}{d_r(t)} f_{rs}(t) \tag{10}$$

If $\pi_{rs}(t)$ is constant over time and if the emission of job migrants is proportional to the labour force, one arrives at a Markov process with stationary transition probabilities. If the transition matrix is denoted by R, the dynamics of spatial labour force allocation can be described as follows:

$$\underline{l}^*(t+1) = R \, \underline{l}^*(t) \tag{11}$$

where $\underline{l}^*(t+1)$ is an Rx1 vector with share elements $l_r^*(t)$ (r=1, ..., R) defined as:

$$l_r^*(t) = l_r(t) / \sum_{k=1}^{K} l_k(t) \tag{12}$$

If R is irreducible, the process converges to a steady-state distribution.

However, equations (8) and (10) provide us with potential sources of instability:

i) changes in the emission rate of migrant workers. For example, given that the young have a higher propensity to move, ageing of the work force may reduce the emission rate.

ii) changes in the pull indicators of potential destinations.

iii) changes in the competitiveness of origins.

iv) changes in the frictional cost of reallocation. This is not likely to be a source of instability since, for example, an improvement in communication through new technology would have a proportional effect on all frictional costs f_{rs}.

In conclusion, shifts in technological and socioeconomic conditions determine the dynamics of the spatial system concerned.

In absolute terms, the time trajectory of the size of the labour force in each region r can be represented by means of the following fundamental growth equation:

$$l_r(t+1) = \{1+g_r(t)\}l_r(t) + m_{.r}(t) - m_{r.}(t) \tag{13}$$

where $g_r(t)$ is the rate of 'natural' increase of the labour force in period t in region r, reflecting the net increase to the labour force through:

i)   a change in the size and age composition of the population (a function of the demographic processes of fertility and mortality).

ii) a change in age-specific labour force participation, which is a function of socioeconomic and cultural phenomena (e.g., emancipation and prolongued education) and labour market disequilibria (e.g., the discouraged and additional worker effects).

Substitution of (1) and (2) into (13) yields the following result:

$$l_r(t+1) = \{1+g_r(t)\}\, l_r(t) + \varepsilon_r(t)\, p_r(t)\, a_r(t)^{\mu r} - \delta_r(t) c_r(t) d_r(t)^{\gamma r} \tag{14}$$

It may be assumed here for the moment that agglomeration size is a proxy for intrinsic push and pull and, thus, that $p_r(t)$ and $c_r(t)$ are related to $l_r(t)$. Therefore, one may use the following auxiliary equations (cf. Anselin 1984):

$$p_r(t) = l_r(t)^\kappa \tag{15}$$

and

$$c_r(t) = 1_r(t)^\lambda \tag{16}$$

Substitution of (15) and (16), and also of (6) and (7), into (14) gives the following expression:

$$1_r(t+1) = \{1+g_r(t)\} \; 1_r(t) \; +$$

$$\alpha(t)^{\mu_r} \varepsilon_r(t) \; 1_r(t)^\kappa \; \{ \sum_{s=1}^{R} \delta_s(t) \; 1_s(t)^\lambda \; d_s(t)^{\gamma_s-1} \; f_{rs}(t) \}^{\mu_r} -$$

$$\alpha(t)^{\gamma_r} \delta_r(t) \; 1_r(t)^\lambda \; \{ \sum_{s=1}^{R} \varepsilon_s(t) \; 1_s(t)^\kappa \; a_s(t)^{\mu_s-1} \; f_{rs}(t) \}^{\gamma_r} \tag{17}$$

This is a nonlinear system of first-order difference equations. Apart from a degenerate case, it is impossible to solve this system analytically (see Nijkamp and Poot 1985). But this system has extremely interesting dynamic properties, which have been studied fairly extensively in population dynamics.

In order to study some of these properties, one may assume a logistic growth process for $g_r(t)$:

$$g_r(t) = v_r \{ 1 - 1_r(t)/\bar{1}_r \} \tag{18}$$

where $\bar{1}_r$ is a saturation level (or carrying capacity) of the labour force in region r; the parameter v_r is a tuning coefficient that determines the velocity of adjustment. Then equation (17) has some very intriguing properties regarding its time trajectory. Two situations will be briefly discussed here, viz. a case without migration and a case with migration. Without migration, (18) will result in a stable spatial labour force allocation if - provided a certain initial condition regarding levels is satisfied - the rate of adjustment parameter v_r falls in the following range: $0 < v_r < 2$. When $v_r > 2$, the spatial system may exhibit cyclical or chaotic behaviour (see for a treatment of the stability properties of this equation in population dynamics May 1974, 1976).

In the presence of spatial interaction through labour migration, (18) has to be substituted into (17), which yields a complicated nonlinear dynamic model. Suppose, for instance, a simple double constrained trip distribution model (i.e., $\gamma_r = \mu_s = 0$). Then (17) becomes:

$$l_r(t+1) = \{1 + v_r(1 - l_r(t)/\bar{l}_r)\}l_r(t) + \varepsilon_r(t)l_r(t)^\kappa \delta_r(t) \; l_r(t)^\lambda \quad (19)$$

This equation may again generate stable or unstable time trajectories, depending on the values of the adjustment rate v_r, on the parameters κ and λ, and on the external forces $\varepsilon_r(t)$ and $\delta_r(t)$. Further analysis of the equilibrium properties of this model can be found in Nijkamp and Poot (1985). Spatial complementarity and spatial competition (leading to competitive exclusion) may both be generated by this model).

Thus the conclusion may be drawn that - depending on initial conditions and on the speed of adjustment - the dynamic spatial system described above may exhibit various time processes which are to some extent also induced by technological progress. The latter issue will be further taken up in the next section.

4.   TECHNOLOGICAL CHANGE AND SPATIAL INTERACTION

So far technology has only been treated as an exogenous factor: technology determined both the labour market push and pull effects of a spatial system. However, every spatial reallocation of people implies a change in residential - and hence urbanisation - patterns. Consequently, an agglomeration induced technological change (based on the breeding place or incubator principle) leads to a new spatial configuration that affects the existing agglomeration economies and causes - in turn - a spatial change in the incubator functions of cities and regions.

Such dynamic feedback effects have to be integrated in our spatial interaction model. It should be noted that the effects of a spatial reallocation may be quite diverse. As part of the diffusion process, technological progress may be embodied in the human capital that is transferred through migration. Through this and other breeding place phenomena technological revival in existing agglomerations may be generated which, in turn, attracts more people, while on the other hand, agglomerations may suffer from congestion phenomena (or, in general, capacity bottlenecks) beyond a critical size.

If we denote technological change by z, one may assume that the relative pull features of settlements in area r is determined by z_r as follows:

$$p_r(t) = \theta_r \, z_r(t)^{\eta_r} \tag{20}$$

Clearly, equation (20) now replaces the auxiliary equation presented in (15). This part of the breeding place principle states that technology exerts a positive impact on the relative pull effects of a city through a qualitative improvement of the urban development potential.

On the other hand, technology is - in turn - positively influenced by city size, while beyond a critical level c diseconomies of scale will occur. This can be indicated as follows:

$$z_r(t) = \varphi_r \, \exp \, (c_r(t) - \hat{c}_r)^{\nu_r} \tag{21}$$

(with $\varphi_r > 0$ and $\nu_r > 1$). Substitution of (21) into (20) gives

$$p_r(t) = \theta_r \, \varphi_r^{\eta_r} \, \exp \, (c_r(t) - \hat{c}_r)^{\nu_r \eta_r} \tag{22}$$

Next, we may substitute (15) into (22):

$$p_r(t) = \theta_r \, \varphi^{\eta_r} \, \exp \, (l_r(t)^{\lambda} \, \hat{c}_r)^{\nu_r \eta_r} \tag{23}$$

Finally, substitution of (16) and (23) into (14), followed by a substitution of (6) and (7) into the resulting expression leads to a complicated nonlinear expression for the labour market development in all places of the spatial system at hand. The final result has of course similar properties as the above mentioned May model, but has even additional interesting properties as it encompasses a turning point for urban growth in all places of the interwoven capital system. Consequently, cyclical spatial developments are likely to occur in a spatial system, as soon as the breeding place principle is integrated with technological progress and diseconomies of scale.

By closing the model expressed in (14) with (18) and the pairs (15) and (16), or (15) and (23), we have effectively expressed the dynamics of the system in terms of the following mapping (or endomorphism):

$$1 = \Omega \{1(t)\} \tag{24}$$

with $1(t)$ the vector $(1_1(t), 1_2(t), ..., 1_R(t))$. The mapping Ω is nonlinear and cannot be expressed in an analytically closed form (since the mapping depends on the levels of the system push and pull factors which are, in turn, a function of $1(t)$). It should be noted that there is no guarantee that equilibrium exists (i.e., that Ω has a fixed point). Moreover, even when an equilibrium would exist, this may be unstable. Thus, the combined growth and spatial interaction model presented here is sufficiently general to reproduce the perturbations that are commonly observed in regional development.

5. CONCLUDING REMARKS

This paper has dealt with two issues. First, it has made an attempt at designing a general dynamic model for spatial movements of people, based inter alia on labour market dynamics. Clearly, technological change is one of the key forces for such dynamic developments. The conditions under which a stable or unstable equilibrium might emerge have also been discussed. Next, technology was endogenised, so that it could be treated as an endogenous driving force (together with other key factors) for spatial dynamics. It was demonstrated that the resulting model bears a close resemblance to some models from population dynamics, whose equilibrium conditions have been studied quite extensively in the literature.

REFERENCES

Alonso, W., 'A theory of movements', in Hansen, N.M. (ed), Human Settlement Systems, Ballinger, 1978, pp. 197-211.

Anselin, L., 'Implicit functional relationships between systemic effects on a general model of movement', Regional Science and Urban Economics, 12, 1982, pp. 365-380.

Anselin, L., 'Specification tests and model selection for aggregate spatial interaction: an empirical comparison', Journal of Regional Science, 24, 1984, pp. 1-15.

Anselin, L. and Isard, W., 'An Alonso's general theory of movement', Man, Environment, Space and Time, 1, 1979, pp. 52-63.

Fisch, O., 'Contributions to the general theory of movement', Regional Science and Urban Economics, 11, 1981, pp. 157-173.

Hua, C., 'An exploration of the nature and rationale of a systemic model', Environment and Planning, A12, 1980, pp. 713-726.

Kleinknecht, A., Innovations Patterns in Crisis and Prosperity, MacMillan, London, 1985.

Ledent, J., 'Calibrating Alonso's general theory of movement: the case of interprovincial migration flows in Canada', Sistemi Urbani, 2, 1980, pp. 327-358.

Ledent, J., 'On the relationship between Alonso's theory of movement and Wilson's family of spatial-interaction models', Environment and Planning, A13, 1981, pp. 217-224.

Malecki, E.J., 'Technology and regional development: a survey', International Regional Science Review, Vol. 8, 1983, pp. 89-126.

Malecki, E.J. and Varaiya, R., 'Innovation and changes in regional structure', in: Nijkamp, P. (ed), Handbook in Regional Economics, North-Holland Publ. Co., Amsterdam, 1986 (forthcoming).

May, R.M., 'Biological populations with nonoverlapping generations: stable points, stable cycles, and chaos', Science, 186, 1974, pp. 645-647.

May, R.M., 'Simple mathematical models with very complicated dynamics', Nature, 261, 1976, pp. 459-467.

Myrdal, G., Economic Theory and Underdeveloped Regions, Duckworths, London, 1957.

Nijkamp, P., 'Reflections on gravity and entropy models', Regional Science and Urban Economics, 5, 1975, pp. 203-225.

Nijkamp, P. and Poot, H.J., Dynamics of Generalised Spatial Interaction Models, Research Memorandum, Department of Economics, Victoria University of Wellington, New Zealand, 1985.

Poot, H.J., 'Models of New Zealand internal migration and residential mobility', Unpublished PhD Dissertation, Victoria University of Wellington, New Zealand, 1984.

Porell, F.W., 'Intermetropolitan migration and quality of life', Journal of Regional Science, 22, 1982, pp. 137-158.

Porell, F.W. and Hua, C.H., 'An econometric procedure for estimation of a generalised systemic gravity model under incomplete information about the system', Regional Science and Urban Economics, 11, 1981, pp. 585-606.

Tabuchi, T., 'The systemic variables and elasticities in Alonso's general theory of movement', Regional Science and Urban Economics, 14, 1984, pp. 249-264.

ON THE PRODUCTION AND DIFFUSION
OF TECHNOLOGICAL CHANGE
Jan Rouwendal

1.   INTRODUCTION

The economics of technological change is a topic which in recent years
has received a great deal of attention among economists (see Stoneman
1983 for an overview). Although the assumption of exogenous technological change is questioned, still the production and diffusion of new
technologies are often described as being exogenous in many respects.
In this paper an approach will be outlined by which both phenomena can
be described in a more endogenous way. The basic idea is that the development of new production techniques by means of R&D can be viewed
as a production process and described by means of a production function.

The structure of the model is basically that of a two-sector growth
model. In Sector 1 a composite consumption-investment good is produced, while Sector 2 produces only knowledge, i.e., more efficient
production techniques. The production function is both sectors is
assumed to be of the Cobb-Douglas type. A complication is that in the
production of Sector 2, productivity increases give no immediate returns. This implies that outlays on R&D have to be financed out of
savings.

In the present paper some implications of this model for the diffusion
of technological knowledge from advanced to lagging regions will be
pointed out. The paper should be viewed as a progress report of research underway. The model has to be elaborated further and the results reached here have a preliminary character, e.g., we use only a
two-region system in our analysis.

It is readily admitted that the use of a macroeconomic production
function for R&D is even more problematic than that for a composite
consumption-investment good, e.g.,R&D faces much more uncertainty in
its outcomes than usual production processes. On the other hand, the
assumption that there is a more or less consistent link between inputs

and outputs seems reasonable even for R&D. So one may judge the production function approach adopted here a reasonable first approximation although it certainly is not an ideal assumption.

It should be mentioned that the dynamic structure of the present model is more complicated than that of the usual neo-classical model (e.g., Solow 1956) and more or less comparable to two-sector growth models with exogenous technical progress. An important source of dynamics is the way productivity in Sector 2 changes when Sector 1 becomes more and more efficient. Given the stock of pure scientific knowledge it seems reasonable to conjecture that productivity in Sector 2 declines as that in Sector 1 grows. Furthermore, it seems probable that it is easier to improve on the productivity of Sector 1 of a region that lags behind in technological development than on that of a region that leads technological development, since in the former one has the possibility to learn from the experiences of the technology leader. This assumption is the basis for the inferences with respect to diffusion of technological change that are drawn later in the paper.

2.   THE MODEL

In this section, we give a short and formal description of the model for one region. Time (t) is suppressed as often as possible without giving rise to confusion, both in this as well as in the following sections.

The two production factors, capital (K) and labour (L) are both assumed to be homogeneous and are both employed in the two sectors. The goods producing sector is determined by an underindex 1, the knowledge-producing one by a 2.

$$L = L_1 + L_2 \tag{1}$$

$$K = K_1 + K_2 \tag{2}$$

It is assumed that labour and capital are being paid the same wage rate (w) and rental rate (r) respectively in both sectors. The incomes earned in both sectors can thus be defined:

$$Y_1 = wK_1 + rK_1 \tag{3}$$

$$Y_2 = wL_2 + rK_2 \tag{4}$$

while total income to the sum of these two:

$$Y = Y_1 + Y_2 \tag{5}$$

Capital and labour are paid according to their marginal products in Sector 1. We assume that production takes place under constant returns to scale so that the revenues from production in Sector 1 are exactly equal to the payments for labour and capital. Since the production of knowledge about more efficient production technologies generates no immediate revenues the production factors employed in Sector 2 have to be paid out of the savings in the economy. Outlays on R&D thus have much the same character as those on capital investments.

Assuming equilibrium in the economy, savings (S) have to be equal to the sum of investments in capital and R&D:

$$S = \overset{\cdot}{K}_1 + \overset{\cdot}{K}_2 + Y_2 \tag{6}$$

In this equation, $\overset{\cdot}{K}_1$ stands for dK/dt, and $\overset{\cdot}{K}_2$ has an analogous interpretation. Y_2, income in Sector 2 is of course, equal to outlays on R&D. For simplicity, no depreciation is assumed to take place. Production in Sector 1 is given by a Cobb-Douglas function:

$$Y_1 = A_1 \, L_1^{\alpha} \, K_1^{1-\alpha} \tag{7}$$

In this equation A_1 can be interpreted as an index of (overall) productivity as may be shown as follows. By appropriate choice of units we may set $A_{1t} = 1$ for $t = 0$. If we now compare the amounts of goods that can be generated by fixed amounts of production factors L_1 and K_1 at times t and 0 by taking their ratio we find:

$$\frac{\bar{Y}_{1t}}{\bar{Y}_{10}} = \frac{A_{1t} \, \bar{L}_1^{\alpha} \, K_1^{1-\alpha}}{A_{10} \, \bar{L}_1^{\alpha} \, \bar{K}_1^{1-\alpha}} = A_{1t} \tag{8}$$

It seems to refer to the quotient $\bar{Y}_{1t}/\bar{Y}_{10}$ and thus to the value of A_{1t} as the productivity ratio.

Productivity in Sector 1 may increase as a result of R&D. The increase in A_{1t} is determined by the amounts of production factors devoted to

R&D by means of, again, a Cobb-Douglas production function with constant returns to scale:

$$\dot{A}_1 = A_2 \; L_2^{\beta} \; K_2^{1-\beta} \qquad\qquad (9)$$

It should be noted that $\dot{A}_1$ ($= dA_1/dt$) does not have to be equal to Y_{2t} although a relation between the two will exist (see Rouwendal 1986 for details).

It can be shown that in the model described by equations (1) - (9) steady state growth is possible. In the steady state, capital stocks and incomes in both sectors grow at the same rate g, while the labour force grows in both sectors at the natural rate γ.

3.   PRODUCTIVITY OF R&D

In equation (9) the term A_2 may be interpreted as the productivity of R&D in the same way as A_1 was interpreted as that of goods production.

As long as the stock of pure scientific knowledge can be assumed to be given it seems natural to assume that A_2 varies inversely with A_1. As more and more efficient production techniques are used it becomes ceteris paribus more and more difficult to find still better ones. Thus some kind of decreasing returns to scale phenomenon is assumed to be present.

One may also conjecture that A_2 rises with increases in the stock of pure scientific knowledge. Since, in this paper, this increase is regarded as being exogenous we will not deal with it any further.

Attention will be concentrated however, on a third relation, viz. that between the productivities in different regions. It seems probable that a region that lags behind in technological development is able to increase its productivity much easier than a technology leader. The productivity of R&D in the lagging region is thus assumed to be higher since in that region one may learn from the experiences of the region with more advanced technologies.

It is assumed however, that even to imitate the technologies of the advanced regions, some labour and capital have to be used.

It seems likely that the productivity of Sector 2 in a lagging region becomes higher as the 'technology gap', i.e., the difference between the productivities in Sector 1 of both regions becomes larger. Furthermore, a distance decay effect will probably occur. It is easier to learn from more advanced regions in the immediate neighbourhood than from those further away.

Summarising, we may postulate the following general relationship for A_2 (where an upper index is used to denote the region concerned:

$$A_2^i = f(A_1^i, g(\frac{A_1^j}{A_1^i}, d_{ij}))$$ (10)

Only two regions are assumed to exist: $j = 1, 2$, $i \neq j$. The argument function g denotes the diffusion effect.
We assume:

$$\partial f / \partial A_1^i > 0 \qquad \partial f / \partial g > 0$$ (11)

The diffusion term g is an increasing function of the technology gap A_1^i/A_1^i and a decreasing one of the distance between the two regions d_{ij}:

$$\partial g / \partial (A_1^j/A_1^i) \geq 0 \qquad \partial g / \partial d_{ij} \leq 0$$ (12)

When no diffusion takes place, g is equal to 1.

These assumptions are consequences of the conjectures that were mentioned above.

It seems natural to assume that distance does not matter as long as there is no productivity difference:

$$g(1, d_{ij}) = g(1, 0) = 1$$ (13)

for all $d_{ij} \geq 0$.

Furthermore, it seems natural to assume that any productivity gap, no matter how large, loses its influence as distance increases, i.e.,

$$\lim_{d_{ij} \to \infty} g(\frac{A_1^j}{A_1^i}, d_{ij}) = 1$$ (14)

In this paper, it will be assumed that the advanced region experiences no drawbacks in its R&D productivity from its lead, i.e., a lag decreases A_2 but a lead does not increase it. Formally, this may be denoted as:

$$g(\frac{A_1^j}{A_1^i}, d_{ij}) = 1 \quad \text{for} \quad \frac{A_1^j}{A_1^i} \leq 1 \tag{15}$$

An example of functions that are relatively simple and satisfy the abovementioned requirements is:

$$f = (A_1^i)^{-\varepsilon} g$$

$$g = (A_1^d/A_1^i)^k, \quad k = \exp(\varphi \, d_{ij})$$
$$\text{for } A_1^j/A_1^i > 1 \tag{16}$$
$$g = 1 \quad \text{for } A_1^j/A_1^i \leq 1$$

Using (16) we find for the leading region, denoted by upper index 1:

$$A_2^1 = (A_1^1)^{-\varepsilon} \tag{17}$$

while for the lagging region, we find

$$A_2^2 = (A_1^2)^{-\varepsilon} (A_1^1/A_1^2)^k \tag{18}$$

4. OPTIMAL GROWTH IN BOTH REGIONS

The optimal rate of growth in defined to be the one that maximises the net present value of all future consumption streams per head. Consumption per head is defined as c_t:

$$c_t = \frac{Y_t - S_t}{L_t} = \frac{Y_{1t} - \dot{K}_{1t} - \dot{K}_{2t}}{L_t} \tag{19}$$

Substituting (7) in (19), taking its present value and taking account of the productivity change defined by (14) and (15) gives rise to a dynamic programming problem. As instrument variables $\dot{K}_{1t}$, $\dot{K}_{2t}$ and L_{2t} are used. The programme is written out in the Annex together with the necessary conditions that follow from it.

For the leading region, it is shown there that the necessary conditions for optimal growth as fulfilled for the growth rate g^1:

$$g^1 = [\frac{\alpha(1+\epsilon) + \beta}{\alpha(1+\epsilon) + \beta - 1}]\gamma \tag{20}$$

In this equation g^1 is the growth rate of the capital stocks in both sectors as well as that of the incomes in both sectors. j is the natural rate of growth, and equal to the growth rate of employment in both sectors.

It may be assumed that $\alpha(1+\epsilon) + \beta > 1$ (and this seems reasonable) then g is greater than j, so that consumption per head rises. Productivity in Sector 1 rises at a rate $(g - \gamma)$ while in Sector 2 declines at a rate $(g - \gamma)$.

For region 2, the lagging one, we find a more complicated expression for the optimal rate of growth g^2. This region (s), apart from the expression for productivity in Sector 2 (equation (14)), assumed to be equal to the leading one:

$$g^2 = [\frac{\alpha(1+\epsilon+k) + \beta}{\alpha(1+\epsilon+k) + \beta - 1}]\gamma \quad +[\frac{k}{\alpha(1+\epsilon+k) +\beta - 1}]g^1 \tag{21}$$

Here g^1 is the growth rate of the leading region, given in (20).

In the lagging region, the capital stocks grow in both sectors at a rate g^2, while population employed grows at the natural rate γ in both sectors. Productivity in Sector 1 is growing at a rate $(g^2 - \gamma)$, while that in Sector 2 is declining at a rate $\alpha[\epsilon(g^2 - \gamma) + k(g^2 - g^1)]$.

5. CONCLUSIONS

It can be inferred from (21) that g^2 is greater than g^1, i.e., the lagging region grows faster than the leading one. When the distance between the two regions becomes larger k tends to zero and g^2 approaches g^1. This implies that diffusion of new technologies proceeds faster as the distance between the regions is smaller. This is a remarkable result, not so much because it refers to a relatively well documented empirical fact, but in the first place because our result is concerned with optimality. If distance hampers the exchange of technological knowledge in the way it is assumed in equation (14) then it is optimal for the lagging region to decrease the distance with the leading one at a smaller pace as the distance between the two is greater.

A more intriguing implication of the present analysis is that the lagging region remains growing at the same (higher) growth rate g^2 until the technology gap has disappeared totally. Then region 2 arrives at a situation identical to that of region 1 and will, of course, grow at the same rate g^1. Probably this result is due to the asymmetry in the equations for A_2 in both regions (see equations (14) and (15)).

We conclude the paper with two questions that need further consideration. One may wonder what the implications of the present analysis are for the diffusion of technology in a system of more than two regions, e.g., one may assume a core with a high productivity and around that a periphery of regions with a smaller productivity. Initially, the regions near the core will grow faster than both the core and the peripheral regions, but presumably this will give rise to indirect diffusion from the regions near the core to the most peripheral ones. The general picture thus seems to be clear, but one wonders what the exact pattern will be.

Secondly, we draw attention to the question of the optimal development of (pure) scientific knowledge. So is it more profitable to increase productivity first of all in a central region and let it diffuse from there to the other ones, or is a gradual increase at the same rate in all regions the preferable one? The first strategy has the benefit of less resources needed for the later increase in productivity of the lagging regions, but this is only realised at the cost of considerable inequality in an earlier stage.

ANNEX The programming problem and its first order conditions

Substituting (7) in (16) and taking its net present value results in a target function :

$$v = \int_0^\infty (e^{-rt}/L_t)(A_{1t}(L_t-L_{2t})^\alpha K_{2t}^{1-\alpha} - \dot{K}_{1t} - \dot{K}_{21})dt \tag{A1}$$

We use $\dot{K}_{1t}$, $\dot{K}_{2t}$ and L_{2t} as our instrument variables and denote them by u_{1t}, u_{2t} and u_{3t} respectively. We have to take into account the following conditions:

$$\dot{K}_{it} = u_{it} \tag{A2}$$

$$\dot{K}_{2t} = u_{2t} \tag{A3}$$

$$\dot{A}_{it} = A_{2t} L_{2t}^{\beta} K_{2t}^{+\beta} \tag{A4}$$

In the last equation for A_{2t} one of the relations (14) and (15) should be substituted.

The problem formulated above gives rise to a Hamiltonian function:

$$H = (e^{-rt}/L_t \ (A_{1t}(L_t - u_{3t})^{\alpha} \ K_{2t}^{1-\alpha} - u_{1t} - u_{2t}) +$$
$$+ \lambda_1 u_{1t} + \lambda_2 u_{2t} + \lambda_3 A_{2t} L_{2t}^{\beta} K_{2t}^{1-\beta} \tag{A5}$$

As necessary conditions for an optimal growth path the partial derivatives of H with respect to the instrument variables have to vanish:

$$\partial H/\partial u_{1t} = 0 : \lambda_1 = e^{-rt}/L_t \tag{A6}$$

$$\partial H/\partial u_{2t} = 0 : \lambda_2 = e^{-rt}/L_t \tag{A7}$$

$$\partial H/\partial u_{3t} = 0 : (e^{-rt}/L_t) \ \alpha \ A_{1t}(L_t - u_{3t})^{\alpha-1} \ K_{1t}^{\alpha} =$$
$$= \lambda_4 \ \beta \ A_{2t} \ u_{3t}^{\beta-1} \ K_{2t}^{1-\beta} \tag{A8}$$

Furthermore, the partial derivatives of H with respect to K_{1t}, K_{2t} and L_{2t} should be equal to respectively, $-\dot{\lambda}_1$, $-\dot{\lambda}_2$ and $-\dot{\lambda}_3$:

$$\partial H/\partial K_{1t} = -\dot{\lambda}_1 : (e^{-rt}/L_t)(1-\alpha) \ A_{1t}(L_t - u_{3t})^{\alpha} \ K_{1t}^{-\alpha} = -\dot{\lambda}_2 \tag{A9}$$

$$\partial H/\partial K_{2t} = -\dot{\lambda}_2 : \lambda_4(1-\beta) \ A_{2t} \ u_{3t}^{\beta} \ K_{2t}^{-\beta} = -\dot{\lambda}_3 \tag{A10}$$

$$\partial H/\partial A_{1t} = -\dot{\lambda}_3 : (e^{-rt}/L_t)(L_t - u_{3t})^{\alpha} \ K_{1t}^{L\alpha} -$$
$$\tag{A11}$$
$$- \lambda_4 \ (\partial A_{2t}/\partial A_{1t}) \ u_{3t}^{\beta} \ K_{2t}^{1-\beta} = -\dot{\lambda}_4$$

If (14) is true we have

$$\partial A_2^2 / \partial A_1^2 = (-\varepsilon - k) \, A_1^{2^{-\varepsilon}-1} \, (A_1^1/A_1^2)^k \tag{A12}$$

while if (15) is true:

$$\partial A_2^1 / \partial A_1^1 = - \, A_1^{-\varepsilon-1} \tag{A13}$$

In these equations, λ_4 can be interpreted as (e^{-rt}/L_t)-times the price of one percentage point productivity increase in Sector 1. Equation (A8) then implies that the marginal productivities of labour in both sectors have to be equal, while (A9) and (A10) have the same interpretation for the marginal productivities of capital.

The optimal growth path is a solution to the equations (A6) - (A11), with the appropriate expressions for $\partial A_1 / \partial A_1$ substituted in it.

It can be checked that a steady growth rate fulfils all these equations (substitute an exponential function with growth rate g for K_1 and K_2 and one with growth rate j for L_1 and L_2 and derive the implications from it.

From Rouwendal (1986) we use the conclusion for the optimal growth rate of the technology leader (that can be easily checked):

$$g^1 = [\frac{\alpha(1+\varepsilon) + \beta}{\alpha(1+\varepsilon) + \beta - 1}] \gamma \tag{A14}$$

If $\alpha(1+\varepsilon) + \beta > 1$ g^1 is positive, greater than γ, a linear increasing of j and a decreasing one of α, β and ε. The optimal growth will thus be smaller if the tradeoff between the productivities in both sectors becomes stronger.

For the region that lags behind, it can in the same way (i.e., by substituting exponential growth at a rate g for K_1 and K_2 and at a rate γ for L_1 and L_2) be found that:

$$g^2 = [\frac{\alpha(1+\varepsilon+k) + \beta}{\alpha(1+\varepsilon+k) + \beta - 1}] \gamma + [\frac{k}{\alpha(1+\varepsilon+K) + \beta - 1}] \, g^1 \tag{A15}$$

REFERENCES

Intrilligator, M.D., Mathematical Optimization and Economic Theory, Prentice Hall, Englewood Cliffs, 1971.

Rouwendal, J., Endogenizing Technological Change in a Neoclassical
    Growth Model, Research Paper, Free University, Amsterdam, 1986.

Solow, R.M., 'A contribution to the theory of economic growth', Quar-
    terly Journal of Economics, 1956.

Stoneman, P., The Economic Analysis of Technological Change, Oxford
    University Press, Oxford, 1983.

INNOVATION AND THE URBAN LIFE-CYCLE:
PRODUCTION, LOCATION AND INCOME DISTRIBUTION ASPECTS
Roberto P. Camagni

"Cities have existed since prehistoric time. They are multi-
centuried structures of the most ordinary way of life. They are
also multipliers, capable of adapting to change and helping to
bring it about. One might say that cities and money created
modernity; but conversely (...) modernity - the changing mass of
men's lives - promoted the expansion of money and led to the
growing tyranny of the cities. Cities and money are at one and
the same time motors and indicators; they provoke and indicate
change."
(Fernand Braudel, Afterthoughts on Material Civilization and Capitalism)

1. INTRODUCTION

Undoubtedly, one of the most interesting models of urban growth proposed in the last decade is Hall and Hay's 'patterns of metropolitan
growth' model (1980), subsequently developed in the 'urban life-cycle'
model by the researchers of the CURB Project (van den Berg et al.
1982, Klaassen et al. 1981).

In spite of its mainly geographic approach and its purely descriptive
nature, it has exerted a 'discrete fascination' on scholars and urban
planners, due to its elegance and conceptual simplicity. The empirical
uniformities it reveals have proved to hold in different spatial contexts (Aydalot 1983, Kawashima 1984, Camagni, Curti and Gibelli 1984),
and on its axis medium term forecasts and policy prescriptions in different urban contexts have been put forward.

The four urban stages of urbanisation, suburbanisation, disurbanisation and reurbanisation, possibly amplified to cover all the possible
combinations of relative population growth in the core, ring and total
metropolitan areas, may in fact be taken as good descriptions of post
war urban development in advanced countries (Figure 1), even though
their indications had to be reinforced by other 'urban problem' variables in order to ascertain the real distressed urban areas in the
case of the European Community (Cheshire, Hay and Carbonaro 1984).

383

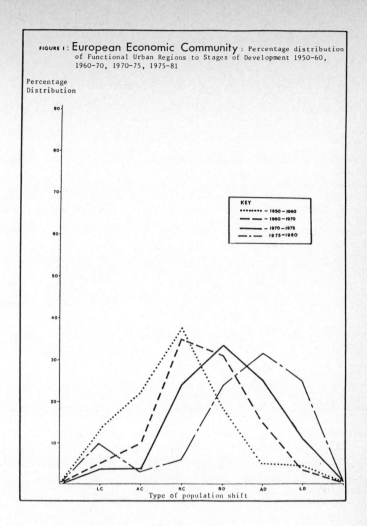

Source: Cheshire and Hay 1984.

As far as the economic interpretation of these stages is concerned,
once an urban economies vs. diseconomies approach has been rejected as
tautological, we are left with a widely non-satisfactory state of the
theory in that it relies on poorly explained dynamics of labour costs
and on the evolution of the urban environmental quality.

As in other well known 'stage of development' and 'life-cycle' hypotheses, it is of course very difficult to explain theoretically under
which quantitative conditions an upturn or downturn will take place or
a new phase will begin. Nevertheless, the interest and the good empirical validation of the model deserved wider theoretical attention.

The main elements, which in my view remain insufficiently explained or even untouched in the present research work on the urban life-cycle hypothesis are the following:

1. what is the _primum mobile_, the driving force of the process;
2. what is the frequency and length of the cycle;
3. which kind and size of cities does it encompass;
4. which lags are likely to be expected in different spatial contexts and along the urban hierarchy;
5. which economic relationships (or 'contradictions') link the metropolis and the countryside;
6. which limits may be fixed to a mechanistic and deterministic interpretation of the cycle and by what extent may successive cycles be considered as similar;
7. which actual symptoms can allow us to forecast a near upturn of the urban cycle in the direction of a 'reurbanisation process.

The aim of the present paper is to present some reflections on these themes, together with some empirical results concerning the northern Italian urban system.

We are not concerned here with another approach to the problem of metropolitan decline which interprets it as a 'clean break' with respect to the past; in this case in fact one should rely on some exogenous macrohistorical elements, not easily tested, like sudden and widespread anti-urban psychological attitudes (Vining and Kontuly 1978) or equally sudden refusals of the market mechanism both in the economic interpersonal relationships (Aydalot 1984). In fact these attitudes are likely to appear in some advanced phases of the regional and urban growth process, characterised by bureaucratisation of industrial relationships, worsening of the social and built environment, lack of entrepreneurial capabilities, pursuit of new and natural values, as Schumpeter reminded us in his last works; but these elements could be easily embodied in a long run cyclical vision of the spatial dynamics, thus enriching the model with new, necessary, noneconomic elements (Camagni 1984a).

Through this paper, we are mainly interested in the relative performances of the _entire_ metropolitan areas, and not in the simple core-ring dialectics within it. In terms of the well known core-ring population change graph, drawn in _absolute_ terms, we will focus on the relative position of the urban systems with respect to the zero-growth line, i.e. to the 45° negatively sloped line passing through the origins. In fact we are interested here in long periodic changes, linked to production, distribution and relative prices elements, while core-ring relationships are related mainly to ecological and physical space needs by both population and firms.

2. THE DRIVING FORCE OF URBAN GROWTH

The urban life-cycle model fails to indicate which forces lie beyond the metropolitan growth process and determine its dimensions and pace, and this shortcoming is due to the overwhelming attention paid only to the visible effects of these forces; population and employment change in space. No hypothesis is put forward on the primary elements that break the stationary state, and that economic theory indicates as the innovation processes; technological change, product and process innovation, change in managerial models and discovery of new markets, all factors which should be included in dynamic models of urban growth (Nijkamp and Schubert 1983). Through the creation of profit opportunities, innovation shapes investment and income cycles and consequently employment and population change over space.

The links between innovation and the urban environment are well known in theory (Rosenberg 1976, Pred 1977) and have been empirically tested recently in different spatial contexts (Oakey et al 1982, Goddard et al. 1984, Camagni 1984b). Due to the presence of information and communication infrastructures, technological and managerial services, skilled labour, R&D activities and abundance of private financial capital, the large metropolitan areas are the natural birthplace of first innovations, and exploit to a certain extent the multiplier effects of the early phase of the long waves of capital accumulation.

These elements have been recently introduced into an urban dynamics simulation model, where the 'structural' growth of each centre is linked to the (random) appearance or attraction of new, higher order urban functions or goods; these new functions generate higher production benefits (APB-F1, APB-F2, ... in Figure 2) and allow the centre to overcome the rising location costs (ALC) which are linked to its size. After each innovation 'jump', urban growth continues through multiplier effects to the point where urban location costs exceed

386

production benefits - along the so called 'constrained growth ' -
(Ao-Ao', A1-A1', A2-A2') (Camagni and Diappi 1984).

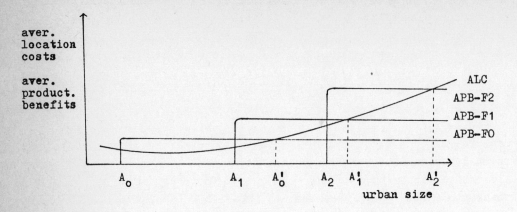

Figure 2   Efficient urban size for different urban functions and
          paths of urban growth
Source: Camagni and Diappi (1984)

3.   FREQUENCY AND LENGTH OF THE CYCLE

The randomness of the appearance pattern of urban innovations i.. the
previous model refers mainly to micro spatial elements, and namely
determines which centres will show an innovation process in a given
time interval; on the other hand this randomness does not refer to the
time dimension, as both theoretical and empirical works have widely
shown that innovations do not appear randomly but tend to cluster
around specific points in time.

Schumpeter in particular theorised the presentation of innovative entrepreneurs by 'groups', owing to the presence of rapid imitation processes and the appearance of 'grapes' of interrelated innovations
(Schumpeter 1971, Ch. VI). Recently, Mensch and Marchetti have empirically demonstrated the relative stability and continuity of innovation
cycles in the last two centuries, deeply related to the general Kondratiev long cycles of the entire economy (Mensch 1979, Marchetti
1980) and there is nowadays fairly widespread agreement on the fact
that changes in 'technological paradigm' are the 'major feature of
each successive growth cycle' (Freeman 1984). Much questioned and
still debated are Mensch's findings about the clustering of innovations some 10 to 15 years before the upswings of the long Kondratiev
cycles, at time intervals of 50 to 60 years around the years 1770,

1825, 1886 and 1935 (Mensch 1978, Freeman et al. 1982, Ch. 3, Klein-knecht 1981).

Even if the time distribution of first innovations is still debated, it is nevertheless widely accepted that the diffusion within the entire economy of the so called 'technological systems', clusters of interrelated and pervasive innovations, follows an S-shaped path; this process takes place thanks to a fast intra- and intersectoral diffusion; allowed by a cycle of aggregate profitability and class relationships and by the cyclical nature of the social, political and institutional resistance to the new technological 'style' (Mandel 1981, Peres 1983, Camagni 1984b).

These hypotheses and the historical uniformities they reveal, if interpreted together with the previous reflections on the metropolitan bias of early innovations, brings support to the idea of the innovation related nature of the urban cycle (Nijkamp 1984).

Looking at the Northern Italian case, and considering that industrial growth in this country took place during the last two Kondratiev waves, it is possible to check that in fact the four major metropolitan areas taken together grew in a cyclical way with respect to the total northern population, with peaks that are perfectly coincident with the peaks of the industrial employment cycle (1861, 1911, 1971). The cores of the four areas (Milan, Turin, Genova, Bologna) show the same regularities, though somehow hidden by the general growth trend; the only downturn in this case is evident in the 1971-1981 period, bringing some support to a possible structural 'clean break' with respect to the past (Figure 3).

Charting the core-ring (municipality-test of the province) relative performance of these areas in the same period and considering the changes in the share of each centre on northern population in order to control for natural growth of population and war destruction, two entire cycles appear in the case of both Milan alone and the four cities together. Each cycle lasts 50-60 years, and three periods fall beneath the zero (relative) growth line, indicating a process of relative disurbanisation; 1861-1871, 1911-1921 and 1971-1981 (Figure 4).

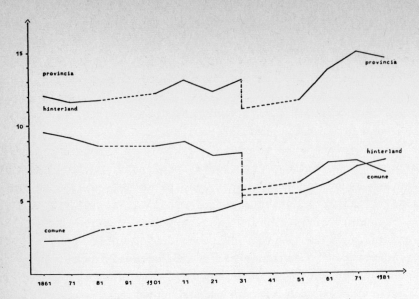

Figure 3 Population share of the four major provinces in
Northern Italy (1861-1981)

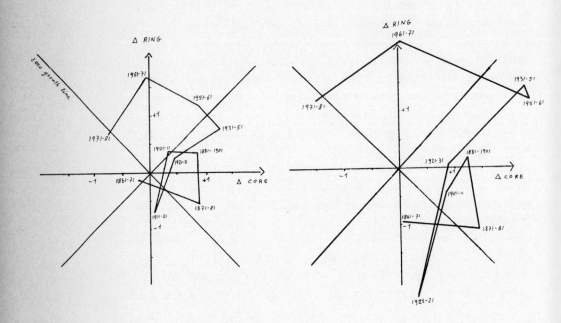

Figure 4 Core-Ring dynamics in Northern Italy (1861-1981)
Changes in population share of decades

4.   WHICH CITY SIZE IS INVOLVED IN METROPOLITAN DECLINE?

According to the superficial view that urban diseconomies are the main factors of metropolitan decline, one would expect cities to decline once they overcome some, not precisely defined, 'optimal size'. Giant metropoli should enter the vicious cycle first, and the others should follow.

Empirical evidence, and most recent refinements to the optimal city size hypothesis, suggest that not only big, but also medium sized and even small cities have declined contemporaneously in the last decade. This fact brought to the idea that an optimal, or better, an 'interval of efficient city size' exists for each urban rank of the hierarchy, deeply tied to the growing benefits of the different productions which are typical of each rank. In other words, the concept of efficient city size is a _relative_ concept, which depends on the functions per-formed by each city and, in a dynamic setting, on its ability to at-tract new and higher order functions. A maximum efficient urban size shows up on each urban rank (A0', A1', A2' in Figure 2), and a sta-tionary state or a decline may begin beyond it, if an innovation does not occur, shifting the centre to a higher rank (Camagni, Curti and Gibelli 1984).

Under this wider approach, urban decline may occur over the entire ranking of the metropolitan areas, especially in periods when the in-novation pace slows down.

5.   ARE THERE LAGS IN THE URBAN CYCLE?

As said before, according to the model presented above, it is not nec-essarily true that small metropolitan areas should decline after the bigger ones. In fact, no relevant time lag showed up in the case of the Po Valley urban system, which encompasses all Northern Italian regions, with the exception of Liguria.

The core-ring graph drawn in the 1951-1981 period (in percentage terms, in order to allow intercity comparisons) shows a perfect anti-clockwise trend in all metropolitan areas. Only Milan shows some lead in the hierarchy in the first subperiod, lying in the 'relative suburbanisation' pattern, the core growing less than the ring, while the opposite condition (core growing more than the ring) shows up for almost all other centres. But on the other hand, in all other subperiods and especially in the last one, the dynamic pattern of Milan is similar to that of all larger centres and of a significant share of smaller centres. In the 1971-1981 subperiod, all cores approach a zero growth rate or an absolute decline (Figure 5).

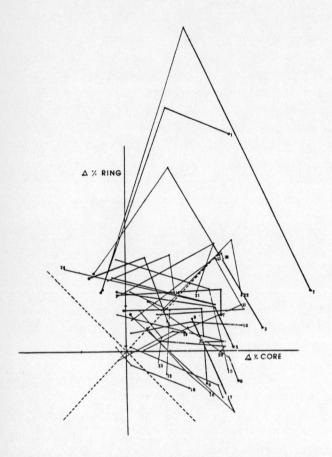

Legenda: 1 Milano; 2 Torino; 3 Bologna; 4 Venezia; 5 Verona; 6 Padova; 7 Brescia; 8 Modena; 9 Parma; 10 Ferrara; 11 Ravenna; 12 Reggio E.; 13 Rimini; 14 Bergamo; 15 Vicenza; 16 Forlì; 17 Piacenza; 18 Novara; 19 Alessandria; 20 Trento; 21 Como; 22 Varese; 23 Cesena; 24 Treviso; 25 Pavia; 26 Busto Arsizio

Figure 5   Core/Ring Dynamics on the Po Plain (1951-1981) (% growth rates)

Source: Camagni, Curti and Gibelli 1984.

Some aid to a filtering-down process along the urban hierarchy of the same regional system in favour of lower rank centres may derive, and may have derived in fact, from the characteristics of technical progress in the last decade. The appearance of what Blair calls 'decentralising technologies' in manufacturing, clerical and professional work, which lower the minimum efficient production size, together with the possible crisis of mass production - replaced more and more by differentiated and personalised goods (Blair 1972, Sabel 1982) - could have lowered the minimum urban size necessary to perform the different urban functions, thus making smaller centres competitive with larger ones.

The technological characteristics of the previous long wave of Italian economic growth, with its emphasis on economies of scale, worked for sure in the opposite direction, creating stronger advantages for bigger metropoli.[1]

If wide lags are not likely to show up within the same urban system, as said before, the opposite may be true among systems characterised by different economic development levels. Regional and urban takeoffs on a macro spatial scale do not take place simultaneously, but depend on complicated historical and geographical 'preconditions'. Anyhow, an innovation or a cluster of innovations always lie at their basis, which in general, for late-comer systems, is not at all a 'first' innovation, but an imitation process of foreign models, innovatively integrated into the local socioeconomic structure.

Once these regional takeoffs have occurred, the following growth pace may be supposed to spread in space and time according to the lag distribution by which big innovation waves spread over the territory from central systems towards the 'peripheries'. This process is by no means mechanical and mechanically repetitive, as it is based on local ability to quickly attract innovations; nevertheless, it shows many 'conservative' characteristics linked to 'traditions' of industrial culture, long standing learning processes and high reaction capabilities clustered in the already developed areas that force past events to deeply determine future ones (Camagni 1984b).

According to this interpretation, in the time when a central urban system may find itself in a declining and desurbanisation phase, an intermediate development system may be booming, as it might build its industrialisation and urbanisation processes upon already well known but innovatively interpreted technological and organisational models.

6. ECONOMIC RELATIONSHIPS, OR CONTRADICTION, BETWEEN METROPOLIS AND COUNTRYSIDE

Under the 45° negatively sloped line of Figure 4, the metropolitan areas show an absolute or relative decline with respect to surrounding rural areas. This conditions is the effect of a decentralisation or diffusion process, typical not only of the Italian urban system during the last decade, but of most western countries, both European and American; it has been described and explained theoretically mainly through location advantage arguments, product life-cycle and filter-down hypotheses connected to relative factor costs (Camagni and Cappellin 1982), or through an innovation diffusion argument, as in previous pages of this article.

Very little research work has been devoted on the contrary to an interpretation based not just in terms of physical production, but in terms of relative prices between the metropolis and the rural areas in modern societies and in terms of income distribution among factors. An approach of this latter kind could introduce us to the challenging but complicated field of the 'domination' relationships in space and the 'contradiction between city and countryside'. In fact, domination or hierarchical relationships are at least as important as 'functional' relationships - which determine the allocation of resources under optimisation criteria - in shaping 'economic space' (Friedmann 1979, Camagni 1980). Physical productivity ratios and location advantages supply us with only one part of the picture, as a strong countervailing element could come from terms-of-trade changes among regions or between city and countryside. Some preliminary notes on this subject will be proposed hereafter.

A simple Ricardian-Schumpeterian model may show us the distributive effects of urban innovations. Putting urban land, endowed with information and communication facilities, on the X axis in decreasing order of centrality and hypothesising a constant land/labour ratio, we can draw:

a) a decreasing curve of marginal productivity of labour, linked to the decreasing access to central information, and

b) a curve of marginal labour costs or, more generally, of reproduction costs of the labour force, increasing along with city size

(Figure 6a). Thus, an initial stationary equilibrium condition is found in stage 0, where labour receives its marginal product (Wo) and land receives a rent (the area OWoRo) in direct proportion to its centrality as a premium for accessibility to information. No rent is paid on marginal urban land ULo.

At this stage profits are absent, and they may appear only thanks to an innovation which pushes the marginal productivity of labour upward (from MgPLO to MgPL1). Average profits (AO) show up indeed in Stage 1, the other distributive shares remaining unchanged in absolute terms. But this is only a transitory disequilibrium condition: due to imitation processes the city expands to UL2, along what we called earlier a 'constrained' path, and the benefits of the innovation waves are split between labour and, especially, rent, as Schumpeter expected.

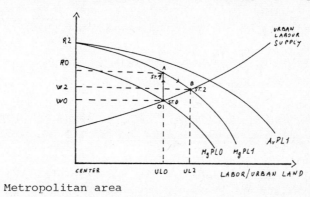

6a   Metropolitan area

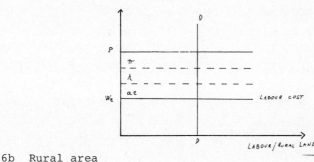

6b   Rural area

Figure 6   Income Distribution in an Urban/Rural Context

Urban profits are washed out by the expansion of urban rent, which in our model also encompasses the incomes of the information-linked factors; extra salary to labour, rewards to professional and top management occupations which create the urban information cluster and the preconditions for innovation, and which are locationally linked to central urban land.

In Stage 2, the city stops growing (and may even decline), but production may be pursued in the rural areas, outside the metropolitan areas, thanks to innovation diffusion processes, both centrally pushed (controlled) and pulled by the periphery. In fact we may hypothesise in the rural areas the same price for products and a lower labour cost; in addition no urban rent is paid, but only an average agricultural land price (ar), which leaves a substantial surplus to be distributed in the form of royalties on patents (λ) and profits on local capital services (π) (Figure 6b).

The ratio $\lambda/(\lambda + \pi)$ may be taken as an index of 'external control' or 'urban domination' upon the countryside, and depends on three elements: the economic distance between city and countryside in terms of skilled factors endowment, the economic and technical 'appropriability' characteristics of the innovation, and time (along which the previous elements become more and more favourable to the countryside).

The two extreme values of the index, 1 and 0, represent respectively a case of colonisation, where the metropoli completely exploits and controls the countryside through its knowhow and capital, and a case we may call the periphery's revenge, which implies an immediate, costless transfer of information and knowhow from the centre, driven by indigenous capital and entrepreneurship in the periphery.

In the equilibrium spatial distribution of income, the city gets, beyond wages on ordinary labour, rents on urban land, rents on the spatial monopolistic control of the urban information cluster, and royalties on patents and direct investments from the countryside; the countryside on the other hand gets wages and profits.

The dimension of the city is limited by rent and by its innovation rate; the dimension of rural production on the contrary is limited only by aggregate demand constraints (DD in Figure 6b).

City is continuously threatened by the ghost of stationary state and decline, and it is condemned to continuously innovating. One the other hand, countryside expands, especially in periods of lower innovativeness of the centre, and its main problem lies in the indigenous control over the growth processes: this goal may be achieved through a strategic appropriation of the precondition for innovation, viz. communication infrastructures and high quality production services and research facilities. But this development in its turn creates new centres and recreates on a more diffused scale a possible antithesis between city and countryside...

As in Adam Smith's description of the relationship between city and countryside, the division of labour among them, based on 'functional' elements, guarantees the entire society the best performance, but may determine 'domination' effects if the distribution of the income generated is affected by unevenly distributed monopoly powers: urban industry vs. agriculture in Adam Smith's times, urban (information) services vs. rural industrialisation nowadays (Smith 1973, Book III).

An uneven distribution of income between city and countryside may derive from another dynamic model, Baumol's well known macroeconomic model of 'urban crisis' (Baumol 1967). If productivity of urban services (both consumer and producer services) is growing less than industrial productivity, and if the employment share of the former sector is growing in the city, then, following Baumol's hypothesis of homogeneous wage increases in the two sectors, we get:

- urban crisis in real terms, if the city is considered per se, as a closed system - and this is Baumol's conclusion -; but on the other hand we get

- urban growth at the expense of the countryside if, properly in our view, the entire economic system is considered, and not just the city. This result comes from the inflationary nature of cities and from the terms-of-trade evolution, favourable to the city which sells its services at increasing relative prices with respect to the (industrial) surrounding areas. This brings us very close to Fernand Braudel's idea of the 'tyranny of the cities', quoted at the beginning.

This second result confirms the need to interpret urban and rural growth cycles not only in locational and employment terms, but also in relative price and income distribution terms.

7. ARE WE CONFRONTED WITH MECHANISTIC CYCLICAL PROCESSES, EVER SIMI-
   LAR TO EACH OTHER?

The answer to the preceding question is simple: no.

Especially in the takeoff and in the revitalisation phases, a host of
local elements come into play, that differentiate each centre's history from the others and determine whether takeoff and revitalisation in
a specific centre will take place at all and when.

Moreover, the successive long waves of innovation and growth show
markedly different characteristics, that have completely different
spatial consequences. Furthermore, once an innovation cycle has come
to an end, the new equilibrium condition its brings about is likely to
be completely different from the initial one, both in terms of income
distribution and of spatial allocation of resources.

In addition, one should not forget the secular trends towards more
balanced infrastructure and educational conditions throughout the national territories, pushed by political reasons, that change the relative locational advantages of the different regions and of the countryside with respect to the city deeply in the long run.

8. SYMPTOMS OF REURBANISATION?

The disurbanisation process hit the urban hierarchy hard in the last
decades. with different intensity according to nations and continents.
Are there theoretical possibilities and empirical symptoms of a reversal of the negative cycle?

From the theoretical point of view, the hypothesis of revitalisation
of big metropolitan areas may find some significant support, not really in the existence of an urban cycle model, but in many reflections
scattered throughout literature. The crisis may be a very strong incubator of new ideas and new opportunities, as it pushes all members of
a society to trying to force the actual negative situation: on the one
hand, it may create new social attitudes and new solidarities among
social actors and classes, and on the other it may help overcome the
cyclical elements that have interrupted the previous growth. We refer
here to the factor prices, both of labour and urban land, and to the

availability itself of these factors that a diminishing concentration and density of activities may recreate. Under these conditions, especially in cities with a still lively downturn and strong historical tradition, and upswing is likely to take place after a certain delay from the emergence of the crisis (Camagni 1984a).

By the same token, in the field of relevant innovations, we quoted on their clustering in crisis periods and their flourishing in economic and employment terms in the following years. This observation led to the hypothesis of a 'depression trigger' in the historical formation of long waves of innovation and to the cautious prediction of a possible push of basic innovations in the next decade (Mensch 1978).

Empirical evidence is scarce on the phenomenon, and it is probably too soon to see it fully defined. Symptoms of this tendency anyway do exist: they encompass the birth of new, small but technologically advanced firms at growing rates in the New York metropolitan area, as well as in the big Northern Italian towns (with the exception of Genova): the appreciation of property value and the new appeal of central cities for the real estate speculation in Boston, Atlanta, Baltimore, Chicago, Philadelphia, Washington and London: the boom of advanced tertiary activities in Paris, Amsterdam, Rotterdam: the gentrification of many big cities pulled by the cultural and information facilities of the core (Isard and Burton 1983, Knight 1984).

Of course, the next cycle big metropolis will be different from the previous one, especially in terms of population density (but not necessary in terms of income density...) of environmental quality and mix of activities. But most important of all, it has to become less 'accidental and unplanned' and more 'willful and intentional' (Knight 1984), as our future international competition will not take place among firms or cities, but among coherent and well structured 'systems'.

9.   CONCLUSIONS

The main conclusion of this paper is twofold.

Firstly, the urban life-cycle, in its aspects concerning the relationships between the entire metropolitan areas and the non urban areas,

is mainly tied in its pace and length to the long waves of basic innovations and national economic development, and the Northern Italian
experience seems to confirm this theoretical hypothesis.

Secondly, the characteristics of the division of labour between city
and countryside and the nature of the innovation process itself determine the need for a theoretical approach to the subject not limited to
the productive and locational aspects, but widened towards the
terms-of-trade and distributive aspects, which impinge on the 'domination' and 'power' elements of our (urban) civilisation.

NOTES

1)   In this respect it is worth noting a result which came from the
     simulation model cited above: in order to 'create', by computer
     simulation, an urban hierarchy, it is not only necessary for the
     successive functions, ranked in rising order of their minimum
     production size and, consequently, of the rank of the correspond-
     ing centre, to show increasing returns, in order to overcome in-
     creasing urban costs, but even their <u>net</u> returns over urban costs
     have to increase along with rank. In other words, the hierarchy
     has to perform under <u>increasing net returns to urban scale</u>, if a
     rank-size distribution of centres, sloping around -1, is going to
     appear (Camagni and Diappi 1984). This element will be taken up
     later in the paper.

REFERENCES

Aydalot, Ph., 'Analyse des phenomenes recents de desurbanisation dans
     les pays occidentaux', paper presented to the XXIII European Con-
     gress, RSA, Poitiers, August, 1983.

Aydalot, Ph., Le dynamisme economiques a-t-il deserté la ville?, Dos-
     siers du Centre Economie Espace Environnement, Cahier n.39,
     Paris, 1984.

Baumol, W.J., 'Macroeconomics of unbalanced growth: the anatomy of
     urban crisis', American Economics Review, no. 57, 1967.

Van den Berg, L. et al., Urban Europe: a Study of Growth and Decline,
     Pergamon Press, London, 1982.

Blair, J.M., Economic Concentration: Structure, Behaviour and Public
     Policy, Harcourt Brace Javanovich, New York, 1972.

Camagni, R.P., 'Teorie e modelli di localizzazione delle attività in-
     dustriali', Giornale degli Economisti, March 1980.

Camagni, R.P. 'Les modeles de restructuration economique des regions
     europeennes pendant les annees '70', in: Aydalot, Ph. (ed), Crise
     et Espace, Economica, Paris, 1984a.

Camagni, R.P., 'Spatial diffusion of pervasive process innovation', XXIV European Congress, RSA, Submitted Papers, Vol. 2, Milan, August, 1984b, forthcoming in the Papers and Proceedings of the RSA, No. 57.

Camagni, R.P. and Cappellin, R., Scenarios of Economic Change in the European Regions, paper presented to the Regional Studies Association Conference, London, April, Studi Economici of the Dipartimento di Economia, Università Bocconi, No. 3, Milan, 1982.

Camagni, R.P., Diappi, L. and Leonardi, G., Urban growth and decline in a hierarchical system: a supply-oriented dynamic approach, paper presented to the II World Congress of the RSA, Rotterdam, June 1984, Regional Science and Urban Economics, 1, 1986, forthcoming.

Camagni, R.P., Curti, F. and Gibelli, M.C., 'Ciclo urbano: le città fra sviluppo e declino', Scienze regionali, no. 3, G. Bianchi and I. Magnani editors, (F. Angeli, Milan), 1984.

Cheshire, P. and Hay, D., The Development of the European Urban System 1971-81 with reference to Berlin, paper presented to the Seminar on 'The future of the Metropolis: the example of Berlin', Berlin, October 1984.

Cheshire, P., Hay, D. and Carbanaro, G., The decline of urban regions in the EEC: some recent evidence and the scope for Community Policy, XXIV European Congress of the RSA, Submitted Papers, Vol. 3, August 1984.

Filippini, C., 'Le onde lunghe di Kondratieff: cicli o fasi storiche?' Note Economiche, no. 1, 1984.

Freeman, C., 'Prometeus unbound', Futures, No. 5, October 1984.

Freeman, C., Clark, J.A. and Soete, L.G., Unemployment and Technical Innovation: a Study of Long Waves and Economic Development, Frances Pinter, London, 1982.

Friedmann, J., 'On the contradictions between city and countryside', in: Folmer and Oosterhaven (eds), Spatial Inequalities and Regional Development, Martinus Nijhoff, Hingham, 1979.

Goddard, J.B. et al., Technological Change and Regional Development, Centre for Urban and Regional Development Studies, University of Newcastle upon Tyne, March 1983 (mimeo).

Hall, P. and Hay, D., Growth Centres in the European Urban System, Heinemann, London, 1980.

Isard, W. and Burton, B., New York City: its future as a world capital, Report for the Committee for a new New York, June 1983 (mimeo).

Kawashima, T., Is Disurbanisation Foreseeable in Japan? A Comparison between US and Japanese Urbanisation Processes, paper presented to the II World Congress, RSA, Rotterdam, June 1984.

Klaassen, L. et al., Dynamics of Urban Development, Gower, Aldershot, 1981.

Kleinknecht, A., 'Observations on the Schumpeterian swarming of innovations', Futures, August 1981.

Knight, R.V., The Advanced Industrial Metropolis: a New Type of World City, paper presented to the Seminar on The future of the Metropolis: the example of Berlin, October 1984.

Mandell, E., 'Explaining long waves of capitalist development', Futures, August 1981.

Marchetti, C., Society as a Learning System: Discovery, Invention and Innovation Cycles Revisited, Technological Forecasting and Social Change, Vol. 18, 1980.

Mensch, G., '1984: A new push of basic innovations?' Research Policy, No. 7, 1978.

Mensch, G., Stalemate in Technology, Ballinger, Cambridge, MA, 1979.

Nijkamp, P., Spatial Dynamics and Innovation: a Long Waves View, XXIV European Congress, RSA, presented Papers, Vol. 2, Milan, August 1984.

Nijkamp, P. and Schubert, U., Structural Change in Urban Systems, Contribution to Metropolitan Study no. 5, IIASA, Laxenburg, Austria, November 1983.

Oakey, R.P., 'Technological change and regional development: some evidence on regional variations in product and process innovation', Environment and Planning A, Vol. 14, 1982.

Peres, C., 'Structural change and the assimilation of new technologies in the economic and social system', Futures, October 1983.

Pred, A.R., City Systems in Advanced Economies, Hutchinson, London, 1977.

Rosenberg, N., Perspectives on Technology, Cambridge University Press, Cambridge, 1976.

Sabel, C.F., Work and Politics, Cambridge, MA, 1982.

Schumpeter, J., Teoria dello Sviluppo Economico, Sansoni, Firenze, 1971.

Smith, A.,Indagine sulla natura e le cause della ricchezza delle nazioni, Mondadori, Milan, 1973.

Vining, D.R. and Kontuly, T., 'Population dispersal from major metropolitan regions: an international comparison', International Science Review, No. 3, 1978.

INDUSTRIAL APPLICATIONS OF INFORMATION TECHNOLOGY:
SPEED OF INTRODUCTION AND LABOUR FORCE COMPETENCE
Börje Johansson and Charlie Karlsson

1. INTRODUCTION

1.1 Regional Specialisation and Spatial Competence Characteristics

Information technology (IT) in the form of computers and microelectronic components as well as information and control systems containing such equipment has a broad set of potential applications in industry. In this paper we present and analyse empirical observations on
the following three sets of IT applications: i) equipment used in administration and management processes, ii) equipment used for production process control, and iii) equipment included as part or component
of the commodity produced. One important objective of the study is to
assess a set of hypotheses about the dynamics of regional specialisation, product cycle development, technological diffusion and technical
change in individual establishments.

Product life cycles were initially discussed with reference to single
firms (Dean 1950). Later the product cycle theory was extended to
cover regional specialisation and relocation processes in an interregional and international context (Vernon 1966). In Andersson and
Johansson (1984) an attempt is made to derive the spatial dynamics of
product cycles from regional variations in i) land values and other
factor prices, and ii) the composition of labour force competence in
each region. In that analysis the birthplace of new products are characterised by accessibility to i) centres of knowledge creation and ii)
labour markets with a rich and responsive supply of knowledge intensive employment categories (Thompson 1968). As a product developed in
such a region matures, becomes standardised and reaches more distant
markets, the initial location of the production ceases to be the most
advantageous place of production. As the production is further automated and the scale increased, the regional advantages shift and it
becomes profitable to locate new production capacities in other

regions which have a cost advantage compared to the regions in which the production was initiated (Krumme and Hayter 1975, Rees 1979).

In the sequel we first discuss characteristics of individual establishments which enable them to introduce new techniques at a faster pace than their competitors. In Section 2 we illustrate with models various processes which bring about i) shifts in regional advantages over a product cycle, ii) a fast introduction of production equipment and automation processes which reduce the cost of production in individual establishments, and iii) R&D efforts and adoption of technological knowledge that can be used in the product development of individual production units.

In Sections 3-5 we present empirical observations and statistical estimation that support the hypotheses introduced in the first two sections. The results in Sections 3-5 confirm that competence, education and knowledge intensity are important development characteristics of each single production unit. In particular, we demonstrate that these characteristics can be used to discriminate between such firms that introduce   automation techniques and processes at a high speed and those firms which adjust and develop their products at a fast pace when new technological knowledge becomes available.

1.2 Introduction of New Techniques and Characteristics of Establishments

In the model discussed in the previous section, the process of change is influenced by the characteristics of the entire labour force and knowledge accessibility in each region. Such overall regional attributes describe the economic environment of individual establishments and indicate their possibility of acquiring knowledge and information pertinent to their production segment. The regional attributes also show which possibilities a production unit has to adjust the competence profile of its staff.

Given the possibilities offered by a regional environment, each single establishment will select a strategy for its development. That includes a gradual adjustment of the labour force competence through a hiring policy and education and training programmes for the existing staff. Also when such adjustments are heavily constrained for the regional economy as a whole, much freedom of choice may be available to the individual establishment.

In a given region, firms belonging to the same industrial sector differ in terms of i) production scale, ii) contact network, iii) labour force competence and many other characteristics. Those differences will to a certain degree reflect the product mix of the individual production unit and the stage of each product on its product cycle. The strategic options of the production units include i) to 'follow the product cycle through' with gradually increased emphasis placed on standardisation, automation, scale efficiency and price competition as the product matures, and ii) to avoid an intensified price competition as the product matures by searching for new products and investing in product development and product renewal. When investment and development efforts are directed towards product development, the objective is to find temporary quasi-monopolistic advantages which last until imitation and production development by competitors reduce the time advantage of the initiators. This form of competition is Schumpeterian in nature (Schmumpeter 1951); in this case the objective of firms is to capture 'disequilibrium profits' which constitute the reward to production units which manage to reach the front before others. However, those profits are slowly disappearing as this front gradually becomes populated by more competitors. Hence, the product development strategy will only generate lasting advantages to a firm if it repetitively succeeds in improving its product mix.

One may add that disequilibrium profits occur also for production units which are able to introduce process changes (innovations) earlier than its competitors. However, usually the time lag between early initiators and their followers is much shorter for process changes than for product changes. One reason for this is that new management and production equipment is produced by other firms who are striving to sell their new products to as many customers as possible.

1.3 Hypotheses and Propositions

The regional environment of a production unit determines to a large extent the likelihood of success attached to each of the two strategic options described above. For a given region and sector, one may at the same time identify a set of characteristics of each single establishment which strongly influence to which extent the investments are allocated to process automation and product development, respectively. Such characteristics also determine the relative speed of adopting new technical equipment and technical solutions. We will organise those characteristics into the following categories:

Production scale and number of employees (1.1)

Availability of investment funds and regional
subsidies such as investment support (1.2)

Labour force competence divided into i) combination
of employment categories, ii) distribution over the
labour force of different kinds of education, and
iii) distribution of technology-specific education and
skills of the labour force (1.3)

Network properties of a production unit such as
i) location of major owner and head office, ii) market
extension, i.e., the share of regional, national and
international sales, iii) customer dependence, i.e. the
degree to which one or a small number of customers buy
the major part of the output, iv) distance to the
regional centre (1.4)

In the empirical part of the paper we examine the following hypotheses:

The introduction of automation processes in production
management is positively influenced by i) the scale of
production and market extension, ii) the possibility of
acquiring investment funds, iii) non-local control of
the production unit, and iv) training of the labour
force in technology-specific skills (1.5)

Product development depends on i) knowledge intensity
and ii) the technology-specific competence of
employees in management position; it is not so strongly
associated with production scale and it is negatively
influenced by having corporation management located
outside the region (1.6)

2.   PROCESS AUTOMATION AND PRODUCT DEVELOPMENT

2.1 Switching of Regional Advantages

In Section 2 we illustrate some basic differences between the two fundamental forms of technological change - process automation and product development. In subsection 2.1 we study how the production technique changes over the product cycle for a given type of product. A gradual increase of automation and standardisation is modelled as a reduction of the   requirements on knowledge intensity and competence together with a simultaneous increase in the demand for land and production workers. We show that such a change process implies that regional cost advantages will switch as time goes by.

In the model outlined below we consider a specific submarket characterised by given price and quantity paths, p(t) and x(t), respectively. The properties or attributes of the product are assumed to remain unchanged as time goes by. Instead we study the effect of gradual but continuing adjustments of the production technology. We describe how such a change process may lead to a switch in the cost advantages of different regions. This type of shift in regional advantages was analysed within a putty-clay framework in Andersson and Johansson (1984). Here we derive similar results when the production technology is given by a Cobb-Douglas type of production function. In a second step we also consider the effects of treating capital equipment as non-malleable.

In the first model version below there is no difference between ex ante and ex post technological possibilities. Our objective is to assess the alternative locations of this production, for which we identify three input categories

    K = capital; ρ = unit price of K
    L = land and labour; w = unit price of L
    N = competence; v = unit price of N

where competence represents the knowledge intensity of a production unit's entire organisation. Let us assume that the production function has the following form in each region r:

$$x_r = A_r \ K_r^\alpha \ L_r^\beta \ N_r^\gamma \ ; \ \alpha, \ \beta, \ \gamma > 0 \qquad (2.1)$$

where A_r is a positive regional parameter. The exercise that follows is an investigation of the cost conditions of potential plants. When cost advantages shift between regions, this may be interpreted as either incentives to relocate a plant from one region to another or as an indication of increased growth possibilities in one region and a simultaneous decline in the likelihood of survival for the same pro- duction in another region.

With reference to formula (2.1) we examine a gradual change of techno- logical possibilities, represented by

$$d\beta/dt = \dot{\beta} > 0$$
$$\qquad\qquad\qquad\qquad\qquad (2.2)$$
$$d\gamma/dt = \dot{\gamma} < 0$$

We assume that

Capital equipment is rented and moveable, that α is
constant, and $\rho_r = \rho$ $\qquad\qquad (2.3a)$

w_r and v_r and opportunities to sell are exogenously
given, i.e.,

$$\Sigma_r \ x_{r(t)} = \tilde{x} \qquad\qquad (2.3b)$$

$\beta + \gamma = h$, where h is a constant $\qquad\qquad (2.3c)$

Regions are similar in the sense that $A_r = A$ for all r $\qquad (2.3d)$

Given the assumptions in (2.3) we can assess cost conditions in each region by differentiating the following Langrangian S, which is de- fined for each point in time

$$S_r = C_r(\tilde{x}) + \mu_r(\tilde{x} - AK_r^\alpha \ L_r^\beta \ N_r^\gamma) \qquad\qquad (2.4)$$

where $C_r(\tilde{x}) = w_r L_r + v_r N_r + \rho K_r$. The formulation in (2.4) implies that we are minimising production costs for a given output level $\tilde{x}$. Differentiating (2.4) yields

$$K_r = \mu_r \alpha \tilde{x}/\rho$$

$$L_r = \mu_r \beta \tilde{x}/w_r \qquad (2.5)$$

$$N_r = \mu_r \gamma \tilde{x}/v_r$$

from which we derive the following equality

$$\tilde{x} = (\mu_r \tilde{x})^\Omega A(\alpha/\rho)^\alpha (\beta/w_r)^\beta (\gamma/v_r)^\gamma \qquad (2.6)$$

where $\Omega = \alpha + \beta + \gamma$. We may now compare the production costs in the two regions 1 and 2 by setting $x_1 = x_2 = \tilde{x}$. Rearranging terms in (2.6) and taking the logarithms we obtain

$$D = \ln \mu_1/\mu_2 =$$
$$\qquad (2.7)$$
$$\beta \ln w_1 + \gamma \ln v_1 - \beta \ln w_2 - \gamma \ln v_2$$

The variable D expresses the difference between $\ln \mu_1$ and $\ln \mu_2$. The term μ_r is a shadow price representing the marginal costs of production in region r. With reference to (2.7) we assume that

$$w_1 > w_2 \text{ and } v_1 < v_2 \qquad (2.8)$$

The inequalities in (2.8) may be interpreted as the outcome of a situation in which competence is more abundant in region 1 than in region2, while the opposite is true for land and labour as a composite factor of production. In Proposition 1 we examine the conditions of production location if the only alternatives are regions 1 and 2.

Proposition 1 Let the assumptions in (2.1), (2.3) and (2.8) be given and assume that location decisions are governed by (2.4). Then we may conclude:

i) Initially, at time t = 0, the production is located in region 1 if D(0)<0;

ii) $D(t) < 0$ iff $G/H > \beta/\gamma$, where $G = \ln v_2/v_1$ and $H = \ln w/w_2$;

iii) $\dot{D} > 0$ iff $\dot{\gamma} < 0$

iv) Production will be relocated to region 2 if γ continues to fall over time.

<u>Proof</u> Part (i) is self-evident and part (ii) follows from (2.7) where $D = \beta H - \gamma G$. Part (iii) is obtained by differentiating $D = (h-\gamma)H-\gamma G$ with respect to time. With regard to part (iv) we observe that C/H is constant and that $\beta = h-\gamma$. This implies that γ can be reduced so that at time t^* we have $\beta(t^*)/\gamma(t^*) = G/H$, with $\beta(t^*-\varepsilon)/\gamma(t^*-\varepsilon) < G/H$ and $\beta(t^*+\varepsilon)/\gamma(t^*+\varepsilon) > G/H$ when $\varepsilon > 0$. Hence, cost minimisation implies that at time $t^* + \varepsilon$ production is relocated from region 1 to region 2. This completes the proof.

This simple model of how regional advantages switch assumes that capital has a putty-putty character with regard to each single production unit. Consider now the following variation of the preceding example. Assume that capital installed at time τ, $K_r(\tau)$, remains fixed in its location and use in the future. Over time part of this equipment will be scrapped. At time t the amount of capital carried over from earlier periods is denoted by $\bar{K}_r(t)$ with an average vintage $\bar{\tau}$. Suppose now that the desired capital at time t is $K_r(t)$. We then assume that $(1-a_r(t))$ is the part of $K_r(t)$ that is already available as a consequence of the existence of $\bar{K}_r(t)$. Hence, the necessary investment is $a_r(t)K_r(t)$, where $0 \le a_r(K_r(t), \bar{K}_r(t), t-\bar{\tau}) \le 1$ and where $t-\bar{\tau}$ is the average vintage difference between new equipment and the existing capital. Moreover, we assume that

$$0 \le a_r(t) \le 1$$

$$a_r(t) = 1 \text{ if } \bar{K}_r(t) = 0$$

$$a_r(t) < 1 \text{ if } \bar{K}_r(t) > 0 \tag{2.9}$$

$$\partial a_r/\partial(\bar{K}_r(t)/K_r(t)) < 0$$

With the assumptions associated with (2.9), we have to observe that $\bar{K}_r(t)$ represents sunk costs. Hence, at time t the cost function $C_r(\tilde{x})$ in (2.4) will now have the following form:

$$C_r(\tilde{x}) = w_r L_r + v_r N_r + \rho a_r(t) K_r(t) \tag{2.10}$$

Proposition 2 Let the assumptions in Proposition 1 be given but modified by (2.9) and (2.10). Assume that D(0)<0 so that the initial production is located in region 1. Then if the 'competence elasticity' parameter γ is reduced at the same speed as in Proposition 1, the relocation (or switch in regional advantages) is delayed and occurs at time t** > t*.

Proof From (2.9) we have that $K_1(0) > 0$ and $K_2(0) = 0$; if relocation has not occurred at time t we still have $\bar{K}_1(t) > 0$ and $K_2(t) = 0$. In addition we have $a_1(t) < 1$ and $a_2(t) = 1$. Next, let D_1 represent the value of $\ln \mu_1/\mu_2$ in Proposition 1 and D_2 the same value when (2.9) and (2.10) apply. Then we can write $D_2 = F + D_1$, where $F = \alpha \ln \rho a_1/\rho a_2 < 0$. At time t* we have that $D_1(t^*) = \beta(t^*)H - \gamma(t^*)G = 0$, while $D_2(t^*) = F < 0$. This means that γ has to be reduced further than $\gamma(t^*)$ in order to reach the switching point. Hence, t** > t* if t** is defined by $F + D_1(t^{**}) = 0$, where $D_1(t^{**}) > 0$. This completes the proof.

2.2 Introduction of Automation Equipment into Individual Establishments

In the preceding subsection we have illustrated for a given product a spatial location effect of its product cycle. In that analysis technological change was entirely exogenous, the production technique was adjusted in perfect response to changes in technological possibilities, while factor prices related to land and labour force were fixed in each location.

In this subsection we discuss with the help of a miniature model how individual production units acquire new techniques (automation of the production process) by buying new equipment as this becomes available over time. The model is used to point out the importance of firm size and competence constraints for this type of investment. It may be thought of as a putty-clay model which allows the introduction of new equipment into the existing structure.

If no change occurs in the production technique of an establishment between period t-1 and t, the profit V is assumed to be

$$V(t) = p(t) \ x(t) \ - \ w(t) \ \ell(t-1) \ x(t) \qquad (2.11)$$

where $x(t)$ denotes output level, $\ell(t-1)$ the input coefficient of labour and similar factors which can be partly replaced by automation equipment, and p output price minus other input costs (except $w \ \ell$) per unit output. We also assume that for each period there is an option to buy equipment $\Delta \ \tau$ which reduces $\ell(t-1)$ by $\Delta\ell(t)$ in period t

$$\Delta\ell = k \ \Delta \ \tau^\beta \ x^{-\alpha}; \ k, \ \beta, \ \alpha > 0 \qquad (2.12)$$

where the term $x^{-\alpha}$ signifies a positive scale factor in case $\alpha < 1$.

From (2.11) and (2.12) we obtain by deleting the time specification

$$V = px \ - \ w(\ell \ - \ \Delta\ell)x \ - \ q \ \Delta \ \tau \qquad (2.13)$$

where q is the (rental) price of one unit equipment. Since we consider a product segment in which price competition gradually becomes tougher, we assume that $\dot{p} < 0$. Improvements in the production of the equipment is reflected by $\dot{q} < 0$. By differentiating (2.13) with respect to x and $\Delta \ \ell$ we obtain

$$\partial V/\partial x = p \ - \ w\ell \ - \ (\alpha-1) \ w \ \Delta \ \ell \leq 0 \qquad (2.14a)$$

$$\partial V/\partial \ \Delta \ \tau = \beta \ wk \ \Delta\tau^{\beta-1} \ x^{1-\alpha} \ - \ q \leq 0 \qquad (2.14b)$$

$$(\partial V/\partial \ \Delta \ \tau) \ \Delta \ \tau = 0 \qquad (2.14c)$$

Condition (2.14c) implies that when q is too high the introduction of the technique is delayed until $q(t)$ has been reduced. From (2.14) we can derive the condition

$$\Delta\tau = (p \ - \ w\ell) \ \beta x \ / \ (\alpha \ - \ 1)q \qquad (2.15)$$

which establishes the following remark:

Remark 1 Consider the system given by (2.12) - (2.15)

i)   If $\partial V/\partial\Delta\tau < 0$ and $\Delta\tau = 0$ at a given point in time, such an establishment will at a later date have an incentive to introduce the equipment only if $0 \geq \dot{p} > \dot{q}$, i.e., if the price of new equipment is reduced at a faster pace than output prices.

ii) If the initial gross profit $p - w\ell(t-1)$ is negative, the new technique will be introduced only if there is a positive scale factor, i.e., if $\alpha < 1$.

iii) If $p - w\ell(t-1) > 0$, there is a solution with $\Delta\tau > 0$ only if $\alpha > 1$ or if there is a constraint such that $x \leq \bar{x}$.

Part iii) of Remark 1 means that (2.13) is replaced by the Langrangian $S = V + \mu (\bar{x} - x)$. Then $\Delta\tau = (p-w\ell-\mu)\beta x/(\alpha-1)q$ and the positive scale effect is counteracted by the constraint on the scale.

The scale constraint may be related to market conditions. For example, the given price in (2.13) may only be valid for $x \leq \bar{x}$. In this case one could also consider to model price as a function of the sales volume such that $\partial p/\partial x < 0$.

The scale constraint can also be assumed to reflect technological conditions. One example would be that the positive scale effect, with a small α, only prevails within certain limits.

Those limits may also be given by the competence level of each production unit. Letting N denote a given competence level we may even assume that the technical change is possible only as long as $x/N \leq a$. Following our earlier arguments we may think of $\bar{x}$ as growing as the coefficient a increases over time, i.e., as competence requirements fall. However, $\dot{p} > \dot{q}$ and $\dot{q} < 0$ represent the basic process that gradually enlarges the set of establishments which have an advantage of introducing the automation technology.

2.3 Technological Change and Product Development

Product development is profoundly different from the type of changes in production technique which was described in the two preceding subsections. Within a given market segment we may indicate the 'level of product development associated with firm i's product by τ_i. This variable will reflect how functional and sophisticated product i is in relation to the preferences and needs of customers within the given market.

Let τ_1 denote the τ-level of an individual establishment's product and $\tau 2$ the same level of its competitors. The basic reason for product renewal is to influence the price in a positive direction. If we let p_1 denote the price on product one, the following conditions should apply $\partial p_1/\partial \tau_1 > 0$ and $\partial p_1/\partial \tau_2 < 0$. Such properties are reflected by

$$p_1 = p_0 + b\ \tau_1^{\alpha}\ \tau_2^{\beta}\ ;\ b,\ \alpha > 0 > \beta \qquad (2.16)$$

Next we introduce a resource factor R_1 representing R&D efforts including a staff with special product development competence. Using (2.16) we can now describe the decision problem of the production unit by formulating the following control problem

$$\text{Max } \hat{V}_1 = \int V(t)\ \exp\ \{-\lambda t\}dt \qquad (2.17)$$

$$\dot{\tau}_1 = a\ R_1^{\varepsilon}\ ;\ 0 < \varepsilon < 1$$

where $V_1 = P_1 - \rho_1 R_1 - c$, ρ_1 is the price/cost per unit R_1, c is other costs per unit output, and λ is a discount parameter. Necessary optimality conditions are obtained by differentiating the Hamiltonian $H = V_1 \exp(-\lambda t) + y_1\ a\ R_1^{\varepsilon}$ which yields

$$y_1 = \rho_1\ \exp\{\ \lambda\ \}\ R_1^{1-\varepsilon/\varepsilon a} \qquad (2.18)$$

$$\dot{y}_1 = -\alpha b\ \tau_1^{\alpha-1}\ \tau_2^{\beta}\ \exp\ \{-\lambda t\} \qquad (2.19)$$

Differentiating (2.18) with respect to time yields a second expression for $\dot{y}_1$ and we obtain

$$\dot{R}_1 = \frac{\lambda\ R_1}{1 - \varepsilon} - \frac{\alpha\ b\ \tau_1^{\alpha-1}\ \tau_2^{\beta}\ \varepsilon\ a\ R_1^{\varepsilon}}{\rho_1\ (1 - \varepsilon)}$$

or $\qquad\qquad\qquad\qquad\qquad\qquad\qquad\qquad\qquad\qquad\qquad\qquad (2.20)$

$$\frac{\dot{R}_1}{R_1} = \frac{\lambda}{1 - \epsilon} \quad \frac{\alpha (p_1(t) - p_0) \epsilon \, a \, R_1^{\epsilon-1}}{\rho_1 (1 - \epsilon) \tau_1} \tag{2.21}$$

which reveals that (2.17) is a game problem, since $\dot{R}_1$ depends not only on τ_1 and R_1, but also on τ_2, the τ-level of competitors. High values of τ_2 speed up the increase of R&D efforts as does high values of R_1 itself. The basic information for regulating the R&D and competence component is the current price information, represented by $p_1(t) - p_0$. From (2.16) we also have that $\dot{p}_1 = 0$ if $\dot{\tau}_1 / \dot{\tau}_2 = -\beta \tau_1 / \alpha \tau_2$.

The effect of the price on the R&D factor may be evaluated for fixed τ_2 as $\dot{R}_1$ approaches zero. Then we have $\rho_1 = (\alpha \, b \, \tau_2^{\beta} \, \epsilon \, a)/(\tau_1^{1-\alpha} \, \lambda \, R_1^{1-\epsilon})$ which means that a low ρ-value corresponds to a high R-value.

3.   INTRODUCTION OF IT-APPLICATIONS

3.1 Selection of Industrial Sector and Type of Variables

The statistical investigation in the subsequent sections may be considered a pilot study of technological change based on IT-applications in the machinery industry of a region. The study is a part of a larger enquiry which covers all sectors in the Swedish region Värmland, located at equal distance between Stockholm and Oslo. The region comprises 3.4 per cent of the Swedish population, 3.2 per cent of the total employment and 4.3 per cent of the employment in building and manufacturing industries in Sweden. Compared to the country as a whole, the machinery industry is overrepresented in the region.

The machinery industry is of special interest, since its IT-applications comprise investment in both process automation and product development. The study is based on a survey including all establishments belonging to the machinery industry. The results presented here are based on statistical analyses of all producing units, staffed by more than one person, around 45 units. This includes all units in the region recorded in the Industrial Statistics of Sweden, a data base including all units with at least five employees.

For each establishment, the data base contains information about the date of introduction for ten different kinds of IT-applications within the administrative area and 18 different types of applications within the area of production process control. IT-applications in product development have not been classified. For each of these applications there is data on i) source of information (knowledge diffusion), investment efforts during a 5-year period, number of persons capable of operating the equipment, and specialist on IT-dependent product development. With regard to product development, there is also an estimate of the value of IT-components as a share of the total product value. Moreover, for each establishment there is information about its size and network properties (market, location, etc.).

The core variables describe the competence profile of each production unit. These are summarised in Table 3.1.

TABLE 3.1

Labour Force Competence Variables

GENERAL EDUCATION	EMPLOYMENT CATEGORIES (Jobs)	IT EDUCATION AND TRAINING
- University engineers	- Natural science	- Length of education (5 classes)
- Other university studies	- Office jobs	- Type of IT education:
- College engineers	- Production Jobs	- elementary
- Other college studies	- Other jobs (transportation etc.)	- administration
		- technical
		- management
		- other types

3.2 Speed of Introduction

The first step in the statistical analysis is to estimate a function with the following logistic form:

$$\ln Z(t) = \alpha_0 + \alpha_1 t \quad ; \quad t = 1, 2, \ldots$$

$$\text{(3.1)}$$

$$Z(t) = f(t)/(1-f(t)) \quad ; \quad 0 \le f(t) \le 1 \, ,$$

where $f(t)$ denotes the share of all establishments which have introduced a given type of IT-application at date t. Now let T be the last date of observation and consider the variable Δf

$$\Delta f = \{1 - f(T)\}/2$$

$$\text{(3.2)}$$

To all units which at date T have not adopted the application studied we assign the date t^* which satisfies

$$f(t^*) = f(T) + \Delta f$$

$$\text{(3.3)}$$

In this way we can for a given application i, attach an application date t_i^k to every establishment. The speed of introduction with regard to establishment k can be expressed with the help of the introduction date t_i^k, in the following way

$$y_i^k = 1/t_i^k$$

$$\text{(3.4)}$$

A compound speed index for different types of applications belonging to either i) management and administration or ii) production processes is obtained as

$$y^k = \sum_{i=1}^{n} y_i^k / n$$

$$\text{(3.5)}$$

where n is the number of various kinds of applications. One may observe that a sequence (y^k) such that $y^k > y^{k+1}$ is a monotonic transformation of the measure $1/f(t)$, $f(0) > 0$. Hence, y^k will express establishment k's position on an introduction curve of the type described in Figure 3.1

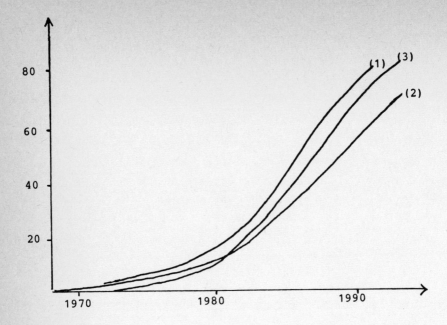

Figure 3.1 IT-introduction in three compound areas of application.

As we describe in Table 3.2, the speed of introduction is significantly correlated with investments and other economic resources that the
individual establishment allocates to the technology. Hence, earlier
adopters also spend more resources than their followers.

TABLE 3.2
Correlation between Speed of IT-Introduction and
Economic Efforts Associated with the Introduction

SPEED OF INTRODUCTION IN :	SHARE OF INVESTMENTS GOING TO INVESTMENTS IN IT-APPLICATIONS
1) Administration and Management	0.6
2) Production	0.7
	VALUE OF IT-COMPONENTS IN PRODUCTS AS A SHARE OF PRODUCT VALUE
3) Product development	0.8

Table 3.3 describes the correlation between the introduction speed with regard to i) all types of applications, ii) production, iii) administration. and iv) product development. The speed index is described in (3.5). As shown in the table, applications to product development display the weakest overall correlation.

TABLE 3.3
Correlation between Various Forms of IT-Applications

	2) Production	3) Administration	4) Product development
1) Compound	0.92	0.87	0.76
2) Production		0.74	0.57
3) Administration and management			0.45

Remark: Compound applications is a weighted average between applications 2) - 4).

As a final overview we describe in Table 3.4 the variation in speed of introduction between a selected sample of specific IT-applications. The analysis presented in Sections 4 and 5 may also be carried out

with regard to each of these specific applications. It is conjectured
that such a detailed analysis will make it possible to establish even
stronger statistical results than those obtained at the aggregate level in Sections 4 and 5.

TABLE 3.4

Introduction speed of IT-Applications
at a Fine Level of Technology Specification

TYPE OF APPLICATION	α_1 = Annual rate of change, %	f(1985) = Share of adopters 1985, %
1. Order, invoicing, etc.	27.0	28
2. IT-components in products	26.3	34
3. Accounting	24.7	55
4. Payments and suppliers ledgers	23.4	19
5. Purchases and stock accounting	22.6	18
6. Budgeting	20.7	34
7. Word and text processing	20.6	12
8. IT production control systems	20.4	30
9. Salary and personnel administration	13.5	20

Remark: α_1 and f(t) are related to each other in formula (3.1) where
$\alpha_1 = \dot{z}/z$.

4. INTRODUCTION OF IT-SYSTEMS FOR PROCESS AUTOMATION IN THE MACHIN-
ERY INDUSTRY

4.1 IT-Applications for Administration and Management Processes

The findings with regard to administration and management processes
can be summarised as follows. Introduction speed is positively influenced by the scale of production (measured by the number of employees). Other variables that reflect scale effects are network properties such as i) large share of non-local sales, and ii) owner located
in other region. We also observe a positive effect on introduction

speed of the share of total employment belonging to the non-specific job category. This may also reflect a scale dependent factor. Finally, specialised IT-education (for administration and management) is shown to have a positive covariation with the introduction speed. Hence, the technological adoption requires investment in the labour force.

The speed index in (3.5) is denoted by y. Using the transformation $Y = 100 \ln y$ the following function has been estimated

$$Y \cong \alpha + \Sigma_i \; \beta_i \; x_i \qquad\qquad (4.1)$$

The estimation results are presented in Table 4.1. The number of observations (consisting of producing units) is 41 and $R^2 = 83$.

TABLE 4.1

Regression of Introduction Speed with Regard to
IT-Systems for Administration and Management

VARIABLE	PARAMETER	t-VALUE
1. Intercept	- 26.2	(19.5)
2. Owner in Sweden but outside the region (dummy)	+ 7.2	(4.9)
3. Share of total sales which are domestic but outside the region	+ 0.04	(2.3)
4. Share of total employment belonging to the non-specified category (distribution jobs)	+ 0.3	(7.1)
5. Share of the labour force with IT-education for managers	+ 1.3	(3.6)
6. Share of the labour force with IT-education for administration applications	+ 0.3	(3.3)

Remark: Variable 2) - 3) represent network properties; 4) - 6) represent labour force competence.

The introduction of automation processes in administration and management does not depend on the general knowledge intensity in the individual establishment. However, it requires special training. This observation is further emphasised in Table 4.2.

TABLE 4.2

Introduction of Computer Support for Administration Purposes

PERCENT OF STAFF THAT CAN OPERATE COMPUTER SUPPORT SYSTEMS IN ADMINISTRATION	INTRODUCTION DATE; DISTRIBUTION OF ESTABLISHMENTS IN PER CENT		
	Late	Early	Sum
Low	80.9	40.0	61.0
High	19.1	60.0	39.0
Sum	100	100	100

χ^2 = 7.2 (Pattern significant at 99 per cent level).

Table 4.2 shows that IT-applications to administration is less investment intensive than IT introduction in other areas. Table 4.3 demonstrates that early adopters have allocated a significantly higher
share of their investments to IT-equipment for administration applications than establishments introducing the equipment at a later stage.

TABLE 4.3

Early and Late Adopters of IT-Systems for
Administration Processes
Distribution in Per Cent

SHARE OF TOTAL INVESTMENTS GOING TO COMPUTERISED ADMINISTRATION SYSTEMS %	LATE ADOPTERS %	EARLY ADOPTERS %
Low	88.9	21.1
High	11.1	78.9
Sum	100	100

χ^2 = 17.1

We shall finally demonstrate in a contingency table that the scale
effect is remarkably strong with regard to IT-systems for administration and management processes.

TABLE 4.4
Scale Effect on the Introduction of
IT-Systems in Administration

COMPUTER SUPPORT IN ADMINISTRATION	NUMBER OF EMPLOYEES		
	1-9	10-99	100-
No use	60.6	19.0	0
Late adopters	30.3	47.6	15.4
Early adopters	9.1	33.3	84.6
Sum	100	100	100

$\chi^2 = 31.6$

4.2 IT-Systems for Production Automation and Control

In the regression analysis in Table 4.5 two samples have been used both containing information about producing units. The smaller sample contains basically units from the Industrial Statistics of Sweden[1], while the larger sample in addition contains establishments with less than five persons in the staff - often only one active person.

Compared to the introduction of automation processes for administration and management, the investment requirements are much stronger in the case of introducing IT-systems for production automation and control. Moreover, the speed of introduction is lower the stronger an establishment's sales are concentrated on a few customers. Knowledge intensity also plays a significant role in stimulating the introduction. There seems to be a critical mass effect, expressed by the number of university engineers.

For a larger sample we may note that the scale effect becomes an important explanatory variable; in this sample the size of production units varies much more than in the small sample. In the larger sample the introduction speed is also positively affected by a non-domestic ownership.

TABLE 4.5

Regression of Introduction Speed with regard
to IT-Production Automation and Control

VARIABLE	PARA-METER	t-VALUE
1. Intercept	- 13.5	(4.7)
2. Share of total investments going to IT-production control equipment	+ 1.7	(7.1)
3. Customer dependence	- 2.8	(3.8)
4. Number of university engineers	+ 4.5	(7.4)
5. Variable (4) in per cent of total staff	- 1.9	(3.9)

Number of observations = 32; R^2 = 88

1. Intercept	- 33.8	(60.8)
II. Number of employees	+ 0.03	(10.8)
III. Investment variable (2) above	+ 0.15	(7.2)
IV. Owner in foreign country (dummy)	+ 7.2	(3.1)

Number of observations = 61; R^2 = 80; (includes units with less than 5 persons on the staff)

Remark: Customer dependence = share of total sales going to the four
largest customers.

The contingency table 4.6 illustrates the existence of a strong scale effect. First, the speed of introduction is strongly correlated with the size of the individual production unit. This scale effect is even stronger than the scale effect for computer based administration processes. Second, IT-specific competence among the staff is also size-dependent.

TABLE 4.6
Scale Effect with regard to IT-production
Automation and Control

COMPUTER SUPPORT IN PRODUCTION	NUMBER OF EMPLOYEES		
	1-9	10-99	100-
No use	84.9	61.9	15.4
Late adopters	12.1	33.3	23.1
Early Adopters	3.0	4.8	61.5
Sum	100	100	100

$x^2 = 33.3$

SHARE OF STAFF THAT CAN OPERATE COMPUTER BASED PRODUCTION EQUIPM.			
Low	87.5	70.6	16.7
High	12.5	29.4	83.3
Sum	100	100	100

$x^2 = 15.5$

The regression in Table 4.5 shows that the investment requirements are strong. The effect of investment size and speed of introduction can also be demonstrated in a contingency table. Another evidence of the importance of investment funds is presented in Table 4.7. There the region has been divided into one subregion that has and another that has not received financial support from the government to investments in production equipment. The former subregion is called 'assisted'. In this region a larger share of the establishments have introduced IT-based production control systems than in the non-assisted region.

TABLE 4.7

Investment Assistance from Central Government

COMPUTER SUPPORT IN PRODUCTION	NON-ASSISTED SUBREGION	ASSISTED SUBREGION
No use	73.3	56.8
Late adopters	10.0	29.7
Early adopters	16.7	13.5
Sum	100	100

$\chi^2 = 3.9$

5. IT-BASED PRODUCT DEVELOPMENT

5.1 IT-Equipment as Components of New Products

It has been argued that innovations are the outcome of a process which is based on the principle 'novelty by combination' (Georgescu-Roegen 1970). This characterisation applies well to the type of innovations analysed here; they comprise product renewal obtained by incorporating microelectronic components and other types of IT-equipment in products.

In contradistinction to the observation of process automation in Section 4 we find here that establishments which have their head office outside the region are less active in product development than other establishments. Product development is positively stimulated by i) the individual establishment's share of employees who are IT-educated for management applications, ii) the number of persons in the establishment with non-engineering university studies. The speed of IT-based product development has been faster the larger the ratio is between the value of IT components used and the value of the final product.

The results summarised above are obtained from a regression equation of the following form

$$Y = \alpha + \Sigma_i \ \beta_i \ \ln x_i \tag{5.1}$$

where Y = 100 ln y as described in relation to formula (4.1). The estimation is presented in Table 5.1. In the second version of the table the distance to the regional centre has been included. No significant distance effect was detected in the analyses of automation processes. We may note that the regional centre contains a university and an airport with good accessibility to the capital cities of Sweden and Norway.

TABLE 5.1

Regression of Introduction Speed with regard to
IT-Based Product Development

VARIABLE	PARA-METER	t-VALUE
1. Intercept	- 16.3	(21.7)
2. Value of IT-input divided by value of product	+ 2.1	(8.0)
3. Number of employees with non-engineering university studies	+ 1.1	(3.3)
4. Share of employees with IT-education for management	+ 0.9	(2.5)
5. Head office in Sweden but outside the region (dummy)	- 5.6	(4.0)

Number of observations = 38; R^2 = 81.

VARIABLE	PARA-METER	t-VALUE
1. (As above)	- 16.2	(22.7)
2. (")	+ 2.3	(8.5)
3. (")	+ 1.2	(3.8)
4. (")	+ 1.1	(3.0)
5. (")	- 5.5	(4.0)
6. Distance to regional centre	- 0.7	(2.1)

Number of observations = 38; R^2 = 83

IT-based product development is positively influenced by the size of the individual establishment. However, as illustrated in Table 5.2 this scale effect is much weaker than it is with regard to introduction of automation processes (compare Tables 4.4 and 4.6).

TABLE 5.2

Scale Effect with regard to IT-Based Production Development

PRODUCTS WHICH CONTAIN IT-EQUIPMENT	NUMBER OF EMPLOYEES 1-99	100-
No	79.6	30.8
Yeas	20.4	69.2

$\chi^2 = 11.9$

5.2 Product Development and Competence

In this section we shall provide further illustration of the association between product development and labour force competence. In Table
5.3 we show that specialised competence of the staff has a clear
effect on how soon a product unit starts to renew its products by introducing IT-equipment as components of products.

TABLE 5.3

Specialised Competence and Product Development

SHARE OF THE EMPLOYEES WHO ARE SPECIALISED IN IT-BASED PRODUCT DEVELOPMENT	TIME AT WHICH AN ESTABLISHMENT STARTS TO INTRODUCE IT-EQUIP-MENT AS PRODUCT COMPONENTS	
	Late	Early
Low	90.5	47.6
High	9.5	52.4
Sum	100	100

$\chi^2 = 9$ (Pattern significant at the 99.5 per cent level).

The pattern in Table 5.3 is further illuminated by the regression described in (5.2), where the share of persons who are specialised in
IT-based product development y, is associated with other competence
characteristics. The regression equation is described below with
t-values within brackets:

$$y = 0.72X_1 + 0.27X_2 - 0.17X_3 \qquad (5.2)$$
$$\quad (15.4) \quad (9.1) \quad (2.7)$$

X_1 = Share of all employees with IT-education for technical applications

X_2 = Number of employees with long IT-education (more than three months)

X_3 = Share of staff with commercial jobs

where the number of observations is 45 and R^2 = 92. We may observe that variable X_3 has a negative effect. In analogous equations for production process automation the sign of the same variable is positive.

6. CONCLUSIONS

By studying one single sector in a region we have demonstrated empirically that the diffusion and adoption of new technologies is strongly influenced by labour force competence and network properties of individual establishments. We have also illustrated the importance of investments in labour force competence. These observations have been interpreted within a theoretical framework comprising models of regional specialisation and product cycles, formulated as dynamic processes. In order to further assess and develop this type of theory, it is necessary to continue our study - first in a multisectoral setting with one region and then in a multiregional setting.

NOTES

1. This data base contains producing units with more than four employees.

REFERENCES

Andersson, A.E. and Johansson, B., 'Knowledge intensity and product cycles in metropolitan regions', IIASA WP-84-13, International Institute for Applied Systems Analysis, Laxenburg, Austria, 1984.

Collins, N. and Walker, D.F. (eds), Locational Dynamics of Manufacturing Activity, London, 1975.

Dean, J., 'Pricing policies for new products', Harvard Business Review, Vol. 28, 1950, pp. 45-53.

Georgescu-Roegen, N., The Entropy Law and the Economic Process, Harvard University Press, 1970.

Krumme, G. and Hayter, R., 'Implications of corporate strategies and product life cycle adjustments for regional employment changes', in: Collins, B. and Walker, D.F. (eds), Locational Dynamics of Manufacturing Activity, London, 1975.

Perloff, H. and Wingo, L. (eds), Issues in Urban Economics, Baltimore, 1968.

Rees, J. 'Technological change and regional shifts in American manufacturing', Professional Geographer, Vol. 31, 1979, pp. 45-54.

Schumpeter, J.A., The Theory of Economic Development, Harvard, 1951.

Thompson, W., 'Internal and external factors in the development of urban economics', in Perloff, H. and Wingo, L. (eds), Issues in Urban Economics, Baltimore, 1968.

Vernon, R., 'International investment and international trade in the product cycle', Quarterly Journal of Economics, Vol. 80, 1966, pp. 191-207.

CAPITAL MOBILITY, LABOUR DEMAND AND R&D INVESTMENT
IN AUSTRIA IN A MULTIREGIONAL CONTEXT
A FIRST ATTEMPT AT ECONOMETRIC MODELLING
E. Brunner and U. Schubert

1. INTRODUCTION

The present contribution is to be seen in the framework of an ongoing
research effort in the field of urban and regional labour market modelling for Austria. The basic spatial unit for which at least some
relevant data are available is the county. Some results of this effort
can be found in e.g. Schubert (1982), Maier and Schubert (1984), Baumann, Fischer and Schubert (1983). This paper focusses on problems of
regional labour demand and investment in the secondary sector. Previous work in on this topic is reported in Schubert (1981).

The hypothesis of regional disparities due to different intensities of
R&D are a widely discussed subject these days. A first attempt at formulating a model which, in principle, could be tested econometrically,
dealing with R&D investment is included in the present contribution.
Unfortunately, the data available for the empirical work are not yet
suitable for this task.

The aims of this paper can be summarised to be:

-   the improvement of the already existing model of regional invest-
    ment and labour demand for Austria (secondary sector without con-
    struction)

-   a first attempt to formulate a model of R&D activities at a re-
    gional scale consistent with the investment and labour demand
    approach mentioned above

-   a discussion of some empirical regional investment and labour
    demand phenomena in the light of the modelling results

-   a brief discussion of the usefulness of regional classifications
    of Austrian regions in connection with the labour market problems

touched upon here. (For various classification schemes of regions in Austria, see J. Kaniak 1983, Maier and Weiss 1985.)

Similar to most industrialised countries, the post war Austrian economy has been characterised by a more or less continuous capital-labour substitution process.

Computing labour input coefficients by dividing employment by production value (in real terms) leads to the following graph (Figure 1). It shows that there are significant differences between the average national development of this indicator compared to the regional time paths. Three types of regions are distinguished, the classification criteria being the level of development, accessibility, etc. (See Maier and Weiss 1985). Differences between the levels as well as the time patterns emerge and it appears that a clear lag structure can be observed.

Economic theory in general and regional growth theory in particular views 'technological progress' as the driving force causing the rise in productivity and providing the potential for new investment possibilities. This process of technological change is fed by various dynamic factors, among which R&D activities tend to rank high as engines of progress. The next table shows R&D expenditures for four federal states of Austria (Vienna, Lower Austria, Upper Austria, Burgenland) which roughly represent the types of regions mentioned above. Unfortunately, the data used are the rather coarse spatial scale of the federal state. The data set represents the results of a sample based survey of firms in Austria, so that a direct comparison or superimposition of data is not possible at present.

TABLE 1
Interregional Differences in R&D 1981

Variable names in R&D model	Absolute	R&D expenditure in mill. AS 'representative firm' (averages)	No. of R&D employees in a 'representative firm'	Investment in equipment (mill.AS) for a 'representative firm'
Federal state				
Vienna	2484.8	16.8	26.6	5.3
Lower-Austria	517.3	5.6	9.6	2.3
Upper-Austria	1777.6	10.6	15.6	4.2
Burgen-Land	27.3	2.3	3.7	1.0
Austria	6572.9	9.9	15.4	3.7

Even the rough estimates for a 'representative firm' presented in this table show significant interregional differences and deviations from the national average, hence these indicators seem to warrant an approach based on various types of regions.

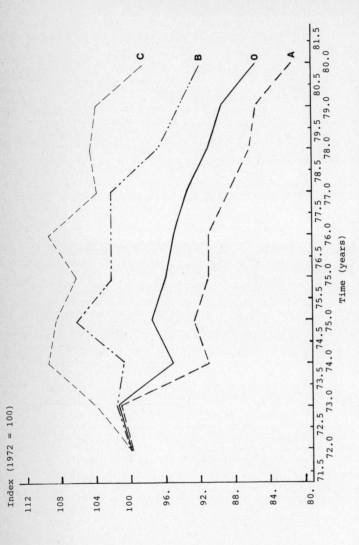

Index (1972 = 100)

Time (years)

Variable 2   Versus Variable labour   Symbol*A Regions with high   level of development
Variable 2   Time Versus Variable input   Symbol*B Regions with medium level of development
Variable 2   Versus Variable coefficients   Symbol*C Regions with low   level of development
Variable 2   Versus Variable (real)   Symbol*D Regions National total

Figure 1. Labour input coefficients (real, secondary sector without construction)

The theoretical question now arises what the determinants of investment, labour demand and R&D expenditures are and to what extent their weights very when different types of regions are considered. These differences is reaction to changes in the decision variables can have two basic causes. There may be genuine differences in the perception and evaluation of those changes that correlate with the development level, or the regional aggregates we are dealing with conceal significant structural differences. The given data set makes a clear distinction between these effects impossible, hence, this question remains unsolved.

The paper proceeds by first looking briefly at the accounting framework underpinning the macro approach taken in this study (Section 2) and the modelling constraints imposed by the data limitations. Section 3 is devoted to a very brief presentation of a microeconomic model of a hypothetical 'representative' multiregional firm, the planning problem of which is to solve a multiregional investment budget allocation problem over time. The optimal control approach adopted here is based on the pioneering work done by Rahman (1963), later modified and operationalised by de Bruyne and van Rompuy (1977). Previous work by Schubert and Hampapa (1979) and Schubert (1981) follows the same lines. The tentative modelling attempts to come to grips with R&D expenditures owes thanks to a recent survey by Malecki (1984) and some considerations by Nijkamp and Schubert (1985).

In Section 4 the theoretical model is transformed into an operational form which allows econometric work. The data restrictions already mentioned obviate an empirical treatment of the R&D expenditure hypotheses. The results of the regression analyses are briefly discussed in this section as well. In Section 5 a few possibilities for further work related to R&D investment are briefly discussed and a short summary is provided.

2. PREREQUISITES FOR MACROMODELLING DATA AND SOME ACCOUNTING PROBLEMS

As mentioned in Section 1 the smallest basic spatial unit at which most of the necessary economic data are available is the county. Since 1972 annual information (for the secondary sector excluding the construction sector) on employment, net and gross production values, investment expenditures as well as the sum of wages are available. Estimates of the capital stock consistent with the regional investment data as well as the national estimates of the capital stock in Austria were made by E. Brunner. Information on various price levels is only obtainable at the national scale. A graph of the Austrian inter-regional transportation system (Kaniak 1983) provides the average travel times used in the calculation of distance effects. The limitations of the R&D related data set were already hinted at in Section 1.

The micromodel of a hypothetical multiregional firm below acknowledges the fact that the interregional mobility of capital has to be taken into account. Especially in the period 1972-1981 considerable suburbanisation of production facilities took place as well as some significant changes in the investment propensities of small towns in several areas (see e.g. Maier and Tödling 1984). A direct test of the model outlined in the following section requires information at the micro-level about interregional investment flows (I^{jk}). This information is not available, only data on the total volume of productive investment at the county level are given. A reduced form approach is hence chosen which makes use of the marginal distribution of a hypothetical capital flow matrix, which which the sum over the rows yields all the investment arriving in the respective region, $I^{\cdot k}$ (the sum over the columns represents all investment emanating from a given region).

$$I^{\cdot k} = \sum_{k=1,n} I^{jk} \qquad (1)$$

The theoretical model of Section 3 attempts to clarify the determinants of I^{jk} for a 'representative firm', in Section 4 the accounting identity just described is utilised to derive a testable macro model, for which data on ($I^{\cdot k}$) for the period 1972-1981 for all 98 counties in Austria are available.

3. PLANNING AT THE MICROLEVEL - THE ALLOCATION PROBLEM OF A MULTIREGIONAL FIRM

3.1 The Decision Problem

In this study only the production factors capital (K), labour (L) and knowledge (T) treated as stock variables, are considered. The respective flows are investment (I), hiring and firing of labour (H), patents (P) and R&D investment (R). Specific combinations of these factors represent 'technologies' by means of which goods (Y) can be produced.

In standard economic analysis it is often assumed that changes in the stocks of production factors cause no <u>internal frictions</u>, often implying temporary losses in output. The installation of new machines or the introduction of a new technology take time in which productivity suffers, however, new labour has to be trained to acquire the specific skills necessary, it usually takes time to find the extra labour required, the expansion of a productive facility on new land takes time in which production is even partly impossible, the increasing need for specialised economic services implies delays, etc. Due to lack of data, the land market issue will not be dealt with in this contribution. These 'product detours' (Böhm - Bawerk 1889, Hicks 1973) imply that a 'production sacrifice' has to be made now, to be able to reach higher production in the future. These considerations lead us to the formulation of the following production function (leaving out time subscripts):

$$\underline{Y} = f(K,L,T,I,H,P,R), \quad f_K, f_L, f_T \gtrless 0, \quad f_I, f_H, f_P, f_R \lessgtr 0 \qquad (2)$$

The f. denoting partial derivatives.

To simplify the analysis we will assume that the productivity losses, due to changes in the productive capacity last only one period, i.e. Y does not depend on:

$$I_{t-\tau}, \; H_{t-\tau}, \; P_{t-\tau}, \; R_{t-\tau}; \quad \tau = 1, 2, \ldots, \bar{\tau} \qquad (3)$$

Investment can be positive or negative (disinvestment). Using an interregional accounting framework, we can (at least theoretically) keep track of all the investment expenditure originating in region (j) and indicate to which regions (k) it goes, as indicated in Section 2, (e.g. Klaassen and Molle 1981a).

As actual, physical transfers of investment are only an exception, a different concept of 'investment flows' underlies this model. The region of origin (j) is to be interpreted mainly as the region where the decision is made and multiregional investment is controlled. The region of destination (k) corresponds to the location of actual investment. This concept finds expression in the hypothetical investment flow matrix.

Investment causes a change in the capital stock, i.e. the 'internal production conditions' of the firm are different because of a decision taken in the past. K^{jk} stands for the productive capital in region (k) controlled by the firm resident in (j). The decision maker has to take dynamic stock-flow conditions into account.

The net change of the capital stock is equal to gross investment minus replacement. Assuming that capital depreciates at the constant rate and measuring time continuously, we obtain:

$$\dot{K}^{jk} = I^{jk} - \delta K^{jk} \tag{4}$$

To produce goods, labour and knowledge are required besides capital (see (2)), hence analogous dynamic constraints have to be observed for labour and knowledge as well.

The net change of labour employed is equal to the number of laborers hired and fired minus the number of laborers leaving the firm (because of retirement, change of job, accidents, etc.).

$$\dot{L}^{jk} = H^{jk} - \gamma L^{jk} \tag{5}$$

where is the labour turnover rate.

The stock of technological and organisation knowhow (T) changes when the firm either buys patents (P) and/or invests in research (R). It is assumed that a constant fraction of this stock of knowledge becomes obsolete in each period.

$$\dot{T}^{jk} = (P^{jk} + R^{jk}) - \varepsilon T^{jk} \tag{6}$$

One allocation problem to be solved by the decision makers is whether
to invest in already available knowledge in the form of patents or to
engage in the risky business of paying for research. At this point no
distinction is made between research done in the firm itself or whether it is contracted out. The change in the stock of knowledge is considered as an output of a knowledge production process, the inputs
into which are 'scientists and other personnel' (S), 'equipment' (E)
and the stock of knowledge given at the time. This production of knowledge is a risky enterprise, hence the production volume is basically
a stochastic variable, whereas buying a patent is practically risk
free.

$$R^{jk} = g(S^{jk}, E^{jk}, T^{jk}, c^{jk}), \ R_S, \ R_E, \ R_T \geq 0 , \qquad (7)$$

where σ is a stochastic disturbance term, reflecting risk.

(Note that we have assumed that E and S are flow variables and that
the change of knowledge is frictionless in this simplified model.)

We further postulate that the labour turnover rate (γ) as well as the
rate of capital depreciation (δ) and (ϵ) are constant and regionally
differentiated.

Profits at each period of time (π) are defined as revenue minus cost.

As we are only considering a one product firm, which can sell its
single product at a given price p^k, total revenue from the sales of
the goods produced in several regions are:

$$\text{Total revenue} = \sum p^k \ y^{jk} \qquad (8)$$

where y^{jk} represents the production volume of a firm located in (k)
and controlled from (j).

The price level p^k signals the demand for the product to the multiregional firm and is assumed to depend on the disposable income in the
demanding regions.

Total factor cost of the production process constitutes total cost.
Let us consider capital and investment expenditures first. Investment

goods are usually bought in a very large market (the world or the national market) in which prices are usually fairly uniform. We suppose then, that the aggregate investment good can be purchased at a spatially invariant price q_1. The total sum to be spent for investments located in several regions is:

$$\text{Total investment goods' cost} = q_1 \sum^k I^{jk} ; \qquad (9)$$

For the existing capital stock at time t opportunity costs have to be paid. Let the interest rate (r) be uniform over the national system, thus implying that the financial markets in a country are 'regionally integrated'.

$$\text{Total capital cost} = rq_1 \sum^k K^{jk} \qquad (10)$$

Besides these direct costs, there are the indirect costs of transferring investment to other locations and the transaction costs of investment in general. There are many components of these, such as the cost of information, which especially for new investment in a region different from the control location, can be quite substantial. Empirical studies, based on surveys (Klaassen and Molle 1981b) have shown that for this reason only very few potential locations are investigated in any detail to find out whether an investment there would be worthwhile. Usually 'nearby' locations are the prime candidates.

Relocation implies that there may also be costs of the physical transfer to be reckoned with, etc. We postulate hence, that the total transaction cost of investment is positively related to the total volume of investment and to the distance of the region of destination from the region of origin, on which information cost as well as physical transfer costs depend.

$$\text{Transation cost of investment} = \sum^k TI(I^{jk},d^{jk}), TI_1, TI_d \geq 0 \qquad (11)$$

Turning to labour now, new labour often has to be trained to acquire the necessary skills, there are filing fees, social security expenses, etc. (Scanlon and Holt 1977). To keep the model as simple as possible, these costs are the same for hiring and for firing (with a negative sign).

$$\text{Sum of wages} = \overset{k}{\Sigma}\ w^k\ L^{jk} \qquad\qquad (12)$$

$$\text{Friction cost} = \overset{k}{\Sigma}\ C(H^{jk})\ ,\ C_H \geq 0 \qquad\qquad (13)$$

The cost of to be borne for the provision of the production factor 'knowledge' (T) consists of the purchasing cost for patents and/or R&D in the form of wages for scientific personnel (S) and equipment (E):

$$q_p\ p^{jk} + (w_S S^{jk} + q_E E^{jk}) \qquad\qquad (14)$$

The already existing stock (T) causes per unit running costs of (r_t). R&D investment expenditures which are not made in the control region cause transaction costs, supposed to rise with the volume of the expenditures and with the distance from the control region:

$$\text{Spatial friction cost of R\&D} = \phi(R^{jk},\ d^{jk}) \qquad\qquad (15)$$

Costs of technological knowhow:

$$q_p\ p^{jk} + (w_S S^{jk} + q_E E^{jk}) + \phi(R^{jk},\ d^{jk}) + r_T T^{jk} \qquad\qquad (16)$$

Collecting terms, we can now compute the total profit of a multi-regional firm at time t.

$$\pi j = \overset{k}{\Sigma}(p^k y^{jk}) - q_I\ \overset{k}{\Sigma}I^{jk} - rq_I\ \overset{k}{\Sigma}\ K^{jk} - \overset{k}{\Sigma}\ TI\ (I^{jk},\ f^{jk}) \qquad\qquad (17)$$

$$- \overset{k}{\Sigma}\ (w^k L^{jk}) - \overset{k}{\Sigma}\ c^k(H^{jk}) - \overset{k}{\Sigma}\ (q_p p^{jk} + w_S S^{jk} + q_E E^{jk} +$$

$$\phi(R^{jk},\ d^{jk}) + r_T T^{jk})$$

3.2 The Demand for Investment Goods, Labour and R&D Investment

The demand for production factors is derived by maximisation of the present value of the hypothetical multiregional firm.

Let be the rate of discount of future earnings, so that the present value (V) of the expected profits is:

$$V = \int_0^{\infty} e^{-\rho t} \pi \ dt \tag{18}$$

The variables the decision maker can control in each period of time, are investment (I), hiring and firing (H), R&D personnel (S) and equipment (E), patents (P), and the volume of production (Y). The stock variables K, L and T are the consequences of past decisions, thus representing the state variables.

The question then is, what levels of the control variables have to be realised in a given period to maximise the present value of the expected future profits arising from these controls.

To solve this kind of cost-benefit analysis we will make use of optimal control theory and the Pontryagin Principle (Pontryagin et al. 1962).

The relevant control problem is:

Maximise V   (see Equations(17) and (18))

given: (2), (4), (5), (6), (7)

(The stock variables K, L and T cannot become negative.)

The Pontryagin Principle (see e.g. Arrow 1968) applied to this problem, postulates (assuming the non-negativity constraints on K, L and T hold):

a) The sum of the marginal effects of a change in the control variables has to be equal to the scarcity prices ( ) of the relevant stock variable at each period (control conditions), where the scarcity price

measures the marginal contribution of the relevant stock variable to
the present value.

$$-q_I - TI_I jk + p^k f_I jk + \lambda_1^{jk} = 0 \tag{19}$$

where λ^{jk} is the 'shadow price' of capital in region K

$$-w^k - C_H^k jk + p^k f_H jk + \lambda_2^{jk} = 0 \tag{20}$$

where λ^{jk} is the 'shadow price' of labour, and

$$p^{k} f_p - q_p + \lambda_3^{jk} = 0 \tag{21}$$

$$p^{k} f_S jk - w_S + R^{jk} R_S jk + g_S jk \frac{\lambda^{jk}}{3} = 0 \tag{22}$$

$$p^{k} f_E jk - q_E jk + \phi_R jkR_E jk + g_E \frac{\lambda^{jk}}{3} = 0 \tag{23}$$

b) As stocks accumulate (or diminish) their scarcities change. So do
their shadow prices. One part of this change is caused by discounting
the future, the second part consists of the gap between marginal cost
and revenue caused by a change in the stocks.

$$\dot{\lambda}_1^{jk} = (\delta + \dot{\rho}) \lambda_1^{rk} + rq_I - p^{f_k} Kjk \tag{24}$$

$$\dot{\lambda}_2^{jk} = (\gamma + \rho) \lambda_2^{jk} + w^k - p^{k} f_L jk \tag{25}$$

$$\dot{\lambda}_3^{jk} = \lambda_3^{jk} (\varepsilon + \rho) - p^{k} f_T jk + \phi_R R_T^{jk} + r_T + \mu g_T \tag{26}$$

Note that the assumption of a very slowly changing transportation and
communication network was made implying constant d^{jk}.

Given 'well behaved' problems, (for a discussion of second order conditions and stability see, Brock and Scheinkman 1977), following these

rules will lead to optimal production, location, investment, R&D, etc. plans. The indicated rules represent a system of simultaneous equations which can be solved to yield the optimal levels of I, H, S, E, P for all locations, i.e. the dynamic demand equations for production factors.

Computing the time derivatives of the control conditions yields equations for the dynamics of co-state variables . Simultaneously the shadow price relations have to hold. Rearranging terms yields solutions of these sets of equations, which, given specific functional forms could be solved for the optimal levels of the control variables as a function of prices, parameters, etc.

The solutions with implicit functional forms are of the following nature:

$$(TI_I^{\cdot}jk) - (p^{\dot{k}}f_Ijk + p^k f_{\dot{I}}jk) - (\delta + \rho)(TI_Ijk - p^k f_Ijk) \quad (27)$$

$$= (\delta + \rho)q_Ijk - \dot{q} + rq_Ijk + p^k f_Kjk \text{ , etc.}$$

4. TOWARDS AN OPERATIONAL MODEL AND SOME EMPIRICAL RESULTS

4.1 From Theory to Testable Hypothesis

In order to be able to attempt an empirical test of the claims just made, more specific assumptions have to be made.

The production function

$$Y^{jk} = A(K^{jk})^\alpha \ (L^{jk})^\beta \ (T^{jk})^\gamma - (aI^{jk} + bH^{jk} + cP^{jk} + \bar{c}R^{jk}) \quad (28)$$

In this special case the marginal frictions are constant, the change over time equals zero.

Let the transaction costs of changing the capital stock be the square of the volume of investment and multiplicatively related to the distance between the region of origin and destination of a capital transfer. To facilitate the analysis we also postulate that these costs are always equally high, independent of whether it is the first investment in a new region or a subsequent one.

$$TI\,(I^{jk},\,d^{jk}) = m(I^{jk})^2 \cdot \psi(d^{jk}) \qquad (29)$$

The cost of changing the labour force changes with the square of the level of change.

$$C(H^{jk}) = h(H^{jk})^2 \qquad (30)$$

The allocation of R&D investment to a region (k) can be assumed to follow a similar rule.

$$\phi(R^{jk},\,d^{jk}) + n(R^{jk})^2\,\psi(d^{jk}) \qquad (31)$$

To simplify matters further and to make the problem tractable from an econometric point of view we approximate marginal products by average products.

Making use of all these special assumptions yields demand equations of the following forms for investment and labour demand.

$$I^{jk} = \frac{1}{2m\psi(d^{jk})}\,\{(\delta + \rho)\,q_1 - \dot{q}_1 + mp^k - \dot{a}p^k +$$
$$\qquad (32)$$
$$rq_I - p^k\,(Y^{jk}/K^{jk})\alpha - 2mI\,\psi(d^{jk})\}\,,\ \text{etc.}$$

Making use of the 'representative firm' concept we assume that the aggregate demand functions for investment and labour demand follow the same pattern as they do for the individual decision maker.

Theoretically, the interregional investment flow matrix of Section 2 could now be filled row by row. Making use of the accounting identity (1) developed in Section 2, we could derive the total investment actually undertaken in a region by summing over the rows. By the same token, the right hand side of the demand equations have to be summed now, yielding a macro formulation of the relevant equations.

Some further, rather ad hoc assumptions were made to cope with the
fact that at present the fuller version of the model including R&D
expenditures cannot be tested due to the lack of appropriate data.
Technological progress, if not explicitly modelled, expresses itself
via capital and labour productivity. The theory of innovation diffusion postulates, applied to the question of the spatial distribution
of productivity, that these are related over space and time. Again
Austrian data at present do not permit a specification of this process
explicitly. To salvage some of this idea we simply computed 'productivity potentials', i.e., distance factor discounted sums of productivities. Note that in the aggregation procedure to derive regional
investment all variables on the right hand side are weighted by the
distance related spatial friction cost variable, the sum over which
yields some aggregate measure of the region's 'accessibility'. This
measure, if not computed explicitly, influences the coefficients of
all variables. This was taken into account by the specification of
separate models for different types of regions, for which this measure
if hypothesised to be fairly homogenous. The explicit calculation of
these accessibility weights raises the problem of the proper cutoff
point - which has not yet been solved satisfactorily.

Another type of problem is raised by the specification of the appropriate factor costs. In the case of the capital goods, the probably
not very heroic assumption of uniform relative capital costs over
space were made. For average industrial wages this assumption notori-
ously does not hold, as our data set clearly revealed. In the absence
of a good econometric grip on the question of wage determination over
time and space to be modelled explicitly, a very simply approach was
tested. No separate simultaneous wage determination model was formulated, but the spatial connectivity of regional labour markets was
expressed by a simple distance discount weighted sum of regional
wages. This specification fared better empirically than the assumption
of spatial independence of wages, i.e., the use of region of destination wages only.

The next specification problem arose out of the fact that no regional
output price indicators are available. An inverse demand function formulation was tried in which the price level depends on the quantity of
output and income as well as on the national rate of inflation. As the
demand for goods in a region arises in the form of domestic plus export demand, incomes in the other regions exert only a 'cost'

(distance) corrected influence, a construct leading to the specification of income potentials - which were calculated for exports to foreign countries separately. As income data on the country level are not
available in Austria, net production values were used as proxies. (For an
exact formulation of the regression equations, see Tables 2 and 3.)

4.2 Some Empirical Results

As mentioned above, the parameters of the equations for different
types of regions contain the same set of independent variables. The
hypothesis to be tested was that investment demand reacts in a different qualitative (i.e. a different set of significant coefficients is
to be expected) as well as quantitative (the elasticities of the variables differ) manner.

Although different estimation techniques were used, the following discussion is based predominantly on the 3 SLS parameter estimates. In
general, it can be observed that in terms of the goodness of fit statistics (R^2, etc.) the investment model proved to be fairly successful
(see Tables 2 and 3), while the labour demand equations came out rather badly on these terms. One has to add, however, that labour demand
is actually estimated in the form of the rate of change of demand, a
fact which usually implies worse goodness of fit characteristics.

In both submodels, the dominance of the 'accelerator hypothesis', i.e.
the strong reactions of the decision makers to changes in the demand
for the respective outputs, is clearly established. Furthermore, productivity changes seem to play an important role. The specification is
terms of potentials to signal the spatial interdependence of technological progress fares better than the inclusion of the productivity
of the region of destination only. This result suggests, however, that
a more theory based approach towards R&D investment seems to be warranted.

A similar argument holds for the wage potential, as a specification
for the wage determination process.

Turning to the investment demand model in more detail now, the results
reveal that the significance of the variables varies greatly over the
different types of regions. For the most developed, the urban regions,
the list of significant variables (t values 1.9) is the longest, as

TABLE 2

The determinants of regional investment demand; regression results (variables in nominal terms)

REGIONS WITH HIGH LEVEL OF DEVELOPMENT

ENDOGENOUS VARIABLE = INV   (INVESTMENT DEMAND)

R SQUARE = .92543

VARIABLE		EXP. SIGN	3-STAGE B	T	ELASTICITY
QR	PRODUCT OF INVESTMENT-GOODS DEFLATOR AND INTEREST RATE	-	-.2843E+03	-.6851E+00	-.23624
DNPW	CHANGE OF NET PRODUCTION VALUE	+	.4519E+00	.3259E+01	.07140
DIDEFL	CHANGE OF INVESTMENT GOODS DEFLATOR	?	-.2975E+05	-.1912E+01	-.21796
KPPO	POTENTIAL OF CAPITAL PRODUCTIVITY	-	-.4650E-01	-.2504E+01	-.62694
NPW	NET PRODUCTION VALUE	+	.1342E+00	.3057E+02	.81209
PNPWPO	PRODUCT OF GNP DEFLATOR AND NET PRODUCTION VALUE POTENTIAL	+	.7277E-04	.3336E+01	.78792
DBNPDEF	CHANGE OF GNP DEFLATOR	?	.5884E+05	.1154E+01	.49449
DPNPWPO	CHANGE OF 'PNPWPO'	?	-.3036E-10	-.3143E+01	-.09091
DBIPRW	CHANGE OF SUM OF GNP'S OF THE MAJOR AUSTRIAN FOREIGN TRADE PARTNERS	?	-.1036E+00	-.1893E+01	-.25059
DINV	CHANGE OF INV. DEMAND		.6331E+00	.9119E+01	.03591
C			.2297E+06	.8212E+00	0.00000

REGIONS WITH MEDIUM LEVEL OF DEVELOPMENT

ENDOGENOUS VARIABLE = INV

R SQUARE = .69355

VARIABLE	3-STAGE B	T	ELASTICITY
QR	.1009E+03	.5115E+00	-.02004
DNPW	.3774E+01	.4312E+01	-.07075
DIDEFL	-.6734E+04	-.8290E+00	-.19893
KPPO	-.2453E-01	-.1933E+01	-.09878
NPW	.2275E+00	.1306E+02	1.06356
PNPWPO	.2719E-04	.2314E+01	.01707
DBNPDEF	-.3093E+04	-.1264E+00	.60437
DPNPWPO	-.2341E-03	-.4200E+01	.06150
DBIPPW	-.1051E-01	-.3700E+00	-.04988
DINV	.5605E+00	.1124E+02	.02931
C	.1866E+05	.1003E+00	0.00000

REGIONS WITH LOW LEVEL OF DEVELOPMENT

ENDOGENOUS VARIABLE = INV

R SQUARE = .82636

VARIABLE	3-STAGE B	T	ELASTICITY
QR	.1445E+03	.3460E+01	.47810
DNPW	.7940E+00	.1970E+01	-.02716
DIDEFL	.9911E+03	.5663E+00	.06347
KPPO	.2391E-02	.7083E+00	.75422
NPW	.2058E+00	.2420E+02	1.08288
PNPWPO	-.2500E-05	-.9980E+00	-.56115
DBNPDEF	-.3457E+04	-.6406E+00	-.19670
DPNPWPO	-.6415E-13	-.1925E+01	-.00413
DBIPPW	.1349E-02	.2218E+00	.12425
DINV	.5008E+00	.8899E+01	.03019
C	-.9256E+05	-.1808E+01	0.00000

TABLE 3

The determinants of regional labour demand; regression results (variables in nominal terms, employment in heads)

REGIONS WITH HIGH LEVEL OF DEVELOPMENT

ENDOGENOUS VARIABLE = D3 (LABOR DEMAND)

R SQUARE =   .44158

			3-STAGE		
VARIABLE		EXP. SIGN	B	T	ELASTICITY
WPO	WAGE POTENTIAL	–	-.5085E+00	-.2244E+01	38.18788
DNPW	CHANGE OF NET PRODUCTION VALUE	+	-.2465E-03	-.1147E+01	.56303
DWPO	CHANGE OF 'WPO'	?	-.2220E+01	-.5591E+01	14.42806
APPO	POTENTIAL OF LABOR PRODUCTIVITY	–	.4458E+00	.3252E+01	-53.72373
NPW	NET PRODUCTION VALUE	+	-.6044E-04	-.8303E+01	3.96963
PNPWPO	PRODUCT OF GNP DEFLATOR AND NET PRODUCTION VALUE POTENTIAL	+	-.3989E-08	-.7922E-01	.21275
DPNPWPO	CHANGE OF 'PNPWPO'	?	.4027E-13	.2689E+01	-1.51285
DBIPRW	CHANGE OF SUM OF GNP'S OF THE MAJOR AUSTRIAN FOREIGN TRADE PARTNERS	+	-.2035E-04	-.2991E+00	.16150
DDB	SECOND DERIVATE OF LABOR DEMAND	?	-.3286E-02	-.1002E+01	-.07027
C			.2542E+03	.9858E+00	0.00000

REGIONS WITH MEDIUM LEVEL OF DEVELOPMENT

ENDOGENOUS VARIABLE = DB

R SQUARE =   .21850

	3-STAGE		
VARIABLE	B	T	ELASTICITY
WPO	.2075E-01	.4495E+00	-38.93738
DNPW	-.1717E-03	-.2285E+00	.80609
DWPO	-.3646E+00	-.3638E+01	-35.21759
APPO	-.5033E-02	-.1386E+00	108.32916
NPW	-.2189E-04	-.1331E+01	-5.09917
PNPWPO	-.4756E-09	-.3273E-01	-28.66904
DPNPWPO	.2606E-13	.5487E+00	1.50456
DBIPRW	-.1666E-04	-.7450E+00	.15329
DDB	.6896E-02	.1879E+01	.18311
C	.2420E+03	.1877E+01	0.00000

REGIONS WITH LOW LEVEL OF DEVELOPMENT

ENDOGENOUS VARIABLE = DB

R SQUARE =   .36504

	3-STAGE		
VARIABLE	B	T	ELASTICITY
WPO	-.9459E-01	-.8640E+00	-41.75710
DNPW	.1508E-02	.3272E+00	3.25483
DWPO	-.2624E+00	-.1261E+01	-37.78120
APPO	.3647E-01	.3457E+00	90.15558
NPW	-.9248E-04	-.1075E+01	-3.04363
PNPWPO	.1757E-07	.4019E+00	-12.20666
DPNPWPO	.7656E-13	.2007E+00	-.40490
DBIPRW	.1633E-04	.3065E+00	-.76560
DDB	-.1126E-01	-.4056E+00	.42654
C	.2447E+03	.5379E+00	0.00000

the development level falls, fewer variables seem to matter. A closer look at these variables reveals that in the regions with a lower development level, it is predominantly demand change and the cost of capital that count, while the full set of variables applies only to the highest development level. Interpreting this result in the light of the product cycle hypothesis, firms in the economic periphery of a country tend to produce either industrial routine products where substitution processes can no longer be set in motion, or very small firms produce for local everyday needs, for which a more or less fixed technology leads to the same results. Expanding the production capacity becomes predominantly a question of the volume of demand for the goods produced. High interest rates make life for these firms difficult, so they tend to wait for better times. In the high development regions the firms generally tend to have a certain range of substitution possibilities at their disposal which implies that all the cost information necessary to make decisions about substitution processes are taken into account. This is particularly true in the rings of the agglomerations, which in the period 1972-1981 represented the industrial heartland of Austria. In the core regions, where many innovations tend to see the light of the industrial day, demand for the products tends to matter more against the cost variables. (In the present contribution however, cores and rings are not distinguished explicitly.)

A similar picture emerges regarding the elasticities. Demand variables (such as NPW, PNPWPO, ...) again take the lion's share of importance, followed by productivity (KPPO), while cost variables (DIDEFL and QR) seem to matter less in terms of the elasticities (computer on the basis of the average level of the respective variables). This is particularly true in the agglomerations. In the less developed regions, the demand variables (NPW and DBNPWPO) which are also significant, are the most important movers of the regional investment activities. In the intermediate group of regions productivity becomes a significant influence on top of the demand variables.

The following figures (2 and 3) illustrate these results by showing the development of investment (I) and the demand for goods (NPW) and the productivity variable (KPPO) over time, to exemplify. Again the graphs reveal that in the less developed regions the time paths of the dependent variable follow the path of the most important variable (NPW) very closely, which is less the case in the highly developed

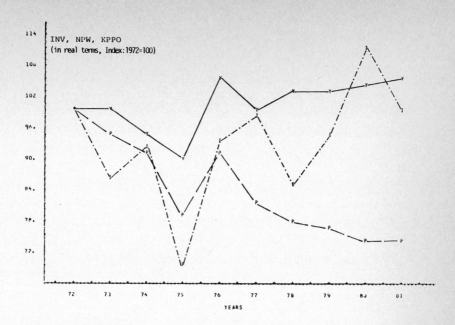

Figure 2.   Investment, net production value and capital productivity potentiel, 1972-1981; in regions of low development level

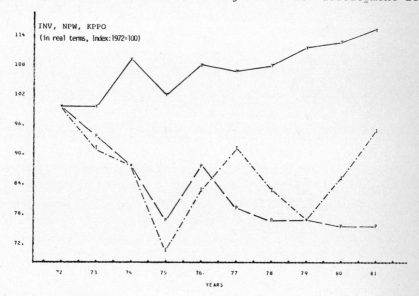

Figure 3. Investment, net production value and capital productivity potential, 1972-1981; in regions of high development level

regions. It is also demonstrated that the ups and downs in the less developed regions are more pronounced while investment activities in the agglomerations tend to be buffered by other considerations than pure changes in the demand for goods.

Turning to labour demand now, as already mentioned, results in terms of the overall goodness of fit were not satisfactory. Additional work seems to be necessary to improve the specification to be tested.

Looking at the respective 't' values first, the labour demand equation responds to the demand as well as to the cost variables. The most significant influence, as in the case of the investment submodel, turns out to be the demand for goods. The highest elasticity may be found in response to changes in the labour productivity, followed by wages. The sign of the productivity coefficient is positive, contrary to the theoretical specification outlined. There could be several reasons for this phenomenon. The use of a productivity potential to capture at least some of the innovation diffusion concept could be misleading, or the separability assumption incorporated into the theoretical model does not hold. It may well be that regions of high labour productivity attract more investment in a lead and lag fashion, which should be explicitly modelled.

5. CONCLUDING REMARKS

Regarding the problem of technological progress, the present contribution seems to indicate that an explicit formulation of R&D activities and innovation could improve the model. Although an approach was outlined which could in principle be empirically pursued with Austrian data, this is clearly not the case at the moment. For a simple cross-section approach there are not enough observations (Austria has nine federal states), and pooling techniques fails as there is only one point in time available at present. Efforts will be made in the future by the statistical office to go down to the country level and to conduct an R&D activities survey of Austria every three years,

But it is not only data problems which need to be solved. Also the theory and particularly the operationalisation leaves much to be desired. Given the model as it now stands, no reasonable assumption about the functional forms of the production function for the increase

in knowhow by R&D investment allow a tractable model formulation for
the demand for R&D personnel and equipment.

Furthermore, the riskiness of undertaking R&D activities needs to be
considered in more detail. How the portfolio choice problem between
the less risky purchase of patents and the risky R&D choice should be
incorporated in the optimal control model, is not yet clear.

By the same token, the various diffusion processes (innovation, wage
determination) should be formulated in a much less ad hoc way. The
data base for a direct empirical approach to the problem does not
exist in Austria, so other avenues will have to be detected.

The strong separability assumptions made in the production functions
should be reconsidered as well to be able to allow for more direct
interaction between the various submodels.

The smaller version of the model, containing only investment and demand produces fairly plausible results. The temporal lag structure
should be investigated in more detail, especially as the length of the
time series information increases (at the moment only ten observation
points over time are available). As the impacts of the national variables can only be estimated on the basis of time series information,
this strategy does not seem warranted at the moment.

REFERENCES

Arrow, K.J., 'Applications of control theory to economic growth', in:
    Dantzig, G. and Veinott, A.F. (eds), Mathematics of the Decision
    Sciences, American Mathematical Society, Providence, RI, 1968,
    pp. 85-119.

Baumann, J.H., Fischer, M.M. and Schubert, U., 'A multiregional labour
    supply model for Austria: the effects of different regionalisa-
    tions in multiregional labour market modelling', Papers of the
    Regional Science Association, Vol. 52, 1983, pp. 53-83.

Böhm-Bawerk, E., Positive Theory of Capital, Vienna, 1889.

Brock, W.A. and Scheinkman, G.A., 'The global assymptotic stability of
    optimal control with applications to dynamic economic theory',
    in: Pitchford, J.D. and Turnovsky, S.J. (eds), Applications of
    Control Theory to Economic Analysis, North-Holland, Amsterdam,
    New York, Oxford, 1977, pp. 173-208.

Bruyne, G. de and Rompuy, P. van, 'Estimation of a system of nonlinear investment allocation functions', Centrum voor Economische Studien, Louvain, Belgium, 1977 (mimeo).

Hicks, J., Capital and Time. A Neo-Austrian Theory, Clarendon Press, Oxford, 1973.

Kaniak, J., Theorie und Methode zur Abgrenzung peripherer Gebiete und zur Messung des regionalen Entwicklungsstandes in Österreich 1961-1973, IIR - Forschung Nr. 1, 1983.

Klaassen, L. and Molle, W., Some General Considerations about Industrial Mobility and Industrial Migration, Paper presented at the International Conference on Industrial Mobility and Migration in the European Community, Rotterdan, 1981a.

Klaassen, L. and Molle, W., Concepts, Measurements and Pitfalls in the Empirical Analysis of Industrial Movement, Paper presented at the International Conference on Mobility and Migration in the European Community, Rotterdam, 1981b.

Maier, G. and Weiss, P., 'The importance of regional factors in the determination of earnings - the case of Austria', International Regional Science Review, Vol. 10, 1985.

Maier, G. and Schubert, U., 'Struktur und Probleme interregionaler Arbeitsmarktmodelle - mit einigen ausgewählten Ergebnissen für Österreich', in: Bahrenberg, G., Fischer, M.M. (eds), Theorie und quantitative Methodik in der Geographie, Bremer Beiträge zur Geographie, Vol. 15, Bremen, 1984, pp. 48-92.

Maier, G., Tödtling, F., Betriebs- und Arbeitsmartentwicklung in Österreichischen Regionen in der Periode der Wachstumsverlangsamung, IIR-Forschung, Nr. 10, 1984.

Malecki, E., 'Technology and regional development. A survey', International Regional Science Review, Vol. 8, No. 2, 1983, pp. 89-125.

Nijkamp, P. and Schubert, U., 'Urban dynamics', in: Brotchie, J, Newton, P., Hall, P. and Nijkamp, P. (eds), The Future of Urban Form - The Impact of New Technology, Croom Helm, London, Sydney, 1985, pp. 79-92.

Pontryagin, L., Boltyanski, R., Gamkredlidze, R. and Mischenko, E., The Mathematical Theory of Optimal Processes, Interscience Publishers, New York, 1922.

Rahman, M.A., 'Regional allocation of investment. An aggregative study in the theory of development programming', Quarterly Journal of Economics, Vol. 77, 1963, pp. 26-39.

Toikka, R.S., Scanlon, W.J. and Holt, C.C., 'Extension of a structural model of the demographic labour market', in: Ehrenberg, R.G. (ed), Research in Labour Economics, an Annual Compilation of Research, Vol. 1, JA1 Press, Greenwhich, Conn., 1977, pp. 305-332.

Schubert, U. and Hampapa, P., A simultaneous model of regional investment and labour demand, IIR-Discussion, Nr. 5, 1979.

Schubert, U., Capital mobility and labour demand in urban agglomerations during the suburbanisation process, an econometric approach, IIR-discussion, Nr. 12, 1981.

Schubert, U., 'REMO - an interregional market model of Austria', Environment and Planning A, Vol. 14, 1982, pp. 1233-1249.

TECHNOLOGICAL CHANGE AND REGIONAL EMPLOYMENT RESEARCH
Manfred M. Fischer and Peter Nijkamp

1. TECHNOLOGICAL CHANGE AND REGIONAL ECONOMIC DYNAMICS IN RETROSPECT

In the recent past economists have placed much emphasis on the role of technological change in the developed economies. Witness the many publications in the field of innovation, long waves and economic dynamics. Especially the present world-wide economic recession has stimulated many research efforts in this area. In many studies, attention has been devoted to the impact of technological change on long term and progressive change processes in the world economy (see e.g. Mensch 1979, Freeman et al. 1982). A major issue in these studies was the problem whether or not basic innovations occur in clusters, especially in periods of economic recession. But in order to understand the role of technological change in a downswing phase, it is far more important to analyse the nature rather than the rate of technological change in existing industries. Any explanation of the nature of technological change, however, has to be based upon an understanding of the determinants leading to innovation, its diffusion patterns and its socioeconomic impacts. Hereby, innovation (whether technical or non-technical, process or product based) may be seen - in accordance with Piatier (1984) - as covering a succession of operations, i.e. the transition from the idea to its materialisation, followed by a result, i.e., the product itself or one of its inputs or the method of its production or sale. Evidently, technological change is not an isolated phenomenon but intertwined with a variety of economic and social processes and adjustments.

So far, however, less attention has been paid to the labour market aspects of long term industrial dynamics. Much of the interest in the issue of technological change expressed by policy makers refers to its effect upon current employment and future job opportunities. Clearly, however, there appears to be only little systematic empirical and theoretical research focussing on the relationship between technological change and employment. It is, for example, still an unresolved

question whether technological change favours positive net employment
effects in the secondary or tertiary sector or whether it has totally
adverse impacts (see also Boyer and Petit 1981). It is indeed rather
difficult to measure the job creating and job replacement effects of
any individual technological change. One of the major difficulties in
analysing technology induced labour market effects is to separate
these effects from all the other changes (such as changes in the
interregional and international division of labour) which are taking
place at the same time. In principle, the adoption of a new technology
provides the potential of job creation. But the creation of new types
of jobs may be offset by the loss of particular types of existing
jobs. Since job creation is indissolubly interlinked with job displacement, it is rather difficult to identify and assess the positive
and the negative employment effects of a specific new technology in a
satisfactory manner without understanding how this technology interre-
lates within a specific production process. Indirect employment effects are even more difficult to ascertain. Indirect labour displacement effects, for example, may arise in cases where industries failing
to introduce improved or new products lose markets and jobs to innovating industries in other regions.

It should be added that technological change does not only affect the
level of employment but also the skill composition. The adoption of
new technologies creates a demand for specific workforce skills. Firms
with large internal labour markets may meet these new skill requirements internally if the in-house supply is limited or does not exist
at all. The balance of these two approaches to supplying the necessary
skill requirements depends upon a wide range of factors such as e.g.
the technical complexity of the innovation and the existing level of
skills of the adopter's employees. This balance as well as the occupational effects are rather hard to predict (see also Cross 1983, for
further details). Furthermore, the use of crude employment data based
on the official classification of employment by occupation and sector
is in many ways inadequate for measuring the impact of new technologies. It is clear that the question how technological change contributes to restructuring the labour market cannot be answered satisfactorily by means of aggregate analysis. There is a strong need for
longitudinal survey based studies at the establishment level in order
to shed some light on the various aspects of employment effects of
well defined new technologies.

An important issue in regional research is the relationship between technological change and regional development. Even though technological change is only one of the driving forces of regional development, new technologies - especially if they are coupled with an appropriate institutional framework - may provide the potential for achieving new prospects for indigenous employment. It is often argued that peripheral regions are generally dependent upon the core regions with respect to sources of technological knowledge and do not provide a supporting environment for innovation (see also the chapter by Goddard and Thwaites in the present volume). Under these circumstances the question arises how policy can stimulate individual entrepreneurs to become more dynamic in utilising new technologies. No doubt, an increasing understanding of the friction between pressures and rigidities for structural adaptation to technological change will provide much scope for a reformulation of regional policy in order to take into account the spatiotechnological dimension.

The present volume served to cover the intriguing research triangle of technological change, employment and urban or regional development. In this book chapters from different disciplinary and also national backgrounds were brought together. This is indicative of the complexity and multidimensionality of the problem as well as of the importance that technological change and employment research has in many societies. A wide range of papers reflecting different interests, different insights and different methodological perspectives have been included in this volume. In the next section of this final chapter, various common findings and conclusions, as well as some major recommendations for future research activities, will be presented.

2.   PERSPECTIVES FOR RESEARCH ON THE TRIANGULAR RELATIONSHIP

It is a striking observation that much current research on technological change is showing the lack of insight in technological change and its implications for socioeconomic systems. This is no doubt an outgrowth of the beginning of some understanding of the complexity of this phenomenon and a recognition of the problems associated with understanding the consequences of this phenomenon upon our societies, especially with regard to the labour market and spatial dynamics. In this context, a reappraisal of Schumpeter's growth theory may stimulate researchers to focus their attention on the development of new interregional growth theories and related econometric growth models encompassing R&D functions as one of their basic elements. This means not only the introduction of production functions in which the state of the art in technology is no longer exogenous but also the mathematical formulation of spatial spillover effects of R&D. These effects are mainly linked to the creation of new production processes and thus with process innovation. But new technical knowledge is also linked with the creation of new products and thus with product innovation. Up to now little attention has been paid to the fact that qualitative structural changes play a dominant role here. In this context, models allowing bifurcation on catastrophe phenomena may be relevant.

The various chapters from the present volume exhibit a wealth of new insights and information on the triangular relationship between technology, employment and regions or cities. Most contributions point to the changing role of big cities and the potential of medium sized cities, but show at the same time a wide diversity of spatial growth patterns in various countries. In the light of these observations, it may be meaningful to identify a limited set of research clusters which may provide a fruitful breeding place for innovative research about the abovementioned triangle. These research areas are: the nature of technological change, information systems about technological change processes, methodological and theoretical frameworks for regional labour market dynamics and integrated policy research. These four clusters will now briefly be pointed out.

2.1 The Nature of Technological Change

Technological change and innovation at both a global-national level and a local-regional level is a much debated issue in various disciplines nowadays. The concept of innovation usually covers both the production process (i.e.., the transition from the idea to its maturity) and the result (i.e., the product or the new process) at one and the same time. Unfortunately, the concept of technological change and/or innovation is rather vague and not always operational, especially for the service sector. In addition to this conceptual problem there are severe measurement problems in empirical research, for example, problems how to measure the innovativeness and the adaptiveness of firms. In consequence, the need for a <u>deeper insight into the nature of technological change in the manufacturing and service</u>

<u>sectors is evident</u>. In particular, we need to obtain more knowledge about the following research issues:

- the sources of technical key inventions and the importance of related managerial and institutional innovation;
- the process of diffusion and adoption of well defined technologies, especially as far as the technology trajectories through different sectors is concerned;
- the life cycle of well defined technologies, in relation to product cycles and urban or regional cycles;
- the development, organisational structure and spatial location of high technology firms, with a special view to the incubation function of cities;
- the institutional and managerial pressures and rigidities for structural adaptation to technological change (especially the rigidities by some forms of state interventions);
- the reaction of agents in capital markets to innovative impulses, particularly as far as the role of venture capital is concerned;
- the role of the public sector in facilitating adjustments through appropriate institutional innovations, including new international cooperative configurations;
- the intra- and intersectoral employment impacts of well defined technologies in the short and in the long run, including consequences for internal and segmented labour markets in certain areas;
- the effects of technological change upon the organisation of the household economy and the informal or shadow sector;
- the impact of office automation on the service sector and the spatial organisation of work;
- the effects of technological improvements in the transport sector (e.g., telematics, logistics revolution) upon the settlement system as a whole;
- the role of large firms, especially multinational companies, in the process of innovation and innovation diffusion, given their usually large expenses for R&D;
- the role of the firm, including the functional-spatial hierarchy of establishments in technological progress at local-regional levels, and its related impact on the structure of local-regional labour markets (in terms of occupational and skill requirements, and primary and secondary markets).

2.2 Information Systems about Technological Change Processes

Given the degree of dynamics of technologies and its related socioeconomic impacts, there is a need for reliable information about technological change processes and thus for a design of monitoring systems over time in order to serve research and policy purposes, in order to achieve a better understanding of the development and diffusion processes of technology at various spatial scales, the restraints on, the barriers to and encouragement of technological change as well as the role of technology in the process of urban, regional, national and international development and redevelopment. This observation directly leads to a call for an <u>international comparison of technological change patterns between areas with different systems of regulations</u> which should provide useful information on both the causes and consequences of technological change processes at local, regional and national levels. Case studies and continuous monitoring may then enable us to identify the generality or specificity of actual trends, impacts and related policies in various countries. There is clearly also the necessity to solve some more or less severe spatial and sectoral categorisation problems first, in order to achieve comparable observations and results.

In this framework, there is also a need for longitudinal research on the functional-spatial structure of firms in the long run, by examining factors behind their production environments, regarding their locational event-histories at the scale of both the centre/periphery and the rural/urban dichotomy. Indepth interviews on the basis of longitudinal statistical data on firms are a necessity to get (more) insight into the types and nature of establishments (branch plants of domestic firms, foreign subsidiaries, etc.). An accounting system, e.g. a demography of establishments, might then be built up in order to portray the dynamics of the different regions.

2.3 Methodological and Theoretical Frameworks for Regional Labour Market Dynamics

The discussion on what is an appropriate methodology for studying the research triangle of technological change, employment and urban or regional development also leads to the need for new modelling frameworks. Traditional macro-analyses of comparative statistics are not very satisfactory for this task. The variety of issues involved in the abovementioned research triangle has emphasised the necessity to model urban/regional processes of adjustment to a variety of changes in various ways. Three types of change processes relevant for the spatial development of cities and regions may be distinguished:

- Fast adjustment processes (up to one year response time) are due to mobility processes of individuals, goods, capital and information within the spatial system.
- Medium speed adjustment processes (2-5 years response time) primarily reflect the transition of the production system caused by technological innovation and changing consumption patterns as well as by world-wide cycles of prosperity and recession, recession and prices, etc.
- Slow speed adjustment processes (3-8 years response time) are concerned with capital-intensive installations having an average lifetime of over 50 years.

These adjustment processes differ widely in terms of response time, duration, level of impact and reversibility. Satisfactory models which attempt to reflect dynamic economic, social, technological and spatial development phenomena in the real world have to distinguish between these types of adjustment processes and have to explicitly recognise their different levels of responsiveness, duration, impact and reversibility. Furthermore, regional, national and international links have to be taken into account as well as the incentive structure, especially the role of the public sector.

One of the most promising frameworks to model the research triangle of technological change, employment and urban or regional development is the catastrophe and bifurcation approach linked with a microeconomic behavioural foundation. Individual based choice-theoretic approaches (e.g., the master equation approach) dealing with choices of agents within constraints offer another promising line of modelling the research triangle. But both modelling paradigms need further development in order to integrate and model the different change processes relevant for the evolution of regional and urban systems.

There is also a need for comparative tests between competing and alternative models. To be able to judge the success of modelling activities it is necessary to have the means by which to compare present ways of modelling and theorising with the alternatives that are being suggested. There are serious deficiencies in the capabilities to test among alternative concepts and models and to determine which of the candidates might be best even within the same modelling paradigm.

Another major field of future research has to be the <u>development and improvement of the theoretical background</u> of such models. There is evidently a number of theoretical approaches like a <u>growth theoretic</u> one (mainly dealing with the analysis of unstable growth paths originating from technological base innovations), <u>(neo-) Schumpeterian and (neo-) Marxist theories</u> (e.g., Mandel's capital theory which takes up and modifies the original ideas of Kondratiev). But all of them fail to stress the importance of space in which we are primarily interested. They are essentially aspatial theories. Furthermore, they do not in general provide an answer to the question how to solve the growing mismatch between technology and institutional environment. Consequently, such modelling approaches would have to be extended with endogenous technological change processes that are linked to both the dynamics of metropolitan or urban growth potentials (the breeding place hypothesis, e.g.) and the life cycles of processes of specific manufacturing or service sectors.

2.4 Integrated Policy Research

The instruments that policy makers have traditionally used to tackle problems of regional development have become less and less effective because the long established relationship between new investments, production and employment growth has broken down in most sectors. Various key questions have been identified in the foregoing chapters. Two major fields of attention for scientific research appear to emerge from these discussions:

- which public policy can stimulate the technological capacity of lagging regions in order to increase local employment opportunities (e.g., by providing advanced telecommunication services, venture capital and other services for small high-tech firms and by supporting local research into new products and processes) and
- how can policy bring pressure to bear on individual entrepreneurs to be more dynamic in the utilisation of new technologies?

The strong need for deregulation is clearly an important point here because in many areas regulatory policies which have been necessitated

by social and environmental concerns in the past resulting from many
forms of market failures have become rigid and inefficient. Various
contributions in this book point out the importance of the role of the
public sector in the transformation process and the need for a regionally based public policy in order to overcome the problems of adjustments in local communities and to provide appropriate initiatives in
both the private and public sphere. Needless to say that this situation will require a more appropriate coordination between scientific
research and planning in the triangle of technological change, employment and regional labour markets.

REFERENCES

Boyer, R. and Petit, P., 'Employment and productivity in the EEC',
    Cambridge Journal of Economics, Vol. 5, No. 1, 1981, pp. 47-58.

Cross, M., 'Technological change, the supply of new skills, and prod-
    uct diffusion', in: Gillespie, A.E. (ed), Technological Change
    and Regional Development, Pion, London, 1983, pp. 54-67.

Freeman, C., Clark, J. and Soete, L., Unemployment and Technical Inno-
    vation, Frances Pinter, London, 1982.

Mensch, G., Stalemate in Technology, Ballinger, Cambridge, MA, 1979.

Piatier, A., 'Long waves and industrial revolutions', CP-84-54, Inter-
    national Institute for Applied Systems Analysis, Laxenburg, Aus-
    tria, 1984.

LIST OF CONTRIBUTORS

Franz-Josef Bade
Deutsches Institut für Wirtschaftsforschung
Königin-Luise-Strasse 5
1000 Berlin 33
Federal Republic of Germany

Huub Bouman
Bureau of Economic Affairs
City of Nijmegen
Nijmegen
The Netherlands

John F. Brotchie
CSIRO
P.O. Box 56
Highett 3190
Victoria
Australia

Ewald Brunner
Interdisciplinary Regional Research Institute
Vienna University of Economics
Augasse 2-6
A-1030 Vienna
Austria

Roberto P. Camagni
Department of Economics
Bocconi University
Via Sarfatti 25
20136 Milano
Italy

Lata Chatterjee
Department of Geography
Boston University
48 Cummington Street
Boston MA 02215
USA

Richard H. Day
Department of Economics
University of Southern California
Los Angeles, CA 90089
USA

Dimitrios S. Dendrinos
School of Architecture and Urban Design
University of Kansas
Marvin Hall 302
Lawrence, Kansas 66045
USA

Hans-Jürgen Ewers
Department of Economics
Technical University Berlin
Uhlandstrasse 4-5
1000 Berlin 12
Federal Republic of Germany

Manfred M. Fischer
Department of Geography
University of Vienna
Universitätsstrasse 7-9
Vienna
Austria

Maria Giaoutzi
Department of Geography
National Technical University
Zographou Campus
Athens
Greece

David Gleave
The Technical Change Centre
114 Cromwell Road
London SW7 4ES
United Kingdom

John B. Goddard
Department of Geography
University of Newcastle
Claremont Bridge
Newcastle upon Tyne NE1 7RU
United Kingdom

Jan Willem Gunning
Social and Economic Research Institute
Free University
P.O. Box 7161
1007 MC Amsterdam
The Netherlands

Günter Haag
Institute for Theoretical Physics
University of Stuttgart
Pfaffenwaldring 57
7000 Stuttgart 30
Federal Republic of Germany

Kenneth A. Hanson
IUI
Grevgatan 34
11543 Stockholm
Sweden

Ad J. Hendriks
Department of Economics
Catholic University Tilburg
Hogeschoollaan 229
Tilburg
The Netherlands

Els Hoogteijling
Central Bureau of Statistics
Voorburg
The Netherlands

Börje Johansson
CERUM
University of Umea
S-90187 Umea
Sweden

Dirk-Jan F. Kamann
Department of Economics
State University of Groningen
P.O. Box 800
9700 AV Groningen
The Netherlands

Charlie Karlsson
University of Karlstad
Box 9501
S-65009 Karlstad
Sweden

Jan G. Lambooy
Department of Economics
University of Amsterdam
Jodenbreestraat 23
Amsterdam
The Netherlands

T.R. Lakshmanan
Department of Geography
Boston University
48 Cummington Street
Boston MA 02215
USA

Peter Nijkamp
Department of Economics
Free University
P.O. Box 7161
1007 MC Amsterdam
The Netherlands

Jacques Poot
Department of Economics
Victoria University
Wellington
New Zealand

Jan Rouwendal
Department of Economics
Free University
P.O. Box 7161
1007 MC Amsterdam
The Netherlands

Uwe Schubert
Interdisciplinary Regional Research Institute
Vienna University of Economics
Augasse 2-6
A-1030 Vienna
Austria

Michael Storper
Department of Urban and Regional Planning
University of California
Los Angeles CA 90024
USA

Alfred T. Thwaites
Department of Geography
University of Newcastle
Claremont Bridge
Newcastle upon Tyne NE1 7RU
United Kingdom

Peter M. Townroe
School of Economic and Social Studies
University of East Anglia
Norwich NR4 7TJ
United Kingdom

Chris van der Vegt
Department of Economics
Jodenbreestraat 23
Amsterdam
The Netherlands

Bram Verhoef
Bureau of Economic Affairs
City of Nijmegen
Nijmegen
The Netherlands

Vol. 184: R. E. Burkard and U. Derigs, Assignment and Matching Problems: Solution Methods with FORTRAN-Programs. VIII, 148 pages. 1980.

Vol. 185: C. C. von Weizsäcker, Barriers to Entry. VI, 220 pages. 1980.

Vol. 186: Ch.-L. Hwang and K. Yoon, Multiple Attribute Decision Making – Methods and Applications. A State-of-the-Art-Survey. XI, 259 pages. 1981.

Vol. 187: W. Hock, K. Schittkowski, Test Examples for Nonlinear Programming Codes. V. 178 pages. 1981.

Vol. 188: D. Bös, Economic Theory of Public Enterprise. VII, 142 pages. 1981.

Vol. 189: A. P. Lüthi, Messung wirtschaftlicher Ungleichheit. IX, 287 pages. 1981.

Vol. 190: J. N. Morse, Organizations: Multiple Agents with Multiple Criteria. Proceedings, 1980. VI, 509 pages. 1981.

Vol. 191: H. R. Sneessens, Theory and Estimation of Macroeconomic Rationing Models. VII, 138 pages. 1981.

Vol. 192: H. J. Bierens: Robust Methods and Asymptotic Theory in Nonlinear Econometrics. IX, 198 pages. 1981.

Vol. 193: J.K. Sengupta, Optimal Decisions under Uncertainty. VII, 156 pages. 1981.

Vol. 194: R. W. Shephard, Cost and Production Functions. XI, 104 pages. 1981.

Vol. 195: H. W. Ursprung, Die elementare Katastrophentheorie. Eine Darstellung aus der Sicht der Ökonomie. VII, 332 pages. 1982.

Vol. 196: M. Nermuth, Information Structures in Economics. VIII, 236 pages. 1982.

Vol. 197: Integer Programming and Related Areas. A Classified Bibliography. 1978 – 1981. Edited by R. von Randow. XIV, 338 pages. 1982.

Vol. 198: P. Zweifel, Ein ökonomisches Modell des Arztverhaltens. XIX, 392 Seiten. 1982.

Vol. 199: Evaluating Mathematical Programming Techniques. Proceedings, 1981. Edited by J.M. Mulvey. XI, 379 pages. 1982.

Vol. 200: The Resource Sector in an Open Economy. Edited by H. Siebert. IX, 161 pages. 1984.

Vol. 201: P. M. C. de Boer, Price Effects in Input-Output-Relations: A Theoretical and Empirical Study for the Netherlands 1949–1967. X, 140 pages. 1982.

Vol. 202: U. Witt, J. Perske, SMS – A Program Package for Simulation and Gaming of Stochastic Market Processes and Learning Behavior. VII, 266 pages. 1982.

Vol. 203: Compilation of Input-Output Tables. Proceedings, 1981. Edited by J. V. Skolka. VII, 307 pages. 1982.

Vol. 204: K.C. Mosler, Entscheidungsregeln bei Risiko: Multivariate stochastische Dominanz. VII, 172 Seiten. 1982.

Vol. 205: R. Ramanathan, Introduction to the Theory of Economic Growth. IX, 347 pages. 1982.

Vol. 206: M.H. Karwan, V. Lotfi, J. Telgen, and S. Zionts, Redundancy in Mathematical Programming. VII, 286 pages. 1983.

Vol. 207: Y. Fujimori, Modern Analysis of Value Theory. X, 165 pages. 1982.

Vol. 208: Econometric Decision Models. Proceedings, 1981. Edited by J. Gruber. VI, 364 pages. 1983.

Vol. 209: Essays and Surveys on Multiple Criteria Decision Making. Proceedings, 1982. Edited by P. Hansen. VII, 441 pages. 1983.

Vol. 210: Technology, Organization and Economic Structure. Edited by R. Sato and M.J. Beckmann. VIII, 195 pages. 1983.

Vol. 211: P. van den Heuvel, The Stability of a Macroeconomic System with Quantity Constraints. VII, 169 pages. 1983.

Vol. 212: R. Sato and T. Nôno, Invariance Principles and the Structure of Technology. V, 94 pages. 1983.

Vol. 213: Aspiration Levels in Bargaining and Economic Decision Making. Proceedings, 1982. Edited by R. Tietz. VIII, 406 pages. 1983.

Vol. 214: M. Faber, H. Niemes und G. Stephan, Entropie, Umweltschutz und Rohstoffverbrauch. IX, 181 Seiten. 1983.

Vol. 215: Semi-Infinite Programming and Applications. Proceedings, 1981. Edited by A. V. Fiacco and K. O. Kortanek. XI, 322 pages. 1983.

Vol. 216: H. H. Müller, Fiscal Policies in a General Equilibrium Model with Persistent Unemployment. VI, 92 pages. 1983.

Vol. 217: Ch. Grootaert, The Relation Between Final Demand and Income Distribution. XIV, 105 pages. 1983.

Vol. 218: P. van Loon, A Dynamic Theory of the Firm: Production, Finance and Investment. VII, 191 pages. 1983.

Vol. 219: E. van Damme, Refinements of the Nash Equilibrium Concept. VI, 151 pages. 1983.

Vol. 220: M. Aoki, Notes on Economic Time Series Analysis: System Theoretic Perspectives. IX, 249 pages. 1983.

Vol. 221: S. Nakamura, An Inter-Industry Translog Model of Prices and Technical Change for the West German Economy. XIV, 290 pages. 1984.

Vol. 222: P. Meier, Energy Systems Analysis for Developing Countries. VI, 344 pages. 1984.

Vol. 223: W. Trockel, Market Demand. VIII, 205 pages. 1984.

Vol. 224: M. Kiy, Ein disaggregiertes Prognosesystem für die Bundesrepublik Deutschland. XVIII, 276 Seiten. 1984.

Vol. 225: T. R. von Ungern-Sternberg, Zur Analyse von Märkten mit unvollständiger Nachfragerinformation. IX, 125 Seiten. 1984

Vol. 226: Selected Topics in Operations Research and Mathematical Economics. Proceedings, 1983. Edited by G. Hammer and D. Pallaschke. IX, 478 pages. 1984.

Vol. 227: Risk and Capital. Proceedings, 1983. Edited by G. Bamberg and K. Spremann. VII, 306 pages. 1984.

Vol. 228: Nonlinear Models of Fluctuating Growth. Proceedings, 1983. Edited by R. M. Goodwin, M. Krüger and A. Vercelli. XVII, 277 pages. 1984.

Vol. 229: Interactive Decision Analysis. Proceedings, 1983. Edited by M. Grauer and A. P. Wierzbicki. VIII, 269 pages. 1984.

Vol. 230: Macro-Economic Planning with Conflicting Goals. Proceedings, 1982. Edited by M. Despontin, P. Nijkamp and J. Spronk. VI, 297 pages. 1984.

Vol. 231: G. F. Newell, The M/M/∞ Service System with Ranked Servers in Heavy Traffic. XI, 126 pages. 1984.

Vol. 232: L. Bauwens, Bayesian Full Information Analysis of Simultaneous Equation Models Using Integration by Monte Carlo. VI, 114 pages. 1984.

Vol. 233: G. Wagenhals, The World Copper Market. XI, 190 pages. 1984.

Vol. 234: B.C. Eaves, A Course in Triangulations for Solving Equations with Deformations. III, 302 pages. 1984.

Vol. 235: Stochastic Models in Reliability Theory. Proceedings, 1984. Edited by S. Osaki and Y. Hatoyama. VII, 212 pages. 1984.

Vol. 236: G. Gandolfo, P.C. Padoan, A Disequilibrium Model of Real and Financial Accumulation in an Open Economy. VI, 172 pages. 1984.

Vol. 237: Misspecification Analysis. Proceedings, 1983. Edited by T. K. Dijkstra. V, 129 pages. 1984.